MW00387872

Fundamental Models in Financial Theory

Fundamental Models in Financial Theory

Doron Peleg

The MIT Press
Cambridge, Massachusetts
London, England

MIT Press books may be purchased at special quantity discounts for business or sales promotional use. For information, please email special_sales@mitpress.mit.edu.

This book was set in Times Ten LT Std by Toppan Best-set Premedia Limited, Hong Kong. Printed and bound in the United States of America.

Disclaimer:
The material in this book is intended for educational purposes only. Although the models presented in this book resemble real-life situations, neither the author nor the publisher guarantee the compatibility, completeness, or accuracy of any information published in this book, and neither the author nor the publisher will be held liable for any consequences resulting from their implementation.

Library of Congress Cataloging-in-Publication Data

Peleg, Doron, 1952–
Fundamental models in financial theory / Doron Peleg.
    p. cm
Includes bibliographical references and index.
ISBN 978-0-262-02667-3 (hardcover : alk. paper)
1. Finance—Mathematical models. 2. Investments—Mathematical models. I. Title.
HG106.P45   2014
332.01'5195—dc23
2013023053

10 9 8 7 6 5 4 3 2 1

Contents

Foreword

From theory to practice: A comprehensive, holistic approach to incorporating financial models into real-life scenarios

Reference books typically present financial theory as a set of separate topics. In this book, I have opted for a different approach. I present the subject matter in a methodical, structured, and logical-mathematical order, starting with the underlying assumptions and progressing through the basic model to more complex models and on to operative conclusions, so as to evolve financial theory from chapter to chapter.

The models describing the world of economics and finance are outstanding for their extraordinary simplicity in a field that claims to be scientific. I assign the introduction to gaining an understanding of the concept of a model, discussing what makes a good model and the methodology used in formulating one. I review the different types and key points of models—descriptive versus normative, deterministic versus statistical—and how to apply them to financial theory.

The basic building blocks of all financial instruments in the market today are bonds (debt certificates) and shares (participating certificates). The demand for and supply of money by individuals and businesses determine the point of equilibrium for interest rates, profits, and dividends. Descriptions of the point of equilibrium and deviations from it are normally to be found in economics textbooks, not in books on financial theory. These concepts are needed to understand "trading in time" and "trading at risk"—key elements of financial theory. The former represents the financial value of the time elapsing from receiving an income to the moment of its actual consumption. The latter distinguishes between favorable future states and unfavorable future states, presenting the financial value of enabling the level of consumption to be smoothed over time. An understanding of how these models are integrated into forecasting economic scenarios is crucial for assessing the value of financial instruments.

The price-to-earnings (P/E) ratio, which is based on the earnings model, and the dividend yield, which is based on the dividend model, are both widely used to assess the value of shares in the market. They too tend to receive only minor mention in the literature on financial theory. The Modigliani-Miller (M&M) cash flow model is deemed by all modern financial experts to be the correct one for appraising the value of a financial asset. To fully understand the advantages and limitations of these models and where each is applicable, it is vital to come to grips with the different assumptions underlying the earnings and dividend models versus the M&M cash flow model.

The conventions for making investment decisions in uncertain conditions are generally discussed in advanced finance textbooks. However, an in-depth understanding of these concepts at an introductory level of financial theory modeling curricula aids in understanding the driving forces in the market and the difference between the value of a financial asset—a bond or a share—and its price as quoted daily in the media covering the various exchanges. Understanding the differences between the two concepts of value and price and whether they can be used to turn a profit is vital to understanding the different models, their limitations, and their advantages.

Markowitz's normative mean-variance model and Sharpe and Treynor's descriptive capital asset pricing model (CAPM) for allocating an optimal, well-diversified portfolio are two separate models with marked conceptual differences. For the first time in a textbook, the Black-Litterman model for building a practical portfolio comprising a small number of assets, and thus not diversified, is presented. The model reduces risk to a minimum using the mean-variance method and allows the presentation and integration of personal views. The book reviews the mathematical background required to understand the theoretical aspects of these models, as well as how to apply them using Excel templates to optimize practical investment portfolios.

A discussion of pure risk trading (future contracts) and the consumption capital asset pricing model (CCAPM) illustrates how to hedge (limit) risk. The development of Black and Schole's mathematical model for options pricing is presented in a manner understandable even by those readers whose strong suit is not mathematics, while providing intuitive interpretations for both interim and final results. I also examine how the option's model is employed for uses other than shares, such as bond pricing or structured asset pricing.

According to Modigliani and Miller, a company's risk is not dependent on its capital structure mix of debt and equity. The difficulty in understanding this concept is the result of the language used in their article, which distinguishes between a world with a corporate income tax and one without a corporate income tax. This depiction is analogous to that of a taxation system that equates the tax rate on two financing channels (debt and equity) with a tax rate that discriminates between the two capital-raising channels. I have chosen to use different terminology to describe Modigliani and Miller's theory, comparing how a dollar earned by a company finds its way into the investor's pocket in a neutral taxation system versus a discriminating taxation system. Arguing the underlying assumptions helps explain the strengths and weaknesses of this important model.

Finance is considered a difficult academic course. I hope that the original presentation of the material and the inclusion of topics not usually addressed in the financial modeling literature will help the reader more easily grasp the material. The problems presented at the end of each chapter are intended to demonstrate the concepts discussed in the chapter and afford a deeper insight into the material. A related website provides discount factor tables, pocket calculator instructions, and Excel instructions in three appendixes to the book, as well as Excel templates, so that readers may gain additional practical use with the models. To further explore the topics discussed, readers may find the limited "further reading" list at the end of each chapter useful. Once listed in a chapter, readings are not repeated in other chapters though they may cover topics mentioned throughout the book. These materials should help readers go beyond theory and start using these new tools to build practical investment portfolios.

Good luck!

I   The Time Value of Capital

1 Introduction

A. Models in Financial Theory

B. The Company's Goals

C. The CFO's Roles

D. Basic Elements in Financial Planning

A. Models in Financial Theory

The word *model* is commonly used in economics and business administration. It is important to define exactly what constitutes a model in order to understand its purpose and its proper implementation.

A model is a conceptual template that assists in solving a certain type of problem.

In the world of exact sciences, it is possible to define a problem and offer an exact model for its solution. Sometimes many parameters are involved and the mathematical tools required for their solution demand extensive knowledge. Business administration models, however, exhibit extreme simplicity for a field claiming to be of a scientific nature, and students occasionally object fiercely to what seems to them a simplistic description of the world outside the classroom.

There are three main reasons for this difference between economic and financial models and models in the exact sciences:

1. *In economics, it is not possible to conduct controlled experiments.* In contrast to other fields in the social sciences, in economics it is not possible to re-create exactly the same conditions and manipulate one parameter at a time in a controlled fashion to study its effects. Economic and financial models are examined through historical samples, and many

parameters vary from one case to the next. As a result, it is not possible to anchor some of the parameters in the different samples. Although statistical tools are available for handling such samples, the results are not always sufficiently significant. Initial attempts carried out in the last decade to conduct controlled experiments have not as yet yielded complete models.

2. *The number of unforeseeable parameters is greater by an order of magnitude than in the exact sciences.*   It is hard (and perhaps impossible) to foresee a variable event such as the attacks of September 11, 2001, or to quantify the effect of such an event on the global asset and financial markets.

3. *We are dealing with people.*   The basic assumption in all financial theory models is that all people are rational and seek to maximize their benefit by maximizing their wealth. This assumption constitutes a basic axiom for the simple reason that no better assumption has been found. But if we were to meet, say, a terrorist (or freedom fighter—it is all in the eyes of the beholder), we would find that his efforts to maximize his personal benefit do not necessarily entail wealth maximization. New theories (whose founders were awarded the 2002 Nobel Prize in Economics) demonstrate that people do not always behave rationally. Later on, we will see there are many who oppose the rationality assumption, and we will explain why we adopt it nonetheless.

There is, however, a point to having models in financial theory. Although a textbook solution such as is possible in engineering cannot be provided, it is still possible to equip students with tools for analyzing and designing solutions that are better than coin-toss decision making.

Since, in light of the above, perfect models cannot be provided, we must consider what constitutes a good model.

A good model eases the mental effort required to solve complex problems.

Methods for Formulating a Good Model

1. *Simplify*—Discuss significant variables while ignoring other, overly complex variables that contribute little to solving the problem. The rule of thumb is that 20% of the variables are responsible for 80% of the results. The problem revolves around identifying the significant variables and understanding their effects. Practically speaking, one begins with a

simplified model and, after understanding it, refines it and increases its complexity by adding parameters.

2. *Separate*—Divide one large problem into easier, independent sub-problems. This method, commonly used in the exact sciences (with mathematical definitions of "independent"), is not so clear-cut in financial theory. Usually we will require only a weak correlation, that is, that the subproblems have only a minor mutual influence. Here too one can start analyzing a problem assuming no correlation between subproblems and only when the problem and the direction of the solution start becoming apparent discard the assumption of independence and develop a more complex model.

3. *Address uncertainty*—Separate the certain variables from the random variables that must be predicted, and develop a forecasting method. This separation process is usually also the first step in separating the problem into subproblems, as described above.

The last item, describing the separation of certain variables from random variables, is an important factor when planning the teaching of financial theory, which usually includes two basic parts:

Part 1—Models concerning the effect of time on the value of capital (money and financial assets) in a world of certainty—

THE TIME VALUE OF CAPITAL.

Part 2—Models concerning the effect of risk on the value of capital (money and financial assets) in a world of uncertainty—

THE RISK VALUE OF CAPITAL.

Models for forecasting under conditions of certainty are *deterministic* in the sense that the numerical answer derived from the model is unique and equals the actual apparent future result in the real world. Models for forecasting under conditions of uncertainty are *probabilistic,* and so the result yielded by the model (e.g., the forecasted average) is only an approximation of the expected future real-world apparent result: actual (future) apparent results will be distributed around this average and are liable (at a low level of probability) to be materially distant from it.

Understanding the advantages and disadvantages offered by probabilistic models is paramount to using financial theory models properly. Even if the probability of losing 90% (or more) of an investment is only one-thousandth of a percent, the chance is still there, and if it materializes, it will constitute 100% of the future outcome!

Normative Models and Descriptive Models

Normative (conceptual) models are based on underlying assumptions (axioms) on which a pyramid of interim conclusions is built, leading to a final conclusion (similar to the laws of trigonometry).

One example of this kind of model is Einstein's theory of relativity. Einstein's underlying assumption is that the speed of light remains constant, while time and distance are not necessarily absolute and fixed. At the time, this assumption was opposed to all commonly accepted assumptions and rules in physics. A certain event—say, turning a light on and off—is observed from two different systems moving relative to each other. The time measured in these two systems for the event will be different and will depend on their relative speed, while both systems operate under the regime of the same fixed measurement for the speed of light. Einstein applied his theory as a pure mathematical model, and the physical conclusions derived from its mathematical developments were astonishing. At this stage, experiments were carried out to confirm or refute the conclusions he reached from developing his model. When these conclusions were confirmed through physical experiments, scientists went back to square one and also examined the new underlying assumption that the speed of light is constant.

Descriptive models are based on a series of actual empirical tests of the correlation between two different quantities. Having found connections between pairs of variables, one can then deduce a description of a system containing several variables. It is also possible to find a connection between several variables at the same time. In this case, the number of correlative descriptions (equations) must equal the number of variables. In the (certain) model correlating speed, acceleration, time, and distance, two different sets of tests were measured:

1. The correlation between distance $S \rightarrow$ and constant speed v, yielding the result $S = v{\cdot}t$.

2. The correlation between variable speed $v_t \rightarrow$ and acceleration a, yielding the result $V_t = v_0 + a{\cdot}t$.

From this, we can correlate the distance $S \rightarrow$ and acceleration a, yielding the result $S = v_0 \cdot t + \dfrac{1}{2} \cdot at^2$.

B. The Company's Goals

The financial problems covered in this book require that a decision be made and a solution be found by an individual or a company. The decision criterion for the individual has already been mentioned: to maximize the individual's benefit by maximizing his or her wealth. The decision criteria for companies are not as self-evident. They depend on the viewpoints and goals of the company's various executives. For example:

Chief Executive Officer (CEO)—One of the classic business administration models (proposed by Theodore Weinschel) describes the CEO's duty as liaising between all company stakeholders, including clients, suppliers, employees, stockholders, debtholders, and so forth. The CEO is required to provide the minimum necessary for each stakeholder to maintain ties with the organization.

Marketing Director—The marketing director's goals are maximizing sales and maximizing market share. Marketing considerations when a product is introduced may be fundamentally different from those near the end of the product's life cycle.

Human Resources (HR) Director—The HR director's goals are maintaining industrial peace, outsourcing operations, and paying attention to environmental quality.

Chief Financial Officer (CFO)—The CFO wishes to maximize profit and positive cash flow.

Production Manager—The production manager's objective is to improve processes and raw material availability while minimizing the defect rate.

The goals of the different executives are legitimate but may conflict with one another. If so, what is the company's shared goal, from which it derives its general operational decision-making criterion?

A company's executives effectively serve as agents for its shareholders. In addition to focusing on their individual responsibilities, they must consider the company's goal from the viewpoint of its owners, the shareholders. From this perspective, the question becomes simpler and brings us back to the realm of the individual. If we assume that the owner of a company is a single person who also carries out all the duties mentioned above, the decision-making criterion is clear: maximizing his wealth.

The fact that there are numerous owners (shareholders) and that they do not carry out the work themselves but through their agents is not meant to change the decision-making criterion for that company's management.

The company's goal is to maximize the company's value for its shareholders.

Studies in this area have shown deviations from the above criterion, which arise from the fact that each officer in the company naturally also tries to maximize his or her own benefit. The conflict between maximizing the agent's personal benefit and the agent's duty to maximize the shareholders' benefit is extensively discussed in the literature as the *agency cost*. It is studied in advanced courses, although most readers are familiar with classic solutions such as executive options schemes.

C. The CFO's Roles

Financial theory is naturally the foundation for serving as CFO of a company (although the basic curriculum is certainly recommended for other executives as well). Under certain circumstances, the CFOs' goals may differ completely from those of his or her colleague directors in the company. A marketing director might wish to sell a product during its market introduction phase, even at a loss. This would (falsely) appear to be contradictory to the duties of the CFO, who is responsible for the company's cash flow.

The CFO receives a work plan from each of the company's executives (production manager, marketing director, etc.) and consolidates them into one comprehensive picture, thus functioning as a systems integrator of sorts.

When a marketing director intends to launch a campaign aimed at significantly increasing sales, it is necessary to make sure that the production manager and the HR director are prepared. If it is necessary to buy another piece of machinery or recruit additional employees, one must calculate whether the entire endeavor is indeed profitable and economical in the long run.

Many projects are routinely proposed by the various divisions in the company. In the above example, it is possible to imagine a scenario in which the motive behind the project was a production manager's proposal to replace an old machine with a new one that would increase production capacity and reduce unit costs. In this case, it would be necessary to check the costs of the marketing department's preparations for the project and its ability to sell the additional products. If the marketing department cannot sell the additional products, then the production manager's entire calculation of the reduction in the unit price is flawed.

The CFO has many additional duties (roles) in the ongoing management of the company:

As *treasurer,* the CFO liaises with the banks; manages cash balances, client credit, supplier credit, and the like.

As *comptroller,* the CFO is responsible for the company's accounting, financial statements, budget formulation and tracking of actual budget implementation, cost accounting, liaising with and reporting to the tax authorities, payroll, employee pension plans, and much else.

As *risk manager,* the CFO drafts and enforces procedures, maintains oversight of internal auditing, handles risk insurance, mitigates currency risks from export/import operations and risks from fluctuations in raw material prices, and the like.

All of the above functions are extremely important but will not be directly covered in this book. The emphasis instead is on strategic financial planning, that is, on decisions concerning the company's project investments, on the one hand, or raising capital on the other. These types of decisions are inherently long-term decisions that do not fall under the company's day-to-day operations.

At this point, it is important to explain the difference between the terms *efficient* and *effective*. A project that is regularly managed with maximum efficiency but that still incurs significant losses is not effective. On the other hand, a project may yield significant profits and funds, that is, it may be extremely effective, but it may not be managed efficiently (it wastes inputs), and therefore its profitability can be improved. The CFO's administrative duties detailed above fall under the category of managing efficiency. Strategic decisions concerning raising capital and project investments fall under the category of sustaining efficacy.

Choosing effective projects determines the company's financial future.

To make the correct effective decisions, a CFO must implement intelligent financial planning. Investment decisions and budgeting decisions regarding financial resources for these investments must be guided by a comprehensive view of the company, not the interests of any one particular department. A company that encourages creativity and continuous development is faced at any given moment with a large number of projects that cannot all be implemented simultaneously.

When setting out to implement financial planning, we must take into account the following points:

Decisions are interdependent. As described earlier, the marketing department's decisions affect other departments as well and require them to make suitable preparations, which affect the company financially. The financial planner must take into account all the cumulative effects. Projects, too, are interdependent, owing to the company's budgetary constraints. Sometimes a company must forgo one project because of a decision to pursue another, costly project. This interdependence due to budgetary constraints is one of the classic problems facing both individuals and companies.

Decisions are made through long-term considerations. Strategic decisions are characterized by their extended setup (investment) time, which may last several years. The subsequent return (income) phase may also last a very long time. The fact that cash inflows and outflows are counted in years is of material importance in financial planning and in the decision-making process.

Each project contributes to the company's overall goal and not only to that project's goals. At first glance, it would seem that a production department initiative that streamlines operations and significantly reduces production costs by acquiring a new, faster machine should be implemented without second thought. However, if the machine produces double or triple the number of products and these products merely pile up in the company's warehouses, the project's effect on the bottom line of the company's income statement will not be to add profits but losses.

Each project contributes to the company's value. The previous item might lead one to think that the company's goal is always to maximize its profits. However, this is not the case. The company's goal is to choose projects according to their overall contribution to the company's value. For example, a marketing department project might lose money in the first few years of developing the product and entering the market. But investors with a long-term view would understand the project's contribution to future profits. The project's contribution to the company's overall value is positive, and will be reflected in its share price.

Risk (which is covered in the second part of this book) also affects the decision-making process. We may opt to choose projects that are less profitable but contribute to reducing the company's overall risk. As a result, that project increases the company's value more than another project that is more lucrative but entails greater risk.

D. Basic Elements in Financial Planning

Financial planning must take into consideration many factors. To make certain all factors are accounted for, it is important that the financial planning process be structured and logical. It should include the following elements:

1. *Examining the company's investment and financing options.* At any given moment the company has more than one option for raising capital (shareholder investments, loans, etc.) and more than one possible project. The company must consider how to raise capital and which projects to implement, subject to its financing (budgetary) options. The first step is to conduct an inventory of possible projects and the company's budgetary constraints.

2. *Forecasting the future results of an investment in each project.* Each project affects the company's cash inflows and outflows differently in terms of the amounts and timing of payments. Each project also affects the company's overall risk. Forecasting all these factors is an essential part of the information-gathering process before making any decision.

3. *Setting the decision-making criteria.* The overall goal of the company's management is to maximize the company's value. Despite this goal being defined unequivocally, the criteria for examining each project's contribution to this goal are not that simple. Therefore, it is necessary to set the decision-making criteria and to be thoroughly cognizant of the assumptions and limitations underlying these criteria.

4. *Choosing alternatives.* After criteria for rating each project are determined, they must be ranked in descending order of efficacy. The decision as to which investment to make depends on budgetary constraints. From the list, the set of projects is chosen that is most effective for the company.

5. *Tracking project progress.* After choosing projects and setting them in motion, it is necessary to track their actual results over time and compare them with projections, while adapting the plan to changing real-world conditions.

Further Reading

Chrisman, J. J., and A. B. Carroll. 1984. Corporate Responsibility: Reconciling Economic and Social Goals. *Sloan Management Review* 25 (Winter): 59–65.

Fama, E. F. 1980. Agency Problems and the Theory of the Firm. *Journal of Political Economy* 88 (2): 288–307.

Findlay, M. F., III, and G. A. Whitmore. 1974. Beyond Shareholder Wealth Maximization. *Financial Management* 4 (Winter): 25–35.

Keynes, J. M. 1936. *The General Theory of Employment, Interest and Money*. New York: Harcourt Brace.

Seitz, N. 1982. Shareholder Goals, Firm Goals and Firm Financing Decisions. *Financial Management* 11 (Autumn): 20–26.

2   Building Blocks: Interest and Dividends—The Basic Model

A. Interest as the Price of Money—Consumption Utility over Time

B. The Company's Production Function—Investment, Profit, and Dividends

C. Basic Capital Markets—Debt and Participation Certificates

D. Primary Institutions in the Capital Market

A.   Interest as the Price of Money—Consumption Utility over Time

This is a classic topic in macroeconomics. However, as it serves as the basis for financial modeling, I introduce the material here as well. In the first chapter we defined an individual's goal as maximizing his or her wealth, while concurrently a company's goal is to maximize the company's value. Regarding individuals, the goal of maximizing wealth actually seeks to meet a more basic need, maximizing consumption. In the models discussed below, we convert actual consumption (e.g., of wheat) into the monetary equivalent required to purchase the same consumption quantity C (of wheat). Thus, for example, it is possible to relate consumption units for wheat to consumption units for clothing through the monetary equivalent of each.

The basic model discussed in this chapter is a two-period model, present and future. Later on, we will expand the model into a multiperiod model, where periods may be days, months, years, or anything we wish.

The basic assumption is that a person always prefers present consumption to future consumption (e.g., prefers to buy a car now than to postpone the purchase to next year). For individuals to postpone a certain amount of consumption in the present, they require a greater quantity of consumption in the future. In an economy where money is the equivalent of consumption, there exists for practical purposes a money market, where one can trade present consumption for future consumption. Shifting consumption from future to present requires paying a fee, while postponing it from present to future requires receiving a fee.

From present to future requires mentioned, for individuals to forgo a certain amount of consumption in the present, they will demand a greater amount of consumption in the future. Let us refer to the required additional consumption as interest and denote it by r (or R), for "rate."

Interest   The additional consumption (money) required to postpone consumption from the present to the future.

Interest is stated as a percent (%) of postponed consumption; for example, $r = 10\%$. For forgoing a consumption level of C_0 in period 0, an individual will demand a consumption level of C_1, which is 10% greater, in the subsequent period 1. We can then state:

$$C_1 = (1+r)C_0.$$

In the above example, the interest rate is 10%: $r = 0.1$.

$$\Rightarrow \quad C_1 = (1+0.1)C_0 = 1.1C_0.$$

Let us assume that individual i (a person out of the general population) has a present amount of money, D_i, which he intends to consume over two periods, 0 and 1—meaning he is limited in budget. We can describe this budgetary constraint in terms of present consumption in period 0 by converting consumption in period 1, which is C_{i1}, to its consumption equivalent in period 0, using the above definition for interest:

$$D_i = C_{i0} + \frac{1}{1+r}C_{i1}.$$

We can also present consumption in terms of the subsequent period and, accordingly, set a budgetary constraint in terms of the next period, H_i (defined in the third equation below). Note that in the above equation, the budgetary constraint D_i was defined in terms of money available to the individual in the present period (now), while H_i is the budgetary constraint in subsequent period (future) terms.

We can therefore present the following set of relations between consumption and budgetary constraints in the present and in the future:

1. $D_i = C_{i0} + \dfrac{1}{1+r} C_{i1}$

2. $C_{i1} = -(1+r)C_{i0} + H_i$

3. $H_i = D_i(1+r)$

If individuals in the population wish to advance their consumption, they must find other individuals willing to postpone consumption in exchange for receiving a suitable fee. This creates a market for trading consumption over time. The consumption over time market is called the "money market," as consumption has been converted into monetary terms. This raises the question, what is the market interest rate R that reflects the "price" of balancing the desires of all individuals wishing to advance consumption with the desires of those wishing to postpone consumption?

To develop our model, let us make two further assumptions concerning the money market:

1. Each individual is too small to affect the interest rate alone.

2. The interest rate is equal for borrowers who advance consumption and lenders who postpone consumption (there are no brokers, or the brokerage costs are zero).

If we add up the desires of all individuals and their monetary con-straints, we end up with the equilibrium interest rate R and a budgetary constraint line for the market, which represents all options available to all individuals for dividing consumption between the present period and the subsequent period. Individuals choose the most suitable point accord-ing to the point where their own utility function is tangent to the budget line.[1]

In figure 2.1 we see the budget line for the entire market, where $D = \sum D_i$ (and $H = \sum H_i$). We added the utility function for two indi-viduals (naming them "Saver" and "Spender"). The tangent of their utility function to the budget line determines the proportional[2] amount of present and future consumption for each individual separately. Note

---

1. The utility function U is a graphic aggregation of all points on the plane of consumption in the present period and consumption in the subsequent period with the same utility (i.e., they are equally beneficial). The higher the function on the graph (up and to the right), the greater is an individual's utility.

2. The absolute amount will be determined by D_i, their own budget constraint. Their budget line will have the same slope, $-(1 + r)$.

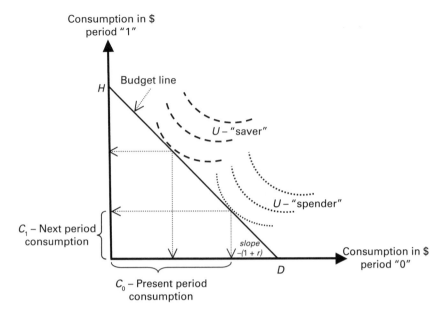

Figure 2.1
Consumption Preference over Two Periods

that the interest rate is dictated by the market, and each of them chooses his proportional present and future consumption accordingly.

B. The Company's Production Function—Investment, Profit, and Dividends

Our description of the market to this point has been partial. Companies also participate in the money market, and they face a different problem: each company has prepared a list of projects requiring present investment, but the fruit of that investment will only be reaped in the future. A similar summary of all companies in the market results in the production possibility frontier (PPF) curve (diminishing marginal return) between investing in income-generating assets in the present and reaping their benefits in the future.

Let us assume that at time 0, the beginning of the present period, the sources available to the company are endowment E_0, the product of past investments. Now, the company can invest part of this output, in the amount I_0, that will produce a yield at the end of period 0 (which is the beginning of the subsequent period 1), the endowment E_1. The

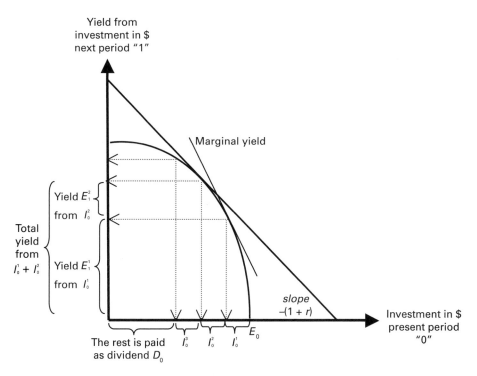

Figure 2.2
Production-Investment, Profit (Yield), and Dividends over Two Periods

residual of the output at the beginning of the period $0 - D_0$ will be distributed to the owners, who will use it for consumption. Note that dividend D_0, which is distributed to the owners in period 0, also serves as their budgetary constraint, before they set out to trade on the money market.

Each company prepares a list of projects in descending economic (output) order. The diminishing marginal yield has already been presented in figure 2.2 by investing equal portions of I_0 (I_0^1, I_0^2, I_0^3, etc.). We plotted the second investment I_0^2 so as to yield the return E_1^2, which is smaller than E_1^1 (diminishing marginal returns).

Figure 2.2 clearly shows that an investment greater than $2 \times I_0$ is not cost-effective since the marginal return on the third project (the tangent to the production curve) will be less than the interest rate available on the market. The company owners will prefer to invest in new projects as long as their return is greater than the price return they can get on the money market.

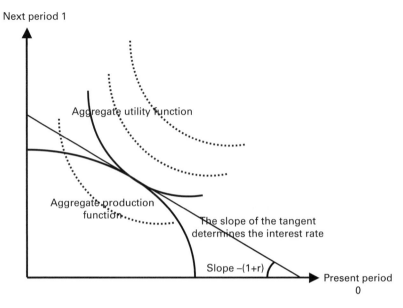

Figure 2.3
Resolution for Two Periods' Pure Interest Rate

In conclusion, assuming that all individuals in the market hold all of the companies' means of production through "participation certificates," then the overall budgetary constraint for all individuals and companies in the market equals the total output of all the companies in the market. The output is available to the individuals at the start of the period for consumption and for investment (through companies) in production, so as to serve as sources of livelihood in the subsequent period as well.

Figure 2.3 merges the two previous figures. It describes the aggregate utility function for all individuals in the market (present consumption versus consumption in the subsequent period) and the aggregate production function. Remember that the aggregate utility function (of present and future consumption) for all individuals in the market is actually a set of curves, and we have emphasized only one utility curve—the one that is tangent to the production function.

The slope of the tangent line at the above point of tangency determines the interest rate in the money market. This interest rate is called the pure interest rate. In the next chapter we will see there is a long list of interest rates that are all derived one from the other. The first rate on that list is the basic (pure) interest rate, which is a result (price) of supply and demand on the money market, assuming a perfect market (though, as we will discuss later, the market is not perfect).

We can define the following:

- *Supply of money*   The sum of postponed consumption for all consumers preferring "saving."

- *Demand for money*   The sum of all investment requirements and early consumption for all consumers preferring "loaning."

- *Price of money*   The slope of the graph tangent (interest rate) at the equilibrium point of money demand and supply.

In figure 2.4, we see how the overall companies' output E_0 at the starting period (time 0) is distributed between the companies' investment

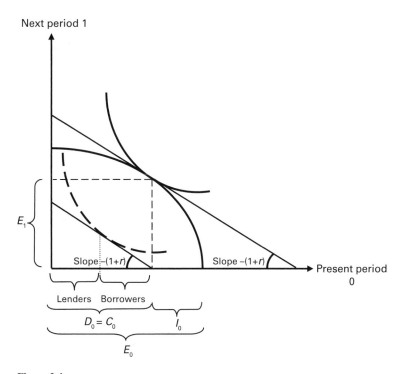

Figure 2.4
General Investment, Production, and Consumption over Two Periods

needs I_0 and the overall consumption of both early consumers (borrowers) and frugal consumers (lenders).

Note: During each period, the companies' beginning period endowment is used in its entirety (for investment and/or consumption).

At the beginning of the subsequent period 1 we will have endowment E_1, which will also be entirely consumed (or invested) during period 1.[3] Consumers who borrowed money in the previous period will need to return (out of distributed D_1) their loan (plus interest), while those who loaned money can increase their consumption in period 1 beyond the dividend they receive, D_1, by the amount of their savings (plus interest).

C. Basic Capital Markets — Debt and Participation Certificates

In our previous discussion, we saw that companies and individuals can lend or borrow money. They do so by drawing up a debt contract (an IOU) stating that one party has loaned money to a second party and that the second party will return the money plus interest in the subsequent period. Since it is easier to trade debt contracts on the money market when they are denominated in standardized amounts, such loan contracts are usually made in round sums of $10, $100, $1,000. . . . These contracts are called bonds and are regularly traded on the market. The original lender can sell the bonds to another party, who from that moment becomes entitled to all future payments under the contract.

In the above model, we also assumed that all individuals in the market hold all the companies' means of production through participation certificates. The percent of participation certificates held by an individual out of the total number of existing participation certificates defines that individual's stake in the output of those companies whose participation certificates he or she holds. These certificates are known as *shares* (or *stock*).

Let us briefly review some basic terms concerning shares and bonds. In the following chapters we will discuss how their value (price) is determined when we wish to buy or sell them on the market.

---

3. By "endowment" we mean the "crop" at the beginning of each period, a yield from the investment made at the beginning of previous period.

Share capital has three legal administrative levels:

1. Authorized share capital

Authorized share capital refers to the number of shares a company can issue from time to time, as determined by the shareholders at the general meeting. At the general meeting, shareholders may also decide to increase the authorized share capital when necessary. Usually (but not necessarily) this will be the maximum amount that can be registered with the company's registrar at a certain fee bracket.[4]

2. Issued share capital

Upon incorporation, the company's founders decide on the number of shares to be issued to the partners as per their prorated share, out of the total authorized share capital. From time to time the board of directors may decide to issue shares to an individual (from among the existing owners, or someone else), provided that the issue is made from the authorized share capital and subject to the company's constituent documents. The percentage of each partner's ownership holdings in the company at any given moment is given by:

$$\frac{\text{Total number of shares issued under one's name, } n_i}{\text{Total number of issued shares, } N}.$$

3. Paid-up share capital

In limited liability companies, the liability of each partner is limited to payment of the sum of shares issued to that partner. Shareholders who have paid the company the required monetary amount for the shares issued to them have paid their debt to the company, and this share capital is called the paid-up share capital. It is only necessary to redeem the shares on liquidation, when those partners who have not paid for their shares are called on to do so.

Company Ownership

Sometimes, according to the company's articles, ownership of shares grants right of first refusal to buy shares issued at a later time, so as to guarantee that the owners' stake in the company is not reduced (i.e., diluted).

---

4. Regulations prescribe different fees for different levels of authorized share capital.

Owners have a basic right to a prorated portion of the dividends paid out of the company's earnings, if and when such dividends are distributed. Shareholders have a right to vote on decisions presented at the general meeting of shareholders (the general meeting), and, on the company's liquidation, shareholders have a right to a prorated portion of the surplus assets after payment of all the company's liabilities.

In its articles, the company can determine that some shares, called *preferred shares*, carry preferred rights. For example, holders of preferred shares can select the managers or directors of a company or may receive predetermined dividends.

A person can acquire (partial) ownership of a company in two ways:

1. By buying shares from existing owners

Current owners sell part of their ownership stake to a new partner and receive the proceeds personally. The number of shares sold passes to the new partner and the seller's holdings in the company decrease (are diluted) accordingly. Let us denote the total number of shares issued N and the number of shares held by partner i as n_i, so that $N = \sum n_i$, and each partner's prorated holdings x_i are $x_i = \dfrac{n_i}{N}$.

2. By investing in the company

A new partner who wishes to use his money to finance new operations in the company and not to put it in the pockets of the current partners will invest his money directly in the company. In this case, the number of shares held by each of the previous partners will remain unchanged and a new number of shares m will be allotted to the new partner out of the authorized share capital. Thus, the number of issued shares increases to $N + m = M$, and the percentage of ownership of all the other partners decreases (is diluted), as now their prorated holdings are

$$x_i = \frac{\text{Total number of shares issued under one's name, } n_i}{\text{New total number of issued shares, } M}.$$

Let us examine these two buy-in options: buying shares from previous owners versus direct investment in the company. Let us denote by V the company's value prior to the transaction, as agreed upon by the buyer and the seller.

Under the first option, the new partner is to buy $x\%$ of the ownership in the company from its previous owners at price P. The percentage of shares he is to buy is $x\% = \dfrac{P}{V}$. The company's value will not change following the transaction, as only the identity of the shareholders has changed.

Under the second option, the partner invests amount I in the company. The company's value will increase to $V + I$. In professional terms, the company's value V is referred to as "pre-money," while the company's value $V + I$ is referred to as "post-money." If the investing partner wants to own $x\%$ of the company, he should invest an amount I, so that

$$x\% = \frac{I}{(V + I)}.$$

Conclusions

When a new partner enters a company, the previous (some or all) shareholders' holdings are diluted:

• When the existing partners sell shares to the new partner, the number of shares under their ownership decreases, but the total number of shares issued does not change. Their relative portion decreases, and the company's total value remains unchanged.

• When the new partner directly invests in the company, the number of shares in the company increases, while the number of shares held by each existing partner remains the same. Their relative holdings decrease, but the company's total value increases, so that the value of their share remains unchanged.

Bonds

Earlier we explained that bonds are written by individuals in the market. In fact, we can expand our model to situations where companies, too, issue bonds; that is, they borrow money (instead of raising capital through participation certificates, that is, shares). Governments, too (which we did not include in our model, to avoid delving too deeply into macroeconomics), can issue bonds when their expenses (government consumption) exceed their income from taxes. Usually a distinction is made between corporate (company) bonds and government bonds since governments can always (in principle) print money to redeem their bonds, whereas companies cannot.

The method of raising capital through loans from commercial banks, or by bond issues through investment banks, will be explained shortly. Bond-related terms are discussed separately in the chapter on bond valuation models.

D. Primary Institutions in the Capital Market

Commercial Banks

The interest rate equilibrium model demonstrates how the ability to borrow or lend money increases individual and corporate utility in the market by allocating consumption over time. The ability to separate the time when income arises from the time that income is actually used, increases utility for all market players and the utility of the overall market in general.

The need to connect lenders and borrowers is the cornerstone of the existence of commercial banks. They serve as intermediaries between those wishing to borrow money and those wishing to lend money, without the two sides having to physically meet. Commercial banks offer owners of savings accounts a lower interest rate on their savings than the rate they charge borrowers. Banks require collateral on the loans they provide and/or charge a premium for the risk that the borrower will default on his repayment. The difference (spread) between the interest rate a bank offers lenders (holders of savings accounts) and the interest rate it charges borrowers, net of bad debts and the bank's operating expenses, forms the basis for the bank's profit. The bank's operation in a competitive market guarantees that the spread and interest rates will be (almost) identical across all banks on the market. Despite the brokerage fee, it is beneficial to use banks' services, as these transactions require unique expertise.

Despite the above, in the models we develop later on, we will use one single interest rate for lenders and borrowers.

Investment Banks

Like any other player on the market, companies can deposit their surplus cash with commercial banks or take out interim loans to finance their operations. For example, orders paid on delivery will usually be bridge-financed by loans from commercial banks.

Sometimes companies need to raise money for new projects. Their funding rounds, characterized by the large sums involved and long repayment periods, are usually financed by issuing new company shares or bonds. Here, too, an intermediary is needed, in the form of investment banks, which connect companies seeking to raise capital and investors seeking to invest in those companies' shares or bonds.

One of the main attributes of these types of loans[5] is the large sums of money involved; in addition, most such transactions take place between institutions and not as offers to individuals.[6] In many ways, investment banks serve as the parties' trustee (partly defined by laws and regulations and partly by practices through which certain banks have acquired their reputation). Investors' ability to check the purposes for which the money is being raised and the risks entailed in their investment is limited. They rely on the investment banks' examination. Investment banks also advise fund-raising companies on the prices they can ask for their shares or bonds, and on the general status of the issue market. Investment banks assume charge of marketing and distributing the issue,[7] and usually also commit to buying the remaining balance of the offering through their own equity, if they fail to distribute the entire issue.[8]

The Central Bank

The basic assumption in our model for finding the pure interest rate in the market was the existence of a perfect market. As mentioned previously, perfect market assumptions require (among other things) that each market player be too small to influence the interest rate. In practice, every country has a central bank whose main role is to control price levels (inflation).[9] Insofar as the main tool available to central banks for this task is setting the market interest rate,[10] the market interest rate ceases to be an internal (endogenous) parameter, determined by perfect market equilibrium, and becomes an external (exogenous) parameter "dictated" to the market. This situation in turn creates a new equilibrium between the demand for money and the supply of money, according to

---

5. Shares are not loans in the regular sense of the word.

6. The institutions involved typically are large-scale investors such as pension funds, insurance companies, investment firms, and the like, all seeking long-term investments.

7. "Issue" in this sense refers to corporate fund-raising by offering shares or bonds for sale.

8. This commitment to purchase the remaining balance of the offering "guarantees" the best judgment for the required price. Such an event does happen occasionally, though not frequently.

9. The central bank's role changes from country to country and includes matters outside macroeconomic policy (e.g., supervision of banks). The main responsibility is always to maintain price levels. Sometimes additional macroeconomic responsibilities are prescribed (such as market growth rate). Most countries avoid expanding responsibilities in order to avoid a conflict of goals.

10. As demonstrated, interest rates affect short-term market consumption and, consequently, price levels.

the dictated interest rate, with the central bank having to meet demand or supply for any gap. It should be recalled that central banks have two main instruments for regulating interest rates:

1. The central bank is by far the largest issuer of bonds (along with companies and households), with a range of terms. Each time, the bank can issue new series of (government) bonds bearing interest rates as per its own policies. In this way it influences the market interest rate for bonds in general.

2. In its role as supervisor of the banking sector, the central bank can change liquidity requirements for banks.[11] From time to time, it also determines the interest rate it pays (charges) commercial banks for their deposits (loans) with the central bank for their liquidity surplus (shortage).

The main and most important conclusion is that the market interest rate is determined primarily by the central bank's policy. As the interest rate is one of the key factors determining the value of financial assets (bonds and shares), the ability to forecast the central bank's policies is an important part of an investor's ability to assess the value of financial assets.

It should be emphasized that monetary policy is not omnipotent but allows for fine-tuning only. If the government's fiscal policy or the market's pure interest rate is too far away from the new equilibrium dictated by the central bank's interest rate, the market may experience hyperinflation or deflation, and the central bank may lose its ability to influence the market interest rate.

Intelligent investors must understand the macroeconomic processes taking place in the country, region (e.g., Europe), and even in the global economy in order to predict interest rate trends and fluctuations in the time frames relevant for their investment. This is because minor changes in interest rates can cause significant short-term capital gains or losses on financial assets.

The Securities and Exchange Commission

An issue of bonds and shares requires a great deal of trust between investors and the issuing company, both in the primary public offer and

---

11. "Liquidity" refers to the percentage of its total deposits that a bank is permitted to provide as loans.

afterward, when these shares or bonds are traded on the secondary market. Buyers and sellers operate in a market "playground." Sellers display their goods and customers examine them, and, as is the case with market playgrounds, the parties offer the amount and price at which they wish to sell or buy. When an agreement is reached, a transaction is made. The market for transactions in financial assets is called the stock market. The market may have a physical location, such as the New York Stock Exchange on Wall Street, or it may exist as a virtual market, such as the NASDAQ (which originally stood for "National Association of Securities Dealers Automated Quotations"), where all bids and offers are gathered, displayed, and carried out online by computers. Such online markets are called over-the-counter (OTC) exchanges. As the goods are "virtual" (contracts), clear and unequivocal rules must apply to the issue and trading of shares and bonds.

In the United States, the body in charge of rule setting and enforcement in the market is the Securities and Exchange Commission (SEC). The SEC also monitors traders and their compliance with its rules and is authorized to investigate and prosecute those who violate the rules for criminal purposes, such as price manipulation. When players violate the rules accidentally, the SEC can impose sanctions, which range from fines to suspension of trading of a certain company's shares.

Note: This book mainly discusses model-building. To ensure that readers are familiar with the terms used, we have briefly reviewed a number of key terms. This review is by no means exhaustive. Readers are encouraged to expand their knowledge in this field through consulting books focusing on the structure, institutions, and rules (laws) of the capital market.

Chapter 2—Questions and Problems

Question 1

A consumer has a money-defined consumption utility function, as follows:

$$U(C_0 ; C_1) = 2.2 \ln C_0 + \ln C_1.$$

The consumer has $3,200,000 at the beginning of period 0 to be used in both periods, 0 and 1 (0 = working age; 1 = retirement). The market interest rate is 10%.

a. How much should the consumer save for his retirement?

b. How would your answer change if the government increased the market interest rate?

Question 2

Show that in the utility function in question 1:

a. The marginal utility from increasing consumption in any period is positive.

b. There is a time preference for consumption. (*Hint:* The function is decreasing and concave.) Explain.

Question 3

You are the CEO of a public company whose money-defined production function is $X_1 = 44 \cdot I_0^{1/2}$. In period 0, you have resources of $W_0 = 800$. The market interest rate is 10%.

a. How much should you invest?

b. How much should you distribute as dividends to owners?

c. What amount of resources will you have at your disposal at the start of the next period?

d. Assuming that conditions do not change in the subsequent period (C_1; C_2), by how much will the dividend distributed to the owners increase (in percent) in the subsequent period over the present period?

e. Assuming that conditions do not change in subsequent periods, what will the dividend growth rate be?

Question 4

Assume a utility function of $U(C_0 ; C_1) = 1.32 \ln C_0 + \ln C_1$. As CEO, you hold all the participation certificates (shares) in the company from question 3, whose production function is $X_1 = 44 \cdot I_0^{1/2}$. The dividend payment is your source of income for all subsequent periods (as noted earlier, all the above equations are defined in money-equivalent terms). At the beginning of period 0, the company has resources of $W_0 = 880$. The market interest rate is 10%.

a. How much should you invest in your company?

b. Assume that your consumption utility function is limited by your short-sighted ability to forecast only your present period. Denote by L_0

the amount of money that you borrow or lend in period 0. What is L_0? What is your consumption C_0 in period 0?

c. Repeat the questions in parts (a) and (b) for period 1 under the same assumptions.

Question 5

Use the same assumptions as in questions 3 and 4 to develop a multipe-riod model for a short-sighted individual who is only able to forecast one period at a time (the present period) for every period n.

a. Develop a recursion formula for a loan amount of L_n and a consumption level of C_n in every period n.

b. Calculate the loan amount L_n and consumption level C_n after a large number of periods by substituting the values for period $n-1, n-2$, $n-3$ ... and using the equation for infinite geometric series:

$$a(1+q+q^2+...+q^n) = \frac{a}{1-q} \quad ; \quad q < 1.$$

c. What is the economic conclusion from the above multiperiod model for the consumption level at equilibrium, and for borrowing recommendations in general?

Question 6

Economists in the State of Utopia (whose economy behaves according to the two-period model described in this chapter) estimate that the aggregate money-defined utility function of all market consumers can be approximated through the equation $U(C_0 ; C_1) = A \cdot \ln C_0 + \ln C_1$ (assuming $A = 1.5$), and that the money-defined aggregate production function for all market manufacturers can be approximated through the equation $X_1 = M \cdot I_0^{1/2}$ (assuming $M = 44$). In period 0, the country has consumption and investment resources of W_0 (assuming $W_0 = 800$).

a. Translate the production function $X_1 = f(I_0)$ (a left-to-right increasing function) into a function of the same kind as the two-period model described in this chapter, $x_1 = f(x_0)$, and show that it is a monotonic *decreasing* function.

b. What is the consumption $C_0 ; C_1$ at equilibrium in this market?

c. What is the pure interest rate at equilibrium in this market?

Question 7

The central bank's main job is to maintain price levels in the market.

Recently, several indices in the previous question's economy have signified rising inflation levels. The central bank's commissioner has announced that from now on, the central bank will issue bonds bearing an interest rate of 11%. Describe how the commissioner's measures will help mitigate inflation (calculate numerically, and explain).

Note: The following questions 8 and 9 are mental exercises to prepare for the next chapter.

Question 8

On January 1, 1998, you deposited a one-time sum of $5,000 in a renewing annual short-term deposit. The interest you received on the deposit at the end of each year varied according to the market interest rate for that year. After five years, you decided to withdraw the money accrued in the short-term deposit. The interest rate in each year was:

1998 5.5%

1999 6.0%

2000 6.3%

2001 6.7%

2002 7.0%

a. What was the amount in your account at the end of the third year?

b. What was the amount at the end of five years?

Question 9

You applied for a loan of $10,000 from your bank, which offers you three interest payment options:

1. Pay 22% interest at the end of the period.

2. Pay 18% interest, but interest is paid on receiving the loan.

3. Pay 10% interest on being granted the loan and another 10% at the end of the period.

a. Calculate the true (effective) interest rate for each of these options.

b. Does the size of the loan affect your ranking of the different options?

Question 10

Define the following terms briefly. Use a library or online references:

a. Short-term loan
b. Short-term deposit
c. Secondary market
d. Investment bank
e. Registered shares
f. Financial broker
g. Issued shares
h. Underwriter
i. Paid-up shares
j. Distribution costs
k. Ordinary shares
l. Public company
m. Preferred shares
n. Private company
o. Face value
p. Prospectus
q. Book value
r. Inside information
s. Securities exchange
t. OTC exchange
u. Primary market

Further Reading

Fisher, I. 1930. *The Theory of Interest*. New York: Macmillan.

Hirshleifer, J. 1970. *Investment, Interest, and Capital*. Englewood Cliffs, NJ: Prentice-Hall.

Jensen, M., and W. H. Meckling. 1976. Theory of the Firm: Managerial Behavior, Agency Costs, and Ownership Structure. *Journal of Financial Economics* 3 (October): 305–360.

Ross, S. A. 1987. The Interrelations of Finance and Economics: Theoretical Perspectives. *American Economic Review* 77 (2): 29–34.

Summers, L. 1985. On Economics and Finance. *Journal of Finance* 40 (July): 633–635.

Teichroew, D. 1964. *An Introduction to Management Science: Deterministic Models*. New York: Wiley.

3 Interest Rates

A. Nominal and Effective Interest Rates

In the previous chapter, we saw that for individuals to forgo a certain amount of present consumption (expressed as a cash equivalent), they will demand a greater amount of money in the future. We defined the compensation required to postpone consumption from the present to the future as interest, and denoted it with the letter r (or R).

Interest rate   Percentage of additional consumption (in cash) required to postpone consumption from the present to the future.

In finance, where we deal with financial asset valuation models, it is convenient to change the above definition and refer to interest in terms of money and not in terms of consumption:

Interest rate   The usage price of money per period of time (stated as a percentage of the cash amount).

In practice, the two definitions are identical, since to postpone consumption (=use money), individuals demand an additional "price." While in the previous model we denoted consumption with the letter C, we will now use that same C to indicate cash. We can still use the same variables in the equations as before.

In the model we developed in the previous chapter for interest as the price of money, and in all the definitions so far, we have included the term "per period of time." The basic model we presented was a two-period model, present and future. As promised, we will now see that the model can easily be expanded into a multiperiod model.

Let's refocus on the definition:

Nominal interest rate   The usage price of money, *for a specific time period.*

If the period is not explicitly specified (e.g., a daily, monthly, etc., interest rate), it is portrayed as being an annual interest rate.

Our model can easily be expanded for two periods by doubling the single-period model, $C_1 = (1 + r)C_0$:

$$C_2 = (1+r)C_1 = (1+r)^2 C_0.$$

In the same way, we can expand the model for three, four, and n periods. In general, we can write the following equation, assuming a fixed interest rate:

$$C_n = (1+r)^n \cdot C_0.$$

If we go back to the above two-period model, we see that the only principal difference between it and the single-period model is that at the end of the first period, we have an amount that equals the base amount plus interest. Thus, at the end of the second period we gain interest not only on the base amount (the principal) but also on the interest accrued during the first period. This yields a new definition:

Compound interest   The interest paid on both the principal and the accrued interest, when there is more than one period.

This last definition requires us to be especially careful with the length of the period. Interest-charging lenders wish to increase their profit by calculating interest over a shorter period. In this manner, they also receive interest on the interest. It is not uncommon to see a nominal interest rate stated for a one-year period, with the fine print stating that the interest amount is calculated on a monthly basis.

Example: A loan of $100 with a 12% nominal annual interest will require the borrower to pay $112 at the end of the period (year). If the interest rate is calculated on a monthly basis, then each month an interest rate of 12%/12 = 1% would be charged. If we calculate the monthly interest paid as monthly compound interest, we would get $100 \times (1.01)^{12}$ = \$112.68, meaning we would pay 68 cents more as interest.

The effective annual interest rate is therefore 12.68%, and not, as indicated by the nominal annual interest rate, 12%.

This leads to a new definition:

Effective interest rate   The true annual interest rate that is paid.

There are different ways of "ballooning" effective interest rates while stating a seemingly lower nominal interest rate. For example, some lenders tend to collect the interest in advance, on granting the loan. Using the numbers from the above example, when the \$12 interest is collected at the start of the period, the borrower would receive $100 - $12 = \$88, while returning \$100 at the end of the period.

In such a scenario, according to the formula

$$C_1 = (1+R)C_0 \quad \Rightarrow \quad R = \frac{C_1}{C_0} - 1,$$

we would end up with an interest rate of

$$R = \frac{100}{88} - 1 = 13.64\%.$$

Therefore, the annual effective interest rate paid would be 13.64% and not 12%, as one might think from the stated nominal interest rate.

We saw that when interest is calculated each month, then each month we are charged for 1/12 of the nominal interest rate. This amount is added to the principal, and in the subsequent months we pay interest (compound interest) on it as well. Similarly, we can calculate the effective interest rate when it is calculated semiannually, quarterly, monthly, weekly, or for any period.

In general, if the nominal interest rate R_{nom} is calculated for n subperiods, for each of which we pay an interest of R_{nom}/n, then in annualized terms we pay an effective interest rate $R_{eff} = (1 + R_{nom}/n)^n - 1$.

If we increase n and calculate interest every month, every week, every day, every hour, every second . . . we end up with the continuous interest rate: $\lim_{n \to \infty} (1 + R_{nom}/n)^n - 1 = e^{R_{nom}} - 1$.

If we calculate the effective interest rate as a continuous interest rate, for the above example we end up with $R_{eff} = e^r - 1 = e^{0.12} - 1 = 0.1274968 \approx 12.75\%$.

We saw how an annual nominal interest rate of 12% balloons to an effective interest rate of 12.68% when calculated on a monthly basis, and to an annual effective interest rate of 12.75% when calculated as a continuously compounded rate.

Therefore, when examining alternatives for a loan or savings, one should calculate the effective interest rate, and not consider the stated nominal interest rate.

B. Inflation and the Real Interest Rate

Economics curricula present inflation as the following:

Inflation   A change (decrease) in the purchasing power of money.

Let's assume we have $10, which at the start of a period suffices to buy one sandwich. If during that same period we have a 10% inflation rate, this means that at the end of the period that same sandwich will cost $11. An individual who loaned his money at a 10% interest rate, expecting to receive compensation for postponing his consumption, which would allow him to consume more in the subsequent period, will find himself at the end of the period (start of the next period) with $11, which is exactly enough to buy that same sandwich. If that individual wanted to guarantee *real* compensation for deferring consumption, he would have to take into account the decrease in the purchasing power of money. Denoting the rate of inflation by Inf, the principal return required is $C_0(1 + Inf)$, and the total required compensation is $C_1 = C_0(1 + Inf)(1 + r)$.

If we compare the last equation with the standard equation for calculating interest,

$$C_1 = (1+R)C_0,$$

we can immediately arrive at the following equation for the price of money:

$$(1+R) = (1+Inf)(1+r).$$

If an individual demands real 12% interest, and we expect 10% inflation, in order for him to receive a real increase in consumption, which would take into account the decreasing purchasing power of money, he should require a nominal interest rate R of

$$1+R = (1+0.10)(1+0.12) = 1.232 \quad \Rightarrow \quad R = 23.2\%.$$

Thus, we define the following:

Real interest rate The interest reflecting the true additional consumption (the nominal interest rate net of inflation).

$$R_{Real} = \frac{(1+R_{Nom})}{(1+Inf)} - 1.$$

This immediately expands our multiperiod model. If we have n periods with an annual nominal interest rate of R_{nom}, and in every period i we expect a certain level of inflation Inf_i, then the real interest rate we receive in each period[1] will be:

$$(1+R_{Real})^n = \frac{(1+R_{Nom})^n}{(1+Inf_1)\cdot(1+Inf_2)\cdot...\cdot(1+Inf_n)}.$$

$$R_{Real} = \sqrt[n]{\frac{(1+R_{Nom})^n}{[(1+Inf_1)\cdot(1+Inf_2)\cdot...\cdot(1+Inf_n)]}} - 1.$$

C. Benchmark Interest Rate and Risk Premium

We assume that borrowers will always repay their loan. This assumption is probably true if we buy U.S. government bonds, as the U.S. government can always print more dollars and repay its debt (the real value of these dollars in terms of purchasing power was discussed in the previous section). Moreover, if we wish to sell these bonds on the bond market, then in light of the huge number of U.S. government bonds traded each day, the chance of not finding a buyer when we are looking to sell is negligible. However, this is not the case if we buy corporate bonds. Companies can find themselves in distress, and in this case it is possible that a company may not be able to repay its debt (and so may initiate restructuring or bankruptcy proceedings).

We can define the benchmark interest rate as follows:

Benchmark interest rate[2] The interest rate for borrowers with no risk of repayment default.

Banks know how to rate borrowers according to the risk of default on their loan.[3] Using historical data and borrower risk levels, banks can

---

1. Note that we assumed a fixed interest rate across all periods.

2. In the finance literature, the benchmark interest rate is also referred to as the basic or risk-free interest rate and denoted by R_f. In the real world, in which interest rates for lenders and borrowers are different, the benchmark interest rate for borrowers is generally called the prime interest rate.

3. Credit rating agencies (e.g., Standard & Poor's, Moody's) specialize in rating corporate bonds by risk levels.

assess the percentage of loans not repaid by borrowers of a certain risk rating. Accordingly, these borrowers are required to pay a premium in addition to the benchmark interest rate (equal to the default rate), to compensate the bank on possible losses. This risk-based premium is called the *default premium*.

When we buy bonds issued by a small company, it is possible that no buyer will be available when we wish to sell the bonds. If we want to sell them quickly, we might need to lower the asking price in order to draw the attention of traders to the bargain and facilitate the purchase of our bonds. In this case the risk involved in holding bonds issued by a small company is reflected in the ability to convert them into liquid cash at any given moment. The harder it is to liquidate and the more we must lower the asking price on our bonds in order to sell them quickly, the higher the premium we require for the ability to "liquefy" our investment.[4] This premium is called the *liquidity premium*.

In general, as lenders keep debt certificates only while the cash is no longer in their hands or under their control, lenders demand a *risk premium* for reconverting their bond holdings into cash.

Risk premium   The addition required on the benchmark interest rate because of possible losses when converting bonds back into cash.

So far, we have seen three main factors affecting the risk premium: inflation (inflation premium), defaults (default premium), and liquidity (liquidity premium). We will now discuss an additional type of premium related to the bonds' lifetime until final repayment.

In the multiperiod model described above, we assumed that the interest rate was fixed and equal in all periods. However, we know that this is not actually the case, and that interest rates may change all of a sudden. Moreover, history shows that the commissioner of the central bank can announce an unexpected significant change in the interest rate in the evening, after the close of trading.[5] Let us examine now how such a change affects the value of bonds.

Assume that the current interest rate is 10%. You buy one-year government bonds with a face (or par) value of $100 (free of default or liquidity risks), meaning you expect to receive $110 at the end of the

---

4. The lower the average daily marketability of a bond, the harder it is to sell.

5. One day the commissioner of the central bank in Israel announced a 2% decrease in the interest rate, and a short time afterward had to announce a 4% increase as a result of the financial market volatility caused by his previous action.

year. Assume further that on the evening of your purchase, the commissioner of the central bank announces a 2% increase in the interest rate. What happens to your bonds?

If you intend to hold them to maturity, then as far as you're concerned almost nothing has happened, except that had you waited one more day, then with the same $100 you could have bought bonds yielding 12%. That is, instead of receiving $110 at the end of the year, you lost a chance to receive $112. You are even worse off if you wish to sell the bonds you bought at $100 the very next day. Since anyone can now buy new bonds bearing 12% interest, no one will want to buy your bonds, which yield only 10% interest, unless you lower the price on your bonds.

Let's assume for the moment that you offer the bonds you bought yesterday at $100, at a price of $95. Would buyers be convinced to buy your bonds? A shrewd investor would jump at the opportunity. If at the end of the year he can expect to receive $110, then (ignoring the day that has passed) he can expect an effective annual interest rate of 110/95 = 15.79%. It is obviously worthwhile buying your bonds, compared with the alternative of buying new bonds offering 12% interest.

This raises the question, at what price would investors be indifferent to buying your bond and buying a new bond on the market? The answer is simple: when the effective interest on the bonds that you offer is identical to the 12% interest on new bonds.

Let us mark this equilibrium price as X:

$$\frac{110}{X} - 1 = 0.12,$$

$$X = \frac{110}{1.12} = 98.21.$$

Thus, if you wish to sell the bonds one day after buying them at $100, you can sell them for no more than $98.21. This means that in one day you lost $100 − $98.21 = $1.79 on every $100 of bonds you bought.

The commissioner's announcement of raising the interest rate by 2% has caused you immediate capital losses of about 1.8%.

An announcement of a reduction in the interest rate would have caused you immediate capital gains (readers are welcome to calculate the capital gain resulting from an announcement of a 2% reduction in the interest rate).

If the bonds you bought were for a two-year period, the losses (gains) incurred following the announcement of an increase (decrease) in interest rates would have been greater, to compensate for interest rate differences over a two-year period (instead of one year). In chapter 5 we will learn how to calculate exactly the capital losses and gains on bonds with a maturity time of several years. At this stage, it is important to note that the longer a bond's maturity time, the greater the change in its price caused by a change in the market interest rate. We can thus say:

The longer the lifetime (maturity time) of a bond, the more sensitive (risky) is its price to changes in market interest rates.

One could think that if we wanted to reduce this risk, then instead of buying two-year bonds we could buy one-year bonds, and upon their maturity at the end of the year buy additional one-year bonds. In reality, this (apparently) simple solution to avoiding the risks of buying long-term bonds is not practical. If we assume that one day after our invest-ment, the commissioner announces a decrease in interest rates, our loss from buying short-term bonds is twofold:

1. The price of one-year bonds would rise by less than had we bought two-year bonds (upon announcement of the interest rate decrease).

2. At the end of the year (upon maturity of the one-year bonds), we would only be able to invest in additional one-year bonds offering a lower interest rate.

The conclusion is that it is not that simple to avoid the risk from the investment period during which we want to save our money. In the fol-lowing chapters, we'll see how these risks can be managed and hedged (mitigated). As a bond investment strategy, we offer the following:

If we expect market interest rates to go down during our investment period → Buy long-term bonds.

If we expect market interest rates to go up during our investment period → Buy short-term bonds.[6]

Let's recap all the risk factors for which a risk premium is required in addition to the benchmark interest rate:

Inflation (for which an inflation premium, IP, is required)

Default (for which a default premium, DP, is required)

Liquidity (for which a liquidity premium, LP, is required)

Maturity (for which a maturity premium, MP, is required)

---

6. Or better, keep the money in a daily deposit account, which bears a minimal interest rate but hedges against capital losses from interest rate increases.

Symbolically, we can say that[7]

$R_{Nom} = R_f + IP + DP + LP + MP$.

D. The Term Structure of Interest Rates

In our multiperiod model, we did not require that interest rates be fixed across all periods. Initially, we expediently assumed it to be fixed, and then we demonstrated how changes in market interest rates affected the value of an investor's bond holdings. Let us now examine the nominal annual interest rate reflected in the prices of bonds with a maturity term of 1, 2, 5, 10, 20, and 30 years.[8]

When we check the nominal annual interest rate on bonds with short, medium, and long maturity terms, historically for different periods, we find that sometimes the graph rises, sometimes it goes down, and sometimes it remains almost level (figure 3.1). This raises the question of what factors affect the graph direction (increasing, decreasing, or level) and what parameters affect its curve.

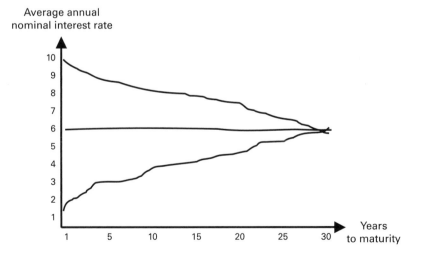

Figure 3.1
The Term Structure of Interest Rates

7. Remember that the inflation premium is not equal to the inflation rate. As we saw before, we must multiply by $(1 + Inf)$.

8. The U.S. government issues short-term (one-year) bonds, mid-term (5- and 10-year) bonds, and long-term (up to 30-year) bonds. Bonds issued several years ago can be found on the market, so that one can actually get the annual interest to maturity for any time period one wishes (actually, almost continuously).

There are several hypotheses that try to explain why the *term structure of interest rates* is expressed as a rising, decreasing, or leveled curve.

Expectations Hypothesis

According to the expectations hypothesis, the curve rises when investor expectations are for future annual interest rates to go up compared to the current market interest rate. The graph decreases if expectations are for interest rates to go down, and the graph remains level when expectations are for interest rates to remain the same. Investors form these expectations mainly on the basis of inflationary forecasts, government economic policies, and expected intervention by the central bank, as explained in the previous chapter.

Market Segmentation Hypothesis

The final chapters of the second part of this book cover risk management theory. For example, one of the most common ways of avoiding risks associated with currency fluctuations between the time an expense is incurred and the time revenues are received is to quote product prices in the same currency in which expenses are paid (e.g., local currency). Similar action can also be taken for the different investment terms. On the market, there are long-term lenders (pension funds and insurance companies) and long-term borrowers (for acquiring housing or equipment with a useful life of many years); there are also medium-term lenders and borrowers (e.g., bus and trucking companies, which need to finance the purchase of a vehicle with a service life of several years); and there are short-term lenders and borrowers. The concept behind market segmentation is that each time frame has a relevant segment of lenders and borrowers, and the interest rate for that time frame is determined (and changes) according to supply and demand at a given point in time. At any given moment, one can plot the supply and demand curve, which is unique for that moment.

Liquidity Hypothesis

In discussing the maturity premium,[9] we argued that the longer a bond's maturity term, the more sensitive (risky) it is to changes in the market

---

9. This should not be confused with the liquidity premium we encountered earlier. Here the name derives from the fact that you are holding bonds and not liquid cash.

interest rate. As this requires a greater risk premium, we would expect the term structure of interest rates to be reflected in a rising curve. Statistical tests have shown a statistical significance only for bonds with a maturity term of less than one year. After one year, data dispersion did not yield significant results.

The fact is that, historically, we also encounter decreasing curves. Therefore, although this hypothesis seems logical, it does not cover all possibilities, and at most we can say that its effect comes in addition to the basic effect of the expectations hypothesis and as an addition to the benchmark interest rate for that market segment at that point in time.

E. Interest Rates and the Stock Market

In the previous chapter, we introduced two instruments used by companies to raise capital: bonds and shares. In our initial discussion above, we saw the effect that interest rates have on a company's bonds. This is important not only for investors who bought that company's bonds but for the company itself. If the company waits until the bonds mature, then it would need to pay the par value of the bonds. Sometimes, if a bond's price on the bond market has gone down due to an increase in the market interest rate, it is preferable for a company to repurchase its bonds (at least in part) at a lower price than their issuing price.

This immediately raises the following question:

Do interest rates also affect the value of a company's shares?

Assuming that such an effect exists (and we will discuss it shortly), then the immediate actionable conclusion is that in periods when a share's value increases *for reasons unrelated to the company* (i.e., regardless of the company's performance), the company should issue shares, as it can raise a greater amount of money for each percentage of ownership allocated. Alternatively, when external factors push a company's share value below the value dictated by its performance, it might be advisable for the company to repurchase some of its shares.[10]

Interest rates affect corporate share prices in two main ways, internally and externally:

Internally—Interest constitutes an expense for companies (financing expenses). Almost every company finances its ongoing operations

---

10. This is not just a theoretical idea but a well-known practice. On more than one occasion, companies have chosen to repurchase bonds or shares.

through bank credit facilities. An increase in interest rates means additional expenses and lower profits. A decrease in a company's financial results (profit) can naturally be expected to be reflected in a decrease in its share value.

Externally—The interest rates offered on bonds compete with the rates of return that investors receive on shares.[11] The higher the market interest rate, the more investors choose to invest in safe U.S. government bonds instead of risky corporate shares,[12] which offer a return that is close to or sometimes even lower than the interest offered on bonds. If investors prefer to invest in bonds and not in shares, the result is a general decrease in share prices. In the short term, companies' operations do not change, and neither do their financial results. Therefore, the return on shares (=financial results divided by share price) increases until it reaches a level where it once again competes with the return on bonds.

The above preliminary analysis clearly shows that a low market interest rate should invigorate the stock market (greater profits for companies and less competition for share issues), while high interest rates should suppress the stock market. This initial analysis is essentially correct. However, as we will see later on, the world consists of many more parameters than just interest rates, and their cumulative effect can drive the market up while interest rates are high, and vice versa.

Chapter 3—Questions and Problems

Question 1

On January 1, the rate of return on five-year government bonds is 10% and the expected inflation rate for the coming year is 5%. You (along with other investors) expect government policies to increase inflation in each of the next three years by 1% each year (to 6%, 7%, and 8%). The benchmark interest rate is 3%. Assume that there is no maturity premium on bonds of up to five years' maturity.

a. What is the average rate of inflation expected in the next four years?

b. What should be the return on four-year bonds?

c. What are your inflation expectations for the fifth year?

11. "Return" here refers to the gains recorded by shareholders divided by the price at which they purchased the shares.

12. It is possible that there will be no profits to distribute, and in extreme cases, bankruptcy is also possible.

Question 2

An investor can invest his money in a two-year savings plan offering 10% interest paid at the end of each year and added to the principal, or buy a short-term bond payable in two years' time, which is currently quoted at 81 points (i.e., bonds with a $100 par value that are currently traded at $81).

a. Which option will he choose?

b. Is the interest rate the only consideration for that investor?

Question 3

Suppose the investor in question 2 lives in Lalaland and all the above given data are in the local currency, the Lay. The investor can also invest in dollar-linked government bonds, which mature in two years. The return at maturity is only 8% (dollar-based).

 The investor chooses not to invest in this option. The dollar exchange rate at the time of his decision is 4 Lays to the dollar. After two years he checks and finds that the exchange rate is 4.7 Lays to the dollar.

a. In retrospect, did he make the right decision?

b. What is the Lay-based profit or loss compared to the profit or loss from his preferred option in question 2, if he invested a total of 100,000 Lays?

Question 4

Fresh, Inc. borrows $3 million from the bank for a two-year period. The loan bears a 12% nominal interest rate. The principal is repaid at the end of the loan term.

a. Interest is paid at the end of each year. What is the effective interest rate paid by Fresh, Inc.?

b. Interest is paid at the start of each year. What is the effective interest rate paid by Fresh, Inc.?

Question 5

As CFO of a company, you request a $2 million loan from your bank for four years, at a stated (nominal) annual interest rate of 11%. The loan, both principal and interest, is to be repaid at the end of the period.

You notice a clause in the contract stating that the interest rate is calculated on a monthly basis. In your negotiations with the bank manager, you are able to have this clause removed from the contract. How much money do you save the company from paying at the end of the period?

Question 6

Inflation projections are 8% for next year, 6% for the year after, and 4% after that. The benchmark interest rate is 2% and the maturity premium is 0.2% for the first year, an additional 0.2% each year for the first five years, and 0% after that.

a. Calculate the interest rate for years 1–5, 10, and 20, and plot the term structure of interest rates for government bonds.

b. Investors are not asking for any default premium on short-term IBM bonds, although 10-year bonds bear a default premium of 0.5%, while 20-year bonds bear a default premium of 1%. Add the curve for the term structure of interest rates on IBM bonds to the curve you plotted in part (a).

Question 7

To finance your final year of economics studies, you need to take out a one-year $10,000 loan. You have several options:

1. A nominal interest rate of 24% on the loan, paid semiannually.

2. A loan linked to the Consumer Price Index (CPI) with an annual interest rate of 12%, paid annually.

3. A CPI-linked loan with an annual interest rate of 8%, paid quarterly, though this loan also adds a risk premium (because you are a student and your ability to repay the loan is doubtful) of 1.5%.

Assume that 20% inflation is expected. Which option would you choose?

Question 8

You have a credit card that allows you to postpone payment by three months and pay the market interest rate for three months of 10.5%.

You bought a product whose regular price is $10,000. You bought the product on sale, such that you will only be billed for the purchase in three months. The seller offers you another option, to pay in cash and receive a 10% discount.

a. Which option would you choose?

b. How much money would you save by choosing the better option?

c. Is the price of the product important, or would your choice always be the same?

Question 9

You need $200,000 to finance a transaction over a three-year period. The bank offers you a loan for three years bearing 15% annual interest or a CPI-linked loan with 6% interest. In both options, interest is paid annually at year's end.

a. What is the minimum inflation forecast for you to prefer the second option?

b. Is there a minimum loan amount after which you would always prefer the second option?

Question 10

You want to buy an apartment in Lalaland, and so on December 30, 1990, you need a loan of 100,000 Lays, with all repayments of principal, interest, and linkage being made in two years' time. The construction company offers you four choices:

1. A loan bearing a nominal annual interest of 25%.

2. A CPI-linked loan bearing a real quarterly interest of 1%.

3. A loan in which the principal is 90% linked to the CPI, while the 0.5% monthly interest is 70% linked to the CPI.

4. A USD-linked (principal and interest) loan bearing an annual interest of 10%.

Additional data: CPI quote for 11/1990–175.6; USD exchange rate as of December 31, 1990–2.048; CPI quote for 11/1989–148.3; USD exchange rate as of December 31, 1989–1.963.

Which loan should you choose, assuming the CPI's rate of increase remains steady, the annual increase in the USD exchange rate is three times higher in 1991 over 1990, and there was an additional 40% increase in the exchange rate between 1991 and 1992?

Further Reading

Ben-Horim, M., and H. Levy. 1986. *Financial Management in an Inflationary Economy, Financial Handbook*. 6th ed. Chichester: John Wiley.

Chambers, D. R., W. T. Carleton, and D. Waldman. 1984. A New Approach to Estimation of Terms Structure of Interest Rates. *Journal of Financial and Quantitative Studies* 19 (3): 233–252.

Coleman, T. S., L. Fisher, and R. Ibbotson. 1992. Estimating the Term Structure of Interest from Data That Include the Prices of Coupon Bonds. *Journal of Fixed Income* 2 (2): 2.

Cox, J. C., J. E. Ingersoll, and S. A. Ross. 1985. A Theory of the Term Structure of Interest Rates. *Econometrica* 53 (2):53.

Culbertson, J. M. 1957. The Term Structure of Interest Rates. *Quarterly Journal of Economics* 71 (4): 485–517.

Day, T. E. 1985. Expected Inflation and the Real Rate of Interest: A Note. *Journal of Banking and Finance* 9 (4): 491–498.

Duffie, D., and K. J. Singleton. 1997. An Econometric Model of the Term Structure of Interest-Rate Swap Yields. *Journal of Finance* 52 (4): 1287–1321.

Fama, E. F. 1975. Short-Term Interest Rates as Predictors of Inflation. *American Economic Review* 65 (June): 269–282.

Fama, E. F. 1984. The Information in the Term Structure. *Journal of Financial Economics* 13 (December): 509–528.

Jarrow, R. A., D. Lando, and S. M. Turnbull. 1997. A Markov Model for the Term Structure of Credit Spreads. *Review of Financial Studies* 10 (2): 481–523.

McCulloch, J. H. 1971. Measuring the Term Structure of Interest Rates. *Journal of Business* 44:19–31.

Meiselman, D. 1966. *The Term Structure of Interest Rates*. Princeton, NJ: Princeton University Press.

Walker, C. E. 1954. Federal Reserve Policy and the Structure of Interest Rates on Government Securities. *Quarterly Journal of Economics* 68 (1): 19–42.

4 Valuation of Periodic Cash Flows

A. Periodic Cash Flows

B. Future Value of Fixed Cash Flows

C. Present Value of Fixed Cash Flows

D. Present Value of Perpetual Cash Flows

E. Present Value of Variable Cash Flows

F. Problems in Future Cash Flow Valuation

A. Periodic Cash Flows

Many transactions involve a series (flow) of incoming or outgoing payments over time: monthly mortgage payments, current interest payments on savings plans, installments on a new car purchase, production machinery bought on supplier credit (paid over several months or even several years), periodic earning distributions paid to shareholders (dividends), or bonds yielding interest from time to time and redeemed on maturity. All these transactions, and many more, involve *periodic cash flows*. Any amount in a periodic (future) cash flow may be negative (outflows) or positive (inflows).

Let us denote by C_i future cash flows, where C (for "cash") indicates the amount paid (negative) or received (positive), while the index i indicates the end of the period in which the inflow or outflow occurs (or is to be made):

$$C_1, C_2, C_3, ..., C_n.$$

Later, we will want to sum up these cash flows, where each sum is translated into its present or future value. In finance terms, this is known as *discounting*.

Since the models developed below frequently use the sum of a geometric series, let us review them briefly.[1]

The sum of a geometric series with n terms is given by

$$S_n = A + A \cdot q + A \cdot q^2 + A \cdot q^3 + \ldots + A \cdot q^{n-1}.$$

Multiply each side of the equation by q:

$$S_n \cdot q = A \cdot q + A \cdot q^2 + A \cdot q^3 + \ldots + A \cdot q^{n-1} + A \cdot q^n.$$

Subtract the second line from the first:

$$S_n - S_n \cdot q = A - A \cdot q^n$$

$$\Rightarrow S_n = A \frac{1-q^n}{1-q} = A \frac{q^n - 1}{q-1}.$$

If the above is an infinite geometric series where $q < 0$ and $n \rightarrow \infty$, then q^n converges to zero and cancels out. Thus the sum of the infinite geometric series is given by

$$S_n = \frac{A}{1-q}.$$

B. Future Value of Fixed Cash Flows

Many savings plans are based on fixed periodic deposits (e.g., monthly) of an amount C deposited at the end of each period. These deposits are usually made for a specific purpose (e.g., buying an apartment, retirement), and we wish to know how much money we will have after n periods. Let us denote by FV the future value of this cash flow after n periods. The first deposit will bear interest over $n - 1$ periods, the next deposit will bear interest only over $n - 2$ periods, while the last deposit will not bear interest at all, as when we deposit it at the end of period n, we will also immediately withdraw it, along with all previously accrued amounts:

$$FV = C(1+r)^{n-1} + C(1+r)^{n-2} + \ldots + C(1+r) + C.$$

This yields a sum of a geometric series where

---

1. A geometric series is a series of terms (numbers) in which each term is greater (smaller) by a factor of q from the previous term, for example, $a_n = q \cdot a_{n-1}$.

$$S_n = A \cdot \frac{q^n - 1}{q - 1} \quad ; \quad A = C \quad ; \quad q = 1 + r$$

$$\Rightarrow FV = C \frac{(1+r)^n - 1}{(1+r) - 1} = C \frac{(1+r)^n - 1}{r}.$$

It is important to note whether deposits are made at the start or at the end of each period. If deposits are made at the start of each period, then each of the amounts will bear interest for one more period. This means we will need to multiply each term by $(1 + r)$. We can factor out $(1 + r)$ and remain inside the parentheses with an expression for deposits at the end of each period. Thus, the equation for deposits at the start of each period is identical to that used for deposits at the end of each period, multiplied by $(1 + r)$.

Instead of calculating the above equation, we can use future value discounting tables, such as table 4.1.

Table 4.1
Future Value Table $FV = \dfrac{(1+r)^n - 1}{r}$
Fixed $1 inflows/outflows at the end of each period, over n periods, at an interest rate of r.

n		1%	2%	3%	4%	5%	6%	7%	8%	9%
							r			
1		1.000	1.000	1.000	1.000	1.000	1.000	1.000	1.000	1.000
2		2.010	2.020	2.030	2.040	2.050	2.060	2.070	2.080	2.090
3		3.030	3.060	3.091	3.122	3.153	3.184	3.215	3.246	3.278
4		4.060	4.122	4.184	4.246	4.310	4.375	4.440	4.506	4.573
5		5.101	5.204	5.309	5.416	5.526	5.637	5.751	5.867	5.985
6		6.152	6.308	6.468	6.633	6.802	6.975	7.153	7.336	7.523
7		7.214	7.434	7.662	7.898	8.142	8.394	8.654	8.923	9.200
8	◀	8.286	8.583	8.892	9.214	9.549	9.897	10.260	10.637	11.028
9		9.369	9.755	10.159	10.583	11.027	11.491	11.978	12.488	13.021
10		10.462	10.950	11.464	12.006	12.578	13.181	13.816	14.487	15.193
11		11.567	12.169	12.808	13.486	14.207	14.972	15.784	16.645	17.560
12		12.683	13.412	14.192	15.026	15.917	16.870	17.888	18.977	20.141
13		13.809	14.680	15.618	16.627	17.713	18.882	20.141	21.495	22.953
14		14.947	15.974	17.086	18.292	19.599	21.015	22.550	24.215	26.019
15		16.097	17.293	18.599	20.024	21.579	23.276	25.129	27.152	29.361

The above table is calculated for $1. We must multiply the value indicated at the proper location in the table by C.

Example: We saved $1,000 at the end of each year in an eight-year savings plan bearing 6% interest. To find out how much we have at the end of the eight years, we first find the value for $1 saved over eight years at an interest rate of 6%, and then multiply it by $1,000 \Rightarrow \$9.897 \times 1,000 = \$9,897$.

As previously explained, had we deposited the same amount at the start of each year, we would need to multiply each of the above amounts by $(1 + r)$, and so all we need to do is multiply the above result by $(1 + r) = 1.06$.

Any financial calculator includes this equation built in (as well as others we will discuss later on). All one has to do is choose the function and type of parameters, such as the number of periods, the interest rate, and whether payments are made at the beginning or end of each period, and the result is calculated automatically. One can also employ these financial functions using Microsoft Excel.

> The online appendixes at http://finmodeling.com/en detail how to apply these tools.

C. Present Value of Fixed Cash Flows

We are frequently faced with the question of how much a future revenue stream is worth today. For example, we won a transportation tender for n years, and consequently bought a bus with a useful life of n years (after which it has zero value). The bus generates a fixed revenue stream C, paid at the end of each year. We are considering an offer we received to sell the contract along with the bus.

Practically speaking, we are asking ourselves what is the present value of the above cash flow fixed revenue stream C. Let us denote it by PV:

$$PV = \frac{C}{1+r} + \frac{C}{(1+r)^2} + \frac{C}{(1+r)^3} + \cdots + \frac{C}{(1+r)^n} .$$

This yields a sum of a geometric series, where:

$$S_n = A \cdot \frac{q^n - 1}{q - 1} \quad ; \quad A = \frac{C}{1+r} \quad ; \quad q = \frac{1}{1+r} \quad \Rightarrow$$

$$PV = \sum_{t=1}^{n} C \cdot \frac{1}{(1+r)^t} = C \cdot \frac{1 - \dfrac{1}{(1+r)^n}}{r} = C \cdot \left[\frac{1}{r} - \frac{1}{r(1+r)^n} \right].$$

Instead of calculating the above equation, we can use a present value discounting table, such as table 4.2.

Table 4.2
Present Value Table $PV = \left[\dfrac{1}{r} - \dfrac{1}{r(1+r)^n}\right]$

Fixed \$1 inflows/outflows at the end of each period, over n periods, at an interest rate of r.

n	r								
	1%	2%	3%	4%	5%	6%	7%	8%	9%
1	0.9901	0.9804	0.9709	0.9615	0.9524	0.9434	0.9346	0.9259	0.9174
2	1.9704	1.9416	1.9135	1.8861	1.8594	1.8334	1.8080	1.7833	1.7591
3	2.9410	2.8839	2.8286	2.7751	2.7232	2.6730	2.6243	2.5771	2.5313
4	3.9020	3.8077	3.7171	3.6299	3.5460	3.4651	3.3872	3.3121	3.2397
5	4.8534	4.7135	4.5797	4.4518	4.3295	4.2124	4.1002	3.9927	3.8897
6	5.7955	5.6014	5.4172	5.2421	5.0757	4.9173	4.7665	4.6229	4.4859
7	6.7282	6.4720	6.2303	6.0021	5.7864	5.5824	5.3893	5.2064	5.0330
8	7.6517	7.3255	7.0197	6.7327	6.4632	6.2098	5.9713	5.7466	5.5348
9	8.5660	8.1622	7.7861	7.4353	7.1078	6.8017	6.5152	6.2469	5.9952
10	9.4713	8.9826	8.5302	8.1109	7.7217	7.3601	7.0236	6.7101	6.4177
11	10.3676	9.7868	9.2526	8.7605	8.3064	7.8869	7.4987	7.1390	6.8052
12	11.2551	10.5753	9.9540	9.3851	8.8633	8.3838	7.9427	7.5361	7.1607
13	12.1337	11.3484	10.6350	9.9856	9.3936	8.8527	8.3577	7.9038	7.4869
14	13.0037	12.1062	11.2961	10.5631	9.8986	9.2950	8.7455	8.2442	7.7862
15	13.8651	12.8493	11.9379	11.1184	10.3797	9.7122	9.1079	8.5595	8.0607

The above table is calculated for \$1. We must multiply the value indicated at the required location in the table by C.

If the contract (and the bus) in the above example are for a 12-year period, and our net annual income is \$100,000, then, at a market interest rate of 5%, the present value of our future cash flow, according to table 4.2, will be

$8.8633 \times \$100,000 = \$886,330.$

Thus, if someone offers to buy the contract (and bus) at an amount greater than the above amount, selling is advisable. Then, if we still want to receive a fixed periodic income and not a lump sum, we can deposit the amount in the bank and receive an annual amount that is greater than the annual income from operating the bus.

The calculation is as follows. Let's assume we are offered \$950,000 for the contract and the bus. If we take this amount and deposit it in the bank in a 12-year savings plan offering 5% interest, with a fixed and equal payment of both principal and interest at the end of each year, how much would we get?

To calculate the amount C that we will receive, we once again use table 4.2. We saw that

$$PV = C \cdot \left[\frac{1}{r} - \frac{1}{r(1+r)^n}\right] = C \cdot (\text{discounting rate})$$

$$\Rightarrow\ C = \frac{PV}{\text{Discounting rate}} = \frac{950,000}{8.8633} = 107,183.5.$$

Thus, instead of receiving \$100,000 each year from operating the contract, we can sell the contract, deposit the money in the bank, and receive \$107,183.50 at the end of each year. Therefore, the transaction is definitely worthwhile.

Once again, we can use a calculator or MS Excel instead of the discounting table.

The online appendixes at http://finmodeling.com/en detail how to apply these tools.

Our final example below is more generally known as a debt settlement template.

We took out a \$500,000 mortgage for 20 years with a 12% nominal annual interest rate (calculated on a monthly basis). The debt is repaid through fixed installments (of principal plus interest) at the end of each month.

Let us denote this fixed payment by PMT (for "payment"). The discounting rate indicated in table 4.2 is denoted by K.

$$PV = PMT \cdot K.$$

$$PMT = \frac{PV}{K} = \frac{\$500,000}{K}.$$

The number of payments is $20 \times 12 = 240$, and the monthly interest rate is 1%.

Using table 4.2, a financial calculator, or a software program (MS Excel), we find that our monthly payment equals \$5,505.43.

Every payment consists of principal plus interest. Interest is paid on the outstanding principal balance for one month. The first payment consists mostly of interest, with a small portion paid on the principal. On the other hand, the final payment (on the last month) is mostly a payment on the principal, with only a small amount going toward interest. To enable borrowers to know the balance of their debt in each period, the bank usually provides an amortization schedule. For each payment, this schedule or table details that part of the payment paid toward the principal, the amount paid as interest, and the outstanding principal balance.

Calculating the amounts in table 4.2 (using a software program) is simple: the fixed payment is known, the outstanding principal balance is known, and the interest paid on that principal in the next month is easy to calculate. The amount of the principal repaid in that payment is the difference between these two amounts. The outstanding principal, on which next month's interest will be calculated, is the previous month's balance minus the calculated principal payment.

We begin our calculation with a principal of $500,000, and so the interest at the end of the first month, at a rate of 1%, equals $5,000.

The difference between our fixed payment ($5,505.43) and the interest indicates that in this payment, we repaid $505.43 of the principal, and so the outstanding principal (used to calculate next month's interest) equals $500,000 − $505.43 = $499,494.56. And so forth. An amortization schedule is shown in table 4.3.

Table 4.3
Amortization Schedule

n	Monthly Payment	Principal	Interest	Outstanding Principal
1	$–5,505.43	$–505.43	$–5,000.00	$499,494.56
2	$–5,505.43	$–510.48	$–4,994.95	$498,984.08
3	$–5,505.43	$–515.59	$–4,989.84	$498,468.49
4	$–5,505.43	$–520.75	$–4,984.68	$497,947.74
5	$–5,505.43	$–525.95	$–4,979.48	$497,421.79
6	$–5,505.43	$–531.21	$–4,974.22	$496,890.58
7	$–5,505.43	$–536.52	$–4,968.91	$496,354.05
8	$–5,505.43	$–541.89	$–4,963.54	$495,812.16
9	$–5,505.43	$–547.31	$–4,958.12	$495,264.85
10	$–5,505.43	$–552.78	$–4,952.65	$494,712.07
11	$–5,505.43	$–558.31	$–4,947.12	$494,153.76
12	$–5,505.43	$–563.89	$–4,941.54	$493,589.87
. . .	. . .	. . .	. . .	. . .
239	$–5,505.43	$–5,396.95	$–108.48	$5,450.92
240	$–5,505.43	$–5,450.92	$–54.51	$0

This type of table is known as a Spitzer amortization table after the person who first introduced it.

D. Present Value of Perpetual Cash Flows

Sometimes we have a perpetual cash flow. For practical purposes, cash flows with extremely long terms, extending, say for 100 years, can also be considered perpetual. The reason for this is simple: our payment 100 years from now is multiplied by the term $1/(1 + r)^n$. If $r = 10\%$, then for $n = 100$ we get a number on the order of 0.0001. The following terms are even smaller.

If we want to calculate the present value of a perpetual cash flow, we end up with a sum of an infinite geometric series.

When we substitute $n \to \infty$ in the expression developed in the previous section,

$$PV_{n \to \infty} = C \cdot \left[\frac{1}{r} - \frac{1}{r(1+r)^n} \right]$$

we end up with:

$$PV = \frac{C}{r}$$

In certain cases, we might want to calculate the present value of a perpetual revenue stream that increases at a fixed rate g (for "growth"). For example, the dividend a company is expected to pay at the end of the coming year is $10 for every $100 par value share. Everyone expects the company's dividends to grow by 6% each year (perpetually). The market interest rate is 10%.

What is the present value of the future cash flow expected from holding this share?

$$PV = \frac{C}{1+r} + \frac{C(1+g)}{(1+r)^2} + \frac{C(1+g)^2}{(1+r)^3} + \cdots + \frac{C(1+g)^{n-1}}{(1+r)^n} .$$

This is the sum of an infinite geometric series, where

$$S_n = \frac{A}{1-q} \quad ; \quad A = \frac{C}{1+r} \quad ; \quad q = \frac{1+g}{1+r} .$$

Substitute A and q into the equation for an infinite geometric series:

$$PV = \frac{C}{r-g} .$$

The result clearly indicates that r must be greater than g (otherwise the series will not converge to a positive number).

Substituting the values from our above example, $C = \$10$, $r = 0.1$, $g = 0.06$, into this equation, we find that the present value of the expected future dividend stream is

$$PV = \frac{C}{r-g} = \frac{\$10}{0.1-0.06} = \$250.$$

E. Present Value of Variable Cash Flows

When each amount in the cash flow is different, that is, $C_1, C_2, C_3, \ldots C_n$, where $C_i \neq C_j$, we must calculate the present value of each amount separately. As we are presenting the most general case, we can also add that the interest changes in each period. The present value of C_i received in i periods is $PV_i = \dfrac{c_i}{(1+r_i)^i}$.

By converting each amount separately into its value at a common point in time (e.g., present value), these amounts can be summed up.

For convenience, we can use the discounting schedule in table 4.4.

Table 4.4

Present Value Table $PV = \dfrac{1}{(1+r)^n}$

Of \$1 received/paid at the end of period n, at an interest rate of r.

n	1%	2%	3%	4%	5%	6%	7%	8%	9%
1	0.9901	0.9804	0.9709	0.9615	0.9524	0.9434	0.9346	0.9259	0.9174
2	0.9803	0.9612	0.9426	0.9246	0.9070	0.8900	0.8734	0.8573	0.8417
3	0.9706	0.9423	0.9151	0.8890	0.8638	0.8396	0.8163	0.7938	0.7722
4	0.9610	0.9238	0.8885	0.8548	0.8227	0.7921	0.7629	0.7350	0.7084
5	0.9515	0.9057	0.8626	0.8219	0.7835	0.7473	0.7130	0.6806	0.6499
6	0.9420	0.8880	0.8375	0.7903	0.7462	0.7050	0.6663	0.6302	0.5963
7	0.9327	0.8706	0.8131	0.7599	0.7107	0.6651	0.6227	0.5835	0.5470
8	0.9235	0.8535	0.7894	0.7307	0.6768	0.6274	0.5820	0.5403	0.5019
9	0.9143	0.8368	0.7664	0.7026	0.6446	0.5919	0.5439	0.5002	0.4604
10	0.9053	0.8203	0.7441	0.6756	0.6139	0.5584	0.5083	0.4632	0.4224
11	0.8963	0.8043	0.7224	0.6496	0.5847	0.5268	0.4751	0.4289	0.3875
12	0.8874	0.7885	0.7014	0.6246	0.5568	0.4970	0.4440	0.3971	0.3555
13	0.8787	0.7730	0.6810	0.6006	0.5303	0.4688	0.4150	0.3677	0.3262
14	0.8700	0.7579	0.6611	0.5775	0.5051	0.4423	0.3878	0.3405	0.2992
15	0.8613	0.7430	0.6419	0.5553	0.4810	0.4173	0.3624	0.3152	0.2745

Each amount is multiplied separately by the appropriate discounting rate.

This table allows us to discount variable cash flows, as well as one-time amounts.

For example, if the amount received or paid in three years is $500 and if the market interest rate on three-year loans is 7%, then the present value of this $500 is (as per the discounting rate in table 4.4[2])

$$PV = \$500 \frac{1}{(1+0.07)^3} \cong \$408.15.$$

If the amount paid or received in four years is $1,000 and the market interest rate on four-year loans is 8%, then the present value of the $1,000 is (as per the discounting rate in table 4.4)

$$PV = \$1000 \frac{1}{(1+0.08)^4} \cong \$735.$$

If these are the only two amounts to be received in the future, then their present value is $PV = \$408.15 + \$735 = \$1,143.15$.

F. Problems in Future Cash Flow Valuation

The above topics are essentially technical. Given the interest rate for each period and the amount for each period, we can easily and accurately calculate the present value of any cash flow. If we must receive or pay a given amount in the present, and in return we must pay or receive a given cash flow in the future with a given payment amount and at a given interest rate, we can easily calculate the present value of that future cash flow.

Our decision criterion for the investment is simple: if the present value PV of a future cash flow which we are expected to receive is greater than our present investment I, then the transaction is economical (and vice versa for future cash flows on a present loan L). Meaning:

For future inflows: $NPV = PV - I > 0 \Rightarrow$ Invest.

For future outflows: $NPV = L - PV > 0 \Rightarrow$ Take the loan.

NPV is the net present value of a financial decision. If it is positive, then the transaction is economical, and if it is negative, the transaction is not worthwhile! (Zero = indifferent.)

So far, everything seems simple, logical, and easy. However, things are significantly more complicated. In most cases, our assumptions that the interest rate in any given period is known with certainty and that amounts

---

2. The expression $\frac{1}{(1+0.07)^3}$ is identical to the value of 0.8163 indicated in the discounting schedule in table 4.4 (see appendix **A** on the website accompanying this book).

are known with certainty do not hold. The interest rate for every period can be derived from the term structure of the interest rate known when making the decision. When we discussed the term structure of interest rates, we emphasized that they are subject to change, and so the data that were available to us when making our decision may turn out to be untrue as circumstances change over time. Cash flow amounts are likewise uncertain.

In the example where we assessed the cost-effectiveness of selling our contract and bus (section C in this chapter), we assumed that our annual income was given and fixed. Clearly, this assumption is far from accurate. In times of recession, budgetary cutbacks, conflict, or disasters, or in times of economic growth, expanding fiscal policies, peace, or even plain old luck, amounts may vary significantly from those assessed and used in our decision.

As mentioned earlier, a good model is one that simplifies the problem. In the first part of this book, our models assume absolute certainty, and we discuss only the effect of time on the value of financial assets and decisions. In the second part we will expand the models and see how they can be expanded beyond the certainty assumption.

Calculation Tools—Online Appendixes (http://finmodeling.com/en):

1. Discounting tables—see appendix A.
2. CASIO FC100 calculators—see appendix B.
3. Financial calculations using Excel—see appendix C.

Chapter 4—Questions and Problems

Question 1

a. You've built an ice cream machine. You expect the machine to yield revenues of $100,000 a year, and the machine has a useful life of only five years. Because of your burning desire to pursue an artistic lifestyle and open a paintbrush manufacturing business, you wish to sell the ice cream machine. Assuming a 6% annual market interest rate, what is the minimum amount for which you would be willing to sell the machine?

b. *Consol* bonds guarantee a certain interest rate from purchase and into perpetuity. What is the present market price of a consol bond if you know that it pays $500 annually in interest? (Assume a market interest rate of 6%.)

Question 2

Instead of paying $6,000 cash for a product, you are offered two alternatives:

1. Six monthly payments of $1,145 each (first installment in cash plus five installments).
2. One payment three years from today with the same effective interest rate as in part (a) of the question.

What is the amount that you will have to pay if you choose option B?

Question 3

Your employer decides to grant all employees a sizable bonus of $1,500. Alternatively, employees may choose to receive $2,200 in four years' time. Assuming that you will remain with the same employer for four years, which option should you choose? (Assume $r = 7\%$.)

Answer the question once in terms of present value and a second time in terms of future value.

Question 4

You started working at age 24. As part of your employment contract, your employer's insurance company offers you executive insurance based on fixed contributions out of your monthly salary, as follows:

• You will contribute 5% of your monthly salary to the insurance policy.
• Your employer will contribute 5% of your monthly salary to the insurance policy.
• Your employer will contribute 8.33% of your salary for severance pay.

Assume the following: Your monthly salary is currently $10,000. Your insured salary is 80% of your present salary (contributions to the insurance policy are based on your insured salary). The insurance company guarantees a fixed annual yield of 5% on your money, covered by special-purpose bonds issued by the government.

a. What is the amount that you can expect to accrue by age 65, assuming that you remain with this company your entire life and your salary does not change over the years?

b. What is the amount can you expect to accrue if, after 21 years, you succeed in improving your terms and update your insured salary to 100% of your monthly salary? (*Note:* The monthly salary itself remains unchanged.)

Question 5

Congratulations! You're 65! When you meet with the insurance company to collect the $1 million that you have accrued over your working life (no connection to the previous question), your insurance company offers you a choice between receiving the $1 million right away or receiving a monthly pension of $4,500 until the end of your life. Assume a market interest rate of 3%.

a. What is the average life span on which the insurance company bases its calculations?

b. Your life span is average. Is it worthwhile for you to choose the insurance option?

Question 6

To upgrade your current production equipment, you require an investment that in the next two years (only) will yield an increase in profits. You have a choice between the following two investments:

	Investment 1	Investment 2
Investment cost	$15,000	$7,000
Increase in profits in year 1	$9,000	$4,000
Increase in profits in year 2	$9,500	$6,000

Investment financing costs are 10%.

Assuming your decision is based on maximizing net present value, which investment should you choose?

Question 7

After buying a luxury vehicle, you do not have any money left to pay for your tuition. Therefore, you have to borrow $2,000 from the bank for four years, at a nominal annual interest rate of 11%, calculated on a monthly basis. Both principal and interest are to be repaid at the end of the period. What is the expected amount of the repayment?

Question 8

You decided to buy a car that costs $80,000. The importer demands 25% cash down when you order the car. The remaining amount is a loan paid in 24 equal monthly installments. The financing loan is provided at a 12% nominal annual interest rate (calculated monthly). What will your monthly payment be?

Question 9

It is time to renew your car insurance policy. Your insurance company offers you two choices for paying your premiums:

1. Five equal monthly installments of $400, with the first paid immediately.

2. Ten equal monthly installments of $220, with the first paid immediately.

What is the interest rate on which your insurance company bases its payment plan? (Assume an identical interest rate in both options.)

Question 10

A possible investment offers forecasted cash flows of $20,000 in years 1–5 and $25,000 in years 6–10. In light of inflation projections, you demand a minimum return of 12% in each of the first five years and 10% from the sixth year on. What is the maximum amount that you should invest in the project?

Further Reading

Golub, S. J., and H. D. Huffman. 1984. Cashflow: Why It Should Be Stressed in Financial Reporting. *Financial Executive* (February).

Greenfield, R. L., M. R. Randall, and J. D. Woods. 1983. Financial Leverage and Use of the Net Present Value Investment Criterion. *Financial Management* (Autumn).

5 Fundamental Bond Valuation Models

A. Yield and Risk

B. Perfect Market — Valuing Financial Assets

C. Basic Models for Bonds

D. Bond Types and Generally Accepted Terminology

A. Yield and Risk

In the two-period, present-future model discussed in the previous chapters, we learned how to mathematically express the fact that money today is worth more than money tomorrow, through the equation $C_0 = \dfrac{1}{1+k} \cdot C_1$. Simple arithmetic derives $k = \dfrac{C_1}{C_0} - 1$, which represents the yield[1] on investment C_0 made at the start of a period, if we know that amount C_1 will be received as a return at the end of the period. Variable k, which in previous chapters was referred to as "interest" or "the discount rate," also fits the definition of yield, so that all three terms may be used interchangeably.

While discussing interest in the previous chapters, we learned that a risk premium is required in excess of the basic rate, and we listed various factors considered in figuring this risk premium, expressed mathematically as $R_{Nom} = R_f + IP + DP + LP + MP$. Even without trying to reach a unique (mathematical) definition of risk (a subject reserved for the second part of this book), we can define a basic functional relation between risk and the required yield:

---

1. "Yield" denotes the profit on an investment, expressed as a percentage of the investment.

The higher the risk, the higher is the premium we require above the basic interest rate (yield).

Mathematically speaking, we require the functional relation between yield and risk to be expressed by an increasing function. In the second part of the book, we will try to define risk in a way that allows us to find a mathematical, functional correlation that enables the discount rate k to be matched with the risk carried by an investment. For now, we can do this in an intuitively empirical fashion. For example, if we are considering whether to invest in bonds or shares issued by a meat product company, we can check the common yield in the market on investments (bonds and shares separately) in the meat industry. If we are considering whether to invest in transportation-related (e.g., an airline or shipping company) securities, we can check the common (required) yield in that specific market. The correlation between the discount rate and yield simplifies matters immensely. All we must do is read reports issued by publicly traded companies in a certain industry, use these reports to calculate the yield required by investors,[2] and then use this calculated yield as our risk-adjusted discount rate (for that industry) for our new investment.

In the second part of this book we discuss models for calculating required yield as a function of both the basic risk-free interest rate, which reflects time preference, and risk: $k = f$(basic interest rate; risk).

B. Perfect Market — Valuing Financial Assets

So far we have discussed only one type of financial asset, bonds. We used bonds to spread individual consumption over time and to enable companies to make investments. In chapter 2 we learned that individuals may advance or postpone their own consumption over time by borrowing (=issuing a bond) or lending (=buying a bond), respectively. Companies, on the other hand, can raise the capital required for physical investments[3] by issuing "IOU certificates," called bonds, or by issuing "participation certificates" in company ownership, called shares. Individuals may wish to buy or sell their holdings of bonds or shares on the capital market (the stock exchange) at any given time.[4]

---

2. The yield on an investment in bonds differs from the yield on an investment in shares.

3. That is, physical as opposed to financial investments.

4. To illustrate the point, there is no practical difference between the capital market and a fish market or a vegetable market. Each market trades according to the rules of supply and demand.

To simplify the development of a model that describes how supply and demand shape financial asset prices on the capital market, we must make several assumptions concerning capital markets. A capital market that meets the following assumptions, or requirements, will be referred to as a *perfect capital market*:

1. Transactions are free of expenses (no brokerage fees); there are no taxes and no administrative restrictions.

2. We can buy any quantity we wish (including bond or share fractions).

3. The capital market is a competitive market (no single player is large enough to influence prices).

4. The market is characterized by perfect information; information is free and available to everyone simultaneously.

5. All individuals in the market make rational decisions based on maximizing their utility expectancy.

The last two items are of particular importance, as they are probably new to readers who until now have studied only commodity supply-and-demand models in basic microeconomics courses.

The fifth item accounts for the uncertainty of future yields. Buyers and sellers in the capital market make decisions based on maximizing their utility expectancy, in contrast to the street markets for commodities, in which buyers may see exactly what they get for their money and decisions are based on maximizing the utility function itself (and not its expected—i.e., average—term). This issue is discussed in greater depth in the second part of this book.

The assumption underlying the perfect information requirement is extremely important (and also applies to commodity markets) and has been the focus of much academic debate, particularly with respect to the capital market. Studies in this matter use a new term, *arbitrage*.

Arbitrage The ability to buy an asset at one price and simultaneously sell an identical asset (or a perfect equivalent) at a higher price.

The assumption underlying the requirement of perfect information effectively prevents any possible arbitrage. The arbitrage reflected in item four dictates that a certain financial asset has only one price at any given point in time, regardless of location. Under this assumption it is not possible, for example, to buy an IBM share on the New York Stock Exchange and simultaneously sell that same share on the Tokyo Stock

Exchange at a higher price.[5] Arbitrage eliminates the possibility of investment- and risk-free profits. It is emphasized that, although this assumption prevails in the vast majority of classical models, in 2001 the Nobel Prize in Economics was awarded to Michael Spence from Stanford, George Akerlof from Berkeley, and Joseph Stiglitz from Columbia University for their separate work on asymmetric information. Their work showed that the last two of the above assumptions are false: information in capital markets is not perfect, and people do not always make rational decisions. Therefore, markets do not always perfectly match supply and demand, which creates price disparities.

To explain the concept behind their work, let's assume that person A has better information than person B about the value of a certain financial asset, and person B is aware of this fact. Akerlof draws on the used-car market to construct an analogy for the capital market: someone who believes that a used car is not in good condition would want to pay a lower price for the car than for a car known to be in good condition. If there is no way of knowing which car is in good condition and which is not (only the seller knows), all buyers would want to pay a lower price. Owners of cars in good condition will not want to trade in this market and sell their cars, as the price is lower than the real price at equilibrium (i.e., the price if buyers knew which cars were in good condition and which were not). This is analogous to the capital market: holders of better financial assets will not want to sell (or issue). The Keynesian model, so familiar to readers who have studied economics, predicts that under certain conditions investments may drop, which would lead to an economic slowdown and unemployment. According to the work done by the above Nobel laureates, it is also possible that the capital market has an inherent capacity for underinvestment or overinvestment, which may cause price bubbles for financial assets, such as the one that characterized capital markets around the world in 2001–2002 and collapsed with great commotion.

The reason why the work by Spence, Akerlof, and Stiglitz was presented is to illustrate once again that financial curricula cannot provide students with the sort of hard-and-fast solutions that engineering curricula, for example, can provide. However, financial curricula provide students with analysis and planning tools, infinitely preferable to coin-toss decision making, that will serve them in real-world

---

5. If we were to have such an option, it would be equivalent to owning a money-printing machine.

situations. Readers must remember that the following models are based on assumptions. When applying these models in real-world situations, we must check just how valid our assumptions are for the matter at hand at that particular point in time. Alternatively, we can use the model as a starting point and then update or adapt it to unique circumstances.

We must differentiate between the term "perfect market" and the term "efficient market," frequently used in connection with capital markets. "Market efficiency" deals with the actual market's closeness to perfect market conditions as defined above. Market efficiency studies mainly focus on the operational aspects of a capital market, as required under the first of the above items, and on a level of perfect information where no individual can make excessive profits, as expressed in the fourth item. Obviously, real-world conditions include transaction expenses, taxes, and administrative limitations, and information is not perfect. Market efficiency studies set out to check the extent to which these deviations from the above assumptions affect our ability to use the perfect market model, and what adjustments must be made to the model. The following chapters discuss several aspects of market efficiency (e.g., taxes) and their effects on the various models.

C. Basic Models for Bonds

The basic bond models are derived from the topics discussed in chapters 3 and 4. The classic historical bond is the *coupon bond*. These bonds are issued as a paper certificate with a face value F (e.g., $100) and a maturity date. The bond includes coupons for denominated interest payments C, with predetermined payment dates (usually annual or semiannual).[6] The bond is redeemed, after T interest payments, at its face value F. We can easily calculate the present value (PV) of the cash flow derived from the bond (B = bond value):

$$B = PV = \underbrace{\frac{C}{1+k} + \frac{C}{(1+k)^2} + \frac{C}{(1+k)^3} + \cdots + \frac{C}{(1+k)^T}}_{PV_C} + \underbrace{\frac{F}{(1+k)^T}}_{PV_F}.$$

6. On the due date, the certificate holder clips the coupon from the certificate and redeems it for cash. In the modern version of these bonds, bondholder titles are recorded electronically (via computer), without paper certificates or coupons, and the stated interest is automatically transferred to bondholders' accounts on the prescribed date.

Separating the last term in the equation from the terms to its left yields the sum of a geometric series with a present value PV_C, and the final term with a present value PV_F. The equation for these two terms was discussed in chapter 4:

$$PV_C = \sum_{t=1}^{T} \frac{C}{(1+k)^t} = C \cdot [\frac{1}{k} - \frac{1}{k(1+k)^T}].$$

$$PV_F = \frac{F}{(1+k)^T}.$$

We can easily calculate the price of this bond by calculating the present value of the cash flows from its interest coupons using a cash flow discounting table (or a calculator or software program). We can then calculate the present value of the payment on the bond's face value at maturity using these same tools, and then add the two sums together.

Example: A 15-year bond with a face value of $100 is carrying an interest rate of 15% (annual coupon of $15). Over 15 years, we have a cash flow of $15 paid at the end of each year. At the end of the fifteenth year we redeem the bond at its face value of $100, in addition to the interest payment (coupon).

Assuming that the bond was issued when the market interest rate was 15%, what was the issue price of the bond?

Let's discount to present value the cash flow, consisting of $15 received every year over 15 years at a 15% annual interest rate. Using the discounting table or a calculator, we find that the present value of this cash flow is $87.71. Discounting the $100 face value to be received on the bond after 15 years, we find that its value upon issue is $12.29. Adding these two numbers together, we end up with $100. Therefore, the bond was issued at face value.

Let's assume that we want to sell the bond after three years. Assuming that the market interest rate is still 15%, at what price will we sell the bond?

There are still 12 years until the bond's maturity. Discounting the cash flow consisting of $15 coupons received every year over 12 years at an annual interest rate of 15%, we find that its present value is $81.31. Discounting the $100 face value to be received after 12 years, we find that its present value is $18.69. Adding the two numbers together, we get $100.

Therefore, assuming that market interest rates stay the same, a (risk-free) bond issued at an interest rate equal to the market interest rate will be issued and sold at its face value throughout its lifetime (figure 5.1).

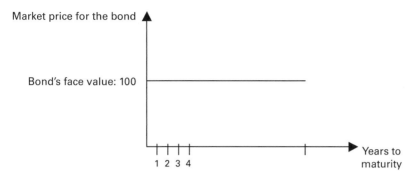

Figure 5.1
Bond's Market Value When the Interest Rate Is Fixed over Time

But is this actually the case?

Let's assume that we sell the bond one year after its issue, either

1. One day before payment of the interest coupon, or

2. One day after payment of the interest coupon.

The bond's price one day after the coupon payment will indeed be calculated using the above formulas, and will always be $100.

However, what happens if we sell the bond one day before the coupon payment?

Clearly, the difference between the two prices is the coupon value ($15), paid when moving from one day to the next. As one day after the coupon payment, the bond's price is $100, then one day before, its price is $115. If we focus on the first two years in figure 5.1, the price of that bond will behave as graphed in figure 5.2.

Let's also assume that after one year (immediately after payment of the first coupon), the market interest rate drops to 10% and is expected to remain at this level for a long time (the next 20 years). In chapter 3 we saw how changes in market interest rates cause bondholders to incur profits or losses. Our discussion in chapter 3 was quantitative only for one-year bonds, and qualitative for bonds maturing over a period of several years. We now have at our disposal the tools to calculate both cases.

Using the discounting tables or a calculator, we discount the cash flows, which consist of $15 each year over 14 years (the number of years remaining until the bond's maturity) with 10% interest, and find a present value of $110.50. We discount the $100 payment to be received after 14

Market price of the bond

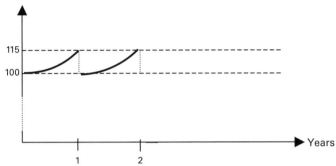

Figure 5.2
Bond's Market Value When the Interest Rate Is Fixed over Time — Zoomed-in View

years, for a present value of $26.33. Adding the two numbers together, we find that the bond's market value is $136.83.

This means that if an investor decides to sell the bond one day after payment of the coupon, its market price would be $136.83. In one year, that investor received (for every $100 invested) $15 in interest and another $136.83 from selling the bond, for a total of $151.83.

Let's define the equation for the interest coupon payment as the *interest yield,* and denote it by k_I. Then $k_I = 15\%$.

Now, let's define the yield on the difference in the bond's buying/selling price as the *capital gains yield*, and denote it by k_P. Then $k_P = 36.83\%$.

The *total yield* on the investment in this bond, k_B, is equal to the sum of these two figures: $k_B = k_I + k_P = 15\% + 36.83\% = 51.83\%$.

A bond that is traded above its face value is referred to as a *premium bond.*

If a bondholder holds the bond to maturity, he will continue to receive the same $15 every year, plus the $100 upon maturity, so as far as that particular investor is concerned, nothing has changed.

It would seem that we have turned a profit out of thin air, but one must remember that if, after selling our bond, we were to buy another in its stead, we would only receive a 10% return each year. If we manage our portfolio skillfully (let's assume that we expected the interest rate to go down a year in advance following an economic analysis of market conditions), then after realizing our excess yield of 36.83% from the previous year, we can now invest our money elsewhere (e.g., in foreign currency), with the hope of recording an excess yield on our investment in the next year as well.

Note that the investor who bought the bond from us at a price of $136.83 can only receive an annual yield of 10% as per market conditions. Although at the end of the year he would still receive a $15 coupon, if we calculate the yield on his investment, we find that it is only $k_I = \$15/\$136.83 = 10.96\%$.

If that investor wants to sell the bond, he would only be able to ask for $135.52.[7]

The capital loss on the sale of the bond is therefore

$$k_P = (\$135.52 - \$136.83)/\$136.83 = -0.96\%.$$

The overall annual yield for the new investor would therefore be as expected: $k_B = 10.96\% + (-0.96\%) = 10\%$.

Note that the bond price goes down every year until it reaches its face value of $100, which is its value at maturity. Accordingly, every year investors will incur a capital loss, but this loss is offset by the excess interest yield, so that the overall annual yield for an investor will be 10%, as per market conditions.

If we assume that the interest rate goes up to 20% after one year and carry out the above calculation, we will see that the present value of the coupon inflow would be $69.16 and the bond would be redeemed at a present value of $7.79, for a total of $76.95. Therefore, in one year we would incur a capital loss of $23.05 for every $100 invested. However, the total annual yield recorded by an investor for holding the bond would be $k_B = k_I + k_P = 15\% + (-23.05\%) = -8.05\%$.

A bond that is traded below its face value is referred to as a *discount bond*.

In summary, if the coupon value matches the market interest rate, the bond price will be equal to its face value (or, at a higher resolution, as detailed above, it will follow a saw-toothed pattern, i.e., it will show a pattern of sudden drops, followed by gradual recoveries). If the market interest rate is higher than the coupon interest rate, the bond will be traded below its face value, and vice versa when the market interest rate is lower than the coupon interest rate (figure 5.3 below).

Note: If the interest rate is changed, for example, eight years after issue (seven years before maturity), then the capital gain or loss recorded as a result of the interest rate change will be smaller than above. As already demonstrated in chapter 3, the longer the maturity time of a bond, the

---

7. If we discount a $15 coupon over 13 years at 10% interest, we get $106.55. The face value in 13 years at 10% interest equals $28.97. In total, the bond's value will be $135.52.

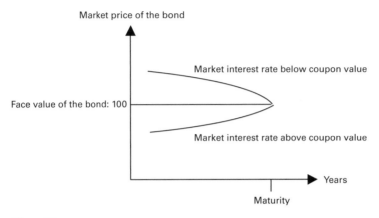

Figure 5.3
Bond's Market Value over Time When the Coupon Interest Rate Is Different from the Market Interest Rate

greater the changes in that bond's price caused by interest rate changes (i.e., the more sensitive it is to such changes). Therefore, these bonds will require a greater risk premium (as reflected in a maturity premium).

Bonds are also issued in other forms, such as zero-coupon bonds. Payment is made for the face value of these bonds only upon maturity. If such a bond is issued with a face value of $100, then according to our above calculation, its value upon issue (with a medium-term market interest rate of 15%) is only $12.29. The issuing company will receive $12.29 for every $100 face value bond issued. Therefore, if we wished to invest $100, we would buy 100/12.29 = 7.14 bonds.

If after one year the market interest rate goes down to 10%, the value of each bond redeemable in 14 years will change to $26.33, for a gain of

26.33/12.29 − 1 = 114.24%.

If after one year the interest rate increases to 20%, then the value of each bond redeemable in 14 years will change to $7.70, for a loss of

7.70/12.29 − 1 = −36.62%.

As we can see, these bonds are more sensitive to market interest rate fluctuations than the previous coupon bond.

The reason for this is simple. With coupon bonds, where interest is paid annually, the first coupon paid after the interest rate change is affected only by the interest rate change for one year. The coupon paid in two years' time will be affected by the change for two years, and so on. With noncoupon bonds, payment of both principal and interest is made together at the end of the period, and so all interest coupons are affected by the change for the entire period until maturity.

The more sensitive a bond to interest rate fluctuations, the more "risky" it is. The quotation marks indicate that this sensitivity may work to our advantage (if market interest rates go down) or to our disadvantage (if market interest rates go up). More sensitive bonds are generally referred to as being riskier. We can define a risk measurement index as the percent change in a bond's price as a result of market interest rates changing by 1%.

We saw that

$$B = \frac{C}{1+k} + \frac{C}{(1+k)^2} + \frac{C}{(1+k)^3} + \cdots + \frac{C}{(1+k)^T} + \frac{F}{(1+k)^T} = \sum_{t=1}^{T} \frac{C}{(1+k)^t} + \frac{F}{(1+k)^T}.$$

Instead of finding the *relative* change in the bond price B (i.e., $dB/_B$) caused by a relatively small change in interest rate k (i.e., $dk/_k$), we may, for the sake of mathematical convenience, consider an (even smaller) relative change in $(1 + k)$, which constitutes the denominator in the last equation for the bond value (i.e., $\frac{d(1+k)}{(1+k)}$).[8]

To find the *absolute* change in the bond's price $\frac{dB}{d(1+k)}$ we need to derivate B with respect to $(1 + k)$:

$$\frac{dB}{d(1+k)} = -\left\{ \frac{C}{(1+k)^2} + \frac{2 \cdot C}{(1+k)^3} + \cdots + \frac{T \cdot C}{(1+k)^{T+1}} + \frac{T \cdot F}{(1+k)^{T+1}} \right\}.$$

To find the *relative* price change as a percent of the bond's price B, that is, $\frac{dB}{B}$, as the percent change of $(1 + k)$, that is, $\frac{d(1+k)}{(1+k)}$, we can divide the numerator by B and the denominator by $(1 + k)$:

$$\frac{dB/B}{d(1+k)/(1+k)} = \frac{(1+k) \cdot dB}{B \cdot d(1+k)}$$

$$= -\frac{1}{B}\left\{ \frac{C}{1+k} + \frac{2 \cdot C}{(1+k)^2} + \frac{3 \cdot C}{(1+k)^3} + \cdots + \frac{T \cdot C}{(1+k)^T} + \frac{T \cdot F}{(1+k)^T} \right\}$$

$$= \frac{\displaystyle\sum_{t=1}^{T} t \cdot \frac{C}{(1+k)^t} + T \cdot \frac{F}{(1+k)^T}}{\displaystyle\sum_{t=1}^{T} \frac{C}{(1+k)^t} + \frac{F}{(1+k)^T}}$$

8. That is, $\frac{dk}{k} \approx \frac{d(1+k)}{(1+k)}$ for small k.

The denominator in the last term, $\sum_{t=1}^{T} \dfrac{C}{(1+k)^t} + \dfrac{F}{(1+k)^T}$, is the bond value B itself:

$$\frac{dB/B}{d(1+k)/(1+k)} = \frac{\displaystyle\sum_{t=1}^{T} t \cdot \frac{C}{(1+k)^t} + T \cdot \frac{F}{(1+k)^T}}{B} = \sum_{t=1}^{T} \frac{t \cdot \dfrac{C}{(1+k)^t}}{B} + \frac{T \cdot \dfrac{F}{(1+k)^T}}{B}.$$

If we look closely at the last term, we see that it is composed of the sum of the weighted payment dates t. Each payment date t is multiplied (weighted) by the portion (percent) of the present value of that payment $\dfrac{C_t}{(1+k)^t}$ out of the overall present value of the bond B, that is, $t \cdot \left(\dfrac{C_t}{(1+k)^t} \Big/ B \right)$.[9] By summing all these weighted times, we arrive at the duration (average lifetime to maturity) of the bond, denoted DT.

Note that "duration" and a bond's "sensitivity to interest rate changes" are two different terms for the same thing.

The longer a bond's duration (DT), the more sensitive (risky) its price is to interest rate changes:

$$DT = \frac{dB/B}{d(1+k)/(d(1+k))}.$$

At any given moment, bonds are traded at a different price than their face value. Investors are not interested in the price at which a bond is traded at a given moment but in the (internal) rate of return used to discount the bond in order to derive its price on the market.[10] Only a comparison of the internal rates of return offered by two bonds can provide us with actionable information as to which bond we should invest in, the one with the higher return.[11]

A bond's internal rate of return is referred to as its yield to maturity.

As mentioned, there are many different types of bonds on the market. For example, bonds carrying variable annual interest rates (linked to the market interest rate), CPI-linked bonds, unlinked bonds, and others. For each type of bond, we can calculate its net present value, as explained in

9. Note that for the last period T, accounting also adds the present value of the payment for the face value, out of the total value of the bond.

10. We can also consider the internal interest rate as the retrospective yield if we buy the bond at its stated market price and hold it to maturity.

11. The scenario assumes they have the same risk.

chapter 4, and then factor in the various risk premiums for each bond. The fact that a bond offers a higher yield to maturity does not necessarily make it more attractive. Most likely, the difference in yield is due to higher risk premium factors required. The multitude of different bond types does not allow us to develop a separate model for each type. The calculation tools and conceptual aids provided so far (as well as those to come) suffice for intelligent investment decision making in the bonds market.

D. Bond Types and Generally Accepted Terminology

This topic is extensive and requires particular specialization. We will now discuss several key terms that are important to assessing the risks inherent in each type of bond.

A bond is an instrument for long-term capital raising. As in every long-term investment (e.g., buying an apartment), the asset purchased with this capital is usually mortgaged. If no real asset exists for mortgaging, a bond is issued without collateral guaranteeing repayment. These kinds of bonds are known as *debentures*.

In order to pay a lower interest rate on their bonds, issuing companies sometimes include a special incentive with a bond to entice investors to buy it. One common way to do this is to grant an option to convert each bond into a set number of shares.[12] These bonds are known as *convertible bonds*. Holders of such a bond to maturity will be able to check whether the value of the (converted) shares is higher than the face value of the bond. If so, they may convert the bond and receive a larger sum. If the conversion value is higher than the bond's discounted value, the market price of the bond will track the market share price. If the conversion value is lower than the discounted value, the bond price will equal the discounted value (of the face value, plus interest). The bond effectively becomes a share substitute, with two main advantages:

1. It guarantees a fixed minimum yield through interest (regardless of dividend distributions), with the possibility of even higher yields through the conversion option into shares.

2. It has a minimum price, so that even if share prices drop significantly, bondholders will still receive the face value of their bond.

---

12. An option, not an obligation.

These advantages[13] allow issuing companies to offer these bonds at a lower interest rate than they would need to if they offered the bonds without this incentive, thereby reducing financing expenses.[14] A similar type of bond offers the benefit of buying a set number of shares at a predetermined price instead of the conversion option. These bonds are known as *warrants*.

The above cases aim to swap (trade) bond-related risks, thereby reducing interest payments. Sometimes companies wish to reduce bankruptcy risks. In that case, they can issue bonds that pay interest only if the company has sufficient profit. These bonds are known as *income bonds*. Although they reduce a company's risk of bankruptcy, they increase the risk for investors, who might not receive interest or might have their interest payment delayed, and therefore the bonds must compensate investors for the extra risk by offering a higher yield.

In the previous section, we discussed the most common types of bonds:

• Classic, or coupon-bearing bonds

• Zero-coupon bonds, whose yield to maturity is determined by discounting their face value upon maturity

• Floating-rate bonds, which offer variable interest rates

• CPI-linked or indexed bonds, and others that are linked to currency exchange rates

In addition to bond type–related risks, bonds are subject to risk from formal contractual conditions (indentures) between bondholders and bond issuers. For example, these contractual conditions may (or may not) obligate bond issuers to set up a "sinking fund" in which they deposit a certain amount each year so as to guarantee they have enough cash to redeem the bond at maturity; they may or may not entitle a company to force a buyback of bonds if market interest rates fall below a certain level; and so forth. Each condition included or excluded from the contract affects a bond's risk level, and therefore affects the yield required by investors, who take into account the risk premium, so that they will be willing to buy the bond.

Investors must take into account a great many parameters. Some, such as those related to interest rate fluctuation risks, are easily measured.

---

13. These advantages can also be valued. However, the necessary mathematical models are covered only in the second part of the book and in advanced courses.

14. There are no free meals, though. Although company owners (shareholders) expect a higher yield on their shares through lower financing expenses, it is quite possible that their holdings will be diluted when the bonds are converted into shares.

Others, mainly those related to current interest and principal payments on maturity, are harder to account for and may even vary throughout a bond's lifetime. Ordinary investors cannot track these parameters themselves over a bond's lifetime. Since the start of the twentieth century, rating agencies have been established to rate bond risk levels. The best known of these are Moody's and Standard & Poor's. These companies rate bonds from AAA (triple A)—excellent for investment; to BBB (triple B)—OK; BB (double B)—speculative; and so on through to junk bond status, assigned to bonds issued by companies facing bankruptcy.

Rating agencies take into account additional parameters beyond those discussed above. This book focuses on models, and so we will not discuss the issue in depth. Readers are encouraged to expand their knowledge through financial textbooks dealing with institutional entities. This topic was presented in brief so as to inform readers that there are other bond valuation tools available in addition to the models presented in this chapter.

Chapter 5—Questions and Problems

Question 1

A company issues coupon bonds with a face value of $1,000 and carrying 6% annual interest paid at the end of each year. The bonds are issued for 15 years. As of today (the issue date), these bonds are traded at a price of $720.

a. Calculate the market interest rate for these bonds.

b. What price would you expect to receive for 10-year coupon bonds with an identical risk premium, a face value of $1,000, and bearing an interest rate of 6.5% paid at the end of each year?

Question 2

Assume an eight-year, government-issued coupon bond with a face value of $1,000 and 12% interest paid at the end of each year. Assume that the yield to maturity on this bond is 7%.

a. Calculate the price of the bond.

b. Calculate the bond's price assuming a 12% interest rate on the bond, paid semiannually (6%). The bond's face value, lifetime, and yield to maturity remain the same. Note that the yield to maturity is the annual yield to maturity.

c. Calculate the duration of both bonds (in parts (a) and (b)). Explain your results.

Question 3

The following table details January 2010 prices on zero-coupon government bonds with a $100 face value, free of any default or liquidity risks. Calculate the term structure of the interest rates.

Maturity Date	Price
January 2011	$96.153
January 2012	$91.573
January 2013	$86.383
January 2014	$80.721

Question 4

Bonds with an infinite lifetime are referred to as consol bonds. Assume a consol bond with a face value of $5,000 and an interest rate of 7% paid at the end of each year.

a. Calculate the bond's price on November 1, assuming the annual yield to maturity required on the market is 9%.

b. If the bond price on January 1 is $6,800, what is the market interest rate for this type of bond?

c. An investor bought this bond at $4,200 on January 1, and sold it after seven years. Assuming the annual yield to maturity did not change over the years, what is the price of the bond?

Question 5

On January 1, 1995, Success Inc. issued a 10-year coupon bond with a face value of $8,000 and an interest rate of 4%, paid at the end of each year. An investor bought the bond on January 1, 1997, at a price of $7,000, and sold it after three years at a price of $7,600. What is the average annual rate of return for the bond recorded by the investor?

Question 6

You want to invest in order to buy a car five years from now. You have the following bond investment options:

• Consol (perpetual) bonds, 80% linked to the CPI and bearing 6% interest, traded at 103 points (every $100 par value costs $103); or

• Consol bonds, 100% linked to the CPI and bearing 6.5% interest, traded at 90 points; or

• Ten-year coupon bonds bearing 8% unlinked interest, with linkage on the principal, traded at 100 points.

Assume an average annual inflation rate (in perpetuity) of 8%.

a. Which bond should you invest in?

b. Should you compare only the real interest rate? How would your answer change (if at all) if additional factors were at play?

Question 7

The market offers only two investment channels:

1. A 10% interest, seven-year savings plan offering. Principal and interest are both paid at the end of the period.

2. Seven-year bonds with a $100 face value and an annual coupon of $10, traded at face value.

You decide to invest $1,000 in bonds, while your friend Miguel decides to invest $1,000 in the savings plan. Immediately after you both make your investments, the commissioner announces that from now on, only 9% interest bonds will be issued. This interest rate is expected to last at least for the next 15 years.

a. What is the effective interest rate in the market?

b. In your opinion, as of the day following the commissioner's announcement, whose was the better investment, yours or Miguel's? What is the difference in profit?

Question 8

You bought a short-term loan with a one-year maturity term at 91 points and sold it after six months at 98 points. What is the nominal (annual) capital gain (yield) on your investment? (Only the capital gain is required!)

Question 9

On January 1, 2008, you invested in a perpetual government bond with a face value of $100,000 and offering a 6% coupon paid at the end of each year (December 31). The market interest rate has been 8% for a long time. That same night, the commissioner of the central bank announced a 2% interest rate decrease. The interest rate is expected to remain unchanged for many years.

One year later (December 31, 2009), you decide to sell your entire investment.

a. What was the bond price on January 2, 2008? At the start of each year (after payment of the interest coupon)?

b. What is the capital gain (in percent) on your investment?

c. What is the interest yield (gain) on your investment?

d. What is the overall yield on your investment?

e. Would your answer change if you were to sell one day later (disregard one-day interest differences)?

Question 10

You bought a 15-year, 7% government bond on its issue date at a price of $133.40. Several years later (the present), the bond is traded at $108.20. The market interest rate is 4% and fixed for the entire lifetime of the bond.

a. You forgot when you bought the bond, and need to calculate the time remaining until maturity.

b. Calculate the present duration.

c. What is the bond's sensitivity to market interest rate changes? Give a specific number, and explain.

Further Reading

Amihud, Y., and H. Mendelson. 1991. Liquidity, Maturity, and the Yields on U.S. Treasury Securities. *Journal of Finance*: 46.

Bierwag, G. O., G. G. Kaufman, and A. Toevs. 1983. Duration: Its Development and Use in Bond Portfolio Management. *Financial Analysts Journal*: 38.

Black, F., and J. Cox. 1976. Valuing Corporate Securities: Some Effects of Bond Indenture Provisions. *Journal of Finance* (May): 351–367.

Brennan, M. J., and E. S. Schwartz. 1977. Convertible Bonds: Valuation and Optimal Strategies for Call and Conversion. *Journal of Finance* (December): 1699–1715.

Brick, I. E., and A. Ravid. 1985. On the Relevance of Debt Maturity Structure. *Journal of Finance* (December): 1423–1437.

Chua, J. H. 1984. A Closed-Form Formula for Calculating Bond Duration. *Financial Analysts Journal* (May/June).

Fama, E. F. 1984. Term Premiums in Bond Returns. *Journal of Financial Economics* (December): 529–546.

Malkiel, B. G. 1962. Expectations, Bond Prices, and the Term Structure of Interest Rates. *Quarterly Journal of Economics* (May): 197–218.

McCulloch, J. H. 1975. An Estimate of the Liquidity Premium. *Journal of Political Economy* (January/February): 95–119.

Merton, R. C. 1974. On the Pricing of Corporate Debt: The Risk Structure of Interest Rates. *Journal of Finance*: 22.

Morris, J. R. 1976. On Corporate Debt Maturity Decisions. *Journal of Finance* (March): 29–37.

Standard and Poor's. 1996. *Standard and Poor's Corporate Ratings Criteria*. New York: McGraw-Hill.

Weinstein, M. I. 1977. The Effect of a Rating Change Announcement on Bond Price. *Journal of Financial Economics* (December): 329–350.

Woodward, S. 1983. The Liquidity Premium and the Solidity Premium. *American Economic Review* (June): 348–361.

Yu, F. 2002. Modeling Expected Return on Defaultable Bonds. *Journal of Fixed Income*: 122.

Zwick, B. 1980. Yields on Privately Placed Corporate Bonds. *Journal of Finance* (March).

6 Fundamental Share Valuation Models—The Earnings Model and the Dividend Model

A. Assumptions

The basic share valuation model is a normative model that defines share value as follows:

Share value   The present value of the rights to future income.[1]

This model is regarded as normative because other definitions can also be proposed. Thus, for example, if holding a share bestows ownership of a company, the definition can include the value derived from the power to appoint managers, to distribute salaries and dividends as one sees fit, and so forth. Let us start with a simple model, which can be elaborated on later.

In this chapter and the next, we discuss the question:

What constitutes the rights to future income that is to be discounted?

This preliminary model applies a basic approach whereby future income actually consists of a company's future profits. Similar to the model discussed in chapter 2, this model makes the following assumptions:

1. Companies are financed only through shares.

2. In each period t, a company has profits of E_t.

---

1. Unless stated otherwise, all values (variables, denoted by letters) are per share (i.e., price per share, dividend per share, earnings per share, etc.).

3. Some of these profits are distributed to shareholders as dividends, D_t.

4. Companies invest undistributed profits (I_t) in new projects intended to increase their future profits.

5. Each investment has a fixed yield (return on investment, RI) into perpetuity.[2]

Let's assume that we bought a share at a price of P_0 immediately after the company posted its earnings at the end of the previous period, which we will designate E_0. Our starting time 0 is immediately after the dividend distribution and investment at the end of the previous period.

We expect earnings of E_1 at the end of the first period and in each of the subsequent periods. These earnings are a result of investments made by the company before we bought the share. According to company policy, part of earnings E_1 is to be distributed as dividend D_1 (the percentage distributed as dividends will be designated DR, for "dividend ratio") and the remainder (designated PB, for "plowed back") is to be invested in business-related projects, yielding a fixed return (RI). Let's also assume that the company's risk-adjusted discount rate is known and designated k_S.

The above definitions immediately lead us to the following equations:

$$DR \equiv \frac{D}{E}$$
$$PB \equiv \frac{E-D}{E} \qquad \Rightarrow \quad PB = 1 - DR.$$

If the company does not make any new investments in period $t = 1$ (and in all subsequent periods), earnings E_2 at the end of the second period (and all earnings in all subsequent periods) will be equal to E_1 and will be the result of past investments made before we bought the share.

B. The Earnings Model

In each period, the increase in earnings, ΔE, will be the result of the new investments made at the start of that period (the end of the previous

---

2. This assumption is actually derived from the accounting definition of earnings, where each year depreciation is subtracted from income. Assumption 5 states that this depreciation difference, which is in principle a virtual accounting expense, is actually reinvested in the relevant asset at the end of each period. Therefore, the asset is never consumed, and continues yielding a return forever.

period), to the amount of $I = E - D$.[3] This investment yielded returns of $(E - D) \cdot RI$ at the end of that period (and in all subsequent periods).

The earnings growth rate g is defined as follows:

$$g = \frac{\Delta E}{E} = \frac{I \cdot RI}{E} = \frac{E - D}{E} \cdot RI = PB \cdot RI.$$

Lacking growth, share value P_0 is dictated by earnings E_1, which, as mentioned, are derived from investments made before we bought the share. Therefore, we expect to receive an infinite inflow of earnings E_1. As discussed in chapter 4, if we discount these inflows at a rate of k_S, their present value will be equal to E_1/k_S.

If at the start of period 2 (end of period 1) an investment was made in a new project, then at the end of period 2 (and in all subsequent periods), we will receive incremental earnings of ΔE_1.

We can calculate the present value PV of this infinite earnings increment, calculated for the start of each investment period. This calculation can be carried out for the start of each and every period. From each $PV_t(\Delta E_t)$ calculated for the start of the investment period, we can subtract the sum of investment I_t made at the start of that period (the end of the previous period) and find the net present value NPV_t of that investment.

We can define the net present value of the expected growth in earnings as follows:

$NPV(growth) =$ present value of all future $[PV_t(\Delta E_t) - I_t]$.

The first earnings that we will record as new shareholders are E_1, from which we will distribute a dividend and make an investment whose fruits we will see from the end of period 2 onward. In its general mathematical form, the earnings model is therefore

$$P_0 = \frac{E_1}{k_S} + NPV(growth).$$

If there is no investment opportunity offering excess yields, that is, when $NPV(growth) = 0$, then all earnings will be distributed as dividends. Thus, $D = E$, and the equation becomes

$$P_0 = \frac{E_1}{k_S} = \frac{D_1}{k_S}.$$

3. For the sake of convenience, we drop the t index: $E = E_t$, $D = D_t$, etc.

This last equation allows us to define earnings yield. As earnings are identical in all future periods (no increase), we can remove the index "1" from these earnings and write

$$k = \frac{E}{P_0}.$$

For historical reasons, capital markets and the business press commonly use the inverse of this last expression, which is referred to as the "earnings multiplier," $EM = P_0/E$, instead of the "earnings yield." The earnings multiplier is intuitively equivalent to the "return on investment period," or the period (number of years) required for investors to get a return of their investment through earnings (excluding interest). In any case, it should be kept in mind that using the earnings multiplier includes an assumption of zero growth in company earnings.

Caution! As we will see later on, this indicator is not effective for company valuations. It is useful when one wishes to obtain a picture of the overall market condition at a specific point in time or of the condition of any particular market sector relative to the historical average earnings multiplier. This point is discussed further below.

Let's reexamine our model when a fixed percentage of the earnings PB is invested in each period (equivalent to distributing a fixed percentage of the earnings DR as dividends):

E_1—Earnings at the end of the first period (and the start of the second period).

$E_1 \cdot PB$—The investment made at the end of the first/start of the second period.

$E_1 \cdot PB \cdot RI = E_1 \cdot g$—End of the second period earnings yielded by that investment.

$E_1 + E_1 \cdot g = E_1(1 + g)$—End of the second period total earnings, equal to E_1 from the previous period plus the earnings from the investment made at the end of the first (start of the second) period.

Similarly, the earnings at the end of the third period will equal $E_1(1 + g)^2$, at the end of the fourth period $E_1(1 + g)^3$, and so forth. Table 6.1 summarizes the calculation for periods 2, 3, 4, and on to ∞.

Remember that earnings on the investment made at the start of a certain period not only will bear fruit in that period but will remain fixed in all subsequent periods. If we wish to calculate the $NPV(growth)$ for that investment, we must discount the earnings from the investment

Table 6.1
NPV Calculation for Periods' Closing Earnings

		$n=2$	$n=3$	$n=4$
1	Earnings per share	E_1	$E_1(1 + g)$	$E_1(1 + g)^2$
2	Investment at start of period	$E_1 \cdot PB$	$E_1(1 + g) \cdot PB$	$E_1(1 + g)^2 \cdot PB$
3	Earnings from the investment in that period[a]	$E_1 \cdot PB \cdot RI$	$E_1(1 + g) \cdot PB \cdot RI$	$E_1(1 + g)^2 \cdot PB \cdot RI$
4	PV of the earnings[b]	$E_1 \cdot PB \cdot RI \, / \, k$	$E_1(1 + g) \cdot PB \cdot RI \, / \, k$	$E_1(1 + g)^2 \cdot PB \cdot RI \, / \, k$
5	NPV of the earnings[c]	$E_1 \cdot PB \, (RI - k) \, / \, k$	$E_1(1 + g) \cdot PB \, (RI - k) \, / \, k$	$E_1(1 + g)^2 \cdot PB \, (RI - k) \, / \, k$

a. The investment made in that year generates earnings in all subsequent periods.
b. Discounting cash flows generated by that year's investment. The present value is for that year (and not for time 0).
c. Line 5 is derived by subtracting line 2 (the investment) from line 4 (discounted cash flows generated by that investment).

made in that period into perpetuity, and do so for each of the investments made in each investment period.

Each term in line 5 of table 6.1 is actually the net present value for the investment made at the start of that period into perpetuity. In this way, if we discount all the terms in line 5 using discount rate $k(=k_s)$, we will actually end up with the present value (at time 0) of all future investments, $NPV(growth)$. Note that the terms in line 5 are members of a geometric series that grows by g in each period. Therefore, we can apply the equation for an infinite series growing at a fixed rate:

$$PV = \frac{C}{r - g} \quad ; \quad C = \frac{E_1 \cdot PB(RI - k)}{k}$$

$$\Rightarrow \quad NPV(growth) = \frac{C \cdot \dfrac{E_1 \cdot PB(RI - k)}{k}}{k - g} = C \cdot \frac{E_1 \cdot PB(RI - k)}{k \cdot (k - g)}.$$

From here we can go back and calculate the share price using the general model

$$P_0 = \frac{E_1}{k_s} + NPV(growth) = \frac{E_1}{k} + \frac{E_1 \cdot PB(RI - k)}{k \cdot (k - g)}$$

$$= \frac{E_1 \cdot k - E_1 \cdot g + E_1 \cdot PB \cdot RI - E_1 \cdot PB \cdot k}{k(k - g)} = \frac{k \cdot E_1(1 - PB)}{k(k - g)} \quad \Rightarrow$$

$$P_0 = \frac{E_1 \cdot DR}{k - g} = \frac{D_1}{k_s - g}.$$

Once again, when we assume an investment at a fixed percentage of a company's earnings, the earnings model leads us to the conclusion that a company's value is determined by the dividend that company distributes. We've seen this result before when we assumed that there are no investment opportunities and that earnings remain constant:

$$P_0 = \frac{D_1}{k_S} \, .$$

For any earnings-based dividend policy, we can say (without proving in general) that the earnings model leads to a conclusion that a company's value is effectively determined by its dividend distribution.

C. The Dividend Model

The dividend model's underlying assumption ignores the connection between the size of a dividend distributed and the company's business performance. Instead, this model focuses on valuing companies from an investor's standpoint. For individuals, future income from holding a company's shares is reflected in that company's future dividend distributions, plus the future price that can be obtained when selling the shares.

If a share is held for T periods (months, years), that is, $t = 1, 2, 3, \ldots T$, then that share's value is equal to the sum of the dividends that will be received in each period (each dividend is discounted using the shareholders' required risk-adjusted discount rate, k_S[4]) plus the share discounted price on its sale after T periods:

$$P_0 = \left[\sum_{t=1}^{T} \frac{D_t}{(1+k)^t} \right] + \frac{P_T}{(1+k)^T} \, .$$

If T is very large,[5] then the second term in the above sum, the discounted amount received on selling the share after T periods, is small and negligible (because of the large denominator). We can therefore approximate the equation as follows:

$$P_0 \approx \sum_{t=1}^{T} \frac{D_t}{(1+k)^t} \, .$$

4. For convenience, we are dropping the "s" index from k_S until the final step.
5. We can assume that T is very large even if the share passes between numerous buyers if each buyer values the share using the same method.

Let's assume that a company distributes a fixed dividend D (corporate dividend distribution policies are discussed later) and that T is infinitely large. The share price then equals

$$P_0\big|_{T \to \infty} = \frac{D}{k} .$$

This last equation allows us to define a "dividend yield," k_D, as follows:

$$k_D \equiv \frac{D}{P_0} .$$

Going back to the earnings model, we see that we reached a similar result.

Now let's assume that the dividend increases each year at a fixed rate, g. If the dividend at the end of the first period is D_1, then at the end of the second period it is $D_1(1 + g)$, at the end of the third period it is $D_1(1 + g)(1 + g)$, and so on. The model will now state:

$$P_0 = \frac{D_1}{1+k} + \frac{D_1(1+g)}{(1+k)^2} + \frac{D_1(1+g)^2}{(1+k)^3} + ... + \frac{P_T}{(1+k)^T}$$

Here, too, let's assume that T is infinite, and the expression $\dfrac{P_T}{(1+k)^T}$ has a propensity of zero. Then

$$P_0 = \frac{D_1}{1+k} + \frac{D_1(1+g)}{(1+k)^2} + \frac{D_1(1+g)^2}{(1+k)^3} + ...$$

This is the sum of a geometric series growing at a constant rate, whose equation has already been discussed:

$$P_0 = \frac{D_1}{k_S - g} .$$

Once again, the result is identical to the one derived from the earnings model.

These results lead us to the conclusion that the earnings model and the dividend model are identical, although they are based on two different approaches.[6] This means that their underlying assumptions are the same after all: a company invests a fixed percentage of its

---

6. The earnings model is based on management's standpoint; the dividend model is based on a shareholder's (owner's) standpoint.

earnings in new investments and distributes the rest (also a fixed percentage of its earnings) as dividends. If no investments offering attractive returns are available to the company, it will distribute all its earnings as dividends, thus being defined as a fixed-dividends (=earnings) company. Companies whose new investments continuously yield a suitable return are companies with fixed growth in both earnings and dividends.

When a company distributes fixed dividends, its share price is identical in all periods; that is, the share's buying price and selling price (in any period) will be the same. The only return recorded by shareholders is from the dividend distributed each year. However, for fixed-growth companies, the share price increases in each period.

We've seen that the share price at the start of the first period is

$$P_0 = \frac{D_1}{k_S - g}.$$

The share price at the start of the second period is

$$P_1 = \frac{D_2}{k_S - g}.$$

As $D_2 = D_1(1 + g)$, it is also clear that $P_1 = P_0(1 + g)$.

A shareholder who sells his share at the end of the first period will receive a twofold return:

1. A return from the dividend payment.
2. A return from the increase in the share's value.

Therefore, we can name two components that make up the return.

The first component consists of the dividend payment, the yield of which has already been defined as

$$k_D \equiv \frac{D_1}{P_0}.$$

The second component consists of the increase in the share's value:

$$\Delta P = P_1 - P_0 = P_0(1+g) - P_0 = P_0 \cdot g.$$

The yield from the increase in share price (capital gain) is

$$k_P \equiv \frac{\Delta P}{P_0} = \frac{P_0 \cdot g}{P_0} = g.$$

The overall return k_s recorded by a shareholder over one period is therefore[7]

$$k_s = k_D + k_P = \frac{D_1}{P_0} + g.$$

Note: If we were to take the original share price equation $P_0 = \dfrac{D_1}{k_S - g}$ and factor out k_s, we would end up with the same result, $k_S = \dfrac{D_1}{P_0} + g.$

Example

For the past few years, Cars Inc. has been growing by 25% each year. This growth rate is expected to continue in the next two years, after which the company's growth rate will return to normal. The company has a fixed earnings percentage dividend policy. Given $D_0 = \$2$, $k = 14\%$, and $g_n = 6\%$ (n denotes the normal growth rate):

a. What is the current share price at equilibrium?

b. What is the dividend yield?

c. What is the capital gains yield?

Solution

a. What is the present share price?

Calculate P_0:

$$D_1 = D_0(1 + g_s) = \$2 \cdot (1.25) = \$2.50.$$
$$D_2 = D_0(1 + g_s)^2 = \$2 \cdot (1.25)^2 = \$3.125.$$

After two years, investors will have a company with a fixed growth rate g_n. Therefore, the share price in two years will be

$$P_2 = \frac{D_3}{k_s - g_n} = \frac{D_2 \cdot (1 + g_n)}{k_s - g_n} = \frac{\$3.125 \cdot (1.06)}{0.14 - 0.06} = \$41.41.$$

The current share price is

$$P_0 = PV(D_1) + PV(D_2) + PV(P_2)$$
$$= \frac{D_1}{(1 + k_s)} + \frac{D_2}{(1 + k_s)^2} + \frac{P_2}{(1 + k_s)^2}$$
$$= \$2.5 \cdot (0.8772) + \$3.125 \cdot (0.7695) + \$41.41 \cdot (0.7695) = \$36.46$$

---

7. Note that a similar method of dividing overall return into a capital component and a yield-based component was also applied to bonds.

b. What is the dividend return?

$$k_D = \frac{D_1}{P_0} = \frac{\$2.50}{\$36.46} = 6.86\%.$$

c. The capital gains yield consists of the increase in the share price from P_0 to P_1. Therefore, we must first calculate P_1:

$$P_1 = \frac{D_2}{(1+k)} + \frac{P_2}{(1+k)} = \frac{\$3.125 + \$41.41}{1.14} = \$39.07.$$

We can now calculate the capital gains yield:

$$k_p = \frac{P_1 - P_0}{P_0} = \frac{\$39.07 - \$36.46}{\$36.46} = 7.16\%.$$

Indeed, we find that the overall return required by the market is as specified:

$$k_s = k_D + k_p = 6.86\% + 7.16\% = 14.02\% \Rightarrow k_s \cong 14\%.$$

(*Note:* The difference is due to rounding off our calculations.)
    Let us assume that the company's abnormal growth rate in the first two years is now going to last for the next five years. Without recalculating, how would that affect (qualitatively) our answers?

a. The required return on the company's shares k_s is constant and equal to 14% (does not change).

b. If we expect growth to continue for five years instead of two, then P_0 will be greater than before.

c. As D_1 remains constant and P_0 increases, the dividend yield $k_D = \dfrac{D_1}{P_0}$ will decrease.

d. We know that $k_s = k_D + k_p$ (the required return on the shares is equal to the dividend yield plus the capital gains yield). As k_s remains constant on the market, then if the dividend yield k_D decreases, the capital gains yield k_P must increase.

D. The Dividend Model—An Empirical Review

Having been convinced that the earnings model and the dividend model are in fact one and the same, this raises the question of whether dividend payments should have been used as a basis for valuating shares in the first place, considering that the size of a dividend is decided arbitrarily by a company's board of directors. Let's assume that we have two completely identical companies, differing only in that the board of one company always decides to distribute a dividend that is double the dividend distributed by the second company. According to the above models, the value of the first company will also be double that of the second company, although our initial assumption was that the companies are identical.

This contradiction is discussed in the next chapter. However, let us discuss real-world situations and see how dividend distribution and investment decisions are made.

In 1956, John Lintner published an article detailing a theoretical model for determining what portion of a company's earnings should be distributed as dividends. Lintner based his model on data gathered through a series of interviews with corporate executives concerning their dividend distribution policies. After analyzing the data, Lintner reached the following conclusions:

1. Companies have a policy of paying a fixed *percentage* as dividends but in practice pay a fixed *amount* as dividends.

2. Executives give more weight to year-over-year changes in dividend amounts than to their absolute value.

3. As a result, executives tend to define long-term policies whereby dividend amounts increase only if management expects earnings to be maintained over time and the new dividend amount can be maintained in the foreseeable future (especially so as not to be forced to decrease the distributed amount).

Lintner proposed a simple mathematical model describing the way in which executives determine the amount to be distributed as dividends, by mathematical smoothing. According to this model, this year's dividend depends on the year's earnings but also on last year's dividend; the previous year's dividends depend on last year's earnings and on dividends paid two years ago; and so forth. Accordingly, Lintner developed a theoretical model based on mathematical recursive equations. The model provided a good explanation for the numerical data, and confirmed the conclusions 1–3 detailed above.

Chapter 6 — Questions and Problems

Question 1

We are at the start of the year. "Examples R Us" expects earnings of $8M at year's end. The company always distributes 40% of its earnings as dividends, and invests the rest in projects with a 20% return. The company has 2M issued shares, and its risk-adjusted discount rate is 16%. Calculate:

a. The share price according to the dividend model

b. The share's price-to-earnings ratio

c. The present value of the company's growth according to the earnings model ($PV(growth)$).

d. Describe the correlation between the NPV of the investment at the start of each period and your answer for part (c) above.

Question 2

The earnings multiplier is suitable for use only with zero-growth companies. Find the expression for earnings multiplier PM_G for companies with a fixed growth rate.

Denote the following values:

DR — as dividend ratio, the percentage of earnings paid as dividends.

PB — as $1 - DR$, the percentage of undistributed earnings (invested in new projects).

RI — as return on investment, the return on new investments.

Start with Gordon's growth model and demonstrate that the earnings multiplier for fixed growth companies maintains the following:

a. $PM_G = \dfrac{P_0}{E_0} = \dfrac{DR(1+g)}{k-g}$.

b. $PM_G = \dfrac{P_0}{E_0} = \dfrac{1+RI \cdot PB}{r - \left(\dfrac{PB}{DR}\right) \cdot (RI - r)}$.

Thus, for fixed-growth companies, $PM_G = \dfrac{P_0}{E_0} = f(DR,g,k_S) = f(PB,RI,k_S)$. (*Hint:* Use $g = RI \cdot PB$.)

Question 3

Samson & Sons distributes 20% of its earnings as dividends and invests the rest in projects bearing a 10% return. Jackson & Co. distributes 80% of its earnings as dividends and invests the rest in projects bearing a 20% return. The two companies operate in the same industry and so have the same discount rate. You checked and found that earnings per share this year were identical in both companies.

In which company should you invest?

Hints:

1. Use the price-to-earnings ratio and assume a profit of $1.

2. Your answer depends on which discount rate you use. Explain, and find the rate that reverses your decision.

Question 4

The dividend per share paid by Rainy Day Inc. is expected to grow annually by 8% over the next five years only. Thereafter the dividend per share will remain constant. At the end of the year, a dividend per share of $25 is expected, and the market requires a return of 10% on these kinds of shares.

What is the share's market price?

Question 5

You bought a share at $23. Dividends are projected as follows:

Year	Expected Dividend
1	$1.00
2	$1.08
3	$1.11
4	$1.21

a. Calculate the dividend growth rate.

b. Calculate the expected dividend yield in the coming year.

c. According to the above data, can you calculate what the share price will be one year from now? Two years from now?

d. Assuming that the market requires a 12% return on the company's shares, would your answer to part (c) change?

Question 6

Local software company Tip-Chip is experiencing accelerated growth. Therefore, its profits and dividends are expected to grow by 15% in the next two years, by 12% in the third year, and by 7% from the fourth year on. The last dividend distributed by the company was $1.70, and the required return on its shares is 10%.

a. Calculate the share's present value.

b. Calculate the share price at the end of the first and second years.

c. Calculate the dividend yield and the capital gains yield in years 1–3.

Question 7

True Delicacies' earnings grow at a constant rate of 2%. Under its dividend policy, the company distributes a fixed percentage of its earnings. The last annual dividend was distributed yesterday and amounted to $10. This morning, you bought $1,000 worth of company shares, with shares traded at equilibrium at a price of $200. At the end of trading (this afternoon), the company announced that it is launching a new line of sausages that will increase its earnings growth rate to 6% for the next three years only. You decide to sell your investment tomorrow (the next trading day after the announcement).

a. What is the dividend yield on your investment?

b. What is the capital gain you recorded on your investment, in dollars?

Question 8

Bright Futures Inc. is developing a new product, and therefore does not expect its business to grow in the next two years. In the two years afterward (years three and four), while introducing the product, the company expects a 5% growth rate, and from the fifth year on it expects a 10% growth rate. The last dividend was $1 per share, and the cost of equity required on the company's shares is 12%. The company distributes a fixed percentage of its earnings as dividends.

a. What is the share's value at equilibrium?

b. What is the dividend yield and the capital gain yield recorded by a shareholder in the fourth year (only)?

Question 9

The Big Break's share's plummeted last month following an announcement that a competitor was entering the market. Everyone expects that from now on the company's earnings will decrease at an annual rate of

5%. Yesterday, you noticed the company for the first time, being traded at a price of $5.20. The last dividend distributed by the company was $2 (having a fixed earning percentage policy). The required return on shares in the company's industry is 11%.

a. What do you expect the share price to be at the end of three years from today (assuming market equilibrium)?

b. Should you buy this share?

Question 10

Satellite Communications Inc.'s board is considering new investments aimed at expanding business and increasing earnings. The risk-adjusted return required by the company's shareholders is 18%. The investor relations officer claims that the earnings multiplier common in the communications market is no more than 8. The company distributes 40% of its earnings as dividends.

a. What is the minimum required return on new projects in order for them to be approved by the board?

b. What is the minimum growth in the company's earnings expected as a result of its new investments?

Further Reading

Aharony, J., and I. Swary. 1980. Quarterly Dividend and Earnings Announcements and Stockholders' Returns: An Empirical Analysis. *Journal of Finance* (March): 1–12.

Bagwell, L. S., and J. B. Shoven, J. B. 1989. Cash Distribution to Shareholders. *Journal of Economic Perspectives* (Summer).

Baker, H. K., G. E. Farrelly, and R. B. Edelman. 1985. A Survey of Management Views on Dividend Policy. *Financial Management* 14 (3): 78–84.

Bar-Yosef, S., and R. Kolodny. 1976. Dividend Policy and Market Theory. *Review of Economics and Statistics* (May): 181–190.

Basu, S. 1977. Investment Performance of Common Stocks in Relation to Their Price-Earnings Ratios: A Test of the Efficient Markets Hypothesis. *Journal of Finance* (June): 663–682.

Benzion, U., and J. Yagil. 1987. On the Price-Earnings Ratio Model. *Investment Analyst* (April).

Bhattacharya, S. 1979. Imperfect Information, Dividend Policy, and "The Bird in the Hand" Fallacy. *Bell Journal of Economics* (Spring): 259–270.

Black, F. 1976. The Dividend Puzzle. *Journal of Portfolio Management* 2 (2): 5–8.

Black, F., and M. Scholes. 1974. The Effects of Dividend Yield and Dividend Policy on Common Stock Prices and Returns. *Journal of Financial Economics* (May): 1–22.

Einhorn, S. G., and P. Shangquan. 1984. Using the Dividend Discount Model for Asset Allocation. *Financial Analyst Journal* (July/August).

Fama, E. F., and H. Babiak. 1968. Dividend Policy: An Empirical Analysis. *Journal of the American Statistical Association* (December): 1132–1161.

Fama, E. F., L. Fisher, M. Jensen, and R. Roll. 1969. The Adjustment of Stock Prices to New Information. *International Economic Review* (February): 1–21.

Farrell, J. L., Jr. 1985. The Dividend Discount Model: A Primer. *Financial Analysts Journal* (November/December).

Feldstein, M., and J. Green. 1983. Why Do Companies Pay Dividends? *American Economic Review* 73 (1): 17–30.

Fisher, L., and J. H. Lorie. 1977. *A Half Century of Returns on Stocks and Bonds*. Chicago: University of Chicago, Graduate School of Business.

Foster, T., III, and D. Vickrey. 1978. The Information Content of Stock Dividend Announcements. *Accounting Review* (April): 360–370.

Gentry, J. A., and S. A. Pyhrr. 1973. Stimulating an EPS Growth Model. *Financial Management* (Summer).

Gordon, M. J. 1959. Dividends, Earnings and Stock Prices. *Review of Economics and Statistics* 4 (2): 99–105.

Gordon, M. J. 1962. The Savings, Investment and Valuation of a Corporation. *Review of Economics and Statistics* (February): 37–51.

Griffin, P. 1976. Competitive Information in the Stock Market: An Empirical Study of Earnings, Dividends and Analysts Forecasts. *Journal of Finance* (May): 631–650.

Griffin, P. 1977. The Time-Series Behavior of Quarterly Preliminary Evidence. *Journal of Accounting Research* (Spring): 71–83.

Jahnke, G., S. Klaffke, and H. R. Oppenheimer. 1987. Price Earnings Ratios and Security Performance. *Journal of Portfolio Management* (Fall).

Joy, M., R. Litzenberger, and R. McEnally. 1977. The Adjustment of Stock Prices to Announcements of Unanticipated Changes in Quarterly Earnings. *Journal of Accounting Research* (Autumn): 207–225.

Kalay, A. 1986. The Informational Content of the Timing of Dividend Announcements. *Journal of Financial Economics* (July): 373–388.

Kane, A., Y. K. Lee, and A. Marcus. 1984. Earnings and Dividend Announcements: Is There a Corroboration Effect? *Journal of Finance* (September): 1091–1099.

Keim, D. 1985. Dividend Yields and Stock Returns. *Journal of Financial Economics* (September): 474–489.

Lintner, J. 1956. Distribution of Incomes of Corporations among Dividends, Retained Earnings and Taxes. *American Economic Review* 46 (2): 97–113.

Michel, A. 1979. Industry Influence on Dividend Policy. *Financial Management* 8 (Autumn): 22–26.

Rappaport, A. 1986. The Affordable Dividend Approach to Equity Valuation. *Financial Analysis Journal* (July/August).

Shefrin, H., and M. Statman. 1984. Explaining Investor Preference for Cash Dividends. *Journal of Financial Economics* (June): 253–282.

Stern, J. 1974. Earnings Per Share Doesn't Count. *Financial Analysts Journal* (July/August): 39–43.

Sunder, S. 1973. Relationship between Accounting Changes and Stock Prices: Problems of Measurement and Some Empirical Evidence. *Journal of Accounting Research* 11: 1–45.

Woolridge, J. R. 1983. Stock Dividends as Signals. *Journal of Financial Research* (Spring): 1–12.

7 Fundamental Share Valuation Models—Modigliani and Miller's Cash Flow Model

A. Assumptions

B. Modigliani and Miller's Cash Flow Model

C. Earnings, Dividend, and Cash Flow Models—Applications

A. Assumptions

In the previous chapter we discussed what seemed to be a convincing model. Toward the end of the chapter we challenged the assumption of using dividend distributions (determined arbitrarily by a company's board of directors) as the basis for calculating share value. We also discussed how Linton's empirical model fails to support the model's underlying assumptions. In this chapter we will discuss the above contradictions so as to distinguish between the classical theories of the previous chapter, which are still widely used today, and the modern theories discussed in this chapter.

First, let us review the assumptions underlying the earnings/dividend model:[1]

1. In each period i, a company has earnings of E_i.

2. Some of these earnings are distributed to shareholders as dividends, D_i.

3. Companies invest undistributed earnings I_i in new projects that will increase their future earnings.

4. Each investment has a fixed return RI into perpetuity.

In 1961, Modigliani and Miller published an article describing a normative model resolving the contradiction discussed at the end of the

---

1. As mentioned, the two models (earnings and dividend) are in fact one and the same.

previous chapter.[2] The principal difference between their approach and what was common until that time, the earnings/dividend model, was the addition of one further assumption:

5. Companies can raise additional share capital to invest in new projects, or alternatively utilize undistributed earnings not for investment but to buy back their own shares.[3]

Modigliani and Miller's assumptions (presented both formally and implicitly during the model's development) were phrased differently from the above five assumptions, though these changes are immaterial. Their underlying assumptions are as follows:

1. A perfect market obtains.[4]

2. In determining the amount to be distributed as dividends, management's only consideration is maximizing company value (i.e., maximizing share value) for shareholders.

3. All companies can freely issue new shares or buy back previously issued shares at their market price, $P(t)$.

B.   Modigliani and Miller's Cash Flow Model

Modigliani and Miller stipulated the following example:

1. Assume two companies whose equity is comprised only of shares.[5]

2. All future dividends are identical, except for the one dividend paid at the start of the first year ($t = 0$).

3. The companies' commercial operations are identical, that is, their investment plans $I(t)$ are identical over the years. Therefore, their operating cash flows $O(t)$ (revenues from operations less operating expenses are identical over the years.

---

2. Modigliani and Miller's third proposition. Their first and second propositions concerning corporate capital structure are discussed later in this book.

3. Actually, it is a negative capital raising. Although we do not discuss the legal aspects of this equity-reducing process, it should be noted that most stock exchanges in the world permit it under certain restrictions (in the past it was illegal, until the rules were changed).

4. The assumptions underlying the definition of a perfect market were discussed in chapter 5.

5. Companies whose equity is comprised of both shares and bonds are discussed later in this book.

In their article, Modigliani and Miller asked:

Should these two identical companies have a different market value (company value) only because one of them made a different dividend payment at the beginning of the first year?

Based on Modigliani and Miller's assumptions, we can immediately conclude the following:

1. Both companies must balance their cash utilization from sources available to them in each period. Therefore, dividend payments D or investments I in any period t can be financed by operating cash flows $O(t)$, plus cash inflows from issuing new shares in that same period t.[6] Surplus operating cash flows can be utilized to buy back company shares.

2. Both companies are engaged in identical commercial operations, which generate the same operating cash flow (and therefore carry the same risk). Therefore, the yield $k_i(t)$ required on their shares is also identical (the same discount rate).

Modigliani and Miller began developing their model from this last statement. If we calculate the return (yield) on each of these companies for any period $t + 1$ as a function of the known variables at time t, then:

$$k_i(t+1) = \frac{D_i(t+1) + (P_i(t+1) - P_i(t))}{P_i(t)} = \frac{D_i(t+1) + P_i(t+1)}{P_i(t)} - 1.$$

The statement that the yield on both companies' shares, company i and company j, is identical means that $k_i(t) = k_j(t)$.

Manipulating the above equation,

$$k_i(t+1) + 1 = \frac{D_i(t+1) + P_i(t+1)}{P_i(t)}.$$

$$P_i(t) = \frac{D_i(t+1) + P_i(t+1)}{1 + k_i(t+1)}.$$

Modigliani and Miller used the fact that each company's value in any given period $V(t)$ is equal to its share price in that period $P(t)$ times the number of shares $n(t)$ circulating at that time: $V(t) = n(t) \cdot P(t)$.

---

6. Cash cannot be transferred between periods. This does not affect the generality of the proof.

Multiplying both sides of the previous equation for $P_i(t)$ by the number of shares $n(t)$ in circulation at time t yields[7] the equation for that company's value, $V_i(t)$:

$$V_i(t) = \frac{TD_i(t+1) + n(t) \cdot P_i(t+1)}{1 + k_i(t+1)}.$$

The number of shares in circulation at time $(t + 1)$ is equal to the number of shares in circulation at time t, or $n(t)$, plus the number of shares issued in time $(t + 1)$, $m(t + 1)$.[8] Therefore:

$$n(t+1) = n(t) + m(t+1)$$

$\Rightarrow \quad n(t) = n(t+1) - m(t+1)$

Substitute this last equation in the company value equation above:

$$V_i(t) = \frac{TD_i(t+1) + n(t+1) \cdot P_i(t+1) - m(t+1) \cdot P_i(t+1)}{1 + k_i(t+1)}.$$

To pay a dividend of $TD(t + 1)$ and make an investment of $I(t + 1)$, the company will have to utilize available cash, derived from its operations, $O(t + 1)$, plus its cash inflows of $m(t + 1) \cdot P(t + 1)$ from new share issues. This can be expressed mathematically as follows:

$$TD(t+1) + I(t+1) = O(t+1) + m(t+1) \cdot P(t+1).$$

Switching sides:

$$-m(t+1) \cdot P(t+1) = O(t+1) - TD(t+1) - I(t+1).$$

Substituting this last equation for the company's value[9] yields

$$V_i(t) = \frac{O_i(t+1) - I_i(t+1) + V_i(t+1)}{1 + k(t+1)}.$$

Note that we wanted to check how the company value would change if each company distributed a different dividend in the beginning of the first year. The initial equation used in the development of the

---

7. $V(t) = n(t) \cdot P(t)$ and $TD(t + 1) = n(t) \cdot D(t + 1)$, where TD denotes total dividend, as generally only those actually holding shares at time t will receive the dividend distributed at time $t + 1$.

8. The amount $m(t + 1)$ will be negative if the company buys back shares instead of issuing new ones.

9. Remember that the company's value at time $(t + 1)$ is $V(t + 1) = n(t + 1) \cdot P(t + 1)$.

Modigliani-Miller model includes dividends as a variable. However, this final company valuation equation is completely independent of any dividend payment![10] If we consider the logic behind it, this final equation is in no way surprising. If we describe this equation in words, it states: a company's value is determined only by its investment decisions.[11]

Modigliani and Miller lifted the limitation on investments by assuming that any quantity of shares can be issued (or bought back). They also separated the decision concerning the size of the investment from the decision concerning the size of the distributed dividend.[12] A company's board of directors can distribute dividends arbitrarily. If that company needs cash for investment, it will issue additional shares as necessary.

This last equation, stating that dividends are irrelevant for company valuation or for calculating share price,[13] has been developed assuming perfect market conditions (i.e., no taxes, no transaction costs, perfect information, etc.). Of course, changing any of these assumptions (e.g., taxation) can lead to different results, as will be discussed later in the book.

Continuing with the perfect market model, we can now ask, if dividends are irrelevant, which component should we discount? The answer can be found in the above equation for company valuation:

$$V_i(t) = \frac{O_i(t+1) - I_i(t+1) + V_i(t+1)}{1 + k(t+1)}.$$

Definition:

Free cash flows[14]   Revenues net of expenses and investments.

$$FCF_i(t) = O_i(t) - I_i(t).$$

Denoting free cash flow by *FCF* and assuming a constant discount rate k, we can rewrite the last company valuation equation as follows:

---

10. Remember that we assumed that $O(t)$ and $I(t)$ are identical in both companies.

11. $O(t + 1)$ is the result of operations derived from all investment decisions made until time t.

12. This model differs from Lintner's empirical findings. While Lintner's is a descriptive model, that is, it describes how the market actually behaves, Modigliani and Miller's model is normative: it describes how the market should behave rationally.

13. We have already mentioned that $V(t) = n(t)P(t)$. The value of $n(t)$ is constant at time t. Therefore, if a company's value is independent of its dividend distribution, then the market price of its shares is also independent of its dividend distribution.

14. Earlier we defined operating cash flow, $O(t)$. We are now defining free cash flow, $FCF_i(t) = O_i(t) - I_i(t)$.

$$V(t) = \frac{FCF(t+1) + V(t+1)}{1+k}.$$

This is actually a recursive equation. We can write a similar expression for $V(t+1)$, $V(t+2)$, ..., and substitute each expression into the previous one. Such a calculation leads to the following equation, which is referred to as the *net cash flow* model:

$$V_0 = \sum_{t=1}^{T} \frac{FCF(t)}{(1+k)^t} + \frac{V(T)}{(1+k)^T}.$$

Here, too, if $T \to \infty$ (or is very large), the net cash flow model yields

$$V_0 = \sum_{t=1}^{\infty} \frac{FCF(t)}{(1+k)^t}.$$

Divide both sides by n_0, the number of shares at time zero, and the left side yields the share price at time zero ($P_0 = \frac{V_0}{n_0}$), while the right side yields the free cash flow for one share (instead of the present value of the overall free cash flow). For the sake of simplicity, we'll keep the same symbol but note that when discussing a company's value, we are dealing with the overall cash flow, while when discussing the value (price) of a single share we are also dealing with the free cash flow per share.

The net cash flow model can therefore be written as[15]

$$P_0 = \sum_{t=1}^{\infty} \frac{FCF(t)}{(1+k)^t}.$$

This last equation is actually Modigliani and Miller's final conclusion:

A share's value (or a company's value) is equal to value of the future cash flow generated by that company.

"Earnings" is an accounting term that can be manipulated (within certain limits) and is in no way absolute. There are numerous examples of companies that "overstretched" these limits before the 2001–2002 bubble burst. The most famous of these was Enron, and the ensuing scandal also led to the collapse of Enron's auditing firm.[16] Modigliani and

---

15. In this case, $FCF(t)$ will be the free cash flow per share.

16. Enron was an energy company that grew very quickly and reached a market value of hundreds of billions of dollars (the fourth largest company in the United States). Its collapse led to criminal charges and the collapse of accounting giant Arthur Andersen LLC.

Miller's conclusion, which seemed revolutionary at the time, is actually quite simple: a dividend is an arbitrary amount determined by a company's board of directors. What interests company owners is the company's bank balance over time—in other words: how much management succeeds in increasing the company's cash balances (in absolute value) each year.

The increase in cash balances (from operations) is the only relevant value when calculating a company's value.

As in the previous chapter, we can consider the case of a company with a constant, perpetual cash flow. Its share value is

$$P_0|_{T \to \infty} = \frac{FCF}{k}.$$

As these cash flows are from operations, we can define "cash flow yield"[17] k_{FCF}:

$$k_{FCF} = \frac{FCF}{P_0}.$$

Alternatively, we can consider a company with a cash flow growing at a constant rate g. In this case, its share value is

$$P_0 = \frac{FCF_1}{k_S - g}.$$

Thus, the general return k_s for a shareholder over one period is[18]

$$k_s = \frac{FCF_1}{P_0} + g = k_{FCF} + k_P.$$

If a company's net cash flow is constant, the overall return k_s is equal to the cash flow yield k_{FCF}, and its share price will not change. When net cash flow increases, k_s is equal to the cash flow yield k_{FCF}, derived from the increase in cash balances over the past year, and return k_p, derived from the share price increase over the past year (capital gain) resulting from the expected future increases in cash flows, that is, $k_P = \dfrac{\Delta P}{P_0} = g$.

17. This term is derived from accounting terminology, which distinguishes between dividends and capital gains.

18. Note that a similar format for distinguishing between two components comprising the overall return, a capital gain component and a dividend component, was also applied for bonds and for the earnings/dividend model.

C. Earnings, Dividend, and Cash Flow Models—Applications

After discussing the earnings model and dividend model in depth, and having proved that these models are irrelevant for the purpose for which they were developed (share valuation), readers may feel a bit frustrated that we have wasted our time. However, the earnings model and the dividend model were discussed for two reasons:

1. To present historical developments in financial theory thought.

2. For practical purposes.

The earnings model and the dividend model still hold an important place in business practice and in the economic press today, while the cash flow model, which we have designated our model of choice, is used only by financial professionals.

To the best of my knowledge, the cash flow model was first used for company valuation by McKinsey in the early 1980s.[19] If we look at the listed company data in the business section of most daily newspapers or online sites, we find they report only corporate earnings. Some also report dividend distributions, but very few (that I know of) detail free cash flow per share, although this figure could easily be derived from the companies' financial statements.

As mentioned, this book was written in light of Enron's collapse and the exposure of the outrageous business and accounting practices of other energy companies. These energy companies were charged with overstating earnings by trading energy contracts among themselves.[20] One after another, high-profile cases of accounting statement "doctoring" surfaced among listed companies (mainly on the New York Stock Exchange). Even if not all such cases proved criminal or were even found out of compliance with accounting board guidelines, they were intended to "advance" earnings for "everyone's" benefit.[21] Following these events, Standard & Poor's proposed a new method for measuring corporate earnings. In the introduction to its report on this new approach, the rating company noted that all currently available alternatives, that is, reported earnings, operating earnings, and pro-forma earnings,[22] are incomplete,

---

19. To my best knowledge, as I could not find written references of any kind.

20. Energy contracts are future contracts for the supply of energy. Therefore, earnings should have been reported on supply of the contract. By selling contracts among themselves, energy companies could "advance" their earnings against future earnings.

21. "Everyone" means shareholders, option holders, and analysts.

22. Pro-forma earnings refer to expected earnings subject to certain assumptions.

and so defined "core earnings" as those post-tax earnings derived from principal operations. The new guideline was to include only income and expenses related to continuing operations constituting a company's core business.

This excluded gains/losses on disposal of assets, good will, unrealized future transactions (gains/losses on paper), and so forth. Statements were to include expenses such as R&D costs, acquisitions expenses, restructuring expenses, and option-allocation expenses.[23] Standard & Poor's proposal was met with much opposition by capital markets. The application of this new approach, and especially its retrospective application for the prior years (to establish comparative data for the first year of application), would have led to a drastic decrease in the previous years' reported earnings (as compared to the existing method).

S&P's proposal was a step in the right direction, but it still cannot replace the cash flow model. Earnings include off-cash flow components, such as depreciation. We can consider a case of two absolutely identical companies. The only difference between them is in their depreciation policy. In a tax-free world, this would not influence their real operations. Their cash flows would be identical, as the important factor is the actual payment time for equipment and asset acquisitions. The difference in early or postponed reporting of earnings according to the arbitrary policy adopted by each company would not change either company's value. This case can easily be expanded to a world with taxes. Assuming that each company's management tries to minimize expenses: then both would apply the shortest possible depreciation policy permitted by their tax authorities. Further discussion of this matter is best left for the classroom or a course in accounting and taxation.

However, the fact that the dividend model and the earnings model are still widely used raises the question, do these models provide any particular insight? To illustrate this point, let us review in brief a few articles published by the well-known U.S. magazine, *Forbes*.

At the end of the third quarter of 2003, stock exchanges worldwide (led by the New York Stock Exchange) began recording significant gains, following the 2001–2002 contraction.[24] A series of articles in business newspapers and economics journals analyzed this phenomenon and asked whether it truly marked a transition from a bear market to a bull

---

23. Option allocation is a subject in itself. Modigliani and Miller's model takes it into account by including exercised options when counting the number of shares in each period.

24. About a 20–30% price increase over a period of a few months.

market.[25] These articles examined various indicative parameters charac-
teristic of a transition to a long-term bull market, as seen after the 1982
and 1991 contractions. To make these professional articles more acces-
sible to graduates of basic financial theory, it is important for us to discuss
in detail both the dividend model and the earnings model, as well as their
underlying logic. The articles cited the average earnings and dividends
per share for the stock market as a whole:

	Year		
	1982	**1991**	**2003**
S&P 500 earnings multiplier[26]	7.9	15.5	27.7
S&P 500 dividend yield	6.3%	3.75%	1.91%

From these comparative figures, the authors concluded that, as of 2003,
there was no reason to expect a long-term bull market. A comparison of
earnings multiplier and dividend yield data showed that, using the earnings and dividend models, respectively, shares in 2003 were traded at a
premium about twice as high as in 1991 and about three times as high as
in 1982.

In addition to the above indicators, other factors were examined. For
example, in comparing the 2003 market to the 1982 market, the equity
multiplier and the sales multiplier were also examined.[27] The data showed
that whereas in 2003 the equity multiplier was 2.75 and the sales multiplier was 1.3, in 1982 the equity multiplier was less than 1 and the sales
multiplier was about 1/3. These facts, and the data presented in the table
above, led the author of that article to conclude that the 2003 market
was anything but trading at a discount.

Another author who compared 1991 and 2003 data found, among
other things, the portion of shares out of all financial assets held by
institutional entities was 24.4% in 1991, compared to 34.6% in 2003, and
the portion held by households was 17.7% and 29.7%, respectively. This
author reached a similar conclusion.

In retrospect, the analysis offered by these authors was only partially
correct. Contrary to their assessments, the 2003–2006 period is seen as

25. A bear market is a stock market experiencing prolonged decreases; a bull market is a
stock market experiencing prolonged increases. These animal-related terms are historical
terms that originated in the United States and are now commonly used worldwide.

26. The S&P 500 Index is a weighted index derived from the 500 largest companies (by
total share value) on the New York Stock Exchange and used to indicate overall market
performance. It can be used to indicate "share price," "earnings," and "dividends."

27. The equity multiplier is calculated as the company value divided by its equity. The sales
multiplier is calculated as the company value divided by its sales.

one of the longest bull markets in history. However, these years were not characterized by rapid growth in the stock market. In hindsight, we can say that prices on the NYSE and the NASDAQ during this period were flat, with a moderate increase. The second half of 2006 through mid-2007 was characterized by a strong bull market that ended in the last quarter of 2007 to the first quarter of 2008, with the start of a bear market and a financial crisis the likes of which have not been seen since the Great Depression of the 1930s.

In summary, even if the dividend model and the earnings model are not relevant for calculating share prices, they are still valuable indicators when analyzing share market trends, or for other uses as described above. They should be used carefully and intelligently, through an understanding of their limitations, as follows:

Dividends represent arbitrary distribution decisions.

Earnings are influenced by the broad leeway afforded by accounting board guidelines.

Net (quarterly) cash flow into a company's accounts and expected inflows, at least in the short term, is subject to less manipulation than the other indicators and is more significant in calculating a company's value.

Chapter 7—Questions and Problems

Question 1

Success Inc.'s share price is $24. The company's operating cash flow is expected to remain constant in the first three years (while the company is developing a new product); to double in the fourth year (when the product is launched); and then to grow by 5% each year (into perpetuity). The company has one million issued shares, and the required return on these shares is 10%.

What is the company's expected operating cash flow for the first year?

Question 2

You bought a share in Leaders Limited at $50. Historically, the company has a constant cash flow of $10 per share. The next day, on publication of the company's financial statements, the CEO announced that in light of the company's decision to initiate new operations in the tour bus sector, it expected its cash flow to increase by 2% each year (into perpetuity), starting from its next financial statements. After one year, you decide to sell your share.

a. What is the return required by the market on Leaders Limited's shares?

b. What is the new share price after the CEO's announcement?

c. What is your capital gains yield following the CEO's announcement?

d. What are your dividend yield and capital gains yield after holding the share for one year?

e. At what price did you sell the share?

Question 3

As an analyst for a well-known broker, you cover Building and Properties Inc.'s shares. The company, which provides mortgages, published its financial statements yesterday. The company's shares are traded at $270; its last reported net cash flow per share is $10, and its historical financial statements indicate that these cash flows grow on average by 8% each year. The mortgage-issuing sector requires an 11% average return on shares.

a. What is your recommendation concerning Buildings and Properties Inc.'s shares? Explain your recommendation in terms of return.

b. Formulate a new recommendation in terms of target share price. Explain.

Question 4

In the board of directors' meeting, someone stated that the market price of the company's shares had to be increased, as most people believed it to be too low. All board members agreed that the share price should be increased by at least 20%, and that this increase could be achieved by increasing the company's growth rate by 1%. Older board members proposed that dividends be decreased by 20% to meet this target, while younger board members suggested increasing sales activities to achieve a rapid increase in net cash flow. To resolve the disagreement among the board members, you have been appointed financial adviser. Your initial examination found that the required return in the company's industry is 15%.

Assuming a perfect capital market:

a. What is the normal company growth rate that justifies the solution proposed by the older board members?

b. What is the normal company growth rate that justifies the solution proposed by the younger board members?

c. Given that the company's normal growth rate is 10%, what is your principal recommendation?

Question 5

Global Inc.'s per share cash flow is expected to grow by 8% per annum for five years only (from the end of this year), and then to remain constant. For the end of this year, cash flow per share is expected to be $2.50, while the return required for this type of shares is 10%. What is the share's market price?

Question 6

The computer company Desktop Limited is experiencing rapid growth. Therefore, its cash flow is expected to grow by 15% in the next two years, by 12% in the third year, and by 7% from the fourth year on. Desktop's last posted cash flow per share was $1.70, and the return required on its shares is 10%.

a. Calculate the share's present value.

b. Calculate the share's value at the end of the first and second years.

c. Calculate the free cash flow yield and the capital gains yield in years 1–3.

Further Reading

Bierman, H., Jr., and J. E. Hass. 1983. Investment Cut-Off Rates and Dividend Policy. *Financial Management* (Winter).

Blume, M. E. 1980. Stock Returns and Dividend Yields: Some More Evidence. *Review of Economics and Statistics* (November).

Brennan, M. J. 1971. A Note on Dividend Irrelevance and the Gordon Valuation Model. *Journal of Finance* (December).

Chen, C. R. 1980. The Dividend and Investment Decisions of Firms: A Varying Parameter Approach. *Journal of the Midwest Finance Association* 9.

Partington, G. H. 1985 Dividend Policy and Its Relationship to Investment and Financing Policies: Empirical Evidence. *Journal of Business Finance and Accounting* (Winter).

Richardson, G., S. Sefcik, and R. Thompson. 1986. A Test of Dividend Irrelevance Using Volume Reactions to a Change in Dividend Policy. *Journal of Financial Economics* 17 (2): 313–334.

8 Capital Budgeting—Corporate Investment Decision Criteria

A. Investment in Physical Assets and New Projects

B. Net Present Value as a Decision-Making Criterion

C. Internal Rate of Return as a Decision-Making Criterion

D. Other Decision-Making Tools as Criteria

E. Ranking Investments—The Optimal Method

A.   Investment in Physical Assets and New Projects

In the previous chapter we discussed how a company's value is determined solely by its investment decisions. Management, which aims to maximize company value for shareholders, is expected to choose the best new projects for investment.

In this chapter we discuss several methods (criteria) for choosing which projects are best. We'll discuss the advantages and disadvantages of each method and will recommend the optimal method.

Capital budgeting is the examination and decision-making process applied by companies for investments involving long-term income (and expenditure).[1] Such investments include investments in assets (equipment, structures, etc.) and investments in new projects.

Decision-making processes fall into two categories:

• Comparative decision making: companies need to choose the best of several alternatives (or rank them).

• Specific decision making: companies must decide whether a particular investment opportunity is worthwhile.

---

1. By long term we mean more than one year.

Replacing old equipment falls under comparative decision making. Buying new equipment to increase production capacity because of increased demand is a specific capital investment decision involving absolute economic viability. In both cases an economic threshold must be calculated below which investment is not worthwhile.

In most cases, investment is not bound by the economic viability threshold but rather by budgetary constraints. In such cases, projects must be compared and ranked in descending order, and budgetary constraints will determine the number of projects in which the company will invest. It is important to form a comprehensive understanding of the decision, as even seemingly specific decisions carry a *shadow price* that renders them comparative. For example, deciding to acquire an office building would seem to be a stand-alone decision but is actually opposed to the shadow price of renting the building.

All decision-making processes discussed below are based on net cash flow — how many dollars flow out of or into the company's bank account — and when (on the time axis) these outflows and inflows occur. Until now, we have acquired techniques for handling cash flows, and we will discuss the effectiveness of these and other techniques in capital budgeting below. We assume that cash flows are known and take into account all aspects related to a project's overall impact on a company's cash flow.[2] As discussed in chapter 1, company executives have different responsibilities and may therefore have different perspectives on an investment. It is the CFO's responsibility to see the overall effect on company value. As we saw in the last chapter, Modigliani and Miller's model states that a company's value is determined by its net cash flow. There is no point investing in machinery that reduces production costs by increasing output if the sales department is unable to sell the additional products. Such a decision would increase inventory, increase expenses, decrease net cash flow, and thus decrease company value.

Before discussing the different decision-making methods, let us review the model's underlying assumptions:

1. Income and expenses are realized in cash at the end of each period. In previous chapters we've seen that adjustment for "start-of-period

2. When HP decided to launch its PCS (printer copier scanner) products, it had to take into account not only cash inflows from product sales but also cannibalism (a decrease in sales from internal competition) of its other products such as stand-alone printers, scanners, and copiers, and calculate the overall change in its cash flows, not only changes related to the PCS line.

models" is made simply by adjusting the interest rates, taking into account that each outflow/inflow is moving back by one period.[3]

2. No inflation, and if there is inflation, cash flows are directly "translated" into present purchasing power.[4]

3. No taxes, and if there are, amounts are updated into the net post-tax cash flow. From M&M's model, we know that a company's value is determined by its net cash flow, i.e., only real amounts actually flowing out from or into the company's bank account. The fact that a payment is made to a tax authority is irrelevant. All payments affect a company's actual cash flow, regardless of the beneficiary.

Tax laws may influence cash flows in two ways: by allowing companies to defer tax payments or by changing the absolute tax rate.[5] Taxation is discussed in more detail later in this book. For now, let's assume net post-tax cash flows (or the equivalent, for our purposes).

4. The cost of capital is known and constant. In chapter 5 we discussed the capital market and saw that the return required by company owners (i.e., shareholders) depends on the pure interest rate and reflects the owners' consumption preferences over time, as well as risk. In the first part of this book we discuss models that examine the attractiveness of investments under certain cash flows; in this way we can analyze the time value of capital separately. In the second part of this book, our conclusions will allow us to fine-tune this fundamental model and develop an amended model that takes into account the risk inherent in future cash flows. As an initial approximation, and as we have done since chapter 5, we will use the risk-adjusted, industry-specific rate of return required by the capital market for each sector.

5. Projects are unique and indivisible—they cannot be repeated, and they must be implemented in their entirety.

6. At the end of their useful life, all projects and assets have zero value. If their value is not zero, we assume they are sold at the end of the period, meaning there is a cash inflow at the end of the period.

---

3. Remember, the start of one period coincides with the end of the previous period.
4. "Present" here refers to the time the decision is made.
5. I refer here to tax laws that encourage capital investment.

B. Net Present Value as a Decision-Making Criterion

In chapter 4 we defined net present value (*NPV*) as a general investment criterion. Net present value is formalized as

$$NPV \geq \Sigma \frac{C_i}{(1+k)^i} - I_0,$$

where I_0 is the investment required at the start of the project, when making the decision,[6] while C_i is the net cash flow derived from the project. C_i is positive in case of cash inflows and negative in case of outflows.

Let us examine two possible projects. The cash flow and net present value for these projects are as follows ($k = 10\%$):

	$t = 0$	$t = 1$	*NPV*
A	–1,000	2,000	818
B	–10,000	15,000	3,636

Both projects are presented over one period for illustrative purposes, and in chapter 4 we discussed how to account for cash flows over several periods. Lacking budgetary constraints, we should implement both projects, as both have a positive NPV. If we must choose only one of the two, we should obviously choose project B, as its NPV, the net amount of cash in our bank account "translated" into present value, is greater. If we have a budgetary constraint that does not allow us to invest in project B, it is still worthwhile investing in project A, as its NPV is also positive.

C. Internal Rate of Return as a Decision-Making Criterion

Instead of examining a project's net present value, we can calculate its average internal rate of return (IRR). As long as a project's IRR is higher than the cost of capital required by owners for their shares, investing in the project is worthwhile for the company, as it will increase the net dollar yield on the company's projects portfolio.

The IRR for which we are indifferent to investment equals the discount rate of return that results in a zero NPV.

$$\Sigma \frac{C_i}{(1+k)^i} - I_0 = 0.$$

---

6. In principle, an investment can be distributed over a project's lifetime; nevertheless, we would not need to change the model. We would need to change only the net amounts in each period.

For example, a project is described by the following cash flow:

$$C_0 = I_0 \qquad C_1 \qquad C_2$$
$$-4{,}000 \qquad 2{,}000 \qquad 4{,}000$$

Substituting for these figures yields:

$$-4{,}000 + \frac{2{,}000}{1+k} + \frac{4{,}000}{(1+k)^2} = 0 \Rightarrow k = 28\%.$$

The method for calculating $k = 28\%$ is related to an assumption that NPV is a decreasing function of k.

Then, we can use the discounting tables and find k through trial and error.

Step 1. Substitute $k = 10\% \Rightarrow NPV = 2{,}000 \Rightarrow k$ must be larger.

Step 2. Substitute $k = 50\% \Rightarrow NPV = -889 \Rightarrow k$ must be smaller.

Step 3. Substitute $k \ldots$ until we find a k for which $NPV = 0$.

In fact, we can also solve the problem graphically by plotting different points on the graph, connecting these points (extrapolation), and finding the point where the graph intersects the x-axis (figure 8.1).

Alternatively, we can use a calculator or computer, which can conduct a similar trial-and-error process,[7] as explained in appendixes B and C on

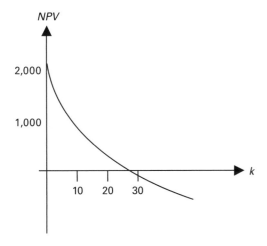

Figure 8.1
Solving the Problem Graphically

7. Usually the Newton-Raphson method is used.

the website accompanying this book (http://finmodeling.com/en). The calculator or software program substitutes different values for k into the equation in a preconfigured manner until it reaches $NPV = 0$. This can take some time, so patience is required.

D. Other Decision-Making Tools as Criteria

NPV and IRR are the two major methods, and will be compared later in this chapter. However, for now, let's discuss two alternative but minor methods:

1. Profitability index (PI)

In our example for the section describing the NPV method, many readers probably felt uncomfortable with our ranking of the projects. Although project B yielded a greater NPV, project A seemed more "efficient" per dollar invested. While project A generates $2 for every $1 investment, that is, a ratio of 1:2, project B generates only $1.50 for every $1 invested.

To account for an investment's efficiency, we can define its profitability index (the return on every dollar invested): $PI = \frac{NPV}{I_0}$.

Let's review each project's cash flow, along with its profitability index.

Project	C_0	C_1	NPV	PI
A	–1,000	2,000	818	0.82
B	–10,000	15,000	3,636	0.36

Each method leads to a different ranking. Which is the better method?

Here we must return to our original assumptions: each project is unique and nonrepeatable. Therefore, we cannot implement ten A-type projects to try to achieve the same investment as in project B. Going back to our discussion of efficient versus effective in chapter 1, the NPV method clearly comes out on top. Although project A is more efficient, project B is more effective (assuming decisions aim to maximize company value). Ultimately, project B provides the required result: maximum cash in the company's coffers.[8]

As mentioned, companies usually do not consider one single project but rather are faced with several projects simultaneously. The first thing that companies do is rank projects in decreasing order of effectiveness

---

8. Under the Modigliani-Miller model, company value is determined by cash flow.

(NPV). To meet budgetary constraints, companies must choose a limited set of projects from this list.[9]

Sometimes different project sets can be chosen that yield essentially the same NPV. In case where project sets are equally effective, and only then, companies can consider project efficiency. Therefore, each project should also include its PI. After forming our project sets, we must also calculate the aggregate NPV and aggregate PI for that set.

This matter is illustrated in the summary example for this section.

2. Payback period

A common method employed by investors is calculating the payback period. Investors calculate project cash flows to see how long it takes each project to pay back the investment in nominal values. Projects are then ranked by payback period, with the project offering the shortest payback period at the top. Investors assume that the shorter a payback period, the lower the risk of losing their investment.[10]

The disadvantages of this method are self-evident:

a. This method sums amounts using nominal values. As we know, one dollar next year is worth more than the same dollar in two or three years, and so adding these amounts makes no economic sense. Advocates of this method sometimes fine-tune their calculations to present value-adjusted payback periods. Each amount is separately "translated" to its present value, and only then is the payback period calculated and the projects ranked.

b. This method does not account for cash flows after the payback period. We can imagine a scenario where a project has a long "maturity time"[11] but in the longer term will generate income many times greater than the income from a project with a shorter maturity time.

c. This method is clearly myopic (short-sighted) and does not meet the requirement of maximizing company value.

---

9. In the exercises for this chapter, we'll see examples where choosing projects in descending order does not necessarily maximize NPV. Sometimes a set of lower-ranked projects maximizes NPV under the given budgetary constraints.

10. This method is similar to using the earnings multiplier $PM = \dfrac{P}{E}$.

11. For example, R&D for biotech projects (such as pharmaceuticals) take years and require significant investment, but subsequent revenues can be many times greater than for a software development project, which usually requires less than one year of development and does not cost much but yields a cash flow many times smaller than the average biotech project.

In the following example, both projects offer the same payback period:

Table 8.1

Project	C_0	C_1	C_2	C_3	C_4
A	−10,000	+5,000	+3,000	+2,000	+1,000
B	−10,000	+2,000	+3,000	+5,000	+6,000

Same payback period (different if value-adjusted)   Cash flow after payback is disregarded

Clearly, if we were to take the cash flow following the payback period into account, then for most real interest rates we would probably prefer project B, which yields a greater NPV.

As was the case in the previous method, this method too can be used as a secondary ranking criterion. After identifying several project sets with an essentially identical NPV, we can apply a secondary ranking of those sets by choosing the one with the shortest payback period.[12]

E. Ranking Investments—The Optimal Method

We stated that NPV and IRR are the two major methods of choice for ranking investments. We also mentioned that the disadvantage of the NPV method is that it does not account for an investment's efficiency. We compensated for this fact by applying a secondary ranking of similar project sets, by comparing their profitability index or their (value-adjusted) payback period.

The IRR method also has its disadvantages:

1. It does not signal profit or loss.

For example:

Project	C_0	C_1	IRR	NPV (10%)
A	−1,000	+1,500	50%	+364
B	+1,000	−1,500	50%	−364

Although both projects are ranked equally under the IRR method, project A obviously is the only viable option. Although the NPV for the

---

12. Note that each secondary method, PI and payback period, may yield a different ranking order.

projects also seems identical, there is a small difference—profitability! In project A, we gain 364, while in project B we lose 364!

In practice, project cash flows definitely do not consist of an investment (outflow) at the start of the project, followed by a series of inflows. Investments are usually distributed over more than one period, among other things because of supplier credit. Project results may also be negative in a different period (e.g., sales losses during market penetration or when attempting to increase market share).

The fact that cash flows can change profitability direction (+/–) in different periods interferes with the IRR method. Losses and gains may yield the same internal rate of return, and we will not be able to tell them apart!

2. Polygons with multiple or no roots are problematic.

In the above example, we assumed a decreasing function. We had a quadratic equation whose graph is a parabola (or an inverted parabola). Quadratic equations can have two roots (solutions), two identical roots (one solution), or zero solutions (figure 8.2).

A polynomial equation of the nth degree, $\Sigma \dfrac{C_i}{(1+k)^n} - I_0 = 0$, derived from a project yielding cash flows over n periods, can have anywhere between zero and n roots (solutions).

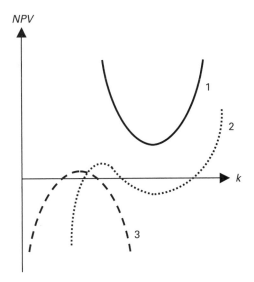

NPV

Figure 8.2
Potential "Roots" for Polynomials

In curve 1, the parabola does not intersect the k-axis (the return axis), and therefore, although the project has a positive NPV for every k, there is no solution, and thus no computable IRR.

For example:

C_0	C_1	C_2	*NPV (10%)*	*IRR*
–3,000	+1,000	+2,500	+339	None

Curves 2 and 3 yield two and three roots (solutions), respectively. Which of these solutions should we use?

Note that for certain values of k, the polynomial equation yields negative NPV values; that is, the project incurs losses. However, other values of k yield a positive NPV; that is, the project is profitable. When our calculations yield several IRR values, it is impossible for us to know under which values the project incurs profits and for which losses.

3. Mutually exclusive projects rank falsely.[13]

Let's use the same example from the NPV method:

Project	C_0	C_1	*NPV*	*IRR*
A	–1,000	2,000	818	100%
B	–10,000	15,000	3,636	50%

As we can see, the IRR method accounts for investment efficiency when ranking projects. Unfortunately, that comes at the expense of effectiveness. If the projects were mutually exclusive, we would make an ineffective choice of project A, as demonstrated previously. Therefore, the IRR method does not account for project size.[14]

4. The method does not account for the term structure of interest rates.

Under the IRR method, we discount the entire future cash flow into one single internal interest rate, while not accounting for interest rate differences across periods, as reflected in the term structure of interest rates (which can be done when calculating NPV).

---

13. Exclusive—replace each other. Mutually exclusive projects—implementing one prevents implementation of the other.

14. As opposed to the NPV method, which accounts for project size but not efficiency. As we've seen, effectiveness is more important than efficiency!

To summarize our above discussion, let's review the following example: Success Inc. is considering the following new investments:

Project	Investment ($M)	NPV ($M)	IRR (%)
A	100	140	15
B	20	20	15
C	50	65	43
D	50	−10	50
E	50	100	50
F	40	32	50
G	20	18	30

The company has a budgetary constraint of $200 million.

If Success Inc. were to apply the NPV method, it would choose projects A, E, and C (in decreasing order).

If it were to apply the IRR method, it would choose projects D, E, and F (all with the same ranking), followed by project C. Note that under the IRR method, the company would choose project D, which is not profitable!

Upon the projects' completion, the company would record an additional income of $305 million under the NPV method, but only $187 million under the IRR method.

The advantages offered by the NPV method are self-evident when compared to the other methods. This method maximizes company value for shareholders, which is derived from net cash flows under the Modigliani-Miller model and has the fewest disadvantages. As mentioned, in certain cases, we will apply this method to choose several similar project sets, and only then will we apply the other methods (including IRR) as a secondary tool in making our investment decision.

In summary, it is also important to enumerate the limitations of the NPV method:

• It does not account for profitability.

• Forecasting future amounts is difficult (with all methods).

• The method includes a hidden assumption that investment can continue under the same terms forever.

• The method does not account for projects of different duration. This point is discussed in further detail in the following chapter, which covers the structure of net cash flows.

Chapter 8—Questions and Problems

Question 1

You are considering an investment yielding the following cash flow:

Year	Cash Flow
0	–1,200
1	800
2	640

Calculate:

a. NPV (12% cost of capital).

b. IRR.

c. Payback period.

d. Profitability index.

Question 2

Below are cash flows from two possible project investments:

Year	Cash Flow A	Cash Flow B
0	–2M	2M
1	6M	–4.5M
2	–7M	4M

a. Calculate the NPV for both cash flows by hand (verify using a calculator).

Assume the cost of capital is 8%.

b. Calculate the IRR by hand. What would the graph of the NPV as a function of cost of capital look like?

c. For which cost of capital values should you invest in each project?

d. How would you rank the projects according to the PI and payback period?

Question 3

The following are cash flows (in $M) for two different projects:

Year	Project A	Project B
0	–400	–330
1	100	100
2	120	60
3	110	110
4	150	110

a. The government wants to encourage companies to implement project B and is therefore willing to subsidize it. If the cost of capital is 10%, what is the subsidy that the government must pay if the subsidy is paid at the start of the project? At the end of the project?

b. At what cost of capital will the government not need to subsidize the project?

Question 4

An economist estimates the following project cash flows (in $K):

Year	Cash Flow A	Cash Flow B	Cash Flow C
0	–800	–900	–1,000
1	362	402	0
2	362	402	0
3	362	402	1,464

a. Calculate the NPV for each project ($k = 10\%$).

b. Calculate the IRR for each project. What is your conclusion in light of part (a)?

c. Calculate the PI for each project. What is your conclusion in light of parts (a) and (b)?

d. Calculate the payback period for each project. What is your conclusion in light of part (a)?

e. Calculate the NPV if the cost of capital is 5% and 15%. What is your conclusion in light of part (a)?

Question 5

A company's cost of capital is 10%. The company decides to limit its investment budget to $30 million. The company has the following investment options:

Project	Investment ($M)	Payback Period (yrs)	NPV ($M)
A	25	6	14
B	10	8	13
C	15	5	20
D	8	7	13
E	5	4	10

What is the optimal project mix?

Question 6

The following are cash flows from two possible projects:

Period	Cash Flow A	Cash Flow B
0	16	–60
1	–100	50
2	100	–30
3	Ended	100

a. Calculate the NPV if the cost of capital is 10%. Which project is more attractive?

b. Calculate the IRR. Which project is more attractive?

c. Draw an approximate graph of the NPV as a function of the cost of capital. For what cost of capital values would your answer change (plot points ∞, IRR; $k = 0$)?

d. What are the problems in comparing project attractiveness?

Question 7

As the CEO of a thriving high-tech company, you have three investment options:

Year	Cash Flow A	Cash Flow B	Cash Flow C
0	–900	–8,500	–12,500
1	400	1,700	7,500
2	400	1,700	7,500
3	400	9,500	7,500

Assume $k = 10\%$

a. Calculate the IRR and NPV for all three options.

b. What investment should you choose under each of these methods? Why?

c. Now assume that the investments are mutually exclusive. Which of the three should you choose under the IRR method and which under the NPV method?

Question 8

Sing-A-Long Limited is considering two mutually exclusive projects:

Project	Year 0	1	2	3	4	5
A	−55,000	18,000	27,000	18,000	17,000	18,000
B	−35,000	13,000	21,000	14,000	12,000	13,000

a. Calculate the IRR for each project.

b. Plot the present value of each project as a function of the cost of capital. (Plot the graphs numerically, i.e., calculate numbers for different values. It is recommended to use Excel, as then it is not necessary to reenter the cash flows for each cost of capital value.)

c. Which project should you choose?

Question 9

Success Inc. has constant operations continuing into perpetuity. The company has 500,000 shares and is traded at a company value of $10 million. The company has a choice of three one-time projects, and its rational CEO, who studied finance, calculated and found that the cost of capital for the projects is 12%. The projects are expected to yield the following cash flows (in $K):

Project	Year 0	1	2
A	−1,000	2,000	4,000
B	−1,750	600	1,200
C	−600	1,400	−100

Assuming the CEO made the right investment decision, what is the new share price?

Question 10

Two possible projects both require an investment of $100,000, and yield:

Project	Year 1	2	3
A	$35,000	$40,000	$35,000
B	$30,000	$50,100	$30,000

To check the cost of capital's effect on the relative attractiveness of each project, your friend suggests you prepare a differential cash flow.

a. Calculate the differential cash flow, subtracting project B from project A, and calculate IRR using a calculator. What is your conclusion?

b. Calculate the differential cash flow, subtracting project A from project B, and calculate IRR using a calculator. What is your conclusion?

c. How would you solve this problem?

Further Reading

Beidlemen, C. R. 1984. Discounted Cash Flow Reinvestment Rate Assumptions. *Engineering Economist* (Winter).

Bernhard, R. H., and C. J. Norstrom. 1980. A Further Note on Unrecovered Investment Uniqueness of the Internal Rate, and the Question of Project Acceptability. *Journal of Financial and Quantitative Analysis* (June).

Black, F. 1988. A Simple Discounting Rule. *Financial Management* (Summer).

Bodenhorn, D. 1964. A Cash-Flow Concept of Profit. *Journal of Finance* (March): 16–31.

Canaday, R. E., P. R. Colwell, and H. Paley. 1986. Relevant and Irrelevant Internal Rates of Return. *Engineering Economist* (Fall).

Ekern, S. 1979. On the Inadequacy of a Probabilistic Internal Rate of Return. *Journal of Business Finance & Accounting* 6 (2).

Fisher, I. 1965. *The Theory of Interest*. New York: Augustus M. Kelley, Publishers.

Fremgen, J. 1973. Capital Budgeting Practices: A Survey. *Management Accounting* (May).

Hirschleifer, J. 1958. On the Theory of Optimal Investment Decisions. *Journal of Political Economy* 66 (August): 329–352.

Hoskins, C. G. 1977. Benefit-Cost Ratio Ranking for Size Disparity Problems. *Journal of Business Finance & Accounting* 4 (2).

Hoskins, C. G., and G. A. Mumey. 1979. Payback: A Maligned Method of Asset Ranking? *Engineering Economist* (Fall).

Narayanan, M. P. 1985. Observability and the Payback Criterion. *Journal of Business* (July).

Nehauser, J. J., and J. A. Viscione. 1973. How Managers Feel about Advanced Capital Building Methods. *Management Review* (November).

Petry, G. H. 1975. Effective Use of Capital Budgeting Tools. *Business Horizons* (October).

Schall, L., G. Sundem, and W. Geijsbeek, Jr. 1978. Survey and Analysis of Capital Budgeting References. *Journal of Finance* (March): 281–287.

Solomon, E. 1956. The Arithmetic of Capital Budgeting Decisions. *Journal of Business* 29 (April): 124–129.

9 Capital Budgeting—Net Cash Flow Construction

A. Net Cash Flow in a World with Taxes

B. Projects with Different Durations

C. Government Intervention

A. Net Cash Flow in a World with Taxes

According to Modigliani and Miller's model, a company's value is determined by its net cash flow. This net cash flow is derived from the company's operations, which in chapter 8 we referred to as "projects." For the sake of simplicity, in chapter 8 we assumed there is no inflation, and if there is, cash flows are adjusted for purchasing power. This requirement is relatively simple: Given a particular cash flow, discounting any amount C_i to its present value PV_i accounts not only for the cost of capital (interest rate) for time t_i but also for the expected inflation rate up to that period. As explained when we discussed the term structure of interest rates (which indicates the cost of capital), interest rates in different periods usually already reflect inflationary expectations. Therefore, no further adjustment is required for inflation when using these rates. In other cases, we can adjust for inflation, as explained in chapter 3.

In chapter 8 we also assumed a world without taxes, and that if any taxes do apply, amounts are "translated" to their net post-tax value in the company's account.

The first part of this chapter discusses net cash flow structure in a world with taxes.

Remember that tax laws may change from time to time, and also differ by country. Further, this chapter is not meant as a substitute for a course in accounting or taxation but rather to illustrate certain fundamental principles used in tax systems throughout the Western world, and the effects of these principles on cash flows. The tax rates applicable at any given moment in any particular country, and expected changes in these rates, should be obtained from tax experts in each country when making any investment decision.

Taxes are an expense like any other. As far as companies are concerned, there is no difference whether a check is made out to a supplier or to the tax authorities. The effect of this payment on their cash balances is the same. As for any other expense, companies are interested in knowing the amount and timing of tax payments. Familiarity with tax laws allows optimal tax planning,[1] which in practice translates into the following:

1. Paying the minimal tax rate.

2. Deferring tax payments to the latest possible date permitted by law (thereby minimizing their present value).

Taxes are not necessarily outflows. Many countries have enacted capital investment encouragement laws, which not only reduce tax rates and defer payments but also provide grants that positively affect corporate cash flows. This matter will be discussed in greater detail later on.

In principle, Western accounting practices distinguish between capital expenses and operational expenses. Capital gains/losses are the result of one-time purchases/sales of "real" assets (buildings, equipment, and even reputation). On the other hand, operational gains/losses are the result of a company's ongoing operations (production, sales). As tax rates and timing are different for each category, the tax authorities' recognition of an expense's classification as a capital or operational expense is of utmost importance. Operational expenses cannot be offset against capital income, and vice versa. A classic disagreement between tax authorities and companies, for example, has to do with the classification of R&D expenses or marketing expenses for launching a new product. Tax authorities tend to classify such expenditures as capital expenses, while

1. Tax planning does not mean tax evasion. Tax planning is legitimate so long as it falls under a company's regular course of business. When artificial commercial actions are taken whose whole purpose and result is a tax decrease, those actions are considered unlawful. The line between tax planning and tax evasion is a fine one, and sometimes can only be decided by the courts.

companies tend to classify them as operational expenses. The reason for this classification dispute is simple: tax authorities recognize operational expenses as immediate expenses reducing annual reported profit and thereby annual tax payments. Capital expenses are recognized only in portions over the real asset's lifetime.

This recognition policy derives from an understanding that the wear of the real asset must be recognized throughout its useful life as a production-supporting expense. Although a capital expense was incurred immediately when the asset was acquired, this expense is recognized for tax purposes over time (and is referred to as *depreciation*). Therefore, immediate profits reported to the tax authorities are greater, while future profits are smaller. The immediate tax payment is greater, and the future payment is smaller.

Capital investment incentive laws usually include accelerated depreciation clauses. These clauses permit companies to write down assets over a shorter period, which reduces immediate reported profits and immediate tax payments. It is noted and emphasized that the total nominal tax payment remains constant, regardless of the depreciation period. There is no nominal reduction in tax payments[2]; the difference is due only to the timing of tax payments. As the present (discounted) value of the tax benefit (recognition of expenses) is greater the earlier an expense is recognized by the tax authorities, it is in a company's interest to report expenses as soon as possible and when permissible.

When assessing a company, its reported profit for tax purposes as dictated by accounting and tax laws is different from its actual cash flow. As mentioned, cash expenses are made in cash at a specific point in time and have an immediate effect on the company's bank account. Tax recognition of that expense is determined by the depreciation period and method.[3] Reported annual depreciation is not a real outflow of cash (which actually occurred when the company acquired the asset) but only a tool for tax calculation.

If we wish to calculate a company's cash flow in each period, we must subtract the entire amount of the capital expenditure from its cash

2. Equal to the corporate income tax rate times the expenditure on the capital asset.

3. The most common depreciation method is the straight-line method: a constant depreciation rate is recognized each year throughout the depreciation period. Some methods allow higher depreciation rates during the initial years, which then decrease over time. In each method, the total write-off will equal 100% of the asset's cost.

balances at the actual time of payment,[4] and credit the depreciation charge back to the company's cash balances each time it is debited from the company's expense accounts.

Depreciation methods assume that capital assets have no value at the end of the depreciation period, and that during the amortization period their real value is equal to their value on the company's books, that is, their purchasing price less accrued depreciation up to that time. Sometimes capital assets are sold during the amortization period at a price that is higher or lower than their book value. This leads to capital gains or losses, respectively, which are subject to capital tax. Capital tax rates are lower than the operational tax rate, that is, the corporate income tax. Needless to say, if assets are sold after the end of the amortization period at a price greater than zero, they generate capital gains.

The above taxation method presentation is summarized in the following example.

Example: Unable to meet demand for its products, Success Inc. is considering stepping up production by buying additional machinery. The new machine costs $500,000.

Sales will increase by an additional 100,000 units, which can be sold at $2 per unit.

The machine requires fixed maintenance costs (regardless of the number of units produced) of $25,000 a year.

Variable production costs are $0.50 per unit.

Depreciation on the machine is allowed over 10 years using the straight-line method. The corporate income tax is 40% and the capital gains tax is 30%.

The required cost of capital on investment is 9%.

The production manager stated that the machine should be sold after seven years at an estimated price of $210,000 (scrap value), instead of wasting effort on increasing maintenance.

Should the company implement this new project?

The first step in making any financial decision is to "draw" the net cash flow (in thousands of dollars).

---

4. Sometimes suppliers provide credit or allow payment in installments. Amounts will be debited from the cash account on actual payment to a supplier.

Symbol	Item	Year 0	1	. . . .	6	7
I	Investment (acquisition)	500	0		0	0
Rev.	Revenues		200	. . . .	200	200
FC	Fixed costs		–25	. . . .	–25	–25
VC	Variable costs		–50	. . . .	–50	–50
Dep.	Depreciation		–50		–50	–50
EBIT	**Earnings before interest and taxes**		**75**	**. . . .**	**75**	**75**
T_C	40% corporate income tax		–30	. . . .	–30	–30
NI	**Net income from operations**		**45**	**. . . .**	**45**	**45**
	Extraordinary income/expenses		0		**0**	**210**
	Capital gains tax[a]		0		**0**	**–18**
	Total reported net income		45	. . . .	45	237
Dep.	Offsetting virtual cash flows (depreciation)		+50	. . . .	+50	+50
NCF	**Net cash flow**	**–500**	**+95**	**. . . .**	**+95**	**+287**

a. Book value is $500 - 50 \times 7 = 150$. Capital gain is $210 - 150 = 60$. Capital gains tax is $60 \times 30\% = 18$.

Depreciation is subtracted from revenues as an expense for tax calculation purposes only! In calculating cash flow, we wrote off the asset's entire value I[5] upon acquisition (–$500,000). After calculating the company's income tax T_C,[6] we must add back this virtual expense (the next-to-last line) to obtain the net cash flow.

Calculating the NPV with a discount rate of 9% yields $83,161. Therefore, buying the machine is worthwhile.

A word of caution: Although we explained that adjusting cash flows for inflation is simple, it must be done correctly. A similar adjustment is made for currency exchange differences. In some cases we can adjust only the final line of the cash flow. At other times the adjustment is applied differently for each line. Depreciation can sometimes be linked to inflation (according to local law), and sometimes must be kept constant using nominal values. Currency fluctuations may only influence revenues, if they are derived only abroad; or they may influence only

5. I denotes "investment."
6. T_C denotes "tax corporate."

direct expenses, if these refer to raw materials imported from overseas. There is no one method for solving all possible problems, and it is necessary to consider all possible influences on each line and the way that these influences affect the bottom line: net cash flow.

B. Projects with Different Durations

Let's continue with the above example. Success Inc.'s CFO disagrees with the production manager and recommends not to sell the machine but to continue operating it for the full 10-year period (scrap value = 0).

As always, before making any financial decision we should "draw" the net cash flow:

Year			
	0	1	. . .10
Net cash flow	–$500,000	$95,000	. . .$95,000

The NPV for this cash flow is $109,677. The CFO presents these results as justification for his recommendation to hold on to the machine.

Is the CFO correct?

The duration of the first project, as proposed by the production manager, is only seven years, while the duration for the second project, as proposed by the CFO, is 10 years. Can we make such a comparison?

These kinds of problems are referred to as *investments' asymmetrical durations*. The question that arises is, what happens at the end of the project? The project proposed by the production manager (project A) is three years shorter than the project proposed by the CFO (project B). At the very least, we should deposit the scrap value from project A in the bank and calculate the interest received during those three years as an addition to project A's NPV.

However, this is only one possibility.

The production manager insists that, as the machine must be replaced with a new one each time, it is better to replace it every seven years. The CFO insists that the machine should be replaced every 10 years. Who is right?

Let's calculate for a 70-year period (divisible by both 7 and 10).

For project A, in addition to the NPV of $83,161 in the "first cycle," we will receive an additional "payment" every seven years (at the start of every eighth year = end of every seventh year), which constitutes the NPV for the next cycle's cash flow, for a total of nine such payment cycles.

As the annual interest rate is 9%, then for seven-year cycles the interest rate for each period will be

$(1 + 0.09)^7 - 1 = 0.828 = 82.8\%.$

For project B, in addition to the present value of $109,667 in the first "cycle," every 10 years (at the start of every eleventh year = end of every tenth year) we will also receive an additional "payment" that constitutes the NPV for the next cycle, for a total of six additional payment cycles. As the annual interest rate is 9%, then for 10-year cycles the interest rate for each period will be:

$(1 + 0.09)^{10} - 1 = 1.367 = 136.74\%$

Let's "draw" the cash flows for both projects:

Project	Period Length	No. of Periods n	Interest rate R (%)	Payment PMT
A	7 years	10	82.8	83,161
B	10 years	7	136.74	109,667

We now have a solvable problem—we must use a different interest rate for each project, which is directly related to each project's cycle length. As this interest rate is particularly high, then after a relatively small number of cycles, the present value of the discounted amounts will be small and negligible. To save ourselves unnecessary calculations, we can approximate and say that they continue into perpetuity.

To rephrase our problem, we have before us two mutually exclusive projects, and we need to decide which is better. Project A provides an immediate payment of $83,161, plus a perpetual periodic cash flow of equal amounts at an interest rate of 82.8%. Project B provides an immediate payment of $109,667, plus a perpetual periodic cash flow of equal amounts at an interest rate of 136.74%.

As we know, the formula for calculating the present value of perpetual cash flows is $NPV = \dfrac{C}{R}$.

Project A's value is $83,161 + \dfrac{83,161}{0.828} = \$183,597$.

Project B's value is $109,667 + \dfrac{109,667}{1.3674} = \$189,868$.

Thus, the best option would be to replace the machine every 10 years.

Let's check our assumption that the problem can be approximated to an infinite number of cycles:

A 70-year calculation for project A yields $183,156, and for project B $189,413. As we can see, the difference when calculating into perpetuity or for 70 years is negligible.

Moreover, the difference in NPV between the two projects, assuming that they continue into perpetuity, is $6,301, and if they continue for only 70 years it is $6,257. The $44 difference between these two calculation scenarios (perpetuity vs. 70 years) amounts to less than half of one-thousandth of the project value, and is therefore negligible.

Conclusion: the projects can be considered to continue into perpetuity and not to be limited to 70 years.

Caution: When applying financial models, it is necessary to consider the significance of the result. The difference between the two PV's of the projects above is $6,000, which amounts to about 1% of the initial invest-ment in a project that will continue into perpetuity. Financially,[7] there is no practical difference between the projects, as there are many produc-tion floor-related parameters that are difficult, and sometimes impossi-ble, to quantify and include in our calculations.[8]

We can generalize the above example and formulate a model that allows comparison between projects of different durations.[9]

Definition:

$NPV(T)$—Net present value of a project with a duration of T years.

r—Cost of capital (annualized).

R—Cost of capital for a period ("cycle") of T years.

$R = (1+r)^T - 1$.

The present value of a project with a duration of T years implemented periodically an infinite number of times is

$$NPV(T,\infty) = NPV(T) + \frac{NPV(T)}{R} = NPV(T)\frac{1+R}{R}.$$

Developing the inverse[10] expression of $\frac{1+R}{R}$, that is, $\frac{R}{1+R}$, where $R = (1+r)^T - 1$, yields $1 - \frac{1}{(1+r)^T}$, which is similar to the discount

---

7. A 1% difference is insignificant considering possible errors in estimating the various amounts.

8. In this case, where the financial calculation does not indicate a significant advantage, then as CEO I would let the production manager call the shots in his area of expertise.

9. Remember that the model is based on the assumption that the project is repeatable!

10. The inverse of x is $1/x$.

rate used in the discounting tables for \$1 paid over T periods:

$$K(r,T) = \frac{1 - \dfrac{1}{(1+r)^T}}{r}.$$

We can therefore also write the expression for serial projects as

$$NPV(T,\infty) = \frac{NPV(T)}{r \cdot K(r,T)}.$$

One common indicator is the *annual equivalent value* (AEV), which is defined as the average fixed annual cash flow that results in the same NPV for a cyclical project: $NPV(T,\infty) = \dfrac{AEV}{r}$.

From the expression above, we can immediately derive the following:

$$AEV = \frac{NPV(T)}{K(r,T)}.$$

Therefore, if we wish to compare two cyclical projects, we can compare their $NPV(T,\infty)$, or their AEV, and choose the project with the greater value.

C. Government Intervention

In the first section of this chapter we stated that taxes are not necessarily outflows. Many countries have enacted "capital investment encouragement laws." In addition to decreasing tax rates and deferring tax payments, these laws also provide various grants that positively influence corporate cash flows and must be taken into account.

Below we review a number of common investment encouragement methods and how they affect NPV—our best tool in investment decision making.

Subsidized-Interest Loans

In many cases, governments are willing to provide entrepreneurs with subsidized-interest loans. This type of government intervention can also occur in noncommercial, "personal" transactions, such as subsidized-interest loans (mortgages) for young couples or disadvantaged populations. In this context, it is common to refer to the "gift value,"[11] which is

---

11. In each of the cases discussed in this section, "gift value" refers to the benefit value as the difference in net present value calculated with and without the benefit.

the difference between the NPV under normal interest conditions and the NPV under the subsidized interest.

Tax Relief

Governments love to include various types of limited-time tax reliefs (usually lasting 5 to 10 years) in their capital investment encouragement laws. Particularly popular is tax relief on undistributed earnings, sometimes even to the point of making these earnings tax-free. In addition, when dividends are eventually distributed, a tax relief is provided for them as well. The tax effect of these measures is discussed in greater detail later in this book.

Governments favor this kind of encouragement, for two reasons:

• It does not require immediate resource allocation from the government's limited annual budget.

• Government participation occurs only if a company is successful, as a waiver of tax income. This method does indeed encourage entrepreneurs to succeed.

Accelerated Depreciation

As discussed earlier, depreciation does not reduce the amount of tax paid over the years but rather alters the timing of these payments. When a government offers accelerated depreciation benefits, it effectively reduces net income in earlier years (thereby reducing tax payments), while increasing tax payments in later years. As the total nominal taxes paid over the years remains the same, accelerated depreciation defers tax payments, thereby decreasing their NPV and increasing the NPV of the company's cash flow. This benefit can be particularly significant in times of rapid inflation, if no accounting regulations are in effect translating all nominal values to inflation-adjusted real values.

Investment Grants

Older capital investment encouragement laws were formulated for investment-heavy industrial projects, such as chemical factories, energy infrastructure, transportation, and so on. These projects required subsidies in the form of government participation in the initial investment itself. The transition to high-tech projects (software, communications, biotech, etc.) necessitated the enactment of new laws, which mainly provided for tax relief as detailed above. However, many countries still operate investment grant programs. These grants reduce the investment required from independent sources at the start of a project, thereby yielding a greater NPV.

Governments usually allow entrepreneurs a choice of options offering different combinations of the above investment encouragement methods. Investors must consider which of these alternatives is most beneficial.

Chapter 9—Questions and Problems

Question 1

SPM Ltd. is considering whether the following investment is worthwhile:

Investment: $1.5 million; investment duration: 10 years; scrap value: 0.

Corporate income tax: 40%; cost of capital: 12%.
Revenues net of direct expenses: years 1–4: $450,000; years 5–10: $300,000.
Calculate:

a. Payback period.

b. IRR.

c. NPV.

d. PI.

Question 2

Success Inc. is considering investing in a machine that produces 100,000 units a year, which retail at $1.40 per unit. Fixed costs total $60,000 a year, and variable costs are $0.40 per unit. The machine costs $100,000 and has a useful life of 10 years. The cost of capital for the company is 12%. The corporate income tax rate is 40%, and the company accounts for depreciation using the straight-line method.

Should the company invest in the machine?

Question 3

A plastics company that shut down its plastic chairs department owing to lack of demand is resuming operations following a sudden increase in demand. To meet current production requirements, it needs to buy two new machines: one that costs $300,000 and has a useful life of four years, and another that costs $200,000 and has a useful life of five years. In addition, it needs to reacquire old equipment transferred to the plastic utensils department. The scrap value of this equipment in the company's books is 0, but the department director claims that the equipment has a market value of $100,000 and a useful life of four years. The utensils department will have to buy used equipment instead of the current equipment at a cost of $150,000. The department's annual revenues are estimated at $500,000.

Annual expenses are estimated as follows:

Raw materials: $30,000

Wages: $70,000

Other: $10,000

Fixed costs: $84,000

Straight-line depreciation: $115,000 for the first four years, $40,000 in the fifth year

To reopen the department, the company needs to increase its working capital by $400,000. The company will apply for support under the investment encouragement law, which provides a tax exemption for five years.

The company's capital raising costs are $k = 15\%$.

Should the company reopen the department?

Make any reasonable assumptions you need (state them clearly) to assess economic viability, considering the following:

Project duration

Accounting for working capital

Accounting for the investment's scrap value

Cost of old equipment

Question 4

You bought a machine five years ago at a cost of $30,000. The machine is amortized over a 10-year period. The machine's current market value is $10,000. You are offered to replace the machine with a newer one that costs $100,000 and has an expected useful life of 10 years. Both machines offer the same production capacity, but the newer one reduces production costs by $12,000 in each of the first three years and by $20,000 in each of the next seven years.

$K = 10\%$, the corporate income tax rate $= 50\%$, and depreciation is applied using the straight-line method.

The bank has granted the company a loan covering the required investment (think carefully what this means!).

Should the company swap machines?

Question 5

As a project assessment consultant, you are presented with an offer for replacing a production machine. In light of the following, is the project worthwhile?

• The old machine has a book value of $20,000 and a useful life of another 10 years. After 10 years, the machine will have zero value.

• The old machine can be sold for $15,000.

• A new machine costs $40,000. Delivery and installation costs an additional $3,000.

• The new machine has a useful life of 10 years, after which it will be worth $10,000.

• The new machine will reduce annual repair and wage costs by $8,000.

• Depreciation is applied using the straight-line method.

• After 10 years, the factory will shut down and will not need to buy new machinery.

• $k = 10\%$.

• Tax rates:

  50% on ordinary income.

  32% on capital gains and losses (capital gains can be offset against capital losses in the same year).

Question 6

You are the production manager of Knaft Food's pasta line. You have three options for buying production machinery, and you must decide which machine to buy ($k = 10\%$).

Machine	Price ($)	Annual Net Cash Flow ($)	Useful Life (yrs)
A	100,000	25,000	8
B	120,000	26,500	10
C	150,000	33,000	9

Assuming you must sign a long-term contract so that when one machine reaches the end of its useful life you replace it with another of the same kind (prices include return costs):

1. Calculate the NPV for each machine. Which should you choose? Explain.

2. What is the average cash flow generated by each machine? Explain the difference between this figure and the above annual cash flow.

Question 7

A company decides to open a new production line for binders. The company is considering two options for buying the necessary equipment:

Parameter	Option A	Option B
Equipment cost	$1,200,000	$4,800,000
Fixed annual maintenance costs	$100,000	$200,000
Variable production costs per unit	$2	$1
Useful life	4 years	12 years

In both cases the equipment has zero scrap value. Equipment costs are amortized for tax purposes using the straight-line method. The income tax rate for the company is 45%. The annual cost of capital for the company is 8%.

The company's marketing manager claims that at $5 per unit, the company can sell 500,000 binders each year into perpetuity. Which option should the company choose in light of this assumption?

Question 8

You are considering a profitable project that will cost $10 million. Near an industrial center, depreciation is applied over four years using the straight-line method. In rural areas, the government offers accelerated depreciation of 40% in the first year, which then decreases by 10% each year. Administrative costs in rural areas are higher by $15,000 a year (and will remain so), while all other expenses are the same. The net cost of capital is 10%, and the corporate income tax is 40%.

Which option should you choose?

Question 9

Capital investment encouragement laws in Utopia provide two tracks:

1. A 20% grant (straight-line depreciation for the remainder of the investment).

2. A 50% reduction in tax rates.

You are considering buying a machine for $100,000 with a useful life of five years. The machine generates operating cash flows of $40,000 a year. The corporate income tax is 40%, and the company's net cost of capital is 18%.
Which option should you choose?

Question 10

You are bidding in a five-year tender for operating the university cafeteria. The tender is based on the dish price as determined by the student union's menu.
Your inquiries yield the following assessments:

• You can sell 30,000 dishes a month.

• Fixed operating costs are $500,000 a year.

• Variable costs are 50% of the dish's retail price to students (without profit).

• After winning the tender, you will need to replace some of the kitchen equipment, and depreciation will be applied using the straight-line method.

It is very difficult to estimate which equipment will need replacement, and so you have decided that you want to recover your investment (through net operating cash flow) in two years at most. The equipment will have no value at the end of the period.

• The tax rate is 40%.

• The cost of capital is 10%.

What is the minimum dish price you can offer in this tender?
For convenience, assume that all revenues and expenses (except the investment) occur at the end of each year. It would, however, be more accurate to assume that they occur midyear.

Further Reading

Brenner, M., and I. Venezia. 1983. The Effects of Inflation and Taxes on Growth Investments and Replacement Policies. *Journal of Finance*. (December).

Brick, J. R., and H. E. Thompson. 1978. The Economic Life of an Investment and the Appropriate Discount Rate. *Journal of Financial and Quantitative Analysis* (December).

Coen, R. M. 1975. Investment Behavior, the Measurement of Depreciation and Tax Policy. *American Economic Review* (March).

Dammon, R. M., and L. W. Senbet. 1988. The Effect of Taxes and Depreciation on Corporate Investment and Financial Leverage. *Journal of Finance* (June).

Emery, G. W. 1982. Some Guidelines for Evaluating Capital Investment Alternatives with Unequal Lives. *Financial Management* (Spring).

Gronchi, S. 1986. On Investment Criteria Based on Internal Rate of Return. *Oxford Economic Papers* (March).

Howe, K. M., and H. Lapan. 1987. Inflation and Asset Life: The Darby vs. the Fisher Effect. *Journal of Financial and Quantitative Analysis* (March).

Kim, M. K. 1979. Inflationary Effects in the Capital Investment Process: An Empirical Examination. *Journal of Finance* (September).

Lembke, V. C., and H. R. Toole. 1981. Differences in Depreciation Methods and the Analysis of Supplemental Current-Cost and Replacement Cost Data. *Journal of Accounting Auditing and Finance* (Winter).

II The Risk Value of Capital

10 Investment Decisions in Random Markets

A. Statistical Tools in Financial Theory

B. Random Processes—Stochastic Dominance on the Payoff-Probability Plane

C. Random Processes—Stochastic Dominance on the Mean Yield–Risk Plane

D. Making Investment Decisions in a Random Market

A. Statistical Tools in Financial Theory

To better understand the need for this chapter, let us return to our fundamental model definition:

Financial asset value   Present value of expected net future cash flow.

In the first part of this book we used a similar definition for financial value, but without the word "expected." We assumed that all future income was known and certain. Clearly, this is not the case under real-world conditions. In the second part of this book we discuss how to value financial assets whose future income stream is not certain and must be predicted.

Example: Company A is a well-known, well-established bank. Company B is a promising, up-and-coming high-tech company that still needs to prove its commercial potential. Its expected net cash flow is completely identical to that expected for company A.

Obviously, although the expected cash flow is in theory identical for both companies, the two companies cannot possibly have the same financial value. Any reasonable investor would choose to buy shares in company A because of its proven track record. If everyone prefers company A's shares, its share price (i.e., the financial asset value) will be higher than the price for shares in company B. If we try to understand the difference between these two companies, we can sum it up in one intuitive word: risk. We used the term "intuitive" to indicate that we must first define risk before we can transform it into an applicable modeling measure parameter. For now, we will not try to find an accurate definition of risk. That is an exercise better left for the classroom, to illustrate just how complicated that definition can be.

In a random world, there are two extremely challenging preliminary steps that must be carried out before valuing financial assets:

1. We must *predict* their expected future cash flows.

2. We must *assess* the different risks involved in each asset's predicted cash flows.

Our main task (even prior to formulating our models) is to formulate a prediction method.[1] As the saying goes, "It is difficult to make predictions, especially about the future."

The most common mathematical prediction tool is derived from the field of statistics and is based on historical data. True, we can make assessments based on various convictions or beliefs, without using historical statistical data. However, using a more conservative approach, we must first examine past data for a particular financial asset or an asset we believe to be similar and then refine, update, and amend this data using our best judgment.[2]

Let us review some definitions in fundamental statistics[3] and demonstrate their use when applied to financial theory.

Probability   The likelihood (P) of a certain event occurring in a large number of repeating trials: $0 \leq P \leq 1$.

Common "events" in financial theory for which we might like to know the probability might be a particular numerical price value (e.g., of a share or bond), a cash flow (e.g., for projects), a yield, or even the occurrence of various conditions that can affect these values.

Example: The likelihood (probability) of a recession in the coming year is 60% ($P = 0.6$).

---

1. Even assessing risk differences between financial assets is a form of prediction.

2. We discuss incorporating personal beliefs into the model in chapter 15.

3. This will not be a formal review but rather an informal, intuitive mixture of probability models and statistical inference, which are two separate fields.

Probability distribution function   A list of all (mutually exclusive) events i that may occur, with each event being assigned a variable with a value X_i and a probability P_i, where $\sum_1^n P(x_i) = 1$. When x_i gets a specific value, the value is denoted X_i.

If, for example, the variable whose historical data are being examined is a share price (or the monthly yield on that share), we can list all X_i values in the relevant historical period (of either share price or share yield), $i = 1 \ldots n$. Each value is assigned a probability P_i as reflected in the frequency[4] with which that value appeared in the historical sample as presented in figure 10.1.

The historical data might also be market conditions:

Market Conditions	Probability[a]	Share A Yield[b]	Share B Yield[b]
Growth	0.3	2.1%	1.5%
Normal	0.6	1.1%	1.0%
Recession	0.1	–0.8%	0.6%

a. Measured historically or a personal prediction.
b. Historical average yield, measured monthly for the specified condition.

Discrete/continuous distribution function   The range of possible results may be finite/discrete, as in the last example, or infinite/continuous. In the latter case the distribution function will be replaced with a continuous function assigning a probability $f(x)$ to every event value x, such that $\int f(x)dx = 1$, as presented in figure 10.2.

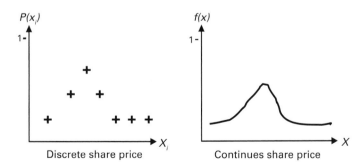

Figure 10.1 and Figure 10.2
Share Price Probability Distributions

4. Frequency is calculated as the number of times the value appears, divided by the total number of observations in the sample.

Share price monthly yield data drawn from a historical sample can be plotted either as discrete values or extrapolated to form a continuous line. Future share prices may have any interim value on the continuous line, even though that exact value did not appear in the historical representative sample.

Cumulative probability function   The probability that any event (value) that is below a certain specific value will become apparent.

In the discrete case, the cumulative probability function will be equal to the sum of all the probabilities for all events up to that specified event value $F(X \leq X_i) = \sum_i P_i$.

In the above example, the share price that serves as the specified event is of a continuous function type, and so the cumulative probability function describing the probability that the share price x will be below (smaller than) a specified value X is $F(x) = \int_0^x f(x)dx$ (figure 10.3).

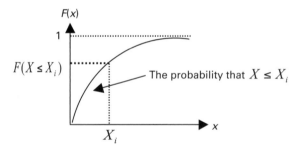

Figure 10.3
Cumulative Probability Function

Having defined basic parameters and statistical functions, let's define a number of mathematical operators (measures) defined over these statistical variables.

Mean   The weighted average of all possible events.

The mean (μ) is the sum of the possible outcomes, multiplied by their respective probability:

$$\mu = E(x) = \sum_{all} x_i \cdot P_i.$$

or for the continuous case,

$$\mu = E(x) = \int_{-\infty}^{+\infty} x \cdot f(x)dx.$$

This statistical measure provides information on the "center of mass" around which the results are distributed. When using a historical sample, we can calculate that sample's mean by multiplying values (e.g., share prices) by their probability (event frequency) and then summing up those amounts, or in the case of continuous data summing up by way of integration. The resulting mean value can serve as a prediction estimator for the future. Assuming that no substantial change occurs either in the company's operations or in the market conditions,[5] we may expect that the future event values, the share prices, will yield a similar mean (weighted average).

If we need to predict the average share price in the coming year, then clearly an estimate derived from historical sample data (adjusted upward or downward, based on our best judgment) is a better predictor than a coin-toss guess (even if that guess is later found to be closer to the mark).

Example:

Market Condition	Condition Probability	Share A Yield	Share B Yield
Growth	0.3	2.1%	1.5%
Normal	0.6	1.1%	1.0%
Recession	0.1	−0.8%	0.6%

We can calculate the expected average monthly yield based on our historical sample:

Share A: $E(X_A) = 0.3 \cdot 2.1 + 0.6 \cdot 1.1 + 0.1 \cdot (-0.8) = 0.63 + 0.66 - 0.08 = 1.21\%$.

Share B: $E(X_B) = 0.3 \cdot 1.5 + 0.6 \cdot 1.0 + 0.1 \cdot 0.6 = 0.45 + 0.6 + 0.06 = 1.11\%$.

If we believe that the market conditions probability for the coming year differs from the probability derived from our statistical sample data (e.g., the expected probabilities will be: growth 0.7, normal 0.3, recession 0), we may want to update our calculation for the future expected value accordingly.

Variance   The average deviation of events' values from their mean (squared[6]):

---

5. Note that this is an extremely significant assumption and must be examined in real-world conditions and on a case-by-case basis.

6. By taking the square we avoid the problem of the deviation sign (+ or −).

$$\sigma^2 = \sum_{i=1}^{n} [x_i - E(x)]^2 \cdot P_i,$$

or for continuous data,

$$\sigma^2 = \int_x [x - E(x)]^2 dx.$$

If we are trying to assess overall variance (for the entire population) by using specific sample data, this measure should be calculated as:

$$\sigma^2 = \frac{\sum_i [x_i - E(x)]^2}{n-1} = \frac{[\sum_i x_i^2] - n \cdot [E(x)]^2}{n-1}.$$

Variance provides a measure of the spread of actual results around their "center of mass." The greater the average (squared) distance, the more dispersed the results. When using historical sample data, we can calculate the mean (center of mass) for that sample, calculate the distance of each event from that mean by subtracting its value from the mean value (using the square of that result so as to avoid negative distances), sum up those results, and divide by the number of events in the sample (or, in case of continuous data, integrate).[7] This sample variance can be used as an estimator measure for the scattering of future values. We expect that if our event is repeated numerous times in the future, it will have a similar variance value.

In the above example:

$$\sigma_A^2 = (2.1-1.21)^2 \cdot 0.3 + (1.1-1.21)^2 \cdot 0.6 + (-0.8-1.21)^2 \cdot 0.1$$
$$= 0.2376 + 0.0073 + 0.4040 = 0.649.$$

$$\sigma_B^2 = (1.5-1.11)^2 \cdot 0.3 + (1.0-1.11)^2 \cdot 0.6 + (0.6-1.11)^2 \cdot 0.1$$
$$= 0.0456 + 0.073 + 0.0260 = 0.145.$$

Standard deviation   The square root of the variance ($=\sigma$).

As we prefer working with linear values, the actual distance from the center of mass is a more intuitive measure than is the square of that distance (variance).

---

7. The statistical inference literature states that in order to avoid bias in this estimate, we must divide by $n-1$ and not by the number of events n. We must distinguish between the mathematical definition of a population mean (and for that purpose, the definition for other measures as well), and its estimated numerical value, inferred from a particular historical data sample.

In the above example, $\sigma_A = \sqrt{0.649} = 0.81\%$, that is, the mean yield expected for share A is $\mu_A = 1.21\%$, and we expect most[8] of the results to be distributed around that value at an average distance (yield) of $\pm 0.81\%$.

Similarly, $\sigma_B = \sqrt{0.145} = 0.38\%$, that is, the mean yield expected for share B is 1.11%, and we expect most of the results to be distributed around that value at an average distance of $\pm 0.38\%$.

Thus, the mean yield for share B is lower than the mean yield for share A. However, this measure alone is insufficient, as we must also note that share A has a greater standard deviation. Therefore, the certainty of a future result being near the expected mean value (whether above or below it) is smaller than for share B, where expected results are more closely packed around the mean value. Therefore, the level of certainty of obtaining a result that is close to the mean value is greater.

So far, we have discussed one variable. However, we frequently wish to examine the statistical tie between two random variables. Sometimes it is difficult to directly predict the future behavior of variable A but easier to forecast the behavior of a co-related variable B. If we know the correlation between variable A and variable B, we can then use this statistical tie to forecast variable A.

Dependent variables A dependent variable measured in an experiment or defined in a mathematical model responds to an independent variable. If A and B are two types of events and there is a connection between the expected outcomes for event A $(X_2, X_2, X_3, ...)$ and the expected outcomes for event B $(Y_1, Y_2, Y_3, ...)$, then we can say that variables x and y have a joint distribution function.

Independent variables A and B are two types of events. If there is no connection between the expected outcomes for event A and the expected outcomes for event B, we can say that variables x and y are independent.

Contingent probability The chance for a certain event out of a set of possible events A to occur,[9] given with certainty (or assuming) that a certain event out of a set of possible events B has occurred.

---

8. As you recall from probability theory, for every distribution we can calculate what percentage of the results will be distributed around the average, in the range $\pm \sigma$ or $\pm 2\sigma$, etc. For example, $X \sim N(\mu, \sigma) \Rightarrow P_r(\mu - 2\sigma < x < \mu + 2\sigma) = 0.95$. This expression means that 95% of all future results are expected to be in the "confidence interval" range of $\mu \pm 2\sigma$.

9. That is, take a specific value.

Covariance A measure on a pair of dependent variables to mutually deviate, each from its own mean value.

A sample's covariance is calculated as follows:

$$\text{Cov}(x, y) = \frac{1}{n} \cdot \sum_{i=1}^{n} [x_i - E(x)] \cdot [y_i - E(y)],$$

or, assuming that we are calculating the general population covariance:

$$\text{Cov}(x, y) = \sum_{i=1}^{n} [x_i - E(x)] \cdot [y_i - E(y)] \cdot P_i.$$

Correlation coefficient A measure of the joint propensity of two dependent variables to deviate mutually from their own mean value. Their covariance is "normalized" on a scale of –1 to 1, with 1 indicating 100% propensity between the two variables, 0 indicating that there is no correlation (independent variables), and –1 indicating 100% inverse propensity, meaning that when one variable increases, the other decreases (by the exact same proportion), and vice versa.

Covariation is "normalized" into this convenient scale as a result of dividing by the standard deviation of both variables.

The reader can find the proof that $-1 \le \rho_{(x,y)} = \dfrac{\text{Cov}(x, y)}{\sigma_x \cdot \sigma_y} \le 1$ in any statistics book.

Calculating the correlation coefficient ρ^{10} for a sample is done as follows:

$$\rho_{(x,y)} = \frac{n \cdot \sum xy - \sum x \cdot \sum y}{\sqrt{\left[n \cdot \sum x^2 - \left(\sum x \right)^2 \right] \cdot \left[n \cdot \sum y^2 - \left(\sum y \right)^2 \right]}}.$$

Linear regression Another way of measuring the covariation of two variables is simply by trying to match them by a linear function. The optimal matching linear function is defined as the line with the smallest sum of error distances (deviation) ε_i between the observation points and the proposed line. This line will serve as the best approximation tool when making future predictions.

The regression calculation is based on the linear function $y = \alpha + \beta \cdot x_i + \varepsilon_i$, or $y = A + B \cdot x_i + \varepsilon_i$.

β is calculated from a sample: $B = \beta = \dfrac{n \sum X_i \cdot Y_i - \sum X_i \cdot \sum Y_i}{n \sum X_i^2 - \left(\sum X_i \right)^2}$

10. The correlation coefficient may also be denoted r.

α is calculated from a sample: $A = \alpha = \dfrac{\sum Y_i - B \sum X_i}{n}$

For example, denote the following variables:

R_A — The yield on share A (dependent variable, graphed on the y-axis in figure 10.4).

R_B — The yield on share B (dependent variable, graphed on the y-axis in figure 10.5).

R_m — The overall market yield (explanatory independent variable, graphed on the x-axis in both figures).

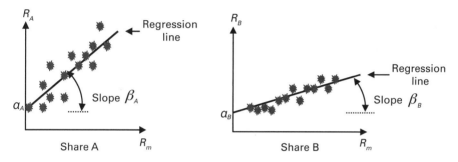

Figure 10.4 and Figure 10.5
Stocks' Yields versus Market Yield Regression Lines

Assume that the general market yield (the explanatory variable) is expected to increase by 2% in the next period. We can calculate the estimated change in the yield expected for share A and share B using the regression lines. Clearly, as the slope for share A's regression line is greater than that for share B, the predicted change in yield is greater.

The divergence of share A's data around the line is also greater than for share B. Therefore, our forecast for share A's expected yield has a lower level of certainty (accuracy) than our forecast for share B.

Stochastic process Up until now, we have introduced the possible outcomes of a single random event. We defined a random variable as a mapping function that assigns value numbers to the possible outcomes of an "experiment," and once a probability is assigned to each value, it is ultimately completely described by a *probability density function* (PDF). In many real-life cases, we have an index time set T, which may be discrete $T = (t_1; t_2; t_3; t_4 \ldots)$ or continuous $T = (0 \rightarrow t)$, on which a process develops. A stochastic process is a "family" (sequence) of random events, that is, random variables $X(t)$ that are defined on this time set, each with possible outcome values.

In the financial models that we will be discussing, we will usually assume a stochastic process of continuous time where the n random variables[11] $X(t)$ $(n \rightarrow \infty)$ have stationary independent increments $X(t_1) - X(t_2)$; $X(t_2) - X(t_3)$; $X(t_3) - X(t_4)$ ..., that is, all $X(t_{i+1}) - X(t_i)$ are independent and have the same normal distribution for all t_i. This means that even if the initial condition (or starting point) is known, the process might take many possible paths, but some paths may be more probable and others less so. Just as number values are assigned to a random variable x, based on the outcome of a random experiment, a stochastic process can also be assigned number values, depending on the outcome of a random process experiment $x(t)$. Thus, we can say that for a specific t, $x(t)$ is a random variable with probability distribution function $F(x,t) = P[x(t) \le X]$ as described in figure 10.6. The same definitions of the mean and the variance for the random variable may be applied now for a stochastic process.

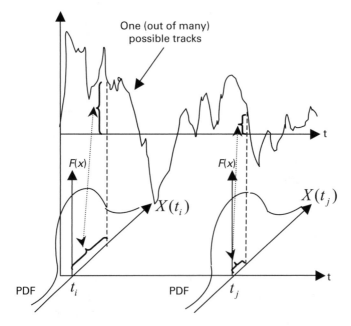

Figure 10.6
Financial Asset Price Stochastic Path (Process)

11. The variables here are denoted by capital letters since they are describing the probability for a specific value X to be obtained at time t.

B.   Random Processes—Stochastic Dominance on the Payoff-Probability Plane

When analyzing random future processes, and developing investment models for different investors, we must take two aspects into account:

1. Future predictions—Assessing outcomes, and their related probabilities.

2. Personal preference—As reflected in each investor's individual utility function.[12]

Is it possible for all investors, despite their different personal preferences (utility functions), to follow the same investment criteria? That is, can future outcomes prediction alone (assuming that it is identical for all investors) be sufficient to dictate investment decision-making criteria?

Such particular conditions are referred to as random processes with stochastic dominance.

The general problem facing investors is choosing among different financial assets. We will discuss a decision involving only two options, and through this solution solve the general problem.[13]

CSD—Complete Stochastic Dominance

When the worst possible outcome expected for asset A is better than the best outcome expected for asset B, then asset A has complete stochastic dominance over asset B.

For example:

Asset A		Asset B	
Probability	**Profit**	**Probability**	**Profit**
0.6	3,000	0.7	1,500
0.4	2,000	0.3	1,000

In choosing asset A, the worst-case scenario yields a profit of 2,000, while the best-case scenario when choosing asset B yields a profit of 1,500. Obviously, any sensible person would choose asset A, regardless of that person's utility function.

---

12. The utility function in an uncertain market is discussed in more depth in chapter 11.

13. In the case of more than two possibilities, we can form preference pairs, and then rank them using the tournament method.

To explain the concepts of first- and second-order dominance, we will use the following three assets:

Asset X		Asset Y		Asset Z	
Probability	**Profit**	**Probability**	**Profit**	**Probability**	**Profit**
0.5	1,000	0.3	2,000	0.3	500
0.3	2,000	0.4	4,000	0.4	1,500
0.2	3,000	0.3	5,000	0.3	2,500

To better compare these assets, we must sort their respective profits and corresponding probabilities. First, we should classify all possible profit outcomes in increasing order, and assign each profit its corresponding probability in each asset. This is illustrated by the following table:

Profit	Probability for Asset X	Probability for Asset Y	Probability for Asset Z
500	0	0	0.3
1,000	0.5	0	0
1,500	0	0	0.4
2,000	0.3	0.3	0
2,500	0	0	0.3
3,000	0.2	0	0
4,000	0	0.4	0
5,000	0	0.3	0

Sorting the data makes our comparison easier than the original three tables, but the interpretation is still too complicated for making an investment decision. The new table allows us to plot our options on one graph, with the y-axis indicating expected profit and the x-axis indicating the cumulative[14] probability.

For example, let's examine assets X and Y. The diagram in figure 10.7 gives us a clear picture of our options and helps in understanding the definitions below. This diagram actually shows the cumulative distribution function, with the axes rotated. In the traditional distribution function, expected values are displayed on the x-axis, while the (cumulative) probability for obtaining those values is plotted on the y-axis.

Rotating the axes for the sake of our discussion does not change anything mathematically. As mentioned, the reason for rotating the axes is strictly didactic, as it is easier to visualize that asset Y is more favorable

---

14. That is, the probability that profits will be smaller than or equal to this value.

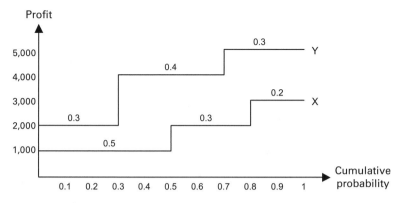

Figure 10.7
Cumulative Distribution Function (Rotated)

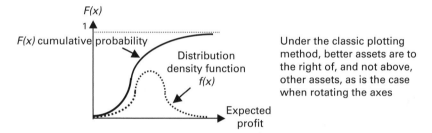

Figure 10.8
Cumulative Distribution Function (Ordinary)

than asset X when plotted as in figure 10.7, with the preferable asset on top. If we were to plot the graph in the classic way, the preferable asset would be to the right (figure 10.8).[15]

In other financial theory books, cumulative probability functions are usually plotted in the classical way. In terms of mathematical accuracy, both methods are correct.

FSD — First-Order Stochastic Dominance

Asset Y has a first-order stochastic dominance over asset X when the cumulative distribution function for the profit from asset Y is preferable to that for asset X for all possible profit values.

---

15. In my experience, students find the graphs with the rotated axes easier to understand.

Obviously, the higher the distribution function on the *y*-axis, the greater the profit offered at any given probability level, and so the more favorable the asset.

This definition is intuitive, and, when presented as above, any investor would clearly choose asset Y. (*Note:* Although in retrospect an event may transpire where we could have earned more had we chosen asset X, in advance, we would always choose Y!)

SSD—Second-Order Stochastic Dominance

Asset X has a second-order stochastic dominance over asset Z if for every profit value chosen for the cumulative distribution function, the mean profit for asset X is higher than the mean profit for asset Z.

Practically speaking, we want to examine the mean profit up to a certain profit value. If we examine the cumulative distribution function, the mean profit up to a certain value is equal to the area confined by the cumulative distribution function up to that value.

If we consider assets X and Z, we see that the cumulative distribution function for asset X is sometimes above and sometimes below that for asset Z. Therefore, this scenario does not qualify as first-order stochastic dominance.

In these situations, is it still possible to define circumstances where one asset has a clear dominance for all possible investors, regardless of their utility function? The area under each asset's PDF is in fact its mean return. While moving the dotted line upward (in figure 10.9) along all profit values in the PDF, the difference between the mean profit for asset X and for asset Z up to that point (shaded area) indicates how much the

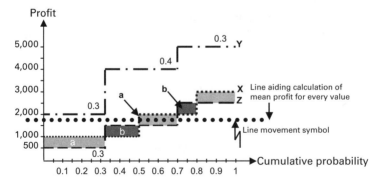

Figure 10.9
Assets X, Y, and Z Cumulative Distribution Functions

mean profit for asset X is greater up to that point than the mean profit of asset Z up to that point. This difference is equal to the sum of the areas confined by the rectangles formed by the two graphs up to that point (shaded area). Note that when asset X is above asset Z, the difference between X and Z as indicated by rectangle *a* in the above example is positive.[16] However, when Z is above X, the difference between X and Z, as indicated by rectangle *b*, is negative.[17]

When the total sum of these rectangles' areas is positive for every probability value, it means that the expected (mean) profit for asset X is always (for any profit value) higher than that for asset Z.

Practically there are two possible situations:

1. The difference is always positive (or negative).

2. The difference varies in sign.

If the difference varies in sign, we cannot determine anything concerning any dominance of one asset over the other. When the difference is always positive,[18] that is, the mean profit from asset X is always greater, we can state that everyone should invest in asset X regardless of their personal preferences.[19]

Although the above models define instances of stochastic dominance, an analysis of those instances covers only a tiny part of all possible circumstances. How, then, can we choose between two assets that do not meet the above criteria? Assets for which, even when checking second-order stochastic dominance, the difference changes sign?

In these instances (which constitute the bulk of cases), we cannot specify absolute criteria for all investors. We must develop a personal model that also takes into account an investor's personal preferences. These models are developed in the following chapters.

C. Random Processes—Stochastic Dominance on the Mean Yield–Risk Plane

In the above models, we discussed the distribution of profit (or yield). In first-order stochastic dominance, we talked about profit/yield, but in our

16. Marked by the light gray rectangle in figure 10.9.

17. Marked by the dark gray rectangle in figure 10.9.

18. And vice versa for negative.

19. Second-order stochastic dominance is the weakest of these three forms, and we can find utility functions where this statement is not true, such as a utility function that accounts not only for mean profit but also for variance.

discussion of second order stochastic dominance we talked about mean (average) profit (or yield). In other words, we were looking at payoff (or mean payoff)–distribution. To broaden our discussion, we must now examine the way stochastic dominance handles more than one parameter — "mean payoff," which is also affected by another parameter, risk. In this section we discuss only the intuitive aspect of risk. Definitions and an in-depth formal discussion of the matter occupy most of the rest of this book.

At the beginning of this chapter, we saw how the level of certainty of obtaining an outcome near the "center of mass," that is, the mean yield, intuitively serves as a risk indicator. If all possible outcomes exactly matched the mean value, then they would not classify such a case as involving uncertainty where outcomes might be distributed over a certain range. Instead, we would classify such a case as being certain. If we know the outcome with certainty, then there is no risk involved, and in Part I of this book we discussed how to analyze such cases. *Risk* is related to the level of uncertainty concerning future outcomes. Whether we define risk in this manner or another, every investor would clearly prefer maximizing his mean yield at minimum risk. Therefore, any investment-supporting model must include at least these two parameters: mean yield and a risk factor.

As in the previous section, here too we must ask ourselves that basic question: Are there instances in which all investors, regardless of their personal preferences and regardless of the formal definition of risk, would follow the same investment rules? That is, would a future prediction of the mean yield on the asset and its inherent risk factor (assuming that these assessments are accepted by all investors) suffice to dictate investment criteria?

It seems that here too, we can describe circumstances of stochastic dominance, and, as in the previous section, these circumstances do not cover all possible situations. Let us plot a general plane of possible assets, with expected (mean) yield on the y-axis and risk (regardless of the definition we choose for the risk factor) on the x-axis (figure 10.10).

If we must choose between asset A and asset B, then clearly, every investor would prefer asset A, as both assets offer an identical yield but asset B carries greater risk. The same is true for assets C and D.

If we must choose between assets A and C, obviously every investor would prefer asset A, as both assets carry identical risk but asset A offers a greater yield.

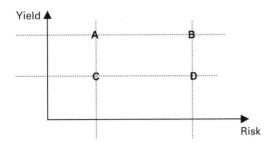

Figure 10.10
Mean Yield–Risk Factor Plane

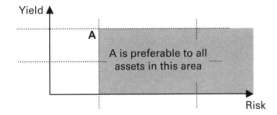

Figure 10.11
Asset A Complete Dominance Zone

If A is preferable to B and B is preferable to D, then A is preferable to D.

In fact, any asset will always be preferable to assets located below and to the right of it, as detailed in figure 10.11.

As in the previous section, here too we have cases with no stochastic dominance:

Which is preferable, B or C? B offers a greater mean yield but also carries greater risk. These instances (which account for the bulk of cases) are discussed in the following chapters.

D.   Making Investment Decisions in a Random Market

The following chapters discuss decision-making models in an uncertain market, based on statistics.

Decision making under these models means making the best possible decision prior to the unfolding of events (a "prospective" decision) and does not guarantee that ex-post results (i.e., retrospective, after events have occurred) will indeed match the prospective recommendation.

For example, if only two results are possible, one at an 80% probability and the other at a 20% probability, the best prospective decision would be to play our cards on the event with the 80% chance of materializing.

This is true even if, retrospectively, actual results showed that the second event occurred. There was, after all, a 20% chance of it occurring! Clearly, if we had to decide all over again, we would still stick to the same prospective decision—we would choose the event with an 80% probability.

During the writing of this book, a large number of hedge funds and financial institutions collapsed. It would not be accurate to say that these institutions made the wrong decisions. Most based their decisions on complex mathematical models developed by the best mathematicians science has to offer. The only mistake was made by investors in those institutions, who failed to understand that their investments involved uncertainty. Even the best of decisions, with a probability of 99%, still have a 1% chance of catastrophe. Therefore, before we continue developing our models, always remember the following statement in all your financial decisions:

Even the best prospective decision never guarantees ex-post results!

Calculation Tools—Online Appendixes (http://finmodeling.com/en):

> 1. Statistical functions in the CASIO FC-100 financial calculator—see appendix B.
> 2. Calculating statistical functions with MS Excel—see appendix C.

Chapter 10—Questions and Problems

Present all calculations in detail! Final calculations may be made using a software program or calculator.

Question 1

Below are the financial statements for Growth Inc. In the past, the company financed its income-generating assets by issuing 1,000,000 shares at $1 each. Data are in thousands of dollars.

	2000	2001	2002	2003	2004	2005	2006	2007	2008	2009
Revenues	250	200	300	400	350	150	200	400	500	100
Fixed costs	100			100			100			
Variable costs (40%)	100			160				160		
Earnings before interest and taxes (EBIT)	50	20			110	−10			200	−40
Interest	0	0	0	0	0	0	0	0	0	0
Earnings after financial expenses	50			140					200	−40
Income tax (40%)	20	8				−4	8			−16
Net earnings	30	12	48	84	66	−6			120	−24
Net earnings per share						−0.06	0.012			
General market yield	6%	5%	8%	10%	7%	4%	5%	10%	11%	3%

a. Fill in the missing data.

b. Calculate the company's mean revenues, its mean earnings before interest and taxes, and its mean net earnings.

c. Calculate the standard deviation for the company's revenues, the standard deviation for its earnings before interest and taxes, and the standard deviation for its net earnings.

d. Calculate the mean net earnings and standard deviation per share.

e. Calculate the mean yield and standard deviation for the general market.

f. Calculate the covariance, correlation coefficient ρ, and regression coefficient β for the yield on the company's net earnings per share as compared to the general market yield.

Note: The question is intended as an exercise of statistical measures only.

According to the models discussed until now, net cash flow is preferable to net earnings when assessing company value.

Question 2

The company in question 1 financed its income-generating assets by issuing one million shares at $1 each. The company decides to double its operations (double its production capacity). It can do so by issuing one million additional shares or obtaining a $1 million loan carrying 3% annual interest (by issuing perpetual bonds). The company decides to take the loan.

Assuming that the company's revenues (and corresponding expenses) will double in the next decade, recalculate the figures in question 1, and try to draw conclusions (assume that the general market yield will repeat its behavior of the past decade).

a. Fill in the data for the company's pro-forma (projected) statements for 2010–2019.

b. Calculate the company's mean revenues, mean earnings before interest and taxes, and mean net earnings.

c. Calculate the standard deviation for the company's revenues, the standard deviation for its earnings before interest and taxes, and the standard deviation for its net earnings.

d. Calculate the mean net earnings and standard deviation per share.

e. Calculate the covariance, correlation coefficient ρ and regression coefficient β for the yield on the company's net earnings as compared to the general market yield.

Note the differences between your results for question 1 and question 2, which are the result of the company's equity structure (share-to-bond ratio). This matter is discussed in detail in the following chapters.

Question 3

Shares A and B offer the following scenarios:

	Market Conditions		
	Growth	**Normal**	**Recession**
Probability	0.5	0.3	0.2
Share A yield	25%	10%	−25%
Share B yield	10%	−5%	35%

a. Calculate the mean yield for each share.

b. Calculate the variance and standard deviation for each share.

c. Calculate their covariance.

d. Calculate their correlation coefficient. Explain the result.

Question 4

This problem illustrates the use of the formula for forming a linear combination of two random variables, $\tilde{X}$ and $\tilde{Y}$; that is, $\tilde{Z} = a\tilde{X} + b\tilde{Y}$ ($\tilde{Z}$ is also a random variable).

	Market Condition			
	I	**II**	**III**	**IV**
Probability	0.1	0.4	0.4	0.1
Share A yield	30%	5%	30%	5%
Share B yield	5%	10%	30%	10%
Share C yield	7.5%	15%	25%	7.5%

a. Calculate the mean and standard deviation for the yield offered by each share.

b. Calculate the covariance for each pair of shares.

c. Calculate the mean yield and standard deviation for a portfolio comprised equally of shares A and B.

d. Calculate the mean yield and standard deviation for a portfolio comprised equally of shares A and C.

e. Calculate the mean yield and standard deviation for a portfolio comprised equally of shares B and C.

f. Compare your answers for sections parts (c) through (e), and explain the risk mitigation offered by holding a portfolio.

Reminder:

$\tilde{Z} = a\tilde{X} + b\tilde{Y}$.

$E[Z] = E[X + Y] = aE[X] + bE[Y].$

$\mathrm{Var}[Z] = \mathrm{Var}[aX + bY] = a^2\mathrm{Var}[X] + b^2\mathrm{Var}[Y] - 2ab\mathrm{Cov}[XY].$

Question 5

a. You are offered the following two investments:

Investment A		Investment B	
Probability	**NPV**	**Probability**	**NPV**
0.20	$1,200	0.50	$2,000
0.60	$1,500	0.50	$3,000
0.20	$1,800		

Complete and explain the following:

Investment _____ has a _____ order stochastic dominance.

b. The yield probabilities for two financial assets are as follows:

Yield	Asset I Probability	Asset II Probability
20%	0	0.7
10%	0.6	0.3
15%	0.2	0
3%	0.2	0

Asset _____ has a _____ order stochastic dominance.
Plot and explain.

Question 6

Assume the following data on the yield distribution for assets A and B:

Yield	Probability for Asset A	Probability for Asset B
2%	20%	10%
8%	30%	25%
–3%	5%	10%
5%	20%	25%
10%	25%	30%

Asset _____ has a _____ order stochastic dominance.
Plot and explain.

Question 7

Share A is priced at $1,000 and share B at $500.

The probabilities for the dollar amount of earnings (loss) on each share in the next period are as follows:

Probability	Share A	Share B	Market condition
0.1	$100	$45	1
0.2	–$20	–$20	2
0.3	$20	–$5	3
0.15	$80	$40	4
0.25	–$40	$30	5

a. Calculate the yield probability distribution for each share.

b. Sort the table by order of increasing yield for both shares.

c. Plot the cumulative yield probability for each share.

d. According to the _____ order stochastic dominance model, share _____ is preferable.

e. Are there other options for checking which share is preferable? (*Hint:* Use two B shares.)

Question 8

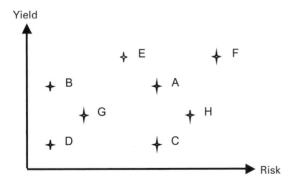

Compile a list of all share pairs (do not duplicate: A ↔ B = B ↔ A).

Determine the complete stochastic dominance relationships. Explain.

Question 9

You are given two shares, both of which trade at $3. All investors believe that one year from now the shares will be priced as follows:

Share A		Share B	
Probability	Price	Probability	Price
0.15	$2	0.05	$3
0.35	$4	0.45	$6
0.30	$5	0.40	$8
0.20	$7	0.10	$12

a. Can a general decision be made for all investors based on stochastic dominance?

b. Assume that the standard deviation serves as the shares' risk indicator. Can a general decision be made for all investors based on stochastic dominance on the yield-risk plane?

c. What is your conclusion after comparing your answers for parts (a) and (b) above?

Further Reading

Alexander, S. S. 1961. Price Movements in Speculative Markets: Trends or Random Walks. *Industrial Management Review* (May): 7–26.

Ali, M. M. 1975. Stochastic Dominance and Portfolio Analysis. *Journal of Financial Economics* (June).

Bawa, V. S., J. N. Bodurtha, Jr., M. R. Rao, and H. L. Suri. 1985. On Determination of Stochastic Dominance Optimal Sets. *Journal of Finance*.

Billingsley, P. 1968. *Convergence of Probability Measures*. New York: Wiley.

Crámer, H. 1961. *Mathematical Methods in Statistics*. Princeton, NJ: Princeton University Press.

Hanoch, G., and H. Levy. 1969. The Efficiency Analysis of Choices Involving Risk. *Review of Economic Studies*: 335–346.

Jarrow, R. 1986. The Relationship between Arbitrage and First Order Stochastic Dominance. *Journal of Finance*. (September).

Jean, W. H. 1980. The Geometric Mean and Stochastic Dominance. *Journal of Finance* (March).

Jean, W. H., and B. P. Helms. 1986. Stochastic Dominance as a Decision Model. *Quarterly Journal of Business and Economics* (Winter).

Kahneman, D., and A. Tversky. 1979. Prospect Theory: An Analysis of Decision under Risk. *Econometrica* (March): 263–291.

Keeney, R. L., and H. Raiffa. 1976. *Decisions with Multiple Objectives: Preferences and Value Tradeoffs.* New York: Wiley.

Larson, A. B. 1964. Measurement of a Random Process in Futures Prices. In *The Random Character of Stock Market Prices*, ed. Paul Cootner, 219–230. Cambridge, MA: MIT Press.

Levy, H., and Y. Kroll. 1976. Stochastic Dominance with Riskless Assets. *Journal of Financial and Quantitative Analysis* (December): 743–778.

Samuelson, P. A. 1965. Proof that Properly Anticipated Prices Fluctuate Randomly. *Industrial Management Review* (Spring): 41–49.

Sobotka, S. P., and C. Schnabel. 1961. Linear Programming as a Device for Predicting Market Value: Prices of Used Commercial Aircraft, 1959–65. *Journal of Business* 34 (January): 10–30.

Von Neumann, J., and O. Morgenstern. 1953. *Theory of Games and Economic Behavior.* Princeton, NJ: Princeton University Press.

Whitmore, G. A., and M. C. Findlay. 1975. *Stochastic Dominance.* Lexington, MA: Lexington Books.

11 Personal Preferences in Uncertain Markets

A. The Utility Function under Uncertainty

B. Risk Aversion on the Payoff-Utility Plane

C. Absolute and Relative Risk Aversion

D. Risk Aversion on the Mean Yield–Risk Plane

E. Rational Decision Making—A Myth?

A. The Utility Function under Uncertainty

At the start of the previous chapter, we discussed how analyzing future random processes and developing investment models for various different investors must account for two aspects:

1. Future predictions: Assessing outcomes and their respective probabilities.

2. Personal preferences: As reflected in each investor's individual utility function.

We discussed cases where the outcomes for each event and the probability distribution of these events are uniform for all investors (e.g., the result of historical statistical data) and suffice to prescribe investment criteria. We showed that in these cases, all investors, regardless of their personal preferences, would make the same choice.

However, the list of possible events is far greater, and we must develop more general models. These models, like all economic analyses, also must account for each investor's personal preferences (figure 11.1). As discussed in the microeconomics literature, personal preferences can be expressed mathematically by defining a utility function.

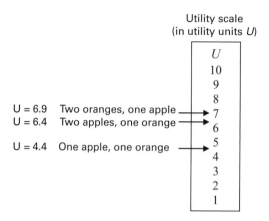

Figure 11.1
Personal (Virtual) Utility Scale

Utility function   A mapping of different "events" on a scale of utility units.

In figure 11.2, each value pair of "apples and oranges" is located on utility curve U. U_1 and U_2 are equal-utility curves, that is, each is a group of different events that have the same utility. Equal-utility curves form a continuum across the entire plane; we plotted these two curves only for illustrative purposes.[1] The more up and to the right a curve is located, the greater is the individual's utility, that is, $U_2 \supset U_1$.[2]

The straight line AB marks an individual's budget constraint for buying apples and oranges. Although they are not plotted, that individual also has additional utility curves, located to the bottom and left of U_1, some of which also intersect the budget line. The point at which the budget line is tangent to the U_1 curve determines the maximum utility for that individual, given his budget constraint AB. Therefore, for that individual, the value pair apples-oranges at that point would serve as his optimal choice.

The use of a utility function was demonstrated in part I of the book, when we discussed consumption preference over time. Figure 11.3 graphs a utility function for two general time periods, present and future.

Utility functions do not necessarily have to be left-to-right decreasing functions. If we plot an investor's risk preference by drawing his utility

---

1. Had we drawn all equal-utility curves, we would have painted the entire plane black.
2. We use the notation $U_2 \supset U_1$ when comparing the utility of one group of points (curve) with the utility of another group of points (curve).

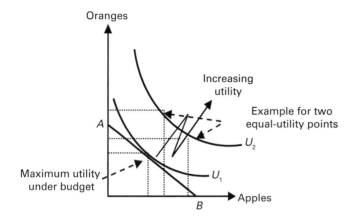

Figure 11.2
Personal Equal-Utility Curves and Budget Line

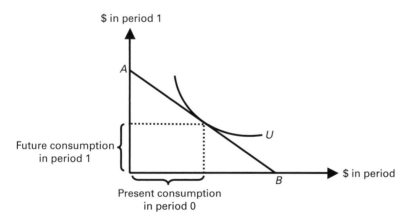

Figure 11.3
Consumption Preference over Two General Time Periods, Present and Future

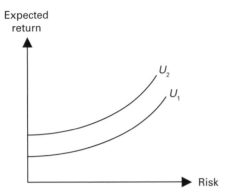

Figure 11.4
Two Investors' Utility Functions on the Mean Yield–Risk Plane

function on the mean yield–risk plane, we get left-to-right increasing function curves like those shown in figure 11.4.

Utility functions on the mean yield–risk plane are necessarily left-to-right increasing functions, since for any additional risk, additional yield is required. In figure 11.4, U_1 and U_2 are equal-utility curves. The higher and to the left a curve is, the greater is that person's utility, that is, $U_2 \supset U_1$.

Up to this point we have discussed the utility function in a certain market. We now want to expand our definitions and assumptions concerning the (mathematical) utility function so as to adapt it to uncertain market conditions. Here we recall the two assumptions on which we based our definition for the utility function under certain market conditions, the assumption of completeness and the assumption of consistency.[3]

Completeness

An individual can always rank his preference for two definite possibilities. If faced with a choice of two options:

- X (e.g., two oranges and an apple)
- Y (two apples and an orange)

a person can state that (where U_x is the utility derived from option X): Either

---

3. The fewer assumptions we need, the better—the more general—is our model.

X is preferable to Y: $\Rightarrow U_X > U_Y$,

or

Y is preferable to X: $\Rightarrow U_X < U_Y$,

or

the individual is indifferent to the choice: $\Rightarrow U_X = U_Y$.

Consistency

If an individual prefers X over Y and Y over Z, then that person prefers X over Z (and the same holds true for indifference).
  For example,

X = buying a motorcycle;

Y = taking a trip around the world;

Z = getting a bachelor's degree.

  According to our assumptions, every person can always make *rational decisions*. Rational decisions can be defined as

• Repeatable[4] decisions based on that person's distinct and invariable utility function;
• Decisions aimed to maximize utility given that person's constraints.

  In random events, in addition to the "outcome" (e.g., receiving an apple, \$10, etc.), there is also the *prospect* of achieving that outcome — its probability P. In order to expand the utility function to account for uncertainty, additional assumptions must be made. From this point on, we will distinguish between certain options (outcomes), which will be indicated by lowercase letters, and random events (outcome plus probability), which will be indicated by capital letters.
  To easily distinguish between symbols and avoid confusing certain options with random options, from here on we will refer to random options as "gambles," denoted by G. We will always discuss gambles with two possible outcomes, X and Y, with probabilities of P and $(1 - P)$, respectively.
  Denote by $G(X, Y, P)$ the random prospect (gamble) for event $X(x,P)$ or event $Y(y,1-P)$ to occur. Below are two additional assumptions, the

---

4. Repeatable decisions mean that an identical decision will be made every time.

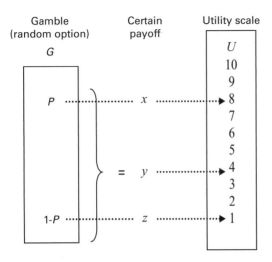

Figure 11.5
The Certainty Equivalent for a Gamble

transposition assumption and the ranking assumption, that must be made to adapt the utility function to uncertain market conditions.

Transposition

If an individual is given three certain options x, y, and z such that $U(x) > U(y) > U(z)$,[5] then we can always find one single probability P where that person would be indifferent to either the certain outcome y or participating in the gamble $G(X, Z, P)$, that is, $U(y) = U[G(X,Z,P)])$ (figure 11.5).[6]

In other words, given a range of certain prospective outcomes $x - z$, arranged so that x offers the maximum utility and z offers the minimum utility, we can always find a probability P to gamble between x and z at which we would be indifferent to choosing the gamble or choosing the certain payoff y, located within the range. We will define y as the certainty equivalent (CE) for the gamble.

This last assumption means that for any gamble we can find one single certainty equivalent that yields the same utility as the gamble.

---

5. One of the symbols can also be smaller or equal, but then P will be either zero or one.

6. In other words, the utility from certainly getting y is equal to the utility from participating in the gamble G.

Ranking

If an individual is faced with four certain options x, y, z, and w such that $U(x) > U(y) > U(z)$ and $U(x) > U(w) > U(z)$, then, if he is indifferent to receiving certain option y or participating in gamble 1, $G(X, Z, P_1)$, that is, $U(y) = U[G(X, Z, P_1)]$, and if he is indifferent to receiving certain option w or participating in gamble 2, $G(X, Z, P_2)$, that is, $U(w) = U[G(X, Z, P_2)]$,

then, if $P_1 > P_2$, then $U(y) > U(w)$,

and, if $P_1 = P_2$, then $U(y) = U(w)$.

In other words, given a range of guaranteed payoffs $x - z$, arranged so that x offers the maximum payoff and z offers the minimum, and there are two gambles in this range, where y is the certainty equivalent of gamble 1 (where the probability of winning x is P_1), and w is the certainty equivalent of gamble 2 (where the probability of winning x is P_2), then $P_1 > P_2$ implies that the utility from certainty equivalent y is greater than the utility from certainty equivalent w (figure 11.6).

The above assumption makes sense, since x has the greatest utility. The greater the probability of obtaining x rather than z, which has a lower probability value $(P_1 > P_2)$, means that it is only logical that the utility from that gamble will be greater as well.

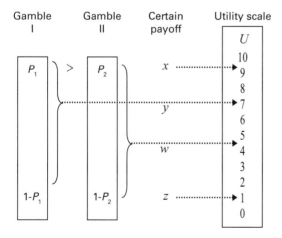

Figure 11.6
Ranking the Utility Derived from Two Different Gambles via Their Prospective Certainty Equivalents

This last assumption means that it is possible to rank the utility derived from two different gambles according to their prospective certainty equivalents.

By adding these two assumptions of *transposition* and *ranking* to the utility function's requirements, we have adapted the utility function to handle uncertainty. An individual whose utility function meets the above four requirements of completeness, consistency, transposition, and ranking can unequivocally state his preference between two random future events.[7]

B. Risk Aversion on the Payoff-Utility Plane

When discussing investment decisions, we always assume they aim to increase wealth, w, so that if $w_1 < w_2$, then $U(w_1) < U(w_2)$. Although this assumption seems self-evident, it still bears mentioning, as reality demonstrates that sometimes people have different motives (e.g., saving face), which may distort this assumption.

When discussing rational decisions in an uncertain market, we distinguish among three personality types: risk seeking, risk averse, and risk neutral. As we have formulated a mathematical definition for the utility function in an uncertain market, we will try to use the utility function to provide a mathematical definition for these three personalities.

Based on the mathematical analogy which holds that a decision in an uncertain market is characterized or defined as participation in a gamble $G(X, Y, P)$, the criterion for measuring risk seeking by investors is their preference or choice between the following:

• Being assured of the expected value, that is, the mean (probability-weighted average) of the gamble, or

• Taking part in the gamble.

An investor who prefers the certainty of receiving the mean value of the gamble rather than participating in the gamble is referred to as *risk averse*. An investor who enjoys (prefers) the uncertainty of participating in the gamble is referred to as *risk seeking*.

For example, individuals are offered two alternatives:

---

7. Formal mathematics requires that we should have added another assumption, namely, that events and gambles are nondependent. We skipped this assumption, as it does not increase understanding of the material.

• Participating in a lottery in which they have a 50% chance of winning $100 and a 50% chance of winning $0, or

• A sure option of receiving $50 (the lottery's mean value).

Remember that when the gamble is repeated numerous times, objectively, the payoff from participating in the gamble should be equal to the payoff from receiving the mean value of the gamble in each round. Because objectively, it makes no difference whether we participate in the gamble or not, we should be indifferent to participation.

In real life, we need to make decisions about events that do not repeat themselves a great many times. Therefore, individuals who prefer certainty and choose not to participate in the lottery are defined as being risk averse, while individuals who enjoy (prefer) participating in the lottery are defined as risk seekers.

Thus, we must compare utilities:

The utility arising from the mean of the values of all possible outcomes

versus

the mean of the individual utilities arising from each possible outcome.

Using the above definitions, we can now mathematically define these personality types:[8]

Risk averse An individual whose utility from the mean value of the gamble is greater than the mean utility of the gamble:

$$U[E(G)] > E[U(G)].$$

Risk seeking An individual whose utility from the mean value of the gamble is smaller than the mean utility of the gamble:

$$U[E(G)] < E[U(G)].$$

Risk neutral An individual whose utility from the mean value of the gamble is equal to the mean utility from the gamble:

$$U[E(G)] = E[U(G)].$$

Thus, we should take the following course of action:

1. Find w_1, the weighted average (mean) for the gamble outcome values:
$w_1 = E[G(X,Y,P)] = x \cdot P + y \cdot (1 - P).$

---

8. The following mathematical definitions will be easier to understand if readers substitute "average" for "mean."

2. Calculate utility U for w_1 $U(w_1) = U[E(G)]$.

3. Find the utility for option x, $U(x)$, and the utility for option y, $U(y)$, and calculate the weighted average (mean) of these utilities: $E[U(G)] = U(x) \cdot P + U(y) \cdot (1 - P)$.

4. Check whether the utility from the mean of the gamble results, $U[E(G)]$, is greater or less than the average of the outcome utilities, $E[U(G)]$.

Alternatively, instead of comparing preferences on the "utility axis" of the function, we can compare preferences on the "payoff axis":

1. Calculate the mean (weighted average) w_1 for the gamble: $w_1 = E[G(X,Y,P)] = x \cdot P + y \cdot (1 - P)$.

2. Find the utility from receiving option x, $U(x)$, and the utility from receiving option y, $U(y)$, and find the mean (weighted average) utility, $E[U(G)]$.

3. Calculate the certainty equivalent w_2, which is the payoff whose utility is equal to the mean utility for the gamble $E[U(G)]$ (calculated in the previous step).

4. Check whether the mean (average) w_1 is greater or less than the certainty equivalent w_2 for the gamble on the utility axis.

Following the above procedure:

Risk averse describes an individual whose utility from being "guaranteed" the average payoff of possible outcomes, w, is greater than the mean of the utilities derived from each option offered by participating in the gamble (figure 11.7): $U[E(G)] > E[U(G)]$.

Alternatively, comparing the payoff axis:

Risk averse describes an individual who prefers to be guaranteed w_1, the average of possible outcomes, rather than rely on w_2, the certainty equivalent derived from his average of the utility functions when participating in the gamble.

Calculate backward (see the arrow direction in figure 11.7) to find the certainty equivalent of $E[U(G)]$, which constitutes w_2, and compare it with w_1, the mean value of the gamble. You will always find that $w_2 < w_1$.

Example: An investor whose utility function is $\ln(w)$ is faced with a gamble offering an 80% chance of winning \$5 and a 20% chance of winning \$30.

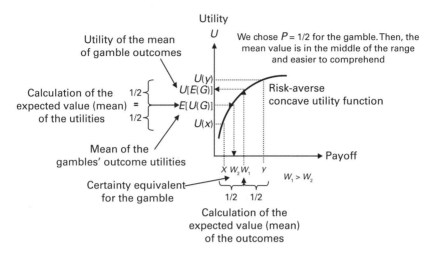

Figure 11.7
Risk-Averse Investor: Concave Utility Function

The mean value for the gamble is

$$w_1 = E(G) = 0.8 \cdot 5 + 0.2 \cdot 30 = \$10.$$

The utility for being guaranteed \$10 (utility from the mean value) is

$$U(10) = \ln(10) = 2.3.$$

The mean of the utilities for both possible events is

$$E[U(G)] = 0.8 \cdot U(5) + 0.2 \cdot U(30) = 0.8 \cdot \ln(5) + 0.2 \cdot \ln(30) = 1.97.$$

Comparing the calculated utility values, we find that 2.3 > 1.97. Alternatively, the mean value for the gamble is

$$w_1 = E(G) = 0.8 \cdot 5 + 0.2 \cdot 30 = \$10.$$

The certainty equivalent for a utility of $U(?) = 1.97$ derived from participating in the gamble is the problem of finding a number when you know its logarithm, called finding the *"antilogarithm"* or sometimes *"exponentiation"*:

$$w_2 = CE = \text{antiln}(1.97) = \$7.17.$$

Comparing the calculated payoffs, we find that \$10 > \$7.17.
Conclusion: the utility function $\ln(w)$ describes a risk-averse individual.

The above discussion assumes that gamblers consider only the outcome of their gamble. Such a discussion is accurate if the results of the gamble do not materially affect a gambler's wealth. Otherwise, instead of considering the outcome of the gamble, we must consider the gambler's wealth before and after the gamble.

Example: A risk-averse individual with a wealth utility function of $\ln(w)$ has an initial wealth of $10. How much would he be willing to pay to avoid participating in a gamble with an 80% chance of losing $5 (i.e., a final wealth of $5) and a 20% chance of winning $20 (i.e., a final wealth of $30)?

In the previous example, we saw that the mean utility for a gamble with the same figures was 1.97 utility units.

The certainty equivalent for the gamble is $CE = \$7.17$.

Define risk premium:

Risk premium (RP) is the amount of money a risk-averse individual is willing to pay to avoid a gamble:

$RP = E(w) - CE.$

The starting wealth was $10. Therefore, the above individual would be willing to pay up to $RP = \$10 - \$7.17 = \$2.83$ to avoid the gamble.

Risk seeking describes an individual whose utility from being guaranteed the mean value of the gamble is smaller than the mean of the utilities derived from each option offered by participating in the gamble (figure 11.8): $U[E(G)] < E[U(G)]$.

Eventually we'll see that $U[E(G)] < E[U(G)]$ and that $w_1 < w_2$.

Therefore, this individual would be willing to pay a premium of $w_2 - w_1$ in order to participate in the gamble.

Risk neutral describes an individual whose utility from the mean value of the gamble is equal to the mean of the utilities derived from each option offered by participating in the gamble (figure 11.9): $U[E(G)] = E[U(G)]$.

C.   Absolute and Relative Risk Aversion

Continuing our discussion on the definition depicted in the previous section, Pratt and subsequently Arrow[9] defined $\rho = RP$ as the risk

---

9. See Pratt (1964) and Arrow (1971).

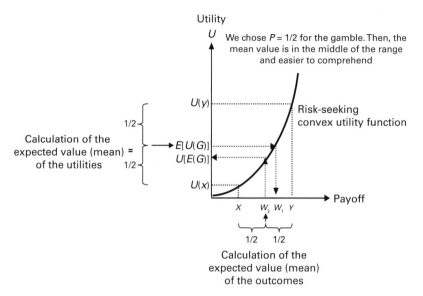

Figure 11.8
Risk-Seeking Investor: Convex Utility Function

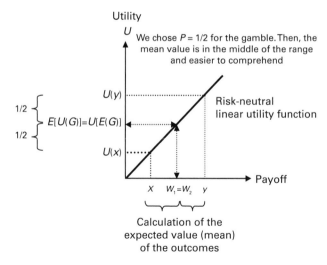

Figure 11.9
Risk-Neutral Investor: Linear Utility Function

premium required by an individual, derived from the equation
$E[U(\bar{w} - \rho)] = E[U(\tilde{w})]$.[10]

In other words, the mean utility of the average wealth net of the
risk premium equals the mean utility of the different wealth statuses
resulting from participating in the gamble. Pratt and Arrow approximated both sides of the equation around an individual's average
wealth using a Taylor series.[11] From the definition, it is clear that since
the initial wealth $\bar{w}$ (when paying the risk premium) and the mean
wealth after taking the gamble $\bar{w}$ are the same, then the mean of the
gamble (which turns the initial wealth $\bar{w}$ into a random variable, $\tilde{w}$) must
be zero.

A Taylor series *approximates* a function $f(x)$ by using a polynomial
series around a point a, that is $(x - a)^n$, where the function value of a,
$f(a)$, is known, as well as the value of all its order derivatives $f'(a); f''(a);$
$\ldots ; f^n(a)$:

$$f(x) = f(a) + f'(a)(x - a) + \frac{f''(a)(x - a)^2}{2!}$$
$$+ \frac{f'''(a)(x - a)^3}{3!} + \ldots + \frac{f^{(n)'}(a)(x - a)^n}{n!}.$$

For developing the equation, let us remember the following:

• Close to point a, that is, where $\Delta x = x - a$ has a small value, higher-order
polynomial terms can be neglected.

• The mean of a nonrandom function is equivalent to the function value
itself.

• The mean value for a function whose random variable is multiplied by
a constant a equals a times the mean of that function.

We will approximate the left side of the equation $E[U(\bar{w} - \rho)] = E[U(\tilde{w})]$
close to the average wealth value $\bar{w}$ by removing higher-order terms:[12]

$$U(\bar{w} - \rho) \approx U(\bar{w}) + U'(\bar{w}) \cdot (\bar{w} - \rho - \bar{w}) = U(\bar{w}) - \rho \cdot U'(\bar{w}).$$

---

10. Up to this point we have discussed discrete situations, or rather two possibilities for
each gamble. The model in this section uses $\tilde{w}$ as a continuous random variable representing all naturally possible post-gamble wealth statuses.

11. The definition of risk premium is the same as given in the previous section. Approximation using a Taylor series limits the use of the utility function to cases where possible
outcomes $\tilde{w}$ are close to the average wealth $\bar{w}$. No such limitation was made in the previous
section.

12. In our case, $a = \bar{w}$, and $x = \bar{w} - \rho$ is a relatively small value.

We will approximate the right side of the equation of function $U(\tilde{w})$ around point $\bar{w}$ as follows:

$$U(\tilde{w}) \approx U(\bar{w}) + U'(\bar{w}) \cdot (\tilde{w} - \bar{w}) + \frac{1}{2} U''(\bar{w}) \cdot (\tilde{w} - \bar{w})^2.$$

The mean value for each of the three terms on the right side of the equation is

$$E[U(\bar{w})] = U(\bar{w}).$$

$$E[U'(\bar{w}) \cdot (\tilde{w} - \bar{w})] = U'(\bar{w}) \cdot E[(\tilde{w} - \bar{w})]$$
$$= U'(\bar{w}) \cdot [E(\tilde{w}) - \bar{w}] = U'(\bar{w}) \cdot [\bar{w} - \bar{w}] = 0.$$

$$E[U''(\bar{w}) \cdot (\tilde{w} - \bar{w})^2] = \frac{1}{2} U''(\bar{w}) \cdot E[(\tilde{w} - \bar{w})^2] = \frac{1}{2} U''(\bar{w}) \cdot \sigma^2.$$

Comparing the results for both sides of the equation,

$$U(\bar{w}) - \rho \cdot U'(\bar{w}) = U(\bar{w}) + \frac{1}{2} U''(\bar{w}) \cdot \sigma^2,$$

we get

$$\rho = -\frac{\sigma^2}{2} \cdot \frac{U''(\bar{w})}{U'(\bar{w})},$$

where $\dfrac{\sigma^2}{2}$ is a constant that is independent of an individual's preferences.

As the value of $(-\dfrac{U''(w)}{U'(w)})$ rises, the greater becomes the required risk premium ρ. Therefore, the last term can serve as an indicator (a measure) of an individual's *absolute risk aversion (ARA)* around a given wealth w:

$$ARA = -\frac{U''(w)}{U'(w)}.$$

We know that a millionaire would consider a $100 gamble (almost) risk-free, but the average man on the street would still approach it with a certain amount of risk aversion. Accordingly, we can define an indicator (a measure) for wealth *relative risk aversion (RRA)*:

$$RRA = -w \cdot \frac{U''(w)}{U'(w)}.$$

This last definition is founded on the idea that an individual with a constant relative risk aversion c has the same risk aversion for losing a certain percentage of his wealth $\frac{c}{w}$ at any given wealth level, even though the absolute value of the loss increases with wealth.

The above definitions indicate that around the average wealth level $\bar{w}$, the greater an individual's absolute risk aversion, the greater is his relative risk aversion, and vice versa.

Let us demonstrate the above model using a binomial utility function of the form

$$U(w) = w^{1-y}; 0 \leq y \leq 1.$$

This function is particularly popular among researchers and formulators of investor behavior models because of the following properties:

1. The utility function $U(w)$ is normalized in the range $0 \leq w \leq 1$, such that $U(0) = 0; U(1) = 1$.

2. It is an increasing function (the greater the wealth, the greater the utility): $U' = (1 - \gamma) \cdot w^{-\gamma} > 0$.

3. The function represents a risk-averse individual whose marginal utility decreases as his wealth increases: $U'' = -\gamma(1 - \gamma) \cdot w^{-\gamma-1} < 0$.

4. The function represents an individual with a constant relative risk aversion $RRA = \gamma$, where

$$RRA = -w \cdot \frac{U''(w)}{U'(w)} = -w \cdot \frac{-\gamma(1-\gamma) \cdot w^{-\gamma-1}}{(1-\gamma) \cdot w^{-\gamma}} = \gamma.$$

Note: Despite its popularity, this is only one of the many utility functions that can be used to describe an individual's investment decision making (gambling).

D. Risk Aversion on the Mean Yield–Risk Plane

In chapter 5 we stated that a risk premium is included in yields required on a financial asset. We now want to find a function that will relate the yield, k, required for holding a given financial asset to both the basic risk-free market interest rate r_f (the time value of capital) and risk:

$$k = f(r_f, Risk).$$

Without defining risk, we may conclude that this function should be an increasing function, so that the greater the risk, the greater is the risk premium required on top of the basic risk-free interest rate.

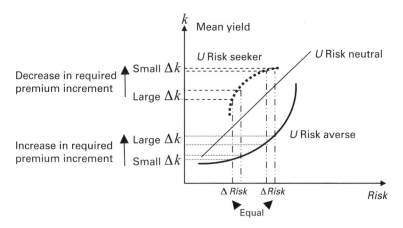

Figure 11.10
Risk Aversion Definition on the Mean Yield–Risk Plane

Here, too, we can define risk-averse and risk-seeking individuals through our definition of risk neutral.

Risk neutral   An individual who for a constant risk increment, $\Delta Risk$, requires a *constant* yield premium increment, Δk, which does not depend on the risk level.

Risk averse   An individual who for a constant risk increment, $\Delta Risk$, requires an *increasing* yield premium increment, Δk, as the risk level increases.

Risk seeking   An individual who for a constant risk increment, $\Delta Risk$, requires a *decreasing* yield premium increment, Δk, as the risk level increases.

It is important to understand that the payoff function between risk and mean yield is an increasing function for both risk-seeking and risk-averse individuals. Thus, both personalities require an additional premium for assuming additional risk. The difference is that while risk-averse individuals require ever-increasing premiums per additional risk unit, risk seekers (who actually enjoy the additional risk) require ever-decreasing premiums per additional risk unit.

Therefore, on the mean yield–risk plane, we will have for risk-averse persons an increasing and concave function, that is, the first derivative is given by $\frac{\partial E(k)}{\partial Risk}\big|_{U=U_0} > 0$ and the second derivative is given by $\frac{\partial^2 E(k)}{\partial^2 Risk}\big|_{U=U_0} > 0$. The function for risk seekers is an increasing and convex function, that is, the first derivative is still $\frac{\partial E(k)}{\partial Risk}|_{U=U_0} > 0$, but now the

second derivative is $\frac{\partial^2 E(k)}{\partial^2 Risk}|_{U=U_0} < 0$.

Note: On the yield–utility plane we will continue to evaluate risk-averse and risk-seeking personalities by comparing their utility from the mean outcome values with the mean utility of the gamble outcome values.

E. Rational Decision Making — A Myth?

One of our basic assumptions at the beginning of this chapter was that everyone makes rational decisions, that is, reproducible decisions that seek to maximize utility. Daniel Kahneman's work, recognized by the 2002 Nobel Prize in Economics, renewed the debate concerning rational decision making in economics and financial theory. Kahneman's models introduce psychological insights into decision-making models in general, and under conditions of uncertainty in particular. The results show that the assumption that investors make rational investment decisions is not necessarily true. The importance of the work carried out by Kahneman (whose training is in psychology) goes beyond the results of his models, as his approach allows controlled scientific experimentation in economics. As mentioned in the first chapter of this book, until Kahneman and other researchers published their studies, economics was considered a science based on observing real-world processes and analyzing these processes through the use of statistical methods. Their work constitutes a material paradigm shift in economic modeling in general and financial modeling in particular.

The attempt to account for human psychology in decision-making theory grew out of the economic models' inability to adequately predict real-world processes. The questions concerning decision-making processes under uncertain conditions deal with issues such as asymmetric information and built-in market mechanisms, which lead, on the one hand, to nonoptimal results, and on the other to irrational human behavior. In 2001 the Nobel Prize in Economics was awarded to a group of scientists who studied asymmetric information. Their work was discussed in chapter 5. Here we describe in brief the work carried out by Kahneman and others concerning rational choice, and its impact on the traditional models to be discussed in the following chapters.

Kahneman set out to demonstrate that a consistent deviation can be found in rationality-based decision making. The assumptions on which we build our models in the coming chapters state that one can assume an investment decision-making "algorithm" that is based on investors' desire to maximize their individual utility. Such a model assumes the decision-making criterion is related only to those parameters concerning the problematic decision confronting investors. Kahneman sought to prove that people tend to evaluate parameters irrationally, that is, not only on the basis of their content but also on the basis of their form. Let us demonstrate Kahneman's approach with two types of nonrational decisions as observed in an actual experiment involving test subjects.

Example 1

An investor buys shares at a price of $4 per share. After a while, the share price increases to $7. If the investor believes the real price of the share to be only $6, he will tend to sell his shares at a profit. Research shows that if the investor bought the shares at $9 per share, and their price then went down to $7, that investor will show a lesser tendency to sell his shares, even if he still believes that their real value is only $6 per share.

Example 2

A. An individual goes to the theater, and when he arrives he discovers that he has lost his ticket, which cost $20.

B. An individual goes to the theater, and when he arrives he discovers that he has lost $20.

The question is, if you the reader were that individual, would you buy a ticket on arriving at the theater? One would think that the answer would be the same regardless of how the problem was presented. An experiment involving numerous test subjects showed that if the problem was presented as in sentence A, most subjects would not buy a ticket; while in those groups who were presented with the problem as formulated in sentence B, most subjects still bought a ticket.

Kahneman's theory is that when applying tools from the field of cognitive psychology,[13] we can demonstrate that people repeatedly make

---

13. Cognitive—decision making through awareness and thought, as opposed to emotional or automatic decision or reaction.

errors in judgment to the extent that under certain circumstances, these errors can be classified and even predicted. The first example is based on people's tendency not to reconcile with their losses. The second example is based on people's tendency to make decisions not necessarily based on a problem's parameters but on the form in which the problem was presented. Herbert Simon, who was awarded the Nobel Prize in Economics in 1978, demonstrated that we use information only partially in decisions involving large amounts of information. For example, we give more weight to newer information such as a share's price in the last week or month.

Kahneman demonstrated a nonconsistent decision-making template that is related to the way in which a problem is presented: once when the problem emphasizes mean utility and once when that same problem emphasizes the risks.

We will demonstrate this point using one of Kahneman's own experiments, in which he presented the same problem in two different ways to groups of subjects, who were then asked to make a decision:

Six hundred people contracted a life-threatening illness. You must choose one of two possible medical treatments.

The first way of presenting these treatments:

1. Treatment A—guaranteed to save 200 lives.
2. Treatment B—a 66% chance that everyone will die.

The second way of presenting these treatments:

1. Treatment A—guarantees that 400 people will die.
2. Treatment B—a 33% chance to save everyone.

Although the objective mortality parameters for each treatment are identical in both presentations, when the problem was presented in its first form, 72% of subjects chose treatment A. However, when the problem was presented in its second form, 78% of subjects chose treatment B.

In the following chapters, we will continue our discussion of modern models commonly used for investment decision making in an uncertain market. These models assume that investors do make rational decisions as defined in our discussion of the utility function in an uncertain market. I believe that because people make recurring decisions in the financial markets where the format nature of the problem is standardized, consistent, and unvarying (the same) over time, they learn how to digest the information in a way that follows rational behavior.

We are not ignoring the new, Nobel-worthy work carried out in the field. In the first chapter we discussed normative models and descriptive models. The coming chapters will demonstrate that modern models can also be described as *normative*, that is, they describe which choices should be made so as to obtain the optimal outcome. The fact that people are not rational and so market behavior does not always match the models (although in both the medium and the long term, it does), allows those people who *are* rational to achieve excess profit. This last statement is based on the assumption that market imbalances (with equilibrium being defined by rational decision models) cannot be maintained over time. They will eventually correct or form price bubbles, which occasionally occur on the stock market. We can demonstrate this point through example 1 above, whereby people tend not to sell their shares at a loss. Assuming people make investments in order to sell them at a certain point in time, then if the real share value of $6 is sustained over time, the yield on those shares would force people to reconcile with their losses and sell.

A person who makes decisions based on "value" models would not have bought the share at $9. On the contrary, he would have seen the option of selling his shares to nonrational individuals as an opportunity for making excess profits.[14]

Calculation Tools—Online Appendixes (http://finmodeling.com/en):

---

1. Statistical functions in the CASIO FC-100 financial calculator—see appendix B.
2. Calculating statistical functions in MS Excel—see appendix C.

Chapter 11—Questions and Problems

Note: Detail all calculations! Final calculations may be made using a calculator or software program.

---

14. The most famous proponent of this approach of value-led transactions is Warren Buffet, chairman and CEO of Berkshire Hathaway. Under his management, Berkshire Hathaway has recorded returns significantly above the market average over three full decades (the company manages tens of billions of dollars in assets).

Question 1

An investor with a starting wealth of $8 million and a utility function of $U(w) = 4w + 0.2w^2$ has three investment options, all of which call for a $4 million investment.

	Investment					
	I		**II**		**III**	
Revenue	4	8	0	12	−4	24
Probability	1/2	1/2	1/2	1/2	1/3	2/3

a. Calculate his final wealth in each possible scenario.

b. Calculate his mean final wealth in each investment scenario.

c. Calculate his utility in each possible scenario.

d. Calculate his mean utility in each investment scenario.

e. Which investment should he choose given only options I and II?

f. Which investment should he choose given all three options?

g. What is the investor's personality, risk averse or risk seeking?

Question 2

An investor with a starting wealth of $8 million and a utility function of $U(w) = \ln(w)$ has three investment options, all of which call for a $4 million investment.

	Investment					
	I		**II**		**III**	
Revenue	5	8	0	12	−3	24
Probability	1/3	2/3	1/2	1/2	?	?

a. Calculate his final wealth in each scenario in options I and II.

b. Calculate his mean final wealth in options I and II.

c. Calculate his utility in each scenario in options I and II.

d. Calculate his mean utility in options I and II.

e. Calculate the scenario probabilities for investment III so that the investor is indifferent between investment III and investment II.

f. Calculate his certainty equivalent in options I and II.

g. Calculate the risk premium.

h. Explain your results and check whether the investor would be willing to make each investment separately given only that one option.

Question 3

An investor with a starting wealth of 10 is given three contracts requiring an investment of 8:

	Contract					
	I		**II**		**III**	
Revenue	10	20	4	24	6	18
Probability	1/2	1/2	1/2	1/2	1/3	2/3

a. Find the certainty equivalent and the risk premium for an individual whose utility function is $U(w) = 6w - 0.1w^2$.

b. Find the certainty equivalent and the risk premium for an individual whose utility function is $U(w) = 6w + 0.1w^2$.

c. Compare your results for parts (a) and (b). What are your conclusions?

Question 4

You are organizing a lottery for individuals whose utility function is $U(x) = 10x + 0.2x^2$, where x is the result of participating in a lottery in which only one ticket in the group wins $100 (everyone else gets $0). Tickets cost $5.

a. Assuming the number of tickets sold is known to everyone, what is the maximum number of tickets you can sell?

b. What is your maximum profit from organizing the lottery?

Question 5

Assume that your utility function is $U(w) = \ln(w)$ and your starting wealth is $6,000.

a. You face a possible gain or loss of $1,000 with a probability of 0.5:0.5. You can buy insurance that would completely cover this risk for a premium of $100 (in this case, the insurer would undertake the entire gamble). Should you buy the insurance or remain exposed to the risk?

b. Assume your starting wealth is $3,000. If you are faced with the same risk and offered the same insurance as before, should you buy the insurance this time? Why?

c. Compare your results for parts (a) and (b). What is your conclusion?

Question 6

"A risk seeker will always participate in a fair game."

Prove this statement graphically. In your answer, state the participation price required to convince a risk seeker not to participate in the game.

Question 7

Assume that standard deviation σ (which, as discussed, indicates the distribution of results around the average) is defined as a risk indicator (measure). An investor has a utility function of $U = 3E(R) - 4.5\sigma^2$ on the mean yield $E(R)$–risk(σ) plane.
    Five financial assets are given on this same plane:

Asset	Mean Yield $E(R)$	Standard Deviation σ
1	12%	19%
2	15%	18%
3	14%	13%
4	19%	24%
5	7%	1%

a. Is the investor risk averse or risk seeking? Explain.

b. In which asset will the investor prefer to invest? Explain.

c. In which asset would a risk neutral investor prefer to invest?

Question 8

An individual with a utility function $U = \sqrt{x}$ has a car valued at \$8,000 (the car constitutes all of that individual's assets). There is a 30% probability that the car will be damaged and its value will decrease to \$2,500, and a 70% probability that it will not be damaged and its value will remain \$8,000. Should this individual insure his car at a cost of \$200?

Question 9

An individual with a utility function of $U(w) = -w^{-1}$ who is faced with an event with a 50-50 chance of winning or losing \$1,000 can buy insurance costing \$500. What level of wealth would make this individual indifferent to incurring the risk or buying insurance?

Question 10

In the previous questions, we demonstrated a number of utility functions describing risk-averse individuals:

1. A parabolic (quadratic) function:

$$U(w) = b \cdot w - a \cdot w^2; \, a > 0$$

2. A logarithmic function:

$$U(w) = a \ln(w)$$

3. Exponential functions:

$$U = \sqrt[n]{w} \text{ or } U = -w^{-n}$$

a. Demonstrate that these functions indeed describe a risk-averse individual.

b. Calculate the absolute and relative risk aversion for the individual described by each of these utility functions.

c. Based on your results for part (a), can you specify which function represents the person with the greatest risk aversion who is faced with a gamble where he could win or lose half his wealth?

Further Reading

Amihud, Y. 1980. General Risk Aversion and an Attitude towards Risk. *Journal of Finance* (June).

Arrow, K. J. 1971. Chapter 3. *Essays in the Theory of Risk Bearing*, 90–133. Chicago: Markham Publishing Co.

Bar-Yosef, S., and R. Meznik. 1977. On Some Definitional Problems with the Method of Certainty Equivalents. *Journal of Finance* (December).

Clarke, R. N. 1985. Certainty Equivalence and the Theory of the Firm under Uncertainty. *International Economic Review* (June).

Cox, J. C., and S. Epstein. 1989. Preference Reversals without the Independence Axiom. *American Economic Review*: 79.

Currim, I. S., and R. K. Sarin. 1989. Prospect versus Utility. *Management Science*: 35.

Friedman, M., and L. J. Savage. 1948. The Utility Analysis of Choices Involving Risk. *Journal of Political Economy* (August): 279–304.

Friedman, M. and Savage, L.J. 1952. The Expected Utility Hypothesis and the Measurability of Utility. *Journal of Political Economy* (December).

Graves, P. E. 1979. Relative Risk Aversion: Increasing or Decreasing? *Journal of Financial and Quantitative Analysis* (June).

Grossman, S. J., and J. Stiglitz. 1976. Information and Competitive Price Systems. *American Economic Review* (May): 246–253.

Hakansson, N. H. 1970. *Friedman-Savage Utility Functions Consistent with Risk Aversion*. *Quarterly Journal of Economics* (August).

Herstein, I. N., and J. Milnor. 1953. An Axiomatic Approach to Expected Utility. *Econometrica* (April): 291–297.

Kudla, R. J. 1980. Some Pitfalls in Using Certainty-Equivalents: A Note. *Journal of Business Finance and Accounting* (Summer).

Miller, S. M. 1975. Measures of Risk Aversion: Some Clarifying Comments. *Journal of Financial and Quantitative Analysis* (June).

Pratt, J. W. 1964. Risk Aversion in the Small and in the Large. *Econometrica* (January–April): 122–136.

Rubinstein, A. 1988. Similarity and Decision-Making under Risk: Is There a Utility Theory Resolution to the Allais Paradox? *Journal of Economic Theory* (October).

Tversky, A., and D. Kahneman. 1986. Rational Choice and the Framing of Decisions. *Journal of Business* 59 (October): S251–S278.

Vickson, R. G. 1975. Stochastic Dominance for Decreasing Absolute Risk Aversion. *Journal of Financial and Quantitative Analysis* (December): 799–812.

Vickson, R. G., and M. Altman. 1977. On the Relative Effectiveness of Stochastic Dominance Rules: Extension to Decreasingly Risk-Averse Functions. *Journal of Financial and Quantitative Analysis* (March): 73–84.

12 The Mean-Variance Model

A. The Evolution of Portfolio Valuation Models
B. Defining Risk for a Single Financial Asset
C. Mean Return and Variance When Holding Two Risky Assets
D. Assets' Correlation Effect on the Investment Opportunities Set
E. Constructing a Multi-Asset Portfolio — The Investment Opportunities Set
F. Constructing a Portfolio in a Market with a Risk-Free Asset
G. Summary of the Markowitz Mean-Variance Model

A. The Evolution of Portfolio Valuation Models

In the early 1950s, professional financial publications began running articles on portfolio analysis. From a historical perspective, these articles led to the development of two different approaches, the mean-variance model and the market model.

The Mean-Variance model — This normative model pioneered by Harry Markowitz was first presented in his 1952 article as a paradigm, and then in his 1959 book as a normative rule to be followed. Markowitz made assumptions concerning the way rational investors should analyze their investments in terms of the mean-variance Taylor series approximation to their expected utility, using probability beliefs where objective probabilities are not known. Markowitz derived the functional relation between the average returns required by investors on portfolios in the capital market and their inherent risk as measured by their variance. Individual investors should then choose from this portfolio's opportunity line their own optimal portfolio, according to their individual utility function.[1]

---

1. This is one of the most important models developed in the second half of the twentieth century (some say *the* most important) as it was the first model in which risk was defined

The Market model—This descriptive model was pioneered by Treynor (1962) and Sharpe (1964). Treynor and Sharpe observed market behavior and applied statistical tools to their observations. They derived the functional relation between the average returns required by investors on portfolios in the capital market and the inherent risk of these portfolios as measured by their correlation with the overall market performance. Again, individual investors then choose their optimal portfolio from this portfolio's opportunity line, according to their individual utility function.

Although the definition of the measure for risk is fundamentally different in each of the models, the assets' returns variance as a measure unit versus the assets' returns correlation with the market as a measure unit, many considered them to be a single model. This is probably because both models were developed during roughly the same historical period, used similar statistical mathematical tools, and reached almost the same conclusions.

This book, however, distinguishes between the two models, emphasizing the differences in their approach and in their definition of a measure for risk.

As discussed in the previous chapter, we want to develop a model that will provide us with a risk-adjusted discount rate for a given financial asset as a function of the basic risk-free interest rate (reflecting only time preference) and risk, which is defined in quantifiable terms.

The discount rate
for a financial asset's
expected cash flow = f (basic interest rate,   risk)

$$k \quad = f \ (\quad r_f \quad ; \quad Risk)$$

B.   Defining Risk for a Single Financial Asset

What criteria guide investors in choosing between risky assets? Only after answering this basic question can we examine an investor's considerations for these criteria.

Markowitz's mean-variance model is a normative model that is based on two assumptions concerning choices made by rational investors:

mathematically and became empirically measurable. Markowitz was awarded the Nobel Prize for his work.

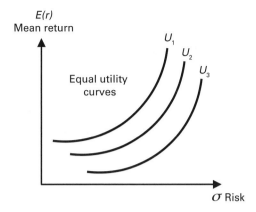

Figure 12.1
Risk-Averse Investors' Equal-Utility Curves

1. Financial assets are chosen strictly according to their mean return and the standard deviation (or variance) from that mean as a measure of risk.

2. Individual investors choose their particular portfolios according to their risk-averse utility function.

Note that the model describes the decision-making criteria people should use, the mean return and standard deviation, and their considerations, risk aversion, and maximum expected utility. However, the model does not state the functional relation between these criteria.

The equal-utility curves for risk-averse investors are shown in figure 12.1.

For such investors, $U_1 \supset U_2 \supset U_3$, or descriptively, the more a curve is located to the left (smaller risk) or upward (greater returns) on the graph, the greater will be that investor's utility.

Remember that this is a normative model, which assumes that $E(R)$ and σ (or σ^2) are the decision-making parameters on which rational investors should base their choice. Later we will see how this assumption can lead to far-reaching conclusions concerning the way people should choose their investment portfolios. Of course, as a mathematical model, its underlying assumption does not require proof, for the very fact that it is an assumption. However, we will discuss the practical significance of this assumption.

As mentioned, the model assumes that investors choose investments strictly according to an asset's mean return and standard deviation. When the model was first justified by Markowitz in his 1959 book explaining the relationships between securities and portfolios, the model's underlying assumption was perceived as having four practical repercussions, two concerning investors' characteristics and two concerning the distribution of the financial assets' returns.[2]

1. *All investors follow a quadratic utility function.*[3]   Mathematically, we can prove that in this case, regardless of the statistical distribution of the financial assets' returns, the utility function will include only the first two moments—mean return and standard deviation.[4]

2. *Investors cannot figure out more than the first two moments.*   The financial assets' distribution may also include higher-order moments, but people disregard them as they cannot utilize this information in their decision-making process.

3. *Financial assets are distributed normally.*   Normal distribution is the only type of distribution that can be defined by only two moments.

4. *Financial assets are distributed in such a way that high-order moments are very small and therefore negligible.*   Following a debate with Pratt and Arrow, who argued that a quadratic utility function could lead to undesirable implications, and others who argued against the approximation of the returns having a normal distribution (see chapter 13), Markowitz co-authored two articles.[5] He and his colleagues conducted a regression of various types of utility functions[6] on their second-order Taylor approximation, which is practically a quadratic function. The values of the original utility functions and their Taylor-approximated functions showed high correlation[7] when calculated over sample data from the annual returns (1958–1967) of 149 mutual funds (portfolios). From my experience teaching students how to derive the maximum of a utility function mathematically, students find it easier to follow an example that applies a quadratic utility function, so I will continue to use

---

2. Propositions 2 and 4 are actually weaker versions of propositions 1 and 3, respectively.

3. Of the type $U(w) = -aw^2 + bw + c$, $a > 0$, where w represents an investor's wealth.

4. The use of the term *moment* comes from mechanics. By analogy, the moment of a distribution function can be used to infer (among other aspects) its symmetry around its "center of mass," that is, its mean. The m-power moment of the distribution of a random variable $\tilde{X}$ is defined as $E(X^m) = \int x^m \cdot f(x)dx$, or, for discrete cases, $E(X^m) = \sum x^m \cdot f(x)$. Readers are referred to chapters on moment-generating functions in the statistics literature.

5. "Approximating Expected Utility by a Function of Mean and Variance," by H. Levy and H. M. Markowitz (1979), and "Mean Variance versus Direct Utility Maximization," by Y. Kroll, H. Levy, and H. M. Markowitz (1984).

6. Similar to those we examined in the questions section of chapter 11.

7. For example, (Utility function actual value) = $0.002 + 0.966 \times$ (Utility function approximated value).

a quadratic utility function here to present the general case. In chapter 14, which shows how to assign weights to a small number of assets when assembling a practical portfolio using the mean-variance approach, I will generalize the result to include any type of (risk-averse) utility function.

C. Mean Return and Variance When Holding Two Risky Assets

In discussing the criteria considered by investors, we must first understand investors' positions (in terms of mean return and risk) when holding a number of different financial assets, as is most often the case.

Assume two financial assets with an uncertain return. For convenience, denote the random expected return for each asset $\tilde{k}_X = \tilde{X}$ and $\tilde{k}_y = \tilde{Y}$ (the tilde indicates that future returns are an uncertain random variable). Assume that we know the mean and variance values for each asset's return and their covariance (or correlation coefficient).

Let's construct an investment portfolio in which the weight (portion) of each asset is:

$a\%$ of $\tilde{X}$, and

$b\%$ $(= 1 - a\%)$ of $\tilde{Y}$.

Let's calculate the mean return k_p and the return variance σ_P^2 for the portfolio P:

$$\tilde{P} = a\tilde{X} + b\tilde{Y}.$$

$$E(\tilde{P}) = E(a\tilde{X} + b\tilde{Y}) = aE(\tilde{X}) + bE(\tilde{Y}).$$
$$\bar{k}_p = a\bar{k}_x + b\bar{k}_y.$$
$$\text{Var}_P = E(\tilde{P} - \bar{k}_P)^2 = a^2\text{Var}(\tilde{X}) + b^2\text{Var}(\tilde{Y}) + 2ab\text{Cov}(\tilde{X}, \tilde{Y}).$$
$$\sigma_P^2 = a^2\sigma_x^2 + b^2\sigma_y^2 + 2ab\text{Cov}(xy) = a^2\sigma_x^2 + b^2\sigma_y^2 + 2ab\rho_{xy}\sigma_x\sigma_y.$$

Example: The distribution of returns offered by two financial assets is as follows:

Condition i	P_i	Y_i	X_i
1	0.2	30%	18%
2	0.2	–6%	22%
3	0.2	12%	–4%
4	0.2	40%	14%
5	0.2	4%	25%

Calculate the mean return for each asset:

$$\bar{k}_x = E(X_i) = \sum P_i \cdot X_i = 15\% = 0.15.$$

$$\bar{k}_y = E(Y_i) = \sum P_i \cdot Y_i = 16\% = 0.16.$$

Calculate the return variance for each asset:[8]

$$\sigma_x^2 = \sum P_i \cdot (X_i - \bar{k}_x)^2 = \sum_i 0.2 \cdot (X_i - 0.15)^2 = 0.0104$$

$$\Rightarrow \sigma_x = 0.102 = 10.2\%.$$

$$\sigma_y^2 = 0.0283$$

$$\Rightarrow \sigma_y = 0.168 = 16.8\%.$$

Calculate the covariance of the two assets' returns:

$$Cov(X,Y) = \sum P_i \cdot (X_i - \bar{k}_x)(Y_i - \bar{k}_y) = -0.0036.$$

And their correlation coefficient:

$$\rho = \frac{Cov(x,y)}{\sigma_x \cdot \sigma_y} = \frac{-0.0036}{0.102 \cdot 0.168} = -0.21.$$

Assume that we are constructing a portfolio where we invest $250 in asset X and $750 in asset Y (thus, $a = 1/4$ and $b = 3/4$):

$$\bar{k}_p = a\bar{k}_x + b\bar{k}_y = 0.25 \cdot 0.15 + 0.75 \cdot 0.16 = 0.1575 \Rightarrow 15.75\%.$$

$$\sigma_p^2 = a^2\sigma_x^2 + b^2\sigma_y^2 + 2ab\,Cov(xy)$$

$$= 0.25^2 \cdot 0.0104 + 0.75^2 \cdot 0.0283 + 2 \cdot 0.25 \cdot 0.75 \cdot (-0.0036) = 0.01522$$

$$\Rightarrow \sigma_p = 0.1234 = 12.34\%.$$

Note: Although the portfolio's mean return is located between the mean return of asset X and the mean return of asset Y ($\bar{k}_x = 20\% > \bar{k}_p = 17\% > \bar{k}_y = 16\%$), the portfolio's return's standard deviation is smaller than the standard deviation for each asset's return when taken separately. In stochastic dominance terms, asset Y is not attractive on its own but only as part of the investment portfolio.[9] (Explain!)

---

8. When calculating the mean, it does not matter whether we use percentage or decimal values. However, decimals should be used when calculating variance.

9. Consider the question, is Y viable? Would anyone even want to buy it? The answer is yes, but why?

D. Assets' Correlation Effect on the Investment Opportunities Set

As discussed above, the formula for calculating a portfolio's variance is

$$\sigma_p^2 = a^2\sigma_x^2 + b^2\sigma_y^2 + 2ab\rho_{xy}\sigma_x\sigma_y.$$

Let's examine the geometric location of $\left(\bar{k}_p;\sigma_p\right)$ on the mean return–risk plane $\left(\bar{k};\sigma\right)$ for different portfolios comprised of assets X and Y, each with a different correlation coefficient[10] ρ_{xy}.

Assume $\rho_{xy} = 1$.

This means the two assets are perfectly correlated (they increase or decrease together at exactly the same rate):

$$\sigma^2{}_p = a^2\sigma_x^2 + b^2\sigma_y^2 + 2ab\ \sigma_x\sigma_y = (a\sigma_x + b\sigma_y)^2$$

$$\Rightarrow \sigma_p = a\sigma_x + b\sigma_y.$$

We get a linear correlation between $\bar{k}_P$ and σ_P on the mean return–risk plane $\left(\bar{k};\sigma\right)$:

$$\bar{k}_P = a\bar{k}_x + b\bar{k}_y = a\bar{k}_x + (1-a)\bar{k}_y = a(\bar{k}_x - \bar{k}_y) + \bar{k}_y$$

$$\sigma_P = a\sigma_x + b\sigma_y = a(\sigma_x - \sigma_y) + \sigma_y$$

$$\Rightarrow a = \frac{\sigma_P - \sigma_y}{\sigma_x - \sigma_y}$$

$$\bar{k}_P = a(\bar{k}_x - \bar{k}_y) + \bar{k}_y = \frac{\sigma_P - \sigma_y}{\sigma_x - \sigma_y}(\bar{k}_x - \bar{k}_y) + \bar{k}_y$$

$$\bar{k}_P = \underbrace{(\frac{\bar{k}_x - \bar{k}_y}{\sigma_x - \sigma_y})}\cdot\sigma_P + \underbrace{(\frac{\bar{k}_x - \bar{k}_y}{\sigma_x - \sigma_y}\sigma_Y + \bar{k}_y)}$$

$$\bar{k}_P = \qquad A\cdot\sigma_P + \qquad\qquad B^{11}$$

Therefore: On plane $\left(\bar{k};\sigma\right)$, the geometric location of the mean return and variance $\left(\bar{k}_P;\sigma_P\right)$ for a portfolio whose two assets have a correlation of $\rho_{xy} = 1$ is a straight line connecting the mean return and the variance for the two assets X and Y. The exact location of a specific

---

10. Unlike the covariance, the correlation coefficient is normalized, and thus meaningful.
11. Remember that σ_x, σ_y, $\bar{k}_x$, and $\bar{k}_y$ are constants (numbers) derived from $\tilde{X}$ and $\tilde{Y}$'s respective distribution. Therefore, A and B are also constants (numbers).

given portfolio's mean return and its variance on this line is determined by the proportionate weights a and b of each constituent asset (see figure 12.2).

Assume $\rho_{xy} = -1$.

This means that the two assets have a perfect inverse correlation (one increases when the other decreases, and vice versa, at exactly the same rate).

$$\sigma_p^2 = a^2\sigma_x^2 + b^2\sigma_y^2 - 2ab\ \sigma_x\sigma_y = (a\sigma_x - b\sigma_y)^2.$$

$$\sigma_p = a\sigma_x - b\sigma_y = a(\sigma_x + \sigma_y) - \sigma_y$$

$$\Rightarrow a = \frac{\sigma_P + \sigma_y}{\sigma_x + \sigma_y}$$

To find the correlation between $\bar{k}_P$ and σ_P, we can again develop the two equations derived as above:

$$\bar{k}_P = a\bar{k}_x + b\bar{k}_y = a(\bar{k}_x - \bar{k}_y) + \bar{k}_y.$$

$$\bar{k}_P = \frac{\sigma_P + \sigma_y}{\sigma_x + \sigma_y}(\bar{k}_x - \bar{k}_y) + \bar{k}_y$$

$$\bar{k}_P = \underbrace{\frac{\bar{k}_x - \bar{k}_y}{\sigma_x + \sigma_y}}_{\downarrow}\cdot\sigma_P + \underbrace{\frac{\sigma_Y(\bar{k}_x - \bar{k}_y)}{\sigma_x + \sigma_y} + \bar{k}_y}_{\downarrow}$$

$$\bar{k}_P = \quad A\cdot\sigma_P + \qquad\quad B$$

Therefore: On the plane $(\bar{k};\sigma)$, the geometric location of the mean return and variance of a portfolio $(\bar{k}_P;\sigma_P)$ whose two assets have a correlation of $\rho_{xy} = -1$ is a broken straight line connecting the mean return and variance for the two assets X and Y, with the line broken at point $\sigma_P = 0$. The exact location of a given portfolio's mean return and variance on this broken line is determined by the proportional weights a and b of each asset in the portfolio (see figure 12.2 below).

The risk σ_P is zero when

$$\sigma_P = a\sigma_x - b\sigma_y = 0 \quad\Rightarrow\quad \frac{a}{b} = \frac{\sigma_y}{\sigma_x}$$

Thus, when the ratio between the assets' weights is *inverse* to the ratio between the assets' standard deviations, then the portfolio risk measure σ_P is zero.

Assume $\rho_{xy} = 0$.

This means the assets are completely independent.

$$\sigma_p^2 = a^2\sigma_x^2 + b^2\sigma_y^2 = (a\sigma_x)^2 + (b\sigma_y)^2.$$

Therefore: The geometric location on plane $(\bar{k};\sigma)$ of the mean return and variance of a portfolio $(\bar{k}_P;\sigma_P)$ whose two assets have a correlation of $\rho_{xy} = 0$ is a parabolic line connecting the mean return and variance of the two assets X and Y. The exact location of a given portfolio's mean return and variance on this line is determined by the proportional weights a and b of each constituent asset (see figure 12.2 below).

We can demonstrate the matter geometrically with the following example. Assume two financial assets:

• Asset X has a mean return of 12% and a standard deviation of 10%.

• Asset Y has a mean return of 6% and a standard deviation of 4%.

We can now plot the set of possibilities (lines) $(\bar{k}_P;\sigma_P)$ on the plane $(\bar{k};\sigma)$ for various correlation coefficients:

Asset weight in the portfolio		Mean return	Portfolio standard deviation σ_p for different correlation coefficients			
a	b	R_p	$\rho_{xy} = 1$	$\rho_{xy} = 0$	$\rho_{xy} = -0.75$	$\rho_{xy} = -1$
1	0	12.00%	10.0%	10.0%	10.0%	10.0%
0.9	0.1	11.40%	9.4%	9.0%	8.7%	8.6%
0.8	0.2	10.80%	8.8%	8.0%	7.4%	7.2%
0.7	0.3	10.20%	8.2%	7.1%	6.2%	5.8%
0.6	0.4	9.60%	7.6%	6.2%	4.9%	4.4%
0.5	0.5	9.00%	7.0%	5.4%	3.7%	3.0%
0.4	0.6	8.40%	6.4%	4.7%	2.7%	1.6%
0.3	0.7	7.80%	5.8%	4.1%	2.1%	0.2%
0.2	0.8	7.20%	5.2%	3.8%	2.2%	1.2%
0.1	0.9	6.60%	4.6%	3.7%	2.9%	2.6%
0	1	6.00%	4.0%	4.0%	4.0%	4.0%

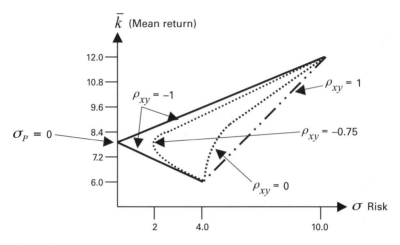

Figure 12.2
Effect of Correlation between Portfolio Assets on the Investment Opportunities Set

Each point along the lines describing the investment opportunities set represents a particular mean and variance value for a given pair of weights (a, b).

Now assume that a risk-free asset R_f is available. The definition of risk leads us to conclude that this asset's variance is zero (i.e., the asset is not a random process variable but rather a certain and specific parameter). Let's also assume that this asset serves as the lending and borrowing interest rate, reflecting the market equilibrium rate for consumption preference over time. Furthermore, only one such asset can be available on the market (why?).

Investors can now invest some of their funds in a risky asset and some in this risk-free asset (the equivalent of giving a loan). Alternatively, they can take a loan and invest their money plus the loan in the risky asset. Now, let's construct a portfolio composed of the risk-free asset X and any risky asset $\tilde{Y}$. The correlation coefficient between the risk-free asset and the risky asset is zero (why?).

$$E(\tilde{P}) = E(aX + b\tilde{Y}) = aE(X) + bE(\tilde{Y})$$

and

$$\bar{k}_x = E(X) = R_f\,;$$

then

$$\bar{k}_p = aR_f + b\bar{k}_y\,.$$

We saw in general that in a portfolio composed of two assets with a zero correlation coefficient, the following obtains:

$$\sigma_p^2 = a^2\sigma_x^2 + b^2\sigma_y^2.$$

For a portfolio where one of the assets, say X, is the risk-free asset, that is, $\sigma_x = 0$:

$$\sigma_p^2 = b^2\sigma_y^2$$

$$\sigma_p = (1-a)\sigma_y$$

$$a = 1 - \sigma_p/\sigma_y$$

$$1 - a = \sigma_p/\sigma_y$$

$$\bar{k}_p = aR_f + (1-a)\bar{k}_y = (1-\sigma_p/\sigma_y)R_f + (\sigma_p/\sigma_y)\bar{k}_y$$

$$\bar{k}_p = \frac{\bar{k}_y - R_f}{\sigma_y}\sigma_p + R_f = A\cdot\sigma_p + B$$

The investment opportunities set is a straight line whose slope is $A = \dfrac{k_y - R_f}{\sigma_y}$, and which intersects the mean return axis at point $B = R_f$.

For the section of the line between the risk-free asset $X = \bar{R}_f$ and the risky asset $\tilde{Y}, 0 < a < 1$, the part invested in the risk-free asset R_f is a, and the part invested in asset $\tilde{Y}$ is $1 - a$.

Extending the line to the right (the dotted line in figure 12.3) indicates that instead of lending a certain amount a of his money ($a > 0$) by

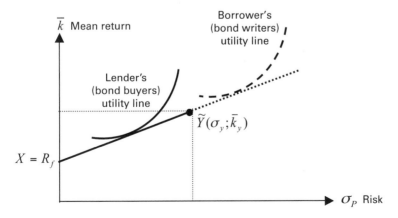

Figure 12.3
Taking a Loan ($a < 0$) to Invest in Asset Y

investing in the risk-free asset R_f, an investor takes a loan (writes a bond at an interest rate of R_f), that is, $a < 0$. The investor uses his money plus the loan to invest in asset $\tilde{Y}$. Because a is negative, the dotted line is portrayed by $\sigma_p = (1 + a)\sigma_y$ (for the absolute value of a).

Taking a loan as part of an investment in a risky asset is referred to as *leveraging*.

Example: An investor has \$1,000 in capital. The investor takes a \$200 loan and invests \$1,200 in an asset with a mean return of 10% and a standard deviation of 8%. The borrowing rate and the lending rate are identical and equal to 5%. What are the mean return and risk for the investor's position according to the mean-variance model?

$a = (-200)/1,000 = -0.2.$

$\bar{k}_p = -0.2 \cdot 5\% + [1 - (-0.2)] \cdot 10\% = 11\%.$

$\sigma_p = (1 - a)\sigma_y = [1 - (-0.2)] \cdot 8\% = 1.2 \cdot 8\% = 9.6\%.$

Thus, the 11% return on the investment is greater than a loan-free investment in the risky asset (offering a 10% return). However, our risk is also greater as the risky asset's standard deviation is 8%, while the standard deviation for our portfolio (i.e., our position) is 9.6%.

In conclusion, when taking a loan with an interest rate R_f, and investing our money plus the loan (which amounts to a% of our original capital) in a risky asset $\tilde{Y}$ with a mean return $\bar{k}_y$ and a variance σ_y, we construct a portfolio with an expected return of

$$\bar{k}_p = -|a|R_f + (1 + |a|)\bar{k}_y = k_y + |a| \cdot (\bar{k}_y - R_f).$$

In other words, on their "own pocket capital" part in the investment, investors can expect a return $\bar{k}_y$, while for the part a taken as a loan, they can expect only an average return that is equal to the difference $(\bar{k}_y - R_f)$ between the mean return on the investment $\bar{k}_y$ and the interest R_f paid on the loan. Compared to a loan-free investment for which investors use only their own capital, when leveraging, the expected average return has increased by $a \cdot (\bar{k}_y - R_f)$. However, their risk has also increased, from σ_y to $\sigma_p = (1 + a)\sigma_y$.

E. Constructing a Multi-Asset Portfolio—The Investment Opportunities Set

We would now like to construct a portfolio comprised of n assets and calculate the portfolio's mean return and variance.

Denote the random return on each asset i as $\tilde{R}_i$.

For asset i, denote its mean return as $E[R_i]$ and its variance as σ_i^2.

Denote the asset's relative weight (asset value in dollars, divided by portfolio value in dollars) in the portfolio as W_i (for "weight").

Denote the correlation between the returns on each asset i and another asset j as ρ_{ij}.

In statistical mathematical terms, the mean is a linear operator (function). Therefore, the portfolio mean return is the sum of the mean return on each component, prorated to its weight in the portfolio:

$$E(R_p) = \sum_{i=1}^{N} W_i \cdot E[R_i].$$

The following result for the portfolio variance is also taken from statistical mathematics:[12]

$$\sigma_p^2 = \sum_{i=1}^{N} \sum_{j=1}^{N} \rho_{ij} W_i W_j \sigma_i \sigma_j.$$

For each asset i, we can determine its contribution to the overall portfolio variance. This contribution is derived from the asset's own variance, plus its covariance with each of the other $n - 1$ assets in the portfolio.

If we sum all the different proportionate contributions for each asset i, that is, $i = 1...n$, we would receive the total portfolio variance.

Table 12.1 provides a better understanding of the notation $\sum_{i=1}^{N} \sum_{j=1}^{N}$.

---

12. This expression is proved to be valid through induction. The expression is proved for two variables (as in the previous chapter), and for three variables. Assuming that it is correct for n variables, it is then proved to be valid for $n + 1$ variables.

Table 12.1

i	j 1	2	...	N	Asset i's partial contribution to overall portfolio variance
1	$W_1^2\sigma_1^2$	$\rho_{12}W_1W_2\sigma_1\sigma_2$		$\rho_{1N}W_1W_N\sigma_1\sigma_N$	$\sum\limits_{j=1}^{N}\rho_{1j}W_1W_j\sigma_1\sigma_j$
2	$\rho_{21}W_1W_2\sigma_1\sigma_2$	$W_2^2\sigma_2^2$		$\rho_{2N}W_2W_N\sigma_2\sigma_N$	$\sum\limits_{j=1}^{N}\rho_{2j}W_2W_j\sigma_2\sigma_j$
3	$\rho_{31}W_1W_3\sigma_1\sigma_3$	$\rho_{32}W_2W_3\sigma_2\sigma_3$		$\rho_{3N}W_2W_N\sigma_2\sigma_N$	$\sum\limits_{j=1}^{N}\rho_{3j}W_3W_j\sigma_3\sigma_j$
⋮	⋮	⋮		⋮	
⋮	⋮	⋮		⋮	
N	$\rho_{N1}W_1W_N\sigma_1\sigma_N$	$\rho_{N2}W_2W_N\sigma_2\sigma_N$		$W_N^2\sigma_N^2$	$\sum\limits_{j=1}^{N}\rho_{Nj}W_NW_j\sigma_N\sigma_j$

Summing up all $i = 1....N$ assets'
partial variance contributions $\longrightarrow$ $\sum\limits_{i=1}^{N}\sum\limits_{j=1}^{N}\rho_{ij}W_iW_j\sigma_i\sigma_j$

Note: $\rho_{ij} = \rho_{ji}$

The weighted variance $w_i^2\sigma_i^2$, located on the diagonal, represents the contribution of asset i's own variance (variation) only. The other terms in each cell of the row i represent the weighted covariance (covariation) of asset i with all other assets j in the portfolio.[13] The sum of all the terms in each row equals the contribution of asset i's partial variation to the overall portfolio variance.

The sum of the column containing all the rows i partial variance contributions constitutes the overall portfolio variance, σ_P^2.

Example: Assume a portfolio consisting of the following shares:

13. Remember, $\rho_{ij}\sigma_i\sigma_j = \text{Cov}(X_iX_j)$.

	Weight in Portfolio	Mean Return	Standard Deviation	Correlation Coefficient between Shares		
				Share 1	Share 2	Share 3
Share 1	0.5	10%	20%	1	0.5	0.3
Share 2	0.3	15%	30%	0.5	1	0.1
Share 3	0.2	20%	40%	0.3	0.1	1

Calculate the mean return for the portfolio:

$$E(R_p) = \sum_{i=1}^{N} w_i \cdot E[R_i].$$

$E(R_P) = 0.5 \cdot 10\% + 0.3 \cdot 15 + 0.2 \cdot 20 = 13.5\%.$

Calculate[14] the variance for the portfolio:
First we calculate the covariances in the following table, where
$\sigma_{ij} = \rho_{ij} \cdot \sigma_i \cdot \sigma_j.$

	Share 1	Share 2	Share 3
Share 1	$20 \cdot 20 \cdot 1 = 400$	$20 \cdot 30 \cdot 0.5 = 300$	$20 \cdot 40 \cdot 0.3 = 240$
Share 2	$30 \cdot 20 \cdot 0.5 = 300$	$30 \cdot 30 \cdot 1 = 900$	$30 \cdot 40 \cdot 0.1 = 120$
Share 3	$40 \cdot 20 \cdot 0.3 = 240$	$40 \cdot 30 \cdot 0.1 = 120$	$40 \cdot 40 \cdot 1 = 1600$

Multiply each cell by $W_i W_j$:

	Share 1	Share 2	Share 3
Share 1	$0.5 \cdot 0.5 \cdot 400 = 100$	$0.3 \cdot 0.5 \cdot 300 = 45$	$0.2 \cdot 0.5 \cdot 240 = 24$
Share 2	$0.5 \cdot 0.3 \cdot 300 = 45$	$0.3 \cdot 0.3 \cdot 900 = 81$	$0.2 \cdot 0.3 \cdot 120 = 7.2$
Share 3	$0.5 \cdot 0.2 \cdot 240 = 24$	$0.3 \cdot 0.2 \cdot 120 = 7.2$	$0.2 \cdot 0.2 \cdot 1600 = 64$
Total	169.00	133.2	95.2

14. This example uses percentages despite our recommendation from a few pages back.

Portfolio variance equals
$$\sigma_P^2 = 169.00 + 133.20 + 95.20 = 397.40$$
$$\sigma_P = \sqrt{397.40} = 19.9\%$$

We may now calculate each share's contribution to the overall portfolio variance.

As the matrix is symmetrical, the sum of each row n and the sum of each column n are identical (check and see that the sum of the column labeled "Share 1" is equal to the sum of the row labeled "Share 1"). The sum of each row or column n in the above table is that share's contribution to the overall portfolio variance of 397.4, that is, $n = 1 \Rightarrow 169.0$, $n = 2 \Rightarrow 133.2$, and $n = 3 \Rightarrow 95.2$, out of 397.4. The proportionate contribution can also be calculated as a percentage.

Let's illustrate graphically (see figure 12.4) how a portfolio is built of three assets, labeled 1, 2, and 3. Each portfolio on the "frontier line," created by using different weights a and b from assets 1 and 2 alone, is effectively a financial asset in itself. For example, portfolio A has a mean return R_A and a variance σ_A, and the fact that it is comprised of two different assets is irrelevant. We can, for all intents and purposes, use it as a regular financial asset. Accordingly, each portfolio on the frontier created by using different weights of assets 2 and 3 alone effectively serves as a single financial asset (e.g., portfolio B).

Assets A and B can also be used to create a frontier for different financial assets by using differing weights of each. This process can be

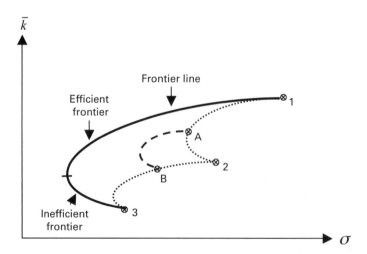

Figure 12.4
Constructing the Efficient Frontier

continued until reaching an "optimal frontier," which yields the maximum return for any given variance (see figure 12.4).

Let us define the following:

Efficient frontier   The curve formed by the set of maximum mean return for any given variance.

The bottom part of the frontier curve in figure 12.4 is not efficient, as the portfolios on the top part offer a higher average return for the same variance. Because of stochastic dominance, only the top part of the curve represents an efficient frontier.

The same efficient frontier concept also applies to portfolios built from any number of financial assets. If we take all financial assets on the market, we can plot the efficient frontier for the entire market. Assets that lie below the efficient frontier will offer inferior performance to portfolios on the efficient frontier line. However, as was the case for a two-asset portfolio numerical example, such assets are still viable and can be held by all investors as part of their portfolios.

F.   Constructing a Portfolio in a Market with a Risk-Free Asset

The existence of a risk-free asset R_f will cause the final efficient frontier to manifest as a straight line departing from point R_f and *tangent* to the initial efficient frontier derived only by the risky assets/portfolios on the market.

Note the emphasis on the word "tangent." Figure 12.5 shows that several lines can be drawn, creating linear combinations of R_f with various portfolios on the efficient frontier for all risky market assets. Figure 12.5 clearly shows that the tangent line is the "highest" possible line, and thus all other lower lines on the graph represent portfolios with the same variance but lower mean returns, that is, inferior portfolios.

The line is tangent to a *particular* portfolio on the initial efficient frontier (derived from all other risky financial assets). This portfolio is referred to as the "market portfolio" and denoted M. This portfolio has a return of R_M and a variance (standard deviation) of σ_M. The final efficient frontier created with the addition of a risk-free asset R_f is therefore a straight line emerging from the risk-free asset and tangent to the market portfolio M.

Example: Assume that the market portfolio offers a 12% return with 16% variance. The risk-free interest rate is 6%. If we construct a

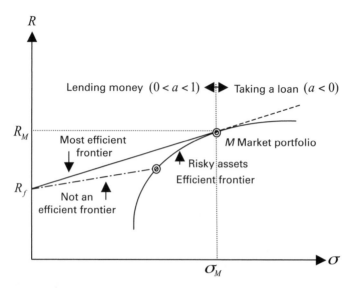

Figure 12.5
Constructing a Portfolio in a Market with a Risk-Free Asset

portfolio half of which consists of the risk-free asset and half of the market portfolio, our portfolio would offer a 9% return with 8% variance.

As we saw previously, extending the line to the right (the dotted line in figure 12.5) indicates that investors take a loan of a% of their equity at an interest rate R_f, and invest their equity plus the loan (in other words, $(1 + |a|) > 1$, $a < 0$) in the market portfolio.

The final line derived from all the efficient portfolios when a risk-free asset is added to the market is called the *securities market line* (SML) (figure 12.6).

To assist in calculating R_i, the expected return for a given portfolio i with a risk of σ_i, we will find the equation for the SML. Denote by R the average return on the portfolios constituting the SML.

We know that the straight-line equation is $R = A \cdot \sigma + B$.

A is the slope, and in our case equals $\dfrac{R_m - R_f}{\sigma_m}$.

B is the intersect with the vertical axis, and in our case R_f.

The SML line equation is therefore $R = \dfrac{R_m - R_f}{\sigma_m} \cdot \sigma \ + \ R_f$.

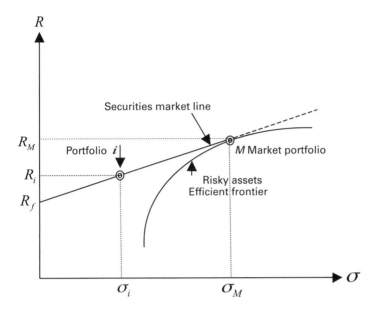

Figure 12.6
The Securities Market Line

G. Summary of the Markowitz Mean-Variance Model

Markowitz presented a normative model that assumes that investors are rational, risk averse, and choose financial assets solely according to the assets' mean return and the standard deviation of that return from the mean.

Capital market portfolios comprised of risky financial assets available on the market and offering the maximum return for any given variance (standard deviation) are known as efficient portfolios and jointly form the line known as the efficient frontier. There is no point holding a solitary share, as it is almost always possible to construct a portfolio that will yield a higher return for the same standard deviation as the share.

When a risk-free asset is available, then the efficient frontier becomes a straight line departing from the risk-free asset and tangent to the efficient curve formed only by the risky assets/portfolios. The portfolio at the tangency point is known as market portfolio M. Through leveraging (taking a loan), investors can extend the efficient frontier beyond the line connecting the risk-free asset and the market portfolio. This line is known as the securities market line.

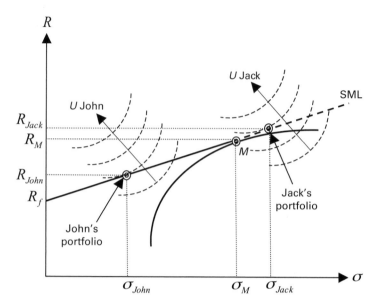

Figure 12.7
Choosing a Personal Portfolio from the Securities Market Line

The market described in figure 12.7 applies to all investors. Every investor will only want to invest in efficient portfolios. John and Jack are two examples of investors in this market.

John and Jack have different utility functions. Figure 12.7 also includes the utility function family for both John and Jack. The family of equal-utility functions (left-to-right increasing functions, as discussed in previous chapters) represents utility (choice) curves balancing return versus risk. The tangency point of each investor's utility function to the SML establishes the portfolio that investor will choose.

In figure 12.7, we see that Jack chooses a portfolio offering a higher mean return but also carrying greater risk (defined as the standard deviation in the portfolio's expected return) than the portfolio chosen by John.[15]

In this way, every investor chooses a portfolio that best suits his or her own preferences (utility function). Each investor constructs his portfolio practically by holding a small part of the market portfolio, and the rest of his investment capital, in a risk-free asset (either lending or borrow-

15. In this example, Jack lends money (buys bonds = gives money in exchange for debt certificates), while John borrows money (sells bonds = writes and issues debt certificates and receives money). Together, they simultaneously create a bond market (a market for trading in consumption timing) and a participation certificate (share) market.

ing). This is the reason why the portfolio is called the *market portfolio*. If each investor holds a small part of the market portfolio, then together they hold the entire market portfolio. As every share is held by an investor, the market portfolio must include all the risky assets available on the market.

We can define the following:

Market portfolio   A portfolio including all the risky assets on the market.

Market portfolio value   The total value of all the risky assets on the market.

When an investor holds a small part of the market portfolio, he actually holds a portfolio that includes prorated portions of all the risky assets on the market.[16]

Chapter 12—Questions and Problems

Question 1

In Utopia, there is only one manufacturing company, Supplier Inc. Its shares are traded on the free market at a current price of 50 (choose whichever currency you like). One risk-free asset is also available on the market. The borrowing rate and lending rate are identical and equal 5% per period. All citizens have the same expectations concerning the probability distribution for the share price at the end of the period, as follows:

Price	60	58	56	55	54	51	49	48	47
Probability	0.05	0.05	0.1	0.15	0.25	0.15	0.1	0.1	0.05

a. Calculate the distribution function for the return on a Supplier Inc. share at the end of the period for each level of probability.

b. What are the mean return and the variance for the end of the period?

c. Using the mean-variance model, what is the return and what is the risk for investors who invest (buy) 20% of their money in the risk-free asset (i.e., lend money) and use the rest of their money to buy shares in Supplier Inc.?

16. Each risky asset's prorated portion is determined by the market value of the risky asset, divided by the entire market portfolio value.

d. Using the mean-variance model, what is the return and what is the risk for investors who issue (sell) a risk-free asset equal to 20% of their equity (i.e., borrow money) and use all their resources to buy shares in Supplier Inc.?

e. Why is Supplier Inc.'s share price uncertain, and why has it been given a probability distribution?

f. In parts (c) and (d), why do investors construct different portfolios (i.e., different positions) at the start of the period?

g. What determines the share price at the start of the period to be 50?

Question 2

Assume a market with three investment portfolios with a correlation of 1 between them (choose their return and risk values as you wish). Plot a graph demonstrating for which range of risk-free asset values (i.e., interest rate) each of these portfolios will have dominance over the others.

Question 3

Assume the following two shares:

| | | | Correlation between Shares | |
	Mean Return	**Standard Deviation**	**Share A**	**Share B**
Share A	10%	15%	1	0.2
Share B	20%	25%	0.2	1

There are five portfolios on the market:

Portfolio	Share A Weight	Share B Weight
1	1	0
2	0.75	0.25
3	0.5	0.5
4	0.25	0.75
5	0	1

a. Calculate the mean return and variance for each portfolio.

b. Plot your answers on the mean return–variance plane.

c. Assume that the lending and borrowing rate (risk-free asset) are both 5%. Are all these portfolios viable? Demonstrate your answer graphically.

d. Explain the fact that the above correlation coefficient matrix has one diagonal with the number 1 while the other diagonal has the number 0.2. Can your answer be generalized for markets with more than two shares? (Explain for a three-share market.)

Question 4

In contrast to the model in which all investors have identical expectations, you live in the real world. You and your wife have different expectations concerning the return offered by a particular share over a one-year period. Despite your disagreement, your wife buys $1,000 worth of these shares. As a compromise, you ask your wife whether you might borrow the shares that she bought, promising to return them at the end of the period. You immediately sell the shares on the market (such a sale of borrowed shares is referred to as a "short sale").

a. Explain and demonstrate why your family's position is now risk-free, even though you promised your wife you would return her shares at the end of the period (and you had better!).

b. What is the correlation between your wife's position after buying the shares (known as a long position), and your position after selling borrowed shares which you promised to return at the end of the period (known as a short position).

Question 5

The correlation between the return on asset X and the return on asset Y is defined by the equation $y = ax + b$, where $a > 0$.

a. Demonstrate that the two assets are perfectly correlated (i.e., correlation coefficient $\rho = 1$).

b. What is required for the correlation coefficient to be perfectly negative?

c. Demonstrate how a risk-free portfolio can be constructed using these two assets. What will the ratio be between the assets in this portfolio?

Question 6

A portfolio is comprised of three shares, whose returns have a variance-covariance (matrix) as follows:

Share	1	2	3
1	2.5	−1	2.4
2	−1	7.5	3.2
3	2.4	3.2	1.2

Note that the table (matrix) is diagonally symmetrical: $(a_{ij} = a_{ji})$ for $i \neq j$!

a. What is the variance on the return offered by a portfolio comprised in equal parts of all three shares?

b. What is the variance on the return offered by a portfolio comprised 10% of share 1, 80% of share 2, and 10% of share 3?

Question 7

Assume a market that accords with Markowitz's assumptions. The risk-free rate is 5%, and the market portfolio offers a 9% return with a 4% standard deviation.

a. A share is at equilibrium and offers a 6% return. What is the share's standard deviation?

b. Joe wants to construct an efficient portfolio with a risk (indicated by standard deviation) of 5%. What is the return on his portfolio? How would he construct such a portfolio?

c. Two shares on the market have a correlation of −1. Given that the first share offers a 3% return with a 2.5% standard deviation, what is the return on the second share if it has a 10% standard deviation?

Question 8

There are 81 shares, each of which has a variance of 900 and a covariance of 400 with each of the other shares.

You have a portfolio comprised 20% of one share and equal parts of all other shares.

a. What is the variance of your portfolio?

b. Approximately how many shares of equal weights do you need in order to construct a portfolio with approximately the same variance?

Question 9

Assume a market that maintains Markowitz's assumptions. The following table details the probability distribution function for the annual return on the market portfolio (long term), as expected by all investors:

R_m	1%	4%	8%	12%	16%	19%
Probability	0.05	0.15	0.30	0.30	0.15	0.05

The risk-free annual interest rate expected by all investors (long term) is 4%, and only one kind of perpetual bond is available.

In the past, you invested $1,000 in a share whose variance is double that of the market portfolio. As of yesterday, the share yields a net cash flow of $2, and its financial results are expected to increase by 7% each year. The share is traded at $23.80. You have an additional $1,000 in cash that you want to invest, and you want to invest only your own money, without taking a loan.

a. Should you invest your other $1,000 in the same asset?

b. In contrast to the other investors, you expect that the central bank will lower the risk-free interest rate to 3% in the near future, and that it will remain at that level for years to come. Assume that this will happen immediately after you make your investment decision. Assuming that this change will not affect the probability distribution function for the market portfolio or the results of the company whose shares you buy, how should you invest, and what is the gain that you expect to earn on your investment (assume that the market will quickly stabilize at the new equilibrium point)?

This question demonstrates how personal expectations concerning interest rates (assuming that they indeed materialize) lead to investment decisions according to the models discussed so far (the share valuation or cash flow model and the mean-variance model). An integrated model for including personal expectations is discussed in the following chapters.

Note on personal expectations:

1. Personal expectations do not guarantee that the "scenario" that guided your decision will indeed materialize!

2. Personal expectations always include "undeclared" assumptions (e.g., that the interest rate reduction will not affect the company's results!).

Further Reading

Aharony, J., and M. Loeb 1977. Mean-Variance vs. Stochastic Dominance: Some Empirical Findings on Efficient Sets. *Journal of Banking and Finance* (June).

Baron, D. P. 1977. On the Utility Theoretic Foundations of Mean-Variance Analysis. *Journal of Finance* (December).

Brown, L., and M. Rozeff. 1978. The Superiority of Analyst Forecasts as Measures of Expectations: Evidence from Earnings. *Journal of Finance* (March): 1–16.

Dybvig, H., and J. E. Ingersoll, Jr. 1982. Mean-Variance Theory in Complete Markets. *Journal of Business* (April).

Elton, E. J., M. J. Gruber, S. J. Brown, and W. N. Goetzmann. 2004. *Modern Portfolio Theory and Investment Analysis.* 6th ed. New York: Wiley.

Kroll, Y., H. Levy, and H. M. Markowitz. 1984. Mean-Variance versus Direct Utility Maximization. *Journal of Finance* 39 (1): 47–61.

Kryzanowski, L., and C. T. Minh. 1987. The E-V Stationarity of Security Returns: Some Empirical Evidence. *Journal of Banking and Finance* (March).

Levy, H. 1973. Stochastic Dominance among Log-Normal Prospects. *International Economic Review* (October).

Levy, H. 1989. Two-Moment Decision Models and Expected Utility Maximization. *American Economic Review*.

Levy, H., and H. M. Markowitz. 1979. Approximating Expected Utility by a Function of Mean and Variance. *American Economic Review* 69 (3): 308–317.

Markowitz, H. M. 1952. Portfolio Selection. *The Journal of Finance* 7 (1): 77–91.

Markowitz, H. M. 1959. *Portfolio Selection: Efficient Diversification of Investments.* New York: John Wiley & Sons. Reprinted by Yale University Press, 1970.

Markowitz, H. M. 1987. *Mean-Variance Analysis in Portfolio Choice and Capital Markets.* Oxford, UK: Blackwell.

Merton, R. 1972. An Analytic Derivation of the Efficient Set. *Journal of Financial and Quantitative Analysis* (September): 1851–1872.

Meyer, J. 1979. Mean-Variance Efficient Sets and Expected Utility. *Journal of Finance* (December).

Michaud, R. 1989. The Markowitz Optimization Enigma: Is Optimized Optimal? *Financial Analysts Journal*: 45.

Modigliani, F., and G. A. Pogue. 1974. An Introduction to Risk and Return: Concepts and Evidence. *Financial Analysts Journal* (March/April): 68–80; (May/June): 69–85.

Reichenstein, W. 1987. On Standard Deviation and Risk. *Journal of Portfolio Management* (Winter).

Sharpe, William F. 1964. Capital Asset Prices—A Theory of Market Equilibrium Under Conditions of Risk. *Journal of Finance* XIX (3): 425–442.

Simkowitz, M. A., and W. L. Beedles. 1978. Diversification in a Three-moment World. *Journal of Financial and Quantitative Analysis* (December).

Tehranian, H. 1980. Empirical Studies in Portfolio Performance Using Higher Degrees of Stochastic Dominance. *Journal of Finance* (March).

Treynor, J. L. 1962. Toward a Theory of Market Value of Risky Assets, unpublished manuscript. A final version was published in 1999, in *Asset Pricing and Portfolio Performance: Models, Strategy and Performance Metrics*, ed. R. A. Korajczyk, 15–22. London: Risk Books.

Wagner, W. H., and S. C. Lau. 1971. The Effect of Diversification on Risk. *Financial Analysts Journal* 27 (November/December): 48–53.

13 The Capital Asset Pricing Model

A. Observation—Beta as a Measure of Risk

B. Building a CAPM Portfolio

C. Comparing the Mean-Variance Model and the CAPM

D. Portfolio Management—Performance Appraisals

E. Empirical Testing

F. Expanding the Market Model

A. Observation—Beta as a Measure of Risk

In the professional literature, the capital asset pricing model (CAPM) is also referred to as the *market model*. It is essentially a descriptive model, which means it first observes market behavior and then develops a theory or correlating formula that describes the observed phenomena.

As previously mentioned, the functional relation we are looking for is

$$k = f(r_f; \ Risk).$$

Markowitz began by defining σ as the measure of risk for a single financial asset, and only then developed his model for choosing an optimal investment portfolio.[1]

In the market model, we begin by observing investment portfolios and then derive a risk measure for a single financial asset. The CAPM risk measure is not the same as that used by Markowitz in his model.

Long before Sharpe and Treynor developed the market model in the early 1960s, it was common knowledge that investors should not put all

---

1. In principle, it does not matter whether we follow Markowitz and define risk as return variance (σ^2) or as the standard deviation of returns (σ).

their money into one financial asset. Investors would hold investment portfolios with several financial assets so as to mitigate risk (which we have yet to define).

The question was:

How many assets are required to build a well-diversified portfolio offering maximum risk mitigation?

Statistical analysis of historical data yields the graph shown in figure 13.1, which describes the connection between the number of assets comprising a portfolio (on the x-axis) and the standard deviation for the portfolio's return (on the y-axis). If we increase the number of assets in the portfolio from 1 to 10, 20, and so on, the standard deviation for the portfolio's returns (its variance) will decrease significantly. If we continue to add more assets, the change in the standard deviation (variance) will decrease further, and after a certain number of assets the incremental change caused by adding another asset to the portfolio will be negligible. The minimum number of financial assets (e.g., shares) required for a well-diversified portfolio is in the range of 25–30 shares.

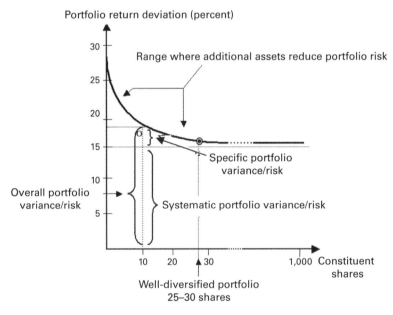

Figure 13.1
Portfolio's Standard Deviation from Average Return as a Function of the Total Number of Constructing Assets

Investors holding portfolios of assets intended to mitigate portfolio return variation consider two types of risk:

Systematic risk (or market risk)   The risk caused by market changes. Each asset or share is correlated to the market, so that if the market return increases or decreases, the portfolio return increases or decreases accordingly. In figure 13.1, we see that no matter how much we increase the number of assets, the annual standard deviation for the portfolio return will not fall below 15%.[2]

Specific risk   The random change in an asset's return, which is independent of market changes. As the specific change in portfolio asset returns is random and independent, if a portfolio includes enough assets, their specific changes will (statistically) cancel each other out.

This directly leads us to conclude the following:

In an efficient mix of enough assets, a portfolio's variance is due entirely to market changes.

The indirect conclusion from this observation is that a risk premium should be paid only for the risk caused by market fluctuations—systematic risk. No risk premium should be charged for specific risk, as it can be avoided "free of charge" through diversification.

As a benchmark for fluctuations in the overall market return, we define the market portfolio M as the portfolio that includes all "risky" financial assets on the market. Each asset's weight in the market portfolio is thus equal to the total value of that asset relative to the total value of all assets in the market portfolio.[3]

We can now measure the return premium, which is the return exceeding the return on a risk-free asset required for incurring the risk in asset i, that is, $R_i - R_f$. We can then compare changes in the return premium with changes in the premium required on the market portfolio M, which likewise exceeds the return on a risk-free asset, that is, $R_m - R_f$. The correlation between the premium required on asset i and that required on market portfolio M can be measured by means of regression and by calculating the regression line slope β.

2. Variance for the annualized stock market return, measured over 20 years by calculating the average monthly return and its standard deviation.

3. Total asset value = share price multiplied by the number of shares (also called a company's market cap).

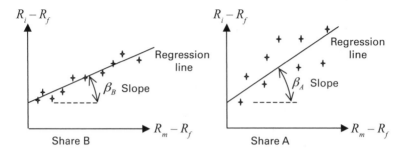

Figure 13.2
Individual Shares' Risk Premium Regression with the Market Portfolio

Example: Assume asset A and asset B, with risk premiums as shown in figure 13.2:

The correlation between the risk premium required for asset i and the risk premium for market portfolio M can be formulated as follows:

$$R_i - R_f = \alpha + \beta_i \cdot (R_m - R_f) + \varepsilon_i$$

with β serving as a measure for asset i's systematic risk and ε_i the error term between the measured risk premium and the regression line.

The larger the β (slope), the more risky the asset, as changes in the overall market return cause greater fluctuations in the return on asset i.

In figure 13.2, slope β_A is greater than slope β_B.

$\beta_A = 1.25$ means that the return premium on asset A changes 1.25 as much as the return premium on the market portfolio M.

$\beta_B = 0.8$ means that the return premium on asset B changes by only 0.8 of the change in the return premium on the market portfolio M.

Note that the random results for asset B are closer to the regression line than those for asset A. This means that asset B's correlation coefficient R^2 is closer to 1 than is asset A's correlation coefficient. This proximity to the regression line is due to various asset-specific reasons that are unrelated to the market.

Remember that this part of the change in returns, which is unrelated to the market, can be canceled out by mixing enough assets in the portfolio. As a risk measure, we need only know that the slope describes the change in the asset's return relative to that of the market portfolio. At this point, we are not interested in the distribution around the line.

If we were to build a portfolio comprised of the above two shares in equal parts (i.e., $w_i = 0.5$ for each share), then to calculate the portfolio's historical return we would have to multiply the return increment exceeding that for a risk-free asset ($R_i - R_f$) for each asset at each point by 1/2,

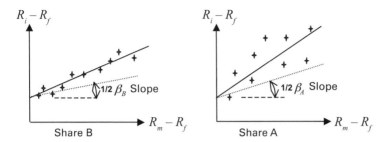

Figure 13.3
Getting 1/2 of Each Share's Risk Premium

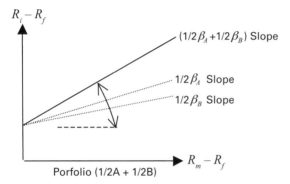

Figure 13.4
Calculating the Weighted Sum of the Two Assets' Slopes

and then add these numbers. Thus, each asset would have a line whose slope equaled one-half of the original slope (figure 13.3).

To calculate the regression line of a portfolio comprised 0.5:0.5 of assets A and B, we must add every point on these new lines. The slope for the portfolio regression line is the weighted sum of the two assets' slopes (figure 13.4):

$$\beta_p = 1/2\beta_A + 1/2\beta_B.$$

In general, if we build a portfolio with n assets, each with a weight of w_i, the return on this portfolio will be equal to the weighted sum of the returns of each of the assets, and the portfolio's risk (measured in terms of β) will be equal to the weighted sum of the risks of each of the assets:[4]

4. Each asset has an expected flow of future net cash flow with a constant and known probability distribution and a constant and known market correlation. For this cash flow, we can calculate its mean return R_i (=mean net cash flow divided by asset price) and its risk factor, β_i.

$$\bar{R}_p = \sum w_i \, \bar{R}_i.$$
$$\beta_p = \sum w_i \beta_i.$$

Thus, whether dealing with a single asset or an asset portfolio, the risk premium (in excess of the risk-free interest rate) required for asset/portfolio i is

$$R_i - R_f = \beta_i \cdot (R_m - R_f).$$

Rearranging the terms in this equation yields the equation for the market-required returns on any given financial asset, known as the *securities market line*:[5]

$$R_i = R_f + \beta_i \cdot (R_m - R_f).$$

B.   Building a CAPM Portfolio

Another study of financial assets found that returns are distributed approximately normally.[6]

An example of the normal distribution of a share's monthly returns is shown in figure 13.5.

In CAPM, Sharpe and Treynor assume a perfect market.[7] Investors build a portfolio with n assets, where the return on each asset has a regular normal distribution (figure 13.6).

• Denote the mean return on each asset i by $E[R_i]$, and the standard deviation of that return by σ_i.

• Denote asset i's relative weight in the portfolio (the asset value divided by the total portfolio value) by w_i.

• Denote the covariance for each asset i with each other asset j by σ_{ij}:

$$E(R_p) = \sum_{i=1}^{N} w_i \cdot E[R_i].$$

$$\sigma_p^2 = \sum_{i=1}^{N} \sum_{j=1}^{N} w_i w_j \sigma_{ij}.$$

5. The resulting equation links the return R_i with the risk measure β_i by a straight-line function, as R_f and R_m are constants.

6. Observations show that daily returns have a "log-normal" distribution. Only monthly or longer returns are distributed approximately normally.

7. Concerning perfect market assumptions, see chapter 4.

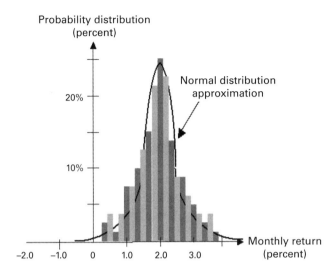

Figure 13.5
Estimating a Normal Distribution to a Share's Monthly Returns

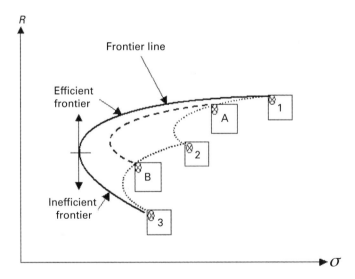

Figure 13.6
Constructing Efficient Portfolios from *n* Assets in a Perfect Market

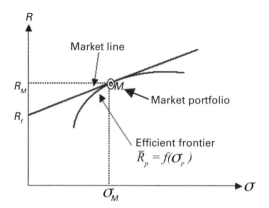

Figure 13.7
Constructing the Securities Market Line

Now let's add a risk-free asset to the market and find the securities market line (using the same criteria as in the previous chapter) (figure 13.7).

On one hand, the securities market line's slope is $\dfrac{R_m - R_f}{\sigma_m}$.

On the other hand, at the securities market line's intersection with the efficient frontier, the securities market line's slope is identical to the first derivative $dR/d\sigma$ of the efficient frontier function $\bar{R}_p = f(\sigma_p)$. To calculate the efficient frontier's slope at point M, we will use portfolio I, which is located very close to the market portfolio and is on the efficient frontier. The geometric location of all the portfolios combining portfolio I with market portfolio M is the efficient frontier connecting the two.

From the general equation for a portfolio P comprised of two assets, I and M, with a weight of a and $b = (1 - a)$, respectively:

$$\bar{R}_p = a\bar{R}_i - (1-a)\bar{R}_m.$$
$$\sigma_p = [a^2\sigma_i^2 + (1-a)^2\sigma_m^2 + 2a(1-a)\sigma_{im}]^{1/2}.$$

When $a = 0$, the portfolio is comprised 100% of the market portfolio M and 0% of portfolio I. Therefore, if we want to find the slope at point M, we can first build portfolio P and calculate the boundary value where $a \to 0$.

Instead of calculating the derivative $\dfrac{dR_p}{d\sigma_p}$ at point M directly (which is hard to do), we can find it indirectly by calculating the partial derivatives for R_p and σ_p[8] (in the above equations) as a function of a, and then divide them by each other:

$$\left. \frac{\partial R_p}{\partial a} \right|_{a \to 0} = R_i - R_m.$$

$$\left. \frac{\partial \sigma_p}{\partial a} \right|_{a \to 0} = \frac{\sigma_{im} - \sigma_m^2}{\sigma_m}.$$

Thus:

$$\frac{dR_p}{d\sigma_p} = \left. \frac{\frac{\partial R_p}{\partial a}}{\frac{\partial \sigma_p}{\partial a}} \right|_{a \to 0} = \frac{R_i - R_m}{(\sigma_{im} - \sigma_m^2)/\sigma_m}.$$

These two expressions for the securities market line slope must be equal:

$$\frac{R_m - R_f}{\sigma_m} = \frac{R_i - R_m}{(\sigma_{im} - \sigma_m^2)/\sigma_m}.$$

Let's rearrange the equation:

$$R_i = R_f + \frac{\sigma_{im}}{\sigma_m^2}(R_m - R_f).$$

If we compare our previous result, $R_i = R_f + \beta_i(R_m - R_f)$, with our present one, $R_i = R_f + \frac{\sigma_{im}}{\sigma_m^2}(R_m - R_f)$, we can immediately conclude that $\beta_i = \frac{\sigma_{im}}{\sigma_m^2}$.

On the securities market line, assume any portfolio P comprised of a risk-free asset R_f with weight a and a market portfolio M with a weight b, where $b = (1 - a)$.

We can write the equation $\quad R_P = R_f + \beta_P(R_m - R_f)$ as

$$R_P = (1 - \beta_P) \cdot R_f + \beta_P \cdot R_m.$$

However, we also know that $\quad R_P = (1 - b) \cdot R_f + b \cdot R_m.$[9]

And therefore, $\qquad\qquad\qquad b = \beta_P.$[10]

---

8. These partial derivatives are $\frac{\partial \sigma_P}{\partial a} = [a^2\sigma_i^2 + (1-a)^2\sigma_m^2 + 2a(1-a)\sigma_{im}]^{-1/2} \cdot [2a\sigma_i^2 - 2\sigma_m^2 + 2a\sigma_m^2 + 2\sigma_{im} - 4a\sigma_{im}]$.

9. As was demonstrated in the previous chapter for assets with a correlation coefficient $\rho = 0$.

10. Note that b is the portion (weight) of the risky asset M (the market portfolio) in portfolio P that we are constructing.

If we calculate the variance for this portfolio, we get:

$$\sigma_p^2 = b^2\sigma_m^2 + (1-b)^2\sigma_{R_f}^2 + 2b(1-b)\rho\sigma_m\sigma_{R_f}.$$

As $\sigma_{R_f} = 0$, $b = \beta_P$, and the correlation between the market portfolio and the risk-free asset is $\rho = 0$, then for market line portfolios we find that $\sigma_p = \beta_p\sigma_m$. In other words, the portfolio's variance is derived only from the market portfolio variance, which is systematic variance.

Our above calculations lead to the following conclusions:

1. Securities market line portfolios have only systematic variance (as predicted).

2. By determining the weight b of the market portfolio in our portfolio, we effectively determine our portfolio's risk β.

3. By determining β, we determine our risk preference.

The graphic representation of return as a function of a portfolio's variance σ is shown in figure 13.7.

To obtain a graphic representation of the return as a function of the portfolio's risk indicator β (and not σ, as plotted so far), we divide the x-axis scale in figure 13.7 by σ_M, which is a constant, and therefore division causes only a linear change in the x-axis.[11]

At the securities market line's tangency with the efficient frontier (the market portfolio), we get $\beta_M = \dfrac{\sigma_M}{\sigma_M} = 1$.

Let's add two investors, John and Jack, to the picture (which does not change but only "shrinks" on the x-axis—see figure 13.8). John and Jack will each choose their risk level and mean return according to their individual utility function.[12]

The CAPM model describes the correlation we looked for between return and risk measured in terms of β (i.e., systematic risk), as shown in figure 13.8.

11. Ultimately, we have defined a basic "standard risk unit" σ_M, the market return standard deviation, similarly to defining "centimeter" or "inch" as a standard unit for measuring length. In the same way that we count the desired quantity of standard length units needed to measure a specific distance, we measure a specific asset's risk by choosing a quantity (multiplier) β of standard risk units σ_M.

12. Their individual utility function ranks their risk-reward preference, where risk is measured in terms of β.

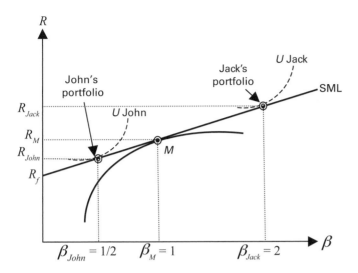

Figure 13.8
Choosing a Personal Portfolio When Risk Is Measured in Terms of β (Systematic Risk)

C. Comparing the Mean-Variance Model and the CAPM

The two ways of defining risk, Markowitz's σ and Sharpe and Treynor's β, are materially different, even though their results seem identical. In the mean-variance model, we *assumed* investors choose an individual risky asset (and consequently choose portfolios) based on only two parameters: mean return and the standard deviation of that return, which is defined as the risk measure. In the market model, we *observed* how asset returns have an approximately normal distribution, and therefore investors choose portfolios (and therefore individual assets) based on their mean returns and their systematic variance β[13] (i.e., the portfolio's covariation with the market), which is defined as the risk measure (see figure 13.9 and figure 13.10).

It is no coincidence that the results yielded by these two models are similar. In both models, we chose efficient portfolios, and therefore both models led us to choose the same portfolio derived from the securities market line and the investor's utility function.

To prove that exactly the same portfolio is chosen under both models, let's return to our results obtained using each model.

---

13. The systematic variance is $\beta \times \sigma_M$.

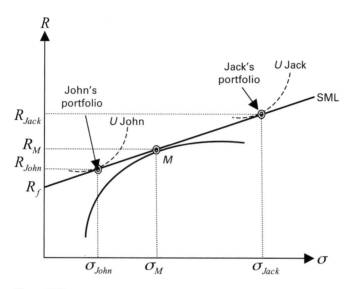

Figure 13.9
Mean-Variance Model

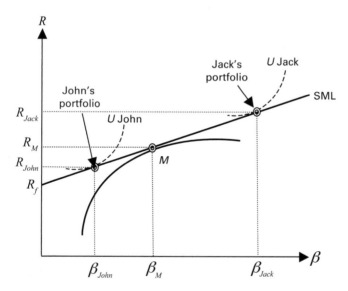

Figure 13.10
Capital Asset Pricing Model

In the mean-variance model, the securities market line equation was

$$R_i = R_f + \frac{\sigma_i}{\sigma_m}(R_m - R_f),$$

while the market model yielded the securities market line equation

$$R_i = R_f + \frac{\sigma_{im}}{\sigma_m^2}(R_m - R_f) = R_f + \beta_i(R_m - R_f).$$

We stated that, under the market model, portfolios on the market line retain the relationship[14] $\sigma_i = \beta_i \sigma_m$, and therefore if we factor β_i out of the last equation and substitute it into the market model, we end up with exactly the same linear equation as in the mean-variance model.

Both models are remarkable for being the first to propose a measurable mathematical definition for risk. They differ, however, in the way they define their risk measure:

In Markowitz's model, risk is defined as the mean dispersal (scatter) of the expected future returns around a financial asset's mean (average) return, measured by the return's standard deviation σ.

In the market model (CAPM), risk is defined as the systematic change of a financial asset's expected future mean return as a result of variation in the expected mean return of the whole market, and is measured by the regression coefficient β.

Ultimately, both models lead investors to the same investment. Practically, in everyday use, the CAPM seems more convenient, as its β measure factor is linear. According to the CAPM, if an investor holds more than one asset, the risk measure β for his portfolio equals the weighted average of the β measures for all portfolio assets. On the other hand, σ is nonlinear. Therefore, the portfolio's risk measure σ_P is not a weighted average of the portfolio assets' σ values, as the portfolio assets' covariances (σ_{ij}) also affect overall portfolio variance (standard deviation). However, we must remember that when holding inefficient portfolios (as is usually the case), we must account for all variance under Markowitz's mean-variance model!

---

14. As discussed in the previous chapter, this correlation means that a portfolio's variance is comprised solely of systematic variance. Remember, the correlation exists only for efficient portfolios located on the securities market line, and does not hold for individual financial assets or portfolios not on the securities market line.

D.   Portfolio Management—Performance Appraisals

Nonprofessional investors do not have the time to thoroughly examine companies in which they are considering investing. Constructing a well-diversified, efficient portfolio with 25–30 assets is no easy task either. Ordinary investors place their money in the hands of professional portfolio managers or invest in mutual funds. Our previous discussions lead us to conclude that it would not be correct to measure a portfolio manager's performance solely by returns, as different portfolios carry different risk.

This raises the question, how can we compare the performance of portfolios with different risk profiles?

First, we should discuss the practical application of risk factor β and its limitations.

The following table is an excerpt from a Merrill Lynch β sheet:

		09/86 CLOSE				RESID STD	STD. ERR			NUMBER
TKR SYMB	SECURITY NAME	PRICE	BETA	ALPHA	R-SQR	DEV-N	OF BETA	OF ALPHA	ADJUSTED BETA	OF OBSERV
DTE1	DETROIT EDISON CO PFD CONV	93.250	.40	.56	.09	4.96	.15	.67	.60	60
DVP	DEVELOPMENT CORP AMER	12.125	1.50	-.56	.30	9.54	.29	1.28	1.33	60
DIN	DEVON RESOURCE INVS DEPOSITA	5.875	.86	-4.68	.04	12.42	.68	3.48	.90	14
DVRY	DEVRY INC	9.500	.62	-.79	.08	7.92	.33	1.43	.75	33
DLCF	DEVELCON ELECTRS LTD	3.438	.21	-4.36	.03	16.28	.69	3.11	.48	30
DWY	DEWEY ELECTRS CORP	3.750	.91	2.29	.02	19.54	.60	2.63	.94	60
DXON	DEXON INC	1.000	2.99	-.98	.12	31.64	.98	4.26	2.32	60
DEX	DEXTER CORP	29.750	.98	.01	.23	7.35	.23	.99	.99	60
DIA9	DI AN CTLS INC	1.313	.28	-.02	.01	18.11	.56	2.44	.52	60
DIG	DI GIORGIO CORP	24.375	.93	.64	.27	6.32	.19	.85	.95	60
DIGN	DIAGNON CORP	1.688	.25	-1.23	.03	20.82	.88	3.49	.50	38
DINO	DIAGNOSTIC INC	7.250	.88	7.28	.01	36.76	1.13	4.95	.92	60
DPC2	DIAGNOSTIC PRUDS CORP	23.000	1.69	.37	.31	10.35	.38	1.55	1.46	51
DRS1	DIAGNOSTIC RETRIEVAL	7.500	1.08	.40	.09	13.10	.40	1.76	1.05	60
DBH	DIAMOND BATHURST INC	16.000	2.07	1.28	.27	13.43	.55	2.28	1.71	37
DMD	DIAMOND CRYSTAL SALT CO	32.500	.37	1.76	.03	7.14	.22	.96	.58	60
DIA	DIAMOND SHAMROCK CORP	10.875	.90	-2.24	.23	6.82	.21	.92	.94	60
SLF	DIANA CORP	11.000	.56	1.48	.04	10.11	.31	1.36	.71	60
DNIC	DIASONICS INC	3.375	1.55	-4.67	.12	15.80	.61	2.50	1.36	43
DXTK	DIAGNOSTEK INC	2.063	1.27	1.67	.00	29.88	1.27	5.82	1.18	29
DBRL	DIBRELL BROS INC	25.000	.95	1.77	.16	8.77	.27	1.18	.96	60
DICN	DICEON ELECTRS INC	19.750	1.12	.13	.13	11.29	.46	2.00	1.08	34
DKJN	DICKEY-JOHN CORP	11.500	.70	-.69	.07	9.87	.35	1.33	.80	60
DCOM	DICOMED CORP	2.250	2.11	-3.22	.31	12.95	.40	1.74	1.74	60
DBD	DIEBOLD INC	39.500	.72	.24	.10	6.51	.26	1.15	.82	60
DIGI	DIGICON INC	.500	1.19	-6.22	.11	13.78	.43	1.94	1.13	60
DILD	DIGILOG INC	6.000	1.11	-.39	.06	16.44	.51	2.21	1.07	60
DEC	DIGITAL EQUIP CORP	89.875	1.21	.21	.23	8.97	.22	1.21	1.14	60
DGPD	DIGITAL PRODS CORP	2.313	.98	-1.88	.02	21.11	.62	2.64	.99	60
DGTD	DIGITECH INC	3.628	.86	6.73	.07	15.76	.49	8.00	2.78	35

$R_m =$ BASED ON S&P 500 INDEX, USING STRAIGHT REGRESSION   PAGE 46

MLPF&S, INC. --- MARKET SENSITIVITY STATISTICS

This table illustrates just how useful these metrics are. A regression is usually made between a share's returns and a portfolio's returns over a five-year period (60 monthly observations). The x-axis in figure 13.11 shows monthly measurements for the market portfolio return, as

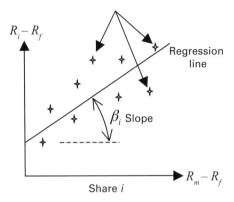

Figure 13.11
Five-Year (60-Observation) Period Data

provided by the S&P 500.[15] The *y*-axis shows the monthly return for a particular share.

The points on this plane indicate a share's monthly return relative to the return recorded that month for the market portfolio, and are used to find a linear regression. If during the five-year observation period a new company enters the market, there will be fewer than 60 observations for that company.

We can choose any historical five-year period and view a different data set and regression line. Of course, the β risk factor derived from one series of five-year observations is different from the β risk factor derived from another group of observations. Therefore, β is not a constant value. β, and its variance, can be measured, as indicated in the two columns connected by a dashed arrow in the Merrill Lynch table. As the table shows, some shares have relatively stable β values, while others have unstable β's. For example, the security DVP (second row, marked with an arrow) has a β of 1.5 and a β variance of 0.29, while the security DLCF (fifth row, marked with an arrow) has a β of 0.2 and a β variance of 0.69.

Note that only a small part of a share's overall variance is explained by changes in the market portfolio (the correlation is indicated by the R^2 values in the dotted rectangle).

---

15. Standard & Poor's daily index (S&P 500), comprised of the 500 leading companies in the U.S. economy, captures about 75% coverage of U.S. equities' value. The return on this portfolio is an excellent approximation of overall equity market return.

If we examine the linear regression function for a share's return against the market portfolio return, $\tilde{R}_i = \alpha_i + \beta_i \tilde{R}_m + \varepsilon_i$, we see that there are three parts to the equation:

α_i—Constant, and therefore has zero variance.

$\beta_i \tilde{R}_m$—Indicates change relative the market portfolio, and therefore indicates systematic variance.

ε_i—The average deviation of data around the regression line, which indicates the asset's specific variance.

Overall variance (denoted by T) is therefore comprised of systematic variance (denoted by s) and specific variance (denoted by ε), as expected:

$$\sigma_T^2 = \beta_i^2 \sigma_m^2 + \sigma_\varepsilon^2 = \sigma_s^2 + \sigma_\varepsilon^2 .$$

The variance values in the dotted rectangle in the above β table indicate specific variance, σ_ε^2. As we can see, some shares have a greater β but a smaller specific variance.

We can now discuss the differences between various ways proposed to compare portfolio performance:

· **Jensen index**

The Jensen index is based on comparing a portfolio's performance (premium) above the risk-free interest rate with that of the market portfolio, using the regression formula $\tilde{R}_i - R_f = \alpha_i + \beta_i (\tilde{R}_m - R_f) + \varepsilon_i$. Assuming an efficient portfolio at market equilibrium, then $\alpha_i = 0$.

If $\alpha_i > 0$, then the portfolio performed above the expected mean return at equilibrium. If $\alpha_i < 0$, then the portfolio performed below the expected mean return at equilibrium.

The higher α_i, the better a portfolio's performance. The problem with this index is that it attributes to α_i equal importance at different risk levels. Thus, two portfolios with a different risk level but the same α_i will be ranked equally.

· **Treynor index**

The Treynor model expands on Jensen's model[16] and accounts for the deviation from equilibrium relative to systematic risk by dividing both sides of the regression formula by β:

16. Though Jensen's model came after Treynor's.

$$\frac{\tilde{R}_i - R_f}{\beta_i} = \frac{\alpha_i}{\beta_i} + (\tilde{R}_m - R_f) + \varepsilon_i^{normalized}.$$

The left-hand side of the equation yields the return per unit of risk β. On the right-hand side, $\dfrac{\alpha_i}{\beta_i}$ assigns linear power per unit of systematic risk. Therefore, a manager of a portfolio with double the β of another portfolio manager must achieve double the premium (in excess of the equilibrium return) in order to be ranked equally.

· **Sharpe index**

Like the Treynor index, the Sharpe index normalizes the Jensen index per risk unit. The difference is that the Sharpe index, a ratio, measures deviation from equilibrium relative to the risk measured by the standard deviation.

Substituting $\beta_i = \dfrac{\sigma_{im}}{\sigma_m^2} = \dfrac{\rho\sigma_i\sigma_M}{\sigma_M^2} = \dfrac{\rho\sigma_i}{\sigma_M}$ into the above regression formula yields

$$\frac{\tilde{R}_i - R_f}{\sigma_i} = \frac{\alpha_i}{\sigma_i} + \frac{\rho(\tilde{R}_m - R_f)}{\sigma_m} + \varepsilon_i^{normalized}.$$

Here, too, the left-hand side of the equation describes the premium on returns per risk unit, although this time the risk-measuring unit is σ.

On the right-hand side, $\dfrac{\alpha_i}{\sigma_i}$ attributes linear power to each risk unit, including σ. Thus, the manager of a portfolio with double the σ (standard deviation) of another portfolio manager must achieve double the premium (in excess of the equilibrium return) to be ranked at the same level.

· **Treynor and Mazuy index**

In addition to providing us with a well-diversified portfolio, we expect portfolio managers to leverage their expertise in predicting market behavior and to change portfolio composition proactively. This is in contrast to nonmanaged portfolios, which keep to a constant structure (at a constant risk level). Savvy portfolio managers will build a high β portfolio if they expect the market to go up and a low β portfolio if they expect it to go down (see figure 13.12).

Retrospectively, we need only check whether a portfolio manager demonstrated the necessary skill. If we were to carry out a linear regression of a managed portfolio's returns on the market portfolio return, we would expect to see considerable second-order elements. Of course, we

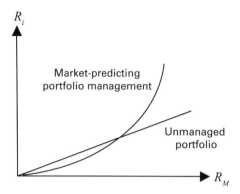

Figure 13.12
Predicting Market Behavior

should also check the direction of these quadratic elements (positive or negative), as otherwise we might find ourselves putting our trust and our money into the hands of a manager whose predictions are exactly opposite to market behavior!

E. Empirical Testing

After acquiring such a convenient model, we should see just how well it describes real-world conditions. Numerous studies have been conducted on this subject, and this book does not provide an exhaustive review of these works or their results or conclusions. Instead, we will discuss a few issues, some of which are econometric in nature, while others are more philosophical and pertain to the theoretical extension of the model.[17]

Let's start with the philosophical issues. Our model (or actually two models) is a prospective model pertaining to start-of-period expectations, while results are measured retrospectively at the end of the period. To better understand the problem, let's look at two securities market lines, retrospective and prospective, as shown in figure 13.13.

The line on the right is an "ordinary" increasing securities market line, while the line on the left seems unreasonable, as the return on the market portfolio should be higher than that for the risk-free asset. In other words, *the risk premium must be positive, while the figure on the right shows a decreasing market line.*

17. Econometrics is the field in statistics that deals with statistical inference methods based on observations.

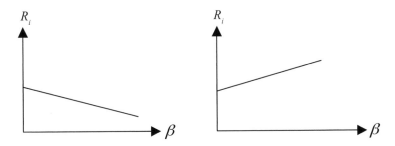

Figure 13.13
Retrospective and Prospective Securities Market Line

The answer lies with the words *prospective* and *retrospective*. When investors are required to choose portfolios prospectively, according to our model, their expectations must reflect the graph on the right. Otherwise, no reasonable investor would invest in the market portfolio. However, by definition, the word "risk" means that it is possible that at the end of the period, that is, retrospectively, investors may find that the return on the market portfolio does not meet expectations. It may be lower than the return on the risk-free asset or even negative. Historical data show that in 2000, the S&P 500 index went down by about 10%, and in 2001 it fell by about 13%. If we were to look at the period 2007–2008, we would find even more significant drops. How, then, can we judge a prospective model using retrospective results?

Although this is a very interesting question, it exceeds the scope of this book, which deals with fundamental models, and so will not be answered here. Suffice it to say at this point that there is an answer to this question.

Another problem arises from the fact that the model is a single-period model, while real-world conditions are certainly not single-period in nature. The model assumes that all investors have a uniform investment range and make uniform assumptions concerning the mean return and variance of all market assets. At the start of each period, each investor chooses which portion of his funds to invest in the market portfolio and which in the risk-free asset, according to his own utility function. Of course, actual human behavior is much more complex and diverse. The model can be expanded into a multiperiod model, given certain assumptions, but again, this is outside the scope of this book. However, these assumptions themselves prove problematic when we want to test the model's validity as an approximation of real-world conditions. Here, too,

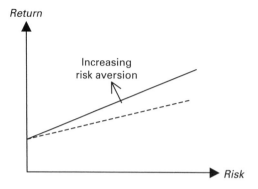

Figure 13.14
Change in SML When Investors' Risk Aversion Increases

readers will be happy to know that advanced courses do offer solutions to these problems.

A third and final philosophical question (though there are certainly many more) concerns changes in investors' risk aversion. These changes can be explained by events such as the September 11, 2001, attacks or a prolonged bear market (as in 2007–2008). Clearly, if investors were risk neutral, we could expect the securities market line to be horizontal. The greater investors' risk aversion, the greater the premium we would expect per additional risk unit. In other words, the securities market line's slope should increase (figure 13.14).

The following seems to conflict with the logic used to develop the model. Continuing the above line of thought, expectations concerning return on assets and concerning the risk-free interest rate are universal. Investors first "calculate" the securities market line and only then choose the ratio between the market portfolio and the risk-free asset according to their utility function. If this is the case, then investors' utility functions should not affect the possibility set, and consequently the securities market line should not change.

This can be solved by a dynamic, not static, explanation:[18] assume that when moving from one period to the next, investors change their utility functions so as to be more risk averse. Each investor's utility function moves to the left, so that he or she willing to incur a smaller risk than before for a given return. Accordingly, each investor would want to change his or her position so as to give the risk-free asset more weight

18. See also the discussion in chapter 15.

in his portfolio while decreasing the market portfolio's weight. If all investors want to reduce their investment in the market portfolio, that is, sell part of the market portfolio, then share prices will go down.

Assuming that the companies' financial results remain the same (their financial results depend on their operations and not on their share prices), then, if share prices at the start of the period go down, and expected profit at the end of the period remains the same, the expected return on these assets (as seen by investors) goes up. The efficient set of portfolios on the market will move upward relative to the previous period. Assuming that the return on the risk-free asset remains constant, the securities market line slope will indeed increase.

Changes in the utility function, and even the aggregate utility function's movement, are not currently measurable. However, changes in the market portfolio caused by changes in the utility function are measurable. As our model requires a utility function in order to determine the securities market line, then as a first-order approximation we can disregard the "source" of the market portfolio's movement (i.e., a change in the utility function, and not changes in financial results) and assume that the utility function remains unchanged between periods.

There are also technical problems with data measurement caused by the model's assumptions or econometric measurement problems. First, there is the fact that the joint distribution of daily returns on financial assets is not normal. Actual data more closely follow a log-normal distribution. We can demonstrate that the model remains valid even assuming a log-normal joint distribution. Another example of underlying assumptions not coinciding with actual phenomena concerns the no-tax assumption. This assumption is false, but it can be rectified relatively easily, as will be demonstrated in the following chapters.

Another fundamental econometric problem is assessing the risk-free asset as a result of inflationary changes over time. Fortunately, inflation will also affect returns by a proportionate amount, so that inflation causes an approximately parallel movement in the securities market line (figure 13.15).[19]

Inflation should also cause utility functions to move upward and to the left. However, even if their movement parallels that of the securities market line, this may change investors' risk preference and their relative holdings in the market portfolio. In this case, the solution is simple: use

19. As a first-order approximation, we add inflation to the interest rate, while it would be more accurate to calculate it as a product: $(1 + R_f)(1 + I_{nf}) - 1$.

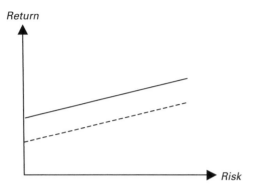

Figure 13.15
Change in SML When Inflation Increases

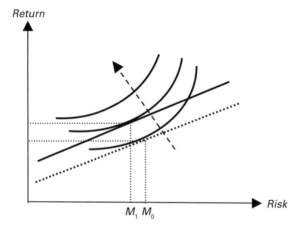

Figure 13.16
Changes in the Market Portfolio Return and Risk When Inflation Increases

the real interest rate, so that no movement should occur in the securities market line (at least theoretically) (figure 13.16).

Equally important is the question concerning the stability of β over time. In other words, is the change in asset returns relative to the market portfolio constant over time? The market portfolio's composition as measured, for example, by the S&P 500 index changes over time, with shares entering and leaving the index. Enron and WorldCom are two examples from the start of the millennium. These two companies were ranked at the top of the S&P 500 index but subsequently collapsed and were removed from the list of the 500 largest companies.

As mentioned, these are no trivial matters, both philosophically and technically. Studies that try to account for all intermediate factors conclude that risk as measured by β does indeed have a linear correlation with a financial asset's return. The main problem indicated by these studies is that this dependence does not statistically explain the majority of changes: R^2 is smaller than expected or, alternatively, specific variance (not explained by changes in the market portfolio) is larger than expected.

In conclusion, it is important to understand that not all assets are located on the securities market line when measured. The market model is an equilibrium model, whereas real-world conditions are dynamic. It is possible that not all assets will be at equilibrium when measured. This situation is not sustainable over time, as investor expectations for an asset will eventually catch up with its actual performance. Investors will want to buy (sell) the asset (according to its deviation above or below the securities market line), and its price will increase (decrease) accordingly. Ultimately, this asset's return will tend toward the securities market line.

F.   Expanding the Market Model

As stated above, statistically, the market model does not explain most of the changes seen in financial asset returns (R^2 is smaller than intuitively expected). Alternatively, the specific variance for financial assets, σ_ε^2—the variance not explained by changes in the market portfolio—is larger than we expect it to be. Below we discuss two attempts to minimize σ_ε^2 by identifying additional parameters that can be assigned "responsibility" for systematic variance, thereby decreasing specific variance.

The first is a descriptive model known as the *multiparameter market model.*

Question: Is there another parameter Q (in addition to the market parameter) that is responsible for systematic changes in the returns of all shares on the market? If this is the case, we must carry out a multivariable regression (in this case, two parameters) to check the changes effected in a given financial asset's returns by the market portfolio M and parameter Q. The extent to which changes in Q (as a percentage) explain changes in the financial asset must be known and measurable.

The regression function can be written as follows:

$$\tilde{R}_i = \alpha_i + \beta_{im}\tilde{R}_M + \beta_{iq}\tilde{R}_Q + \varepsilon_i.$$

There are three parts to this equation:

α_i — Constant, and therefore with zero variance.

$\beta_{iq}\tilde{R}_M$ — Indicates systematic change caused by market portfolio M.

$\beta_{iq}\tilde{R}_Q$ — Indicates systematic change caused by parameter Q.

ε_i — The average distribution of data around the regression line; its variance represents the specific variance.

Overall variance (denoted by T) is therefore comprised of systematic variance caused by the market portfolio (denoted by sm), systematic variance caused by parameter Q (denoted by sq), and specific variance (denoted by ε):

$$\sigma_T^2 = \beta_{im}^2\sigma_m^2 + \beta_{iq}^2\sigma_m^2 + \sigma_\varepsilon^2 = \sigma_{sm}^2 + \sigma_{sq}^2 + \sigma_\varepsilon^2.$$

In addition to the above mathematical-statistical approach, this approach also has economic and financial justification. As discussed in the first part of the book, individuals must decide how much to consume in the present period and how much to invest (with an intent to consume) in a subsequent period. The market model demonstrates how individuals must adjust interest rates to account for investment-related risk. However, the market model paints an incomplete picture, as it may lead one to think that individuals seek to maximize their returns as reflected in financial asset prices, while investors actually seek to maximize their consumption utility over time.

The difference between maximizing returns and maximizing consumption is best illustrated by an example. As you may be aware, energy prices jumped significantly in the period 2006–2008. For the sake of simplicity, let's assume zero flexibility in energy demand; that is, a fixed number of energy units is consumed. Therefore, if energy prices go up, we will be left with fewer resources (money) for other consumption expenses. Conversely, if prices go down, we will be left with more. Volatility in energy prices affects us in two ways:

1. Indirectly, by influencing the return on the market portfolio.

Companies use energy as an input. Increased input prices reduce profits, and vice versa. Fluctuations in energy prices are reflected in fluctuating financial results and similarly in the return recorded by investors. Overall, changes in energy prices affect the return on the market portfolio.

2. Directly, by influencing investors' "disposable income."

In this case, "disposable income" has a different definition: it is the income that can be spent on consumption after paying for energy prices.

If we want to maximize our consumption, we should account for fluctuations in energy prices both as reflected in the market portfolio return, consequently increasing or decreasing our mean future resources, and as reflected in our consumption derived from the mean future fluctuation in disposable income (as defined here).

The second is a normative model known as the *arbitrage model*. The arbitrage model assumes that all financial assets are dependent on a number of parameters. As in the market model, where we used linear regression to express each financial asset's correlation with the market portfolio, here too we can express this correlation through multiparameter regression:

$$R_i = a_1 + \beta_{i1}F_1 + \beta_{i2}F_2 + ... + \beta_{in}F_n + \varepsilon_i.$$

The market model as we know it is therefore a special case of the arbitrage model. If we assume a risk-free asset, then here too we can check the mean return on any financial asset in excess of the return on the risk-free asset (i.e., the risk premium).

The normative approach behind the arbitrage model is that if the actual premium on a financial asset is higher (lower) than required by the market, then investors can build a portfolio yielding a lower (higher) return for the same risk level. Therefore, by buying (selling) the asset, on the one hand, and the new portfolio on the other, both of which have identical risk but a different return, investors can implement arbitrage (= generate money). As everyone would want to do the same thing, prices for inadequately priced assets would increase (decrease) until the returns evened out. Given enough financial assets on the market (a much higher number of assets is required than parameters influencing their price), we can perform a regression' and find all the different β's in the above equation.[20]

Although both these models yield identical results, it is important to understand that they are generated from different viewpoints: one is a

20. Given n parameters (plus the risk-free interest rate), we must solve $n + 1$ financial asset equations (linear algebra).

descriptive model, the other is a normative model. This book introduces only the above multiparameter models, which are discussed in greater depth in advanced courses.

As readers may conclude, these models are much harder to test empirically than the issues discussed in the previous section. The models themselves do not provide a way of defining the parameters (in the same way as the market portfolio is defined) affecting returns on assets (systematically). Instead, they only state that such parameters exist, and leave researchers with the difficult task of defining these parameters, and afterward figuring out how to measure them.

Chapter 13 — Questions and Problems

Question 1

In a CAPM-compliant market that is in equilibrium, an investor holds a portfolio half of which is comprised of four shares (whose weights are detailed in the following table) while the other half consists of the risk-free asset:

Share i	W_i	$\bar{R}_i$	β_i
1	10%	7%	0.4
2	10%	8%	0.6
3	10%	10%	0.8
4	20%	12%	1.2

a. What is the risk-free interest rate and what is the market portfolio return?

b. What are the mean return and risk for the investor's portfolio?

c. Another investor wants to build a portfolio comprised of the market portfolio and a risk-free asset yielding a 12% return. How will the portfolio be constructed?

Question 2

In a CAPM-compliant market that is in equilibrium, the risk-free rate is 6%. The market portfolio has an 11% return with a 12% standard deviation.

An investor holds an efficient portfolio P yielding a 15% return.

a. What is the portfolio risk, expressed in β?

b. What is the portfolio variance, σ_P^2?

c. What is portfolio P's covariance with the market portfolio (σ_{pm})?

d. Using the above data, demonstrate that efficient portfolios are perfectly correlated with the market portfolio.

Question 3

In a CAPM-compliant market that is in equilibrium, the risk-free rate is 6%. The market portfolio has a return of 11%, with a 4% standard deviation.

An investor holds one share (at equilibrium) yielding a 16% return with a total variance of 10%.

a. What is the share's risk, expressed in β?

b. What is its systematic variance?

c. What is its specific variance?

d. What is the risk for this investor as compared to the investor in question 2?

Question 4

The following exercise demonstrates the use of statistical mathematics tools and illustrates how the various model parameters are derived from historical data.

The following data were collected for the period 1990–1999 (see table):

• The market portfolio return R_m (e.g., in the United States, returns on the S&P 500 index).

• The return per share in Success Inc., R_i.

• A risk-free interest rate of 5% (e.g., the return to maturity on one-year government bonds).

On January 1, 2000, a CAPM-guided investor is considering an investment in Success Inc. Help him use the data below to derive the required parameters for a one-year investment.

Year	R_m	R_i	$R_m - \bar{R}_m$	$(R_m - \bar{R}_m)^2$	$R_i - \bar{R}_i$	$(R_i - \bar{R}_i)^2$	$(R_m - \bar{R}_m)(R_i - \bar{R})$
1990	0.25	0.17					
1991	0.12	0.08					
1992	−0.1	−0.07					
1993	0.15	0.1					
1994	0.19	0.12					
1995	0.08	0.05					
1996	0.11	0.08					
1997	−0.05	−0.03					
1998	0.16	0.11					
1999	0.27	0.18					

Note:

1. In addition to historical data, the table includes columns that you must fill out. This calculation will help you understand the significance of the statistical measures used in financial models.

2. Solve the question using MS Excel, with cells containing the appropriate formulas presented at the top of each column, and in the following sections.

   a. Calculate the mean return for the market portfolio, $\bar{R}_m = \dfrac{\sum R_m}{N}$.

   b. Write the equation for the securities market line.

   c. Calculate the variance and standard deviation for the market portfolio, $\sigma_m^2 = \dfrac{\sum (R_m - \bar{R}_m)^2}{N-1}$.

   d. Calculate the mean return for Success Inc.'s shares, $\bar{R}_i = \dfrac{\sum R_i}{N}$.

   e. Calculate the variance and standard deviation for Success Inc.'s shares, $\sigma_i^2 = \dfrac{\sum (R_i - \bar{R}_i)^2}{N-1}$.

   f. Calculate Success Inc.'s shares' covariance with the market portfolio, $\sigma_{im} = \dfrac{\sum (R_m - \bar{R}_m)(R_i - \bar{R}_i)}{N-1}$.

   g. Calculate risk for Success Inc., as expressed by β: $\beta_i = \dfrac{\sigma_{im}}{\sigma_m^2}$.

   h. Is the share at equilibrium? Assuming the share will be at equilibrium at the end of the year, should the investor buy or sell the share?

Question 5

In a CAPM-compliant market that is at equilibrium, John holds an efficient portfolio A with a mean return of 22% and 15% standard deviation.

Assume a risk-free interest rate of 7% and a mean return on the market portfolio of 17%.

a. What is the portfolio risk in terms of β?

b. John has \$1,000 in equity, invested entirely in the securities market. Is he borrowing or lending, and how much?

c. Calculate the mean return on an asset B with a correlation coefficient of 0.7 with the market portfolio and a standard deviation of 20%.

Question 6

Assume a CAPM-compliant market where $R_f = 5\%$, $\sigma_m = 6\%$, and $R_m = 10\%$.

Frozen Greens, a company that markets frozen vegetables, has remained static for years. Its annual dividend has been \$3 for many years and its average share price (at equilibrium) is \$33.33. The company's management announced that it has decided to expand the company and acquire a meat product company (the meat product industry has a β factor of 1.6), which will account for 25% of all business (on acquisition). Following this development in the company's operations, everyone expects its consolidated financial results to grow by 3% per year for many years to come (assume perpetually).

a. What will be the new risk measure (expressed as β) for the company's shares at equilibrium?

b. What will be the new market price for the company's shares at equilibrium following management's announcement?

(*Hint:* The consolidated company can be considered a portfolio.)

Question 7

CAPM: the market portfolio has a mean return of 12% and a standard deviation of 2%. The risk-free rate is 4%.
Your portfolio consists of the following three shares:

Asset	Mean Return	Standard Deviation	ρ_{im}
A	16%	4%	0.9
B	14%	6%	0.5
C	12%	3%	0.6

(*Hint:* The shares are temporarily not at equilibrium according to CAPM.)

a. You need $1,000 in cash immediately. Which of the shares should you sell now? (See hint above).

b. What is the nonsystematic (specific) risk on share A?

c. Your portfolio consists of shares A, B, and C at a market value of $2,000, $3,000, and $5,000, respectively. What is the risk on your portfolio?

d. Assuming you want to invest only in these three shares, after examining macroeconomic data, you decide to change your investment to $5,000 in share A and $2,000 in share C. Assuming that you are a rational individual, what is your assumption concerning the market for the near future?

Question 8

In Capitaland, which has a CAPM-compliant market, there is only one risky asset yielding a return of 8% with a 10% standard deviation, and the risk-free borrowing and lending rates are both 4%. An investor builds an efficient portfolio with a 20% return.

a. What is the portfolio's standard deviation?

b. Assume that the market also has two assets A and B, not at equilibrium, such that $\beta_A = 2\beta_B$. Which of the following statements is true?

   1. The required return on asset A is twice that on asset B.

   2. The systematic variance for asset A is four times that for asset B.

   3. The specific variance for asset A is four times that for asset B.

   4. The total variance for asset A is four times that for asset B.

   5. Statements 1 and 4 are true.

Question 9

Assume a CAPM-compliant market: $R_f = 5\%$, $R_m = 10\%$. An efficient portfolio is comprised of the market portfolio and a risk-free asset and maintains $R_p = 25\%$, $\sigma_p = 12\%$. A share (not at equilibrium) has a correlation coefficient of 0.5 with the market portfolio and a standard deviation of 2%.

a. What is the risk (expressed as β) on the share?

b. At its current market price, the share has a mean return of 12%. Assuming that company's free cash flow is constant and perpetual, you decide to buy the share. What is the capital yield that you expect on the share, assuming you sell it at equilibrium?

Further Reading

Alexander, G. J., and N. L. Chervany. 1980. On the Estimation and Stability of Beta. *Journal of Financial and Quantitative Analysis* 15: 123–137.

Bera, A. K., and S. Kannan. 1986. An Adjustment Procedure for Predicting Systematic Risk. *Journal of Applied Econometrics* (October).

Black, F. 1972. Capital Market Equilibrium with Restricted Borrowing. *Journal of Business* (July): 444–455.

Black, F., M. C. Jensen, and M. Scholes. 1972. The Capital Asset Pricing Model: Some Empirical Tests. In *Studies in the Theory of Capital Markets,* ed. C. Jensen, 79–121. New York: Praeger.

Blume, M. E. 1971. On the Assessment of Risk. *Journal of Finance* 26 (March): 1–10.

Bower, D., R. Bower, and D. Logue. 1984. Arbitrage Pricing Theory and Utility Stock Returns. *Journal of Finance* (September): 1041–1054.

Boyer, M., S. Storoy, and T. Sten. 1975. Equilibrium in Linear Capital Market Networks. *Journal of Finance* (December).

Brown, S. 1978. Earnings Changes, Stock Prices and Market Efficiency. *Journal of Finance* (March): 17–28.

Chen, N. F. 1983. Some Empirical Tests of the Theory of Arbitrage Pricing. *Journal of Finance* (December): 1393–1414.

Cheng, P. L., and R. R. Grauer. 1980. An Alternative Test of the Capital Asset Pricing Model. *American Economic Review* (September).

Cho, D., E. Chinhyung, J. Edwin, and M. J. Gruber. 1984. On the Robustness of the Roll and Ross Arbitrage Pricing Theory. *Journal of Financial and Quantitative Analysis* (March).

Cornell, B., and J. K. Dietrich. 1978. Mean-Absolute-Deviation versus Least-Squares Regression Estimation of Beta Coefficients. *Journal of Financial and Quantitative Analysis* (March).

DeJong, D., and D. W. Collins. 1985. Explanations for the Instability of Equity Beta: Risk-Free Rate Changes and Leverage Effects. *Journal of Financial and Quantitative Analysis* (March).

Dukes, W. P., O. D. Boulin, and S. S. MacDonald. 1987. The Performance of Beta in Forecasting Portfolio Returns in Bull and Bear Markets Using Alternative Market Proxies. *Quarterly Journal of Business and Economics.*

Ehrhardt, M. C. 1987. A Mean-Variance Derivation of a Multi-Factor Equilibrium Model. *Journal of Financial and Quantitative Analysis* (June).

Elton, E. J., M. J. Gruber, and T. Ulrich. 1978. Are Betas Best? *Journal of Finance*: 23.

Fama, E. F., and J. D. MacBeth. 1974. Tests of the Multiperiod Two-Parameter Model. *Journal of Financial Economics* (May): 43–66.

Farrar, D. E. 1962. *The Investment Decision under Uncertainty.* Englewood Cliffs, NJ: Prentice-Hall.

Fisher, L., and J. H. Kamin. 1985. Forecasting Systematic Risk: Estimates of "Raw" Beta that Take Account of the Tendency of Beta to Change and the Heteroskedasticity of Residual Returns. *Journal of Financial and Quantitative Analysis* (June).

Friend, I., R. Westerfield, and M. Granito. 1978. New Evidence on the Capital Asset Pricing Model. *Journal of Finance* (June): 903–917.

Gehr, A. K., Jr. 1975. Some Tests of the Arbitrage Pricing Theory. *Journal of the Midwest Finance Association*: 91–105.

Gibbons, M. R., and W. Ferson. 1985. Testing Asset Pricing Models with Changing Expectations and an Unobservable Market Portfolio. *Journal of Financial Economics* (June): 217–236.

Huberman, G. 1982. A Simple Approach to Arbitrage Pricing Theory. *Journal of Economic Theory*: 183–191.

Jensen, M. 1972. Capital Markets: Theory and Evidence. *Bell Journal of Economics and Management Science* (Autumn): 357–398.

Jensen, M. C., ed. 1972. *Studies in the Theory of Capital Markets*. New York: Praeger.

King, B. F. 1966. Market and Industry Factors in Stock Market Behavior. *Journal of Business*, Security Prices: A Supplement, 39 (January): 179–190.

Levy, H. 1980. The CAPM and Beta in an Imperfect Market. *Journal of Portfolio Management* (Winter).

Levy, H. 1983. The Capital Asset Pricing Model: Theory and Empiricism. *Economic Journal* (March).

Levy, H. 1984. Another Look at the Capital Asset Pricing Model. *Quarterly Review of Business and Economics* (Summer).

Levy, H. 1984. Measuring Risk and Performance over Alternative Investment Horizons. *Financial Analyst Journal* (March/April).

Markowitz, H. M. 1984. The Two Beta Trap. *Journal of Portfolio Management* 11 (Autumn): 12–20.

Markowitz, H. M., and A. F. Perold. 1981. Portfolio Analysis with Factors and Scenarios. *Journal of Finance* 36 (4): 871–877.

Mayers, D., and E. Rice. 1979. Measuring Portfolio Performance and the Empirical Content of Asset Pricing Models. *Journal of Financial Economics* (March): 3–28.

Merton, R. 1973. An Intertemporal Capital Asset Pricing Model. *Econometrica* (September): 867–888.

Mossin, J. 1966. Equilibrium in a Capital Asset Market. *Econometrica* (October): 768–783.

Mullins, D. W., Jr. 1982. Does the Capital Asset Pricing Model Work? *Harvard Business Review* (January/February).

Pettit, R. R., and R. Westerfield. 1974. Using the Capital Asset Pricing Model and the Market Model to Predict Security Returns. *Journal of Financial and Quantitative Analysis* (September): 579–605.

Reilly, F. K., and D. J. Wright. 1988. A Comparison of Published Betas. *Journal of Portfolio Management* (Spring).

Reinganum, M. R. 1981. The Arbitrage Pricing Theory: Some Empirical Results. *Journal of Finance* (May): 313–321.

Roll, R. 1970. *The Behavior of Interest Rates: An Application of the Efficient Market Model to U.S. Treasury Bills*. New York: Basic Books.

Roll, R. 1977. A Critique of the Asset Pricing Theory's Tests. *Journal of Financial Economics* (March): 129–176.

Roll, R. 1984. A Critical Reexamination of the Empirical Evidence on the Arbitrage Pricing Theory: A Reply. *Journal of Finance* (June): 347–350.

Roll, R., and S. Ross. 1980. An Empirical Investigation of the Arbitrage Pricing Theory. *Journal of Finance* (December): 1073–1103.

Rosenberg, B., and V. Marathe. 1979. Tests of the Capital Asset Pricing Hypothesis. *Research in Finance* (January): 115–223.

Ross, S. A. 1976. The Arbitrage Theory of Capital Asset Pricing. *Journal of Economic Theory* 13 (December): 341–360.

Scholes, M., and J. Williams. 1977. Estimating Betas from Nonsynchronous Data. *Journal of Financial Economics* (December): 309–327.

Scott, E., and S. Brown. 1980. Biased Estimators and Unstable Betas. *Journal of Finance* (March).

Sharpe, W. F. 1964. Capital Asset Prices: A Theory of Market Equilibrium under Conditions of Risk. *Journal of Finance* 19 (3): 425–442.

Sharpe, W. F. 1970. *Portfolio Theory and Capital Markets*. New York: McGraw-Hill.

Sharpe, W. F. 1977. The Capital Asset Pricing Model: A "Multi-Beta" Interpretation. In *Financial Decision Making Under Uncertainty*, eds. H. Levy and M. Samat. New York: Academic Press.

Sharpe, W. F., and G. M. Cooper. 1972. Risk-Return Classes of New York Stock Exchange Common Stocks, 1931–1967. *Financial Analysts Journal* 28 (March/April): 46–54, 81.

Stapleton, R. C., and M. G. Subrahmanyam. 1978. A Multiperiod Equilibrium Asset Pricing Model. *Econometrica* (September): 1077–1096.

Treynor, J. L. 1962. Toward a Theory of Market Value of Risky Assets, unpublished manuscript. A final version was published in 1999, in *Asset Pricing and Portfolio Performance: Models, Strategy and Performance Metrics*, ed. R. A. Korajczyk, 15–22. London: Risk Books.

14 Assembling a Practical Portfolio—Allocating a Few Assets

A. Introduction

Modern finance has a number of shortcomings, the most bothersome of which is that the two basic models for constructing an optimal basic investment portfolio, the mean-variance model and capital asset pricing model (CAPM), while so appealing in theory, fall short when we try to apply them. In theory, an asset allocation model should be a handy tool for the portfolio manager. In practice, portfolio managers have found asset allocation models difficult to use and the portfolio they generate is often deceptive. Both the mean-variance model and the CAPM conclude that an investor should hold a well-diversified portfolio or, alternatively, a linear combination of risk-free assets and a market portfolio. By definition, such a market portfolio should include all globally available investment opportunities, thus making it a purely theoretical construct.

It is still possible to make an approximation of a market portfolio through the use of indices such as the S&P 500 for an American market portfolio, or a weighted combination of indices when trying to invest globally. In reality, investors tend to allocate their individual portfolios across only a few asset classes (industries, countries, etc.), either directly in shares or bonds or through ETFs,[1] for reasons (and real-life problems) to be discussed in the next section. Since such an investment practice undermines our basic assumption of a well-diversified portfolio, the convenient CAPM measure of portfolio risk, $\beta_p = \sum w_i \beta_i$, is no longer applicable. With CAPM having showed its limitations, portfolio managers often try using the mean-variance model, only to find that it is extremely sensitive to very small changes in the assets' parameters, and especially to their forecasted expected returns. This is primarily true if the portfolio in question includes a balanced weighting for diverse assets whose returns are highly correlated.

In most business schools, portfolio asset allocation is taught using the Solver tool in Excel. Solver is used to solve linear and nonlinear optimization problems with up to 200 decision variables (in our case, asset weights in the portfolio w_i). Restrictions may be placed on the decision variables, including up to 100 explicit constraints, for example, $\sum_i w_i = 1$, and up to 400 simple constraints, for example, lower and upper bounds on the decision variables w_i. In other words, one need only set up a few basic formulas in Excel to get a portfolio's expected return and variance, and one can then rely entirely on Excel's built-in Solver to find the optimal portfolio asset weights, requesting Solver to find $Max\left\{\sum_i w_i \cdot R_i\right\}$ for any given variance.

Using Solver, portfolio managers do not need to know optimization techniques such as the Lagrange multiplier or how to deal with a large system of linear equations, which would require them to master matrix algebra. Given the sensitivity of optimal portfolio weights to expected returns, one approach practitioners took in the past was to apply relatively tight constraints, forcing Solver to constrain short selling, or putting an upper limit on the weight of certain assets in a portfolio. Another way was to induce high transaction costs, which again allowed the creation of "balanced" portfolios through artificial interventions. If the constraints are not real but rather imposed to achieve reasonable-looking portfolios, then they clearly reflect some inadequacy in the model, and there is no justification for accepting the constrained solution.

The above issue led to two principal schools of thought:

1. The first or "technical" school sought better statistical inference procedures for evaluating the models' parameters, for example, variance-

---

1. ETFs (exchange-traded funds) are index funds that hold assets such as stocks, bonds, or trades and attempt to replicate the performance of a specific market index.

covariance matrix shrinkage methods, a good example of which can be found in Simon Benninga's *Financial Modeling* (MIT Press, 2008) and other books of that genre. Since the practical application of financial models requires extensive use of MS Excel, such books were wrongly denigrated as "cookbooks" and ranked inferior to those defined as offering "pure theory." Unfortunately, technical solutions have only marginally improved the practical results of portfolio management.

2. The second or "theoretical" school, exemplified by Fischer Black and Robert Litterman, suggested avoiding the unacceptable allocation results of the mean-variance model and its sensitivity to forecasted (expected) returns by cross inference between the mean-variance model and the CAPM. This approach enabled practitioners for the first time in financial modeling history to further present a constructive way to deviate from the CAPM equilibrium by introducing a procedure that incorporated personal views.

In this chapter we introduce the Black-Litterman approach to handling the mean-variance model optimizer, while the procedure for incorporating personal views is discussed in chapter 15.

The Black-Litterman model is *the* most confusing, obscure, and difficult-to-apply model in financial theory, by far. For this reason, most textbooks suffice with a verbal presentation of the model, providing only the conceptual approach and its bottom-line result. It is not surprising that this model has not been analyzed and presented in detail by any textbook until now because, unfortunately, when introducing their model, Black and Litterman themselves sufficed with spelling out the model's conceptual approach, the underlying fundamental equations, and their bottom-line result.[2] They did not provide the proper mathematical background or the complete method for deriving those final results. Moreover, their presentation lacks many mandatory details without which no one can apply the model in practice using computerized (Excel) templates.

The model's numerous parameters, which need to be plugged into the Excel template, are simply mentioned by name. However, not all of them are specified to an applicable degree. For example, in chapter 7 of the monograph by Litterman and his colleagues at Goldman Sachs, "Beyond

2. Fischer Black and Robert Litterman, "Asset Allocation: Combining Investors Views with Market Equilibrium," *Journal of Fixed Income* (September 1991); idem, "Global Portfolio Optimization," *Financial Analysts Journal* (October 1992); Robert Litterman et al., chapter 7 in *Modern Investment Management: An Equilibrium Approach* (2003).

Equilibrium," they explain, "In the Black Litterman model, the investor is asked not only to specify a return expectation . . . but also a degree of confidence which is a standard deviation around the expectation" (p. 77). The variance of the views Ω, one of the basic parameters in their fundamental equations, is inversely related to an investor's confidence in the views.[3] However, Black and Litterman do not provide in their publications an intuitive way to quantify this relationship. It is up to the investor to compute the variance of his views. The many publications that followed the Black and Litterman articles tried to cover the missing mathematical components required to derive their bottom-line results, a mandatory preliminary step to understanding the intuition behind the model's different parameters. This information is essential in figuring out how to practically evaluate those parameters when plugging them into computerized (Excel) templates. Nevertheless, even an Excel-oriented book such as Benninga's, which has a chapter titled "The Black-Litterman Approach to Portfolio Optimization" (chapter 13), states, "An application to portfolio modeling can be found in Black and Litterman (1991) and other associated papers. This author finds those papers dauntingly complicated and difficult to implement. A simpler approach . . . is a convex combination of the markets' weights and opinion-adjusted weights." Unfortunately, in the Goldman Sachs monograph, Litterman objects to this approach: "we simply tried to take a weighted average of the investors-specified excess expected returns with the equilibrium values. We found that simply moving away from the equilibrium risk premium in a naïve manner soon leads to portfolio weights that make no sense." This book, *Fundamental Models in Financial Theory* is therefore the first and so far the only textbook to provide a comprehensive review of the Black-Litterman model and its practical application in Excel. I can tell readers from personal experience that Benninga's daring statement that the Black-Litterman model is very difficult to implement in Excel did not shock me in the least. I had the same experience, feeling sure I understood the model until I actually tried to apply it for the first time using Excel, and . . . zilch, nada! Thus, understanding the Black-Litterman model's theoretical approach is not enough when it comes to the model's application, and we will need all the obviously exhausting details spelled out in this chapter and the next.

I cannot sufficiently emphasize the importance of coming to grips with the details. For example, the Black-Litterman model's main objective is

---

3. Jay Walters, The Black-Litterman Model: A Detailed Exploration (2008 rev.), p. 8.

to incorporate personal views (see chapter 15) or, in mathematical terms, to find the parameters $[E(R)]$ and $[\bar{\Sigma}]$ of the joint (equilibrium plus views) distribution in order to plug them into a mean-variance optimizer (discussed next in this chapter). Despite their own central premise, if you try to use their model's bottom-line result for $[\bar{\Sigma}]$ and plug it into the Excel template (or Solver, if you wish), it does not work. Black and Litterman do not actually tell us that $[\bar{\bar{\Sigma}}] = [\bar{\Sigma}] + [\Sigma]$ is in fact the ultimate joint distribution variance-covariance matrix that we should enter. I had to struggle for months to reach this conclusion myself, then recently found support for it in one of the latest revisions of J. Walters's marvelous articles.[4]

Given its complexity, this model has rarely if ever been introduced in any finance textbook. This is quite odd, as no other academic field accepts the notion that its graduates need not know how to apply in practice the models they are taught! MBAs (and practitioners) should and can master this important model comprehensively and know how to apply it in practice.

At this point, readers should be assured that we are not going to try to develop either their Excel or their mathematical skills. These are merely tools required to realize our goal of a holistic approach resulting in hands-on application. Since, realistically, readers may only have used these tools once in the distant past, we will repeatedly use the "review" method to refresh readers' knowledge and present Excel formulas by key strokes to keep it light and simple. Once readers have built the complete spreadsheet, the concept should make itself clear. We should perhaps add that Solver, although widely used in all other textbooks as a tool for finding optimal portfolio allocations, is the antithesis of the Black-Litterman approach. Therefore, we will try to avoid it at all times, even when it might make sense to use it.

B. Problems in Constructing a Portfolio with a Limited Number of Assets

In this chapter, we will follow on Black and Litterman's work and seek to construct a practical portfolio with a small number of assets in such a way that will minimize risk for any given expected return in equilibrium on the portfolio. We will apply Markowitz's mean-variance approach, thus making the following postulations:

4. Readers who can handle high-level mathematics are urged to refer to them; see note 3.

1. The investor defines the standard deviation (σ) of the assets' returns from their mean (expected) return, as the measure of risk.

2. The portfolio risk σ_P^2 depends on the variances of the assets in the portfolio and on the covariances between them.

3. The investor allocates (chooses) the assets' weights (proportion) in the portfolio to minimize[5] the portfolio return risk σ_P^2 for any desired portfolio expected return, R_P.

The Markowitz mean-variance approach offers a solution to the problem of finding the weights of each of the assets in the portfolio in order to obtain a minimum variance for any required portfolio return. Once the expected returns and covariances of the assets are known, it is possible to use the same efficient frontier approach introduced in chapter 12 using more extensive mathematics, but first it is necessary to discuss how many assets in this context are considered "a few."

As explained in chapter 13, roughly 30 assets are required to maintain a well-diversified portfolio. I emphasize "roughly" because if some of the assets are highly correlated, they do not provide a well-diversified portfolio and will result in nonintuitive weights, as demonstrated by the following example[6] of a simple three-asset (I, II, and III) portfolio, with the following variance-covariance matrix and expected risk premium:[7]

Variance-Covariance

Asset	I	II	III	Risk Premium
I	0.06	0.063	0.023	0.054
II	0.063	0.09	0.043	0.072
III	0.023	0.043	0.036	0.038

Calculating the correlation coefficient table ρ_{ij} for the above three assets:

ρ_{ij}

Asset	I	II	III
I	1.000	0.857	0.495
II		1.000	0.755
III			1.000

---

5. Naming the standard deviation σ as a measure of risk is intuitively comprehensible. Using σ^2 is only a question of scale. Minimizing σ^2 is equal to minimizing σ.

6. These assets resemble the Black-Litterman example. The data appear in Tomas M. Idzorek, "A Step-by-Step Guide to the Black-Litterman Model" (2002), pp. 4, 17. The three assets resemble: I—U.S. Large Growth; II—U.S. Small Growth; III—Int'l Dev Equity. The original data from the Black-Litterman example was slightly changed to get a more "educational" (didactic) portfolio.

7. The risk premium is the assets' excess return above the risk-free rate.

The final efficient frontier line will start at the risk-free rate and be tangent to the assets' preliminary efficient frontier at a point at which the weights of assets I, II, and III are 36%, 27%, and 37%, respectively. The result is an intuitively well-balanced $E(R_p) = 5.3\%$, and $\sigma_p^2 = 0.046$.

Now, if we change the covariance between assets I and III in the three-asset portfolio from 0.023 to 0.044 (i.e., $\rho_{13} \approx 0.95$), we get the following variance-covariance matrix:

Original:

Asset	I	II	III
I	0.06	0.063	**0.023**
II	0.063	0.09	0.043
III	**0.023**	0.043	0.036

Changed to:

Asset	I	II	III
I	0.06	0.063	**0.044**
II	0.063	0.09	0.043
III	**0.044**	0.043	0.036

and for ρ_{ij}

Asset	I	II	III
I	1.000	0.857	**0.495**
II		1.000	0.755
III			1.000

Asset	I	II	III
I	1.000	0.857	**0.95**
II		1.000	0.755
III			1.000

The weights of assets I, II, and III will change to 25, 74%, and 1%, respectively (very unbalanced), and in practice the portfolio collapses, to hold only assets I and II.

In chapter 12, we drew the frontier line of a portfolio constructed of two assets, X and Y, with a correlation of $\rho_{XY} \approx 1$ or $\rho_{XY} \approx -1$ (figure 14.1).

One should bear in mind that in a market where short selling[8] is allowed, $\rho_{XY} = 1$ and $\rho_{XY} = -1$ may in practice have an identical risk-return efficient frontier picture. It is only rational that when we introduce a risk-free asset R_f, that is, an asset for which $\sigma_{R_f} = 0$, into a portfolio that contains two (or more) highly correlated X and Y risky assets, such a portfolio will behave erratically.[9]

Practical experience suggests that we should choose assets having a correlation of 0.2 or less to construct a balanced portfolio. The correlation coefficients between the assets in our example are much higher than the recommendation since it includes only indexes. Finding such

---

8. A short sale is a position in which we "borrow" a share in the market (for a fee), sell it, and at the end of the borrowing period buy the share at market price and return it to the lender. If in that period of time the share price falls, we make a profit. Thus, a short sale position has a mirror (reverse) profit picture than the profit picture of holding the share for the long term.

9. We end up having two different assets with $\sigma = 0$ (riskless), but with different expected returns. See also question 2 in chapter 12.

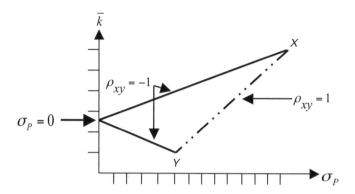

Figure 14.1
Creation of a Riskless Asset (Portfolio) Using Two (or More) Highly Correlated Risky Assets

low-correlated assets is no simple task and is almost impossible if we wish to include ETFs in our portfolio, as is the case with our Black-Litterman example.

For a portfolio that consists of 30 assets, the number of variances that need to be estimated is 30, but the number of covariances that need to be estimated is 435! Moreover, we will have to find 30 such assets for which all 435 correlation coefficients are small, or at least we will need to examine the significance of their higher correlation on the portfolio structure. This seems to be too much for an ordinary investor or even for a professional investment team to handle. Markowitz (1990) acknowledged that "in portfolios involving large numbers of correlated securities, variances shrink in importance compared to covariances."

The above leads us to conclude that "a few" or "a limited number" would really have to be a very small number. Finding even eight low-correlated assets is not a simple task at all. At least 28 covariances need to be estimated and their correlation coefficients calculated, all of which must have a relatively small correlation coefficient, or otherwise be eliminated or replaced.

Now that we have defined the meaning of a limited number of assets, and the covariances of these few assets can be adequately estimated (Benninga's *Financial Modeling* is recommended for that purpose) and selected to have a low correlation, practical experience shows that it is difficult to propose reasonable estimators of market expectation about future returns $E(r_i)$ for these assets. Furthermore, small changes in these expected return estimators for the different assets that are combined in our portfolio make a big change in the proportions (weights) of the assets in the portfolio,[10] and again lead us to nonintuitive portfolio construction. Let's take our above example and change the expected return premium of asset I from 5.4% to 5.9%.[11] The weights of assets I, II, and III will change to become 60%, –5% (short sale), and 45%, respectively. Considering how small the change we have made in the expected return of only one of the assets, starting with an intuitively well-balanced portfolio, we now have a portfolio structure that makes us decidedly uncomfortable. We are looking for "neutral" estimators for the future expected return, based on past history data, so that the predictions of these estimators of actual future returns will give us a balanced portfolio structure.[12] Practical experience also teaches that the lower the correlations between the assets, the less sensitive the portfolio structure (proportional asset weights) will be to changes in the expected returns' estimators.

We can address the market expected returns estimator in many ways.[13] We will discuss just two, to give a feel for the complexity of this issue:

1. Use the past history average return (mean) of each asset i as an estimator for the expected future returns $E(r_i)$.

2. Find the past history[14] β_i of each asset i, and use the CAPM model to calculate an implied estimator[15] for the expected *equilibrium* returns $E(r_i)$.

The historical average returns approach assumes that future expected returns will equal the historical averages. This means that the investor should purchase assets that have performed the best historically and sell those that historically have had poor results. However, calculating the average asset returns for the past five years often results in negative returns for many of the assets. Using these averages as estimators for future parameters in the process of allocating assets according to the efficient frontier method will result in a portfolio structure that is, to say the least, very poor and nonintuitive.

---

10. We will elaborate on this subject and demonstrate it in the next chapter.

11. Note that we have changed the estimator by less than 10% of its original value.

12. We expect that the weights of the assets will not include extreme long or short positions.

13. This book presents only basic models. Finding an estimator for the parameters in any statistical model is a complex issue that should be addressed in advanced courses.

14. β is also an estimator, and one should take into consideration its quality (at least R^2).

15. The implied estimator is formalized as $R_i = R_f + \beta_i(R_M - R_f)$. In a portfolio that contains global equities, bonds, and currencies, we may use Black's global CAPM version (F. Black, *Financial Analysts Journal*, July/August 1989). The required risk premium is given by $\pi_i = R_i - R_f = \beta_i(R_M - R_f)$.

The *implied* expected return does not mean that we assume that all the assets in the market are always in equilibrium. On the contrary, we assume it is not the case; otherwise we could not justify the existence of personal views. We do assume that returns tend not to move too far from their equilibrium state, and when they do, the market will tend to push them back toward equilibrium. We will use these *implied* expected returns estimators in the mean-variance optimizer presented from now on, for the simple reason that Black and Litterman, while working at Goldman Sachs investment bank, found that they generated optimal portfolios that were more balanced and better than the unreasonable results of estimators derived through other methods.

To find the weights of each of the assets (asset allocation) in our portfolio that will minimize variance for any given required portfolio return, that is, to find the efficient frontier, we need to master linear (matrix) algebra, or else apply MS Excel Solver using the implied expected return as estimators and without imposing harsh constrains. Since the introduction of personal views (in the next chapter) can only be presented using linear algebra, we will exercise the matrix version of the mean-variance optimizer in this chapter. We will first conduct a brief and rather informal review of linear algebra, in the hope that it will make it easier for the reader to understand the model developed in this chapter and the next.

C.   Review of Linear (Matrix) Algebra

1. Motivation

Linear algebra has many applications. One of the basic applications is in solving a system of linear equations, which may be presented (expressed) in matrix and vector form by separating the constants from the variables:

$$
\begin{array}{c}
2x_1 + x_2 - 3x_3 = 5 \\
4x_1 - 2x_2 + 2x_3 = 10 \\
x_1 + 4x_2 + x_3 = 12
\end{array}
\text{ is presented by} \Rightarrow
\begin{pmatrix} 2 & 1 & -3 \\ 4 & -2 & 2 \\ 1 & 4 & 1 \end{pmatrix}
\begin{pmatrix} x_1 \\ x_2 \\ x_3 \end{pmatrix}
=
\begin{pmatrix} 5 \\ 10 \\ 12 \end{pmatrix}.
$$

$$
\begin{array}{ccc}
\uparrow & \uparrow & \uparrow \\
Matrix & Vector & Vector \\
A & X & B
\end{array}
$$

When we multiply each of the n elements a_{1j} in the first row of matrix A ($j = 1...3$) with each of the n variables x_i of the column vector X ($i = 1...3$) and sum them up, we obtain the first line in the equation system on the left, and so on.

$[A]$ and $[B]$ represent the constant parameters' matrixes (vector), and $[X]$ represents the variables' vector.

The above example is no more than a notation convention whereby a matrix has n rows and m columns (in the above example, $n = m$). A vector is defined as a matrix that has *one* column or *one* row. Each element in a matrix is denoted as $a_{ij}, i = 1...n, j = 1...m$ (row i, column j).

When we wish to solve a system of n linear independent equations with n variables $x_i, i = 1...n$, without using matrix algebra, we manipulate the constants attached to the different x_i's by multiplying each equation (line) by a (different) constant, adding (subtracting) one equation (line) from the other, thus decreasing the number of variables, until we are left with only one. Following our calculation, we can then go back and solve the remaining variables. In linear (matrix) algebra, we do something similar but in a way that is suitable to solution by computer software programs.

Linear (matrix) algebra is a method of manipulating the parameters of matrix A (and matrix B) to solve the unknown values of the variables in matrix X. As in ordinary algebra, adding, subtracting, multiplying, or dividing both sides of an equation by the same expression keeps the validity of the equality. To do so, we first have to define the regular algebra operators, that is, addition, subtraction, multiplication, and division, for matrixes.

2. Transposition

In linear algebra we sometimes need to shift the content of a *horizontal*

vector (range of cells) $\begin{array}{ccc} A & ; & B & ; & C \\ [a & ; & b & ; & c & ...] \end{array}$ into a *vertical* range $\begin{array}{c} 1 \\ 2 \\ 3 \\ : \end{array}\begin{bmatrix} a \\ b \\ c \\ \ \end{bmatrix}$, or

vice versa, in a form that correlates numerical with alphabetical line with column order: $A \leftrightarrow 1 \quad B \leftrightarrow 2 \quad .....$

The above applies also to matrixes where the content of each *horizontal* line (vector) in the matrix is shifted into a *vertical* range:

$$
\begin{array}{cccc}
 & A & B & C & D \\
1 & \begin{bmatrix} a & b & c & d \\ \end{bmatrix} \\
2 & \begin{matrix} e & f & g & h \\ \end{matrix} \\
3 & \begin{bmatrix} i & j & k & l \end{bmatrix}
\end{array}
\qquad \overset{\longleftrightarrow}{Transpose} \qquad
\begin{array}{cccc}
 & A & B & C \\
1 & \begin{bmatrix} a & e & i \\ \end{bmatrix} \\
2 & \begin{matrix} b & f & j \\ \end{matrix} \\
3 & \begin{matrix} c & g & k \\ \end{matrix} \\
4 & \begin{bmatrix} d & h & l \end{bmatrix}
\end{array}
$$

3. Adding and subtracting matrixes

Let A, B, and C be matrixes of the same $n \times m$ dimension, with a_{ij}, b_{ij}, and c_{ij} elements, respectively. Then, if $A \pm B = C \Rightarrow a_{ij} \pm b_{ij} = c_{ij}$.

Example 1:

$$
\begin{pmatrix} 1 & 2 \\ 3 & 4 \end{pmatrix} + \begin{pmatrix} 1 & -1 \\ -2 & 3 \end{pmatrix} = \begin{pmatrix} 1+1 & 2-1 \\ 3-2 & 4+3 \end{pmatrix} = \begin{pmatrix} 2 & 1 \\ 1 & 7 \end{pmatrix}.
$$

Example 2:

$$
\begin{pmatrix} 1 & 2 \\ 3 & 4 \end{pmatrix} - \begin{pmatrix} 1 & -1 \\ -2 & 3 \end{pmatrix} = \begin{pmatrix} 1-1 & 2-(-1) \\ 3-(-2) & 4-3 \end{pmatrix} = \begin{pmatrix} 0 & 3 \\ 5 & 1 \end{pmatrix}.
$$

4. Multiplying a matrix by a constant parameter (dot product)

Let A and C be matrixes and λ be a scalar (constant parameter).

If $C = \lambda \cdot A \Rightarrow c_{ij} = \lambda \cdot a_{ij}$.

Multiplying matrix A by a scalar λ is equivalent to summing matrix A with itself λ times. Thus, the above definition is straightforward and intuitive.

Example:

$$
5 \cdot \begin{pmatrix} 1 & 2 \\ 3 & 4 \end{pmatrix} = \begin{pmatrix} 5 & 10 \\ 15 & 20 \end{pmatrix}.
$$

5. Multiplying two matrixes (cross product)

Let A, B, and C be matrixes with a_{ij}, b_{ij}, and c_{ij} elements, respectively, so that the number of columns in matrix A equals the number of rows in matrix B; that is, $A(n \times m)$, $B(m \times p)$, and $C(n \times p)$,

Then, if $C = A \times B = AB \Rightarrow c_{ij} = \sum_{k=1}^{m} a_{ik} \cdot b_{kj} = a_{i1}b_{1j} + a_{i2}b_{2j} + \ldots + a_{im}b_{mj}$.

Example:

$$A = \begin{pmatrix} 1 & 2 & 3 \\ 4 & 5 & 6 \end{pmatrix} \text{ and } B = \begin{pmatrix} 1 & 0 & -2 & 0 \\ 3 & 1 & 0 & 0 \\ 0 & 2 & 0 & -1 \end{pmatrix} \quad \Rightarrow$$

$$\begin{pmatrix} 1 & 2 & 3 \\ 4 & 5 & 6 \end{pmatrix} \times \begin{pmatrix} 1 & 0 & -2 & 0 \\ 3 & 1 & 0 & 0 \\ 0 & 2 & 0 & -1 \end{pmatrix} = \begin{pmatrix} 7 & 8 & -2 & -3 \\ 19 & 17 & -8 & -6 \end{pmatrix}$$

$$\left[c_{22}\right] = \sum_{k=1}^{3} a_{2k} \cdot b_{k2} = a_{21}b_{12} + a_{22}b_{22} + a_{23}b_{32} = 4 \cdot 0 + 5 \cdot 1 + 6 \cdot 2 = 17$$

Note: $AB \neq BA$.

In the above example, BA is not even defined since it does not comply with the basic requirement that the number of columns in matrix B equal the number of rows in matrix A. This inequality is always true, even in cases where the prerequisite is met.

6. Division by a matrix

When we want to divide an algebraic equation by, say, x, we may do so by multiplying both sides by its inverse: $x^{-1} = \frac{1}{x}$. Similarly, when we want to divide a matrix algebra equation by a matrix A, we may do so by multiplying both sides by the inverse matrix $A^{-1} = \frac{1}{A}$.

We define the meaning of A^{-1} similar to our definition of x^{-1}. Using the same logic of the equation $x \cdot \frac{1}{x} = x \cdot x^{-1} = 1$, we may define matrix A^{-1} by the equation $A \times A^{-1} = I$, where I is a square[16] matrix with *ones* on the main diagonal and *zeros* everywhere else.

Example:

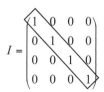

$$I = \begin{pmatrix} 1 & 0 & 0 & 0 \\ 0 & 1 & 0 & 0 \\ 0 & 0 & 1 & 0 \\ 0 & 0 & 0 & 1 \end{pmatrix}$$

16. A square matrix is defined as a matrix that has the same number of rows and columns.

Another rationalization for the definition of matrix I comes from its property $IA = AI = A$, which is equal (parallel) to $1 \cdot x = x \cdot 1 = x$ in common algebra.

7. Determinants

To calculate the different a_{ij}^{-1} elements of the matrix $[A]^{-1}$ or to find the solutions for the values of the different x_i's in the vector X in a system of linear equations, we will have to become familiar with another linear algebra term, the *determinant*. As already mentioned at the beginning of this section, when we wish to manually solve a system of n linear equations for n different x_i's, we manipulate the parameters by multiplying each line by a constant, adding (or subtracting) one equation line from another until we are left with one variable. Using determinants is a process that conceptually replicates this process.

Since this subchapter is only a review, we are not going to prove either the procedure for calculating the a_{ij}^{-1}'s elements or the procedure for calculating the x_i's values. To ease any doubts, let me clarify that their calculation boils down to a tedious procedure that can easily be converted to a computer routine. This routine is executed by command in MS Excel, as demonstrated in detail in the online appendix to this book (http://finmodeling.com/en).

A determinant is a single number of *worth* (a scalar) associated with a square matrix. In this review, we will not explicitly define the function that attaches the value of the scalar (determinant) to the matrix $[A]$ (it is too long), but since we are going to use it further on in this chapter, and very intensively in our next chapter, we will familiarize ourselves with the term by demonstration.

To each square $(n \times n)$ matrix $[A]$ we may attach or define a scalar, called the *determinant*, denoted by $\det[A]$ or $|A|$. Let us now demonstrate the process of calculating this scalar for (1×1), (2×2), and (3×3) matrixes $[A]$, so that it may be intuitively expanded to any matrix size $[A]$.

i. The determinant for (1×1) matrix $[A] = [a_{11}]$ is the scalar a_{11} itself, that is, $|A| = a_{11}$

ii. The determinant for (2×2) matrix $[A] = \begin{bmatrix} a_{11} & a_{12} \\ a_{21} & a_{22} \end{bmatrix}$ is the scalar $|A| = a_{11} \cdot a_{22} - a_{12} \cdot a_{21}$, i.e.,

$$|A| = \begin{vmatrix} a_{11} & a_{12} \\ a_{21} & a_{22} \end{vmatrix} = a_{11} \cdot a_{22} - a_{12} \cdot a_{21}$$

iii. The determinant for (3×3) matrix $[A] = \begin{bmatrix} a_{11} & a_{12} & a_{13} \\ a_{21} & a_{22} & a_{23} \\ a_{31} & a_{32} & a_{33} \end{bmatrix}$ is the scalar

$$|A| = a_{11} \cdot \begin{vmatrix} a_{22} & a_{23} \\ a_{32} & a_{33} \end{vmatrix} - a_{12} \cdot \begin{vmatrix} a_{21} & a_{23} \\ a_{31} & a_{33} \end{vmatrix} + a_{13} \cdot \begin{vmatrix} a_{21} & a_{22} \\ a_{31} & a_{32} \end{vmatrix}.$$

That is, $|A|$ is a linear combination of three "second-order" (2×2) determinants, each multiplied by the matrix's first line elements a_{11}, a_{12}, a_{13} (with switching signs[17]). Each second-order determinant is formed by deleting the line and column of the corresponding leading (multiplying) element:

$$|A| = a_{11} \cdot \begin{vmatrix} a_{11} & a_{12} & a_{13} \\ a_{21} & a_{22} & a_{23} \\ a_{31} & a_{32} & a_{33} \end{vmatrix} - a_{12} \cdot \begin{vmatrix} a_{11} & a_{12} & a_{13} \\ a_{21} & a_{22} & a_{23} \\ a_{31} & a_{32} & a_{33} \end{vmatrix} + a_{13} \cdot \begin{vmatrix} a_{11} & a_{12} & a_{13} \\ a_{21} & a_{22} & a_{23} \\ a_{31} & a_{32} & a_{33} \end{vmatrix}$$

From the above example, the reader can understand how we may extrapolate and obtain the scalar (determinant) $|A|$ by regression, for a fourth-order, fifth-order, or nth-order matrix. All we have to do is delete the line and column of the corresponding leading element that appears on the first line of the nth-order matrix $[A]$ and multiply it (with switched signs) by the remaining matrix of order $n - 1$ (after erasing the corresponding line and column). Just remember, the above tedious process yields a single number (i.e., a scalar).

D. Optimal Portfolio Allocation

We wish to find the relative weights of the assets in our portfolio to minimize variance for any given portfolio return. It is equivalent to finding the maximum portfolio return for a given portfolio variance; that is, both represent the efficient frontier. In chapter 12 we saw that once we introduce a risk-free asset[18] R_f, then the final efficient frontier is a line that starts at R_f and is tangent to the preliminary efficient frontier at point (portfolio) P, which we previously formed from all the risky assets included in the portfolio.

The investment opportunities line (IOL), or the final efficient frontier, is the line the investor faces when establishing his investment position

---

17. Switching signs entails multiplying by $(-1)^{j+1}$.

18. It is risk-free in the sense that not only is its variance (close to) zero but also its correlation between this asset and any other of the assets in the portfolio is (close to) zero.

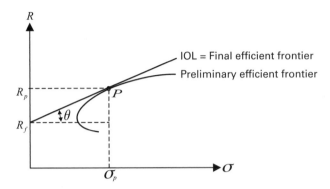

Figure 14.2
The Investment Opportunities Line (IOL)

between the risk-free asset and the risky portfolio P, according to his utility function. Thus, the new efficient frontier line is obtained in practice by maximizing[19] $\tan\theta = \dfrac{R_p - R_f}{\sigma_p}$.

Maximizing $\tan\theta$ is equivalent to finding the relative weights of the assets that give a minimum portfolio variance σ_P^2 for expected returns[20] $R_p - R_f$, or to finding the maximum $R_p - R_f$ for a given portfolio variance σ_P^2. It is exactly the same procedure we planned for deriving the preliminary efficient frontier,[21] but instead of performing the process on R_i, the expected return of each asset, we must use each asset risk premium π_i, that is, the expected returns *above* the risk-free rate $R_i - R_f$.

Note: When we follow this last procedure we will not derive the whole preliminary efficient frontier, that is, a minimum variance for any required expected return, but rather the weights for the assets constructing the particular portfolio P, the portfolio that is tangent to the final frontier straight line. However, this is the portfolio we need, as we do not actually need the whole preliminary efficient frontier.

We may now start our formal optimal asset allocation for our n assets portfolio assembly.

---

19. All the other lines connecting the risky asset with any portfolio on the preliminary efficient frontier will have a smaller θ, that is, a smaller $\tan\theta$. This procedure is similar to finding the SML (securities market line) in chapter 13. The IOL is not necessarily the SML since the preliminary efficient frontier of portfolio P is formed by only a few assets (and not all the existing assets), some of which we will assume in chapter 15, may not be in market equilibrium.

20. To simplify the notation, we have omitted the operator E and used R for expected return in figure 14.2, as well as in the above discussion and hereafter (unless otherwise noted).

21. That is, before introducing R_f.

Let's denote the risky assets' market consensus expected returns *above* the risk-free rate (their risk premium):

$$[\Pi] = \begin{bmatrix} \pi_1 \\ \pi_2 \\ \vdots \\ \pi_n \end{bmatrix} = \text{in our example} \begin{bmatrix} 5.4\% \\ 7.2\% \\ 3.8\% \end{bmatrix}.$$

And their equilibrium[22] market capitalization weights[23] $[w] = \begin{bmatrix} w_1 \\ w_2 \\ \vdots \\ w_n \end{bmatrix}$;

$$[w]^T = [w_1, w_2, \ldots w_n].$$

The expected return premium on our portfolio is therefore:

$$R_P = [w]^T \times [\Pi] = [w_1, w_2, \ldots w_n] \times \begin{bmatrix} \pi_1 \\ \pi_2 \\ \vdots \\ \pi_n \end{bmatrix}$$

$$= w_1 \cdot \pi_1 + w_2 \cdot \pi_2 + \ldots + w_n \cdot \pi_n = \sum_i w_i \cdot \pi_i.$$

The last equation demonstrates how the new matrix notation is translated into the familiar, regular algebraic notation from chapter 12, that is, $R_P = [w]^T \times [\Pi] = \sum_i w_i \cdot \pi_i$.

In a similar fashion, we may denote the market consensus variance-covariance $n \times n$ matrix associated with the n assets portfolio to be $[\Sigma]$.[24]

The variance σ_P^2 of our portfolio is $\sigma_P^2 = [w]^T \times [\Sigma] \times [w]$, where

$$[\Sigma] = \begin{bmatrix} \sigma_1^2 & \sigma_{12} & \ldots & \sigma_{1n} \\ \sigma_{21} & \sigma_2^2 & \ldots & \sigma_{2n} \\ \vdots & \vdots & \ldots & \vdots \\ \sigma_{n1} & \sigma_{n2} & \ldots & \sigma_n^2 \end{bmatrix} = \text{in our example}$$

Asset	I	II	III
I	0.06	0.063	0.023
II	0.063	0.09	0.043
III	0.023	0.043	0.4

22. As explained, we use the *implied* rate of return for R_i, which by definition is the equilibrium rate.

23. $w_1 + w_2 + \ldots + w_n = 1$.

24. Do not confuse the variance-covariance matrix notation $[\Sigma]$ with the summation notation $\sum_{i=1}^{N}$.

Thus, $\sigma_p^2 = [w]^T \times [\Sigma] \times [w] = [w_1, w_2, ... w_n] \times \begin{bmatrix} \sigma_1^2 & \sigma_{12} & ... & \sigma_{1n} \\ \sigma_{21} & \sigma_2^2 & ... & \sigma_{2n} \\ \vdots & \vdots & ... & \vdots \\ \sigma_{n1} & \sigma_{n2} & ... & \sigma_n^2 \end{bmatrix} \times \begin{bmatrix} w_1 \\ w_2 \\ \vdots \\ w_n \end{bmatrix}$

$$= \left[\left(\sum_{i=1}^{n} w_1 \cdot \sigma_{i1} \right) ; \left(\sum_{i=1}^{n} w_2 \cdot \sigma_{i2} \right) ; ... ; \left(\sum_{i=1}^{n} w_n \cdot \sigma_{in} \right) \right] \times \begin{bmatrix} w_1 \\ w_2 \\ \vdots \\ w_n \end{bmatrix}.$$

We get the same results as in chapter 12, namely:[25]

$$\sigma_p^2 = \sum_{i=1}^{n} \left(\sum_{j=1}^{n} w_j \cdot \sigma_{ji} \right) \cdot w_i = \sum_{i=1}^{n} \sum_{j=1}^{n} \rho_{ij} W_i W_j \sigma_i \sigma_j.$$

Once again, the last equation demonstrates how the new matrix notation is translated into the familiar, regular algebraic notation from chapter 12:

$$\sigma_p^2 = [w]^T \times [\Sigma] \times [w] = \sum_{i=1}^{n} \sum_{j=1}^{n} \rho_{ij} W_i W_j \sigma_i \sigma_j.$$

In chapter 12 we discussed how Markowitz et al. conducted a regression of various types of utility functions on their second-order Taylor approximation, which is essentially a quadratic function, and showed that the results are the same for all practical purposes. Students usually find it easier to follow the mathematical derivation of the maximum of a quadratic utility function than to find the maximum of a general utility function.

We will use the quadratic utility function $U = R_P - \frac{\lambda}{2} \cdot \sigma_P^2$ to present the "collective market utility function" when holding a portfolio P, and only then generalize the case to any general risk-averse utility function.

Let's define a scalar λ as the average market risk-aversion coefficient. The market risk-aversion coefficient is a risk-return trade-off in the sense that it implies how much more the expected return will be required if we increase the risk (variance) by one unit. In equilibrium, the market utility function is tangent to the efficient frontier at the market portfolio M,

25. Reminder: $\sigma_{ij} = \rho_{ij}\sigma_i\sigma_j$ for $i \neq j$ and $\sigma_{ij} = \sigma_i^2$ for $i = j$.

that is, $\lambda = {r_M}/{\sigma_M^2} = \tan\theta$, where θ is the securities market line (SML) slope. Empirical studies estimate λ to be in the range of 2.5.

We may summarize our notation so far as follows:

[Π]—The assets' implied (equilibrium) excess return vector ($n \times 1$ column vector).

[Σ]—The variance-covariance matrix of the (excess) returns ($n \times n$ matrix).

[w]—The market capitalization weights of the assets ($n \times 1$ column vector).

λ—The average (market) risk-aversion coefficient.

We will demonstrate the role of the average (market) risk-aversion coefficient λ by maximizing the *representative* quadratic market utility function of our example $U = \Pi_P - \dfrac{\lambda}{2} \cdot \sigma_P^2$ with respect to the weights of the assets w_i for $i = 1, 2, \ldots n$:

$$Max_w \{U(w) = \Pi_P - \frac{\lambda}{2} \cdot \sigma_P^2\}$$

$$\downarrow \qquad \qquad \downarrow$$

$$= Max_w \left\{ \sum_{i=1}^{n} w_i \cdot \pi_i + \frac{\lambda}{2} \cdot \sum_{i=1}^{n} \sum_{j=1}^{n} w_j \cdot \sigma_{ji} \cdot w_i \right\} \text{ in regular math notation;}$$

$$\downarrow \qquad \qquad \downarrow$$

$$= Max_w \left\{ [\mathrm{w}]^{\mathrm{T}} \times [\Pi] - \frac{\lambda}{2} \cdot [\mathrm{w}]^{\mathrm{T}} \times [\Sigma] \times [\mathrm{w}] \right\} \text{ in matrix notation.}$$

To maximize the market utility function $U(w)$, we must equate all of its partial derivatives with respect to each of the k assets' weights w_k to zero,[26] that is:

$$\frac{\partial U(w)}{\partial w_k} = \pi_k - \frac{\lambda}{2} \cdot \sum_{i=1}^{n} 2 \cdot \sigma_{ik} \cdot w_k = 0 \qquad \text{for each asset } k, \qquad k = 1, 2, \ldots n$$

$$\Rightarrow \qquad \pi_k = \lambda \cdot \sum_{i=1}^{n} \sigma_{ik} \cdot w_k \qquad \text{for } k = 1, 2, \ldots n.$$

26. The reader should imagine a graph of $k + 1$ dimensions in which the risk and return are on the k-axis (one for each asset) and the expected utility from holding w_i from that asset is on the z-axis. The utility function at the maximum point has a ∩ shape in any of the k assets' dimension. Thus, the slope of the tangent (derivative) at that point is zero.

Using matrix algebra notation, the last equation may be written as:

$[\Pi] = \lambda \cdot [\Sigma] \times [w]$.

To find vector $[w]$, multiply both sides of the equation by $[\Sigma]^{-1}$.
We get:

$$[\Sigma]^{-1} \times [\Pi] = \lambda \cdot \underbrace{[\Sigma]^{-1} \times [\Sigma]}_{I} \times [w] = \lambda \cdot [I] \times [w] = \lambda \cdot [w] \qquad \Rightarrow$$

$$[w] = \frac{1}{\lambda} \cdot [\Sigma]^{-1} \times [\Pi].$$

We may now generalize the above final result for any utility function.

Small changes in asset weights that result in an increase in our portfolio return must also increase the portfolio risk, $\sigma_p^2 = [w]^T \times [\Sigma] \times [w]$. When we increase/reduce (buy/sell) one of the weights w_k by δ_k, our return will change by $\pm \delta_k \cdot \pi_k$. Denote the corresponding rate of change of σ by $\Delta_k = \pm \partial \sigma / \partial w_k$ (+ for buying, – for selling), and the risk σ will change by $\pm \delta_k \cdot \Delta_k$. Once again, a small change in the weight of asset k results in changes in *both* the return and standard deviation of the portfolio! Choosing the optimal weights that maximize the expected value $E[U(w)]$ means that we are at an extreme point of the expected utility function in the risk-return space.[27] By definition, at that point $\dfrac{\pi_k}{\Delta_k} = \dfrac{\pi_k}{\partial \sigma / \partial w_k}$ must be the same constant for all the assets $k = 1, 2, \ldots n$. Otherwise, we could sell the asset with the smaller ratio and buy the asset with the larger ratio, reaching a higher value for the expected utility function. This means that from the beginning, we were not at the optimal (max) spot.

As the above is true for any market utility function maximum point, the results we obtained for the quadratic utility function that we gave as our example applies to any market utility function, and this constant must be the market average risk-aversion coefficient (constant) λ.

E. The Normalized Variance-Covariance Matrix

In this optimization process we neglected to apply the constraint $\sum_{i=1}^{n} w_i = 1$. We may bypass the constraint and get the desired result $\sum_{i=1}^{n} w_i = 1$ by

27. See note 26.

dividing each of the weights w_i that we obtained in the original optimization process by their sum.

$$\sum_{i=1}^{n} w_i = C \neq 1 \Rightarrow \sum_{i=1}^{n} \frac{w_i}{C} = \frac{1}{C} \cdot \sum_{i=1}^{n} w_i = \frac{1}{C} \cdot C = 1.$$

In this process of "normalizing" the weights w_i so that they add up to
one, the meaning that we gave for λ as the market risk-aversion coefficient cancels out, and in its stead, we get a meaningless proportional
scalar α.

$$\left[w^{normal} \right] = \frac{1}{\lambda \cdot \sum_{i-1}^{n} w_i} [\Sigma]^{-1} [\Pi] \Rightarrow \left[w^{normal} \right] = \alpha \cdot [\Sigma]^{-1} [\Pi]\, ; \alpha = \frac{1}{\lambda \cdot \sum_{i-1}^{n} w_i}.$$

Since α is a scalar representing a proportional relation and has no
other meaning, we may replace it with another scalar τ that directly
multiplies all the parameters in the variance-covariance matrix $[\Sigma]$, so
that the last equation will have the form $[w^{normal}] = [\tau\Sigma]^{-1}[\Pi]$.

For convenience, we will delete the suffix "normal" from $[w^{normal}]$, and
from now on we will use the notation $[w]$ for the normalized matrix.

The matrix $[\tau\Sigma]$ is called the "normalized variance-covariance matrix."
It is normalized in the sense that once it replaces the original variance-
covariance matrix (extracted from past history) when plugged into our
above mean-variance optimizer process, we will automatically receive
the normalized weights vector $[w]$; that is, the results for $[w]$ will sum up
to one right away.

Once again, one could rightly wonder what we have gained from building a matrix form for the mean-variance optimizer rather than using
the convenient black-box optimizer named Solver. So far, Black and Litterman have only let us know that in their extensive experience, it is
advisable to apply the "implied expected returns" for better portfolio
configuration when making use of the mean-variance optimizer, a con-
ception that should yield good results when employing Solver without
forcing artificial constraints, as well. This is true if we do not want to add
any personal views about the expected future returns. As stated in the
Introduction section of this chapter, Black and Litterman "found that
simply moving away from the equilibrium risk premium in a naive
(weighted average) manner quickly leads to portfolio weights that make
no sense." What causes it are the covariances between the assets' returns.

Thus, to employ personal views jointly with market equilibrium expectations, we will need to master the matrix presentation for portfolio

configuration when extracting the joint expected returns and their joint variance-covariances. The normalized variance-covariance matrix, combined with the investor's confidence level, will determine the weight that will be given to the investor's own views about future returns relative to the market equilibrium expectations.

We will present the Black-Litterman approach to integrating personal views in chapter 15. Their process not only makes extensive use of matrix algebra but also uses the normalized variance-covariance matrix $[\tau\Sigma]$, presented above, when "translating" the investor's confidence level in his views into terms of the variance of his expected returns. What we have achieved in chapter 14 is familiarization with the matrix form of presenting the mean-variance optimization process, as well as presenting the notion for the normalized variance-covariance matrix $[\tau\Sigma]$.

The use of the quadratic utility function in the above discussion is, in my opinion, tremendously important for an intuitive understanding of the concept of the mean-variance maximization process in its matrix form. Readers who prefer a more formal approach and who are extremely proficient in mathematics may derive the same result, $[w] = \dfrac{1}{\lambda}\cdot[\Sigma]^{-1}\times[\Pi]$, applying the Euler-Lagrange equations for the function's extreme, extended by the Lagrange multipliers method to take into account possible constraints.

The mean-variance maximization problem can be formally stated as:[28]

$$\begin{cases} \underset{w}{Max} \ \left\{\ [w]^T \times [\Pi]\ \right\} \\ s.t. \ \ [w]^T \times [\Sigma] \times [w] = \sigma^2 \end{cases}$$

where the Lagrange function is

$$L = [w]^T \times [\Pi] - \delta\cdot\left([w]^T \times [\Sigma] \times [w] - \sigma^2\right).$$

F. Optimal Portfolio Construction Using Excel

We shall conduct this part with a numerical example for a four-asset portfolio, using the Excel functions for linear (matrix) algebra (if you are not familiar with them, see appendix C at http://finmodeling.com/en).

---

28. This is the most simple presentation ignoring the constraint $\sum_{i=1}^{n} w_i = 1$, since we have seen that the final result may be adjusted to meet this requirement.

An investor has chosen[29] four assets with the following annual implied excess expected returns and variance-covariance matrix, extracted from historical data for the last five years:

Σ Variance-Covariance Matrix					$E(\pi_i)$
Asset	I	II	III	IV	Implied Returns
I	0.06	0.063	0.023	0.033	0.054
II	0.063	0.09	0.043	0.04	0.072
II	0.023	0.043	0.035	0.02	0.038
IV	0.033	0.04	0.02	0.028	0.037

The average return for the last five years on one-year T-bills was 4%.

1. Calculate the weights for the assets in the optimal portfolio P.
2. Calculate the expected return and the standard deviation of portfolio P.
3. Calculate the normalized variance-covariance matrix $\tau\Sigma$ (of particular importance for the next chapter).

1. We will calculate the weights for the optimal portfolio P in two steps

First calculate $[w] = \dfrac{1}{\lambda} \cdot [\Sigma]^{-1} \times [\Pi]$.

Then calculate $[w^{normal}] = \dfrac{1}{\lambda \cdot \sum\limits_{i=1}^{n} w_i} [\Sigma]^{-1} [\Pi]$.

Step 1. Enter the data into the Excel sheet:

29. We have added one more asset to the three-asset portfolio used thus far in our examples. This additional fourth asset resembles the "Int. Dev. Equity" asset in the Black-Litterman example (see also note 4 in this chapter).

Step 2. Using the mouse, highlight the target range (**B11:B14**) for the vector solution [*w*].

Step 3. Click the **Insert Function** button f_x.

Choose the function **MMULT** and select **OK.**

The following screen is displayed.

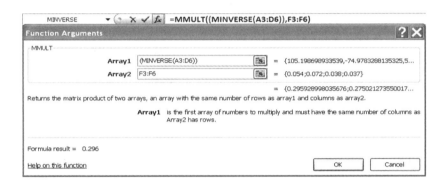

Step 4. In **Array 1**, type **MINVERSE**, followed by the array cells of [Σ], in our example: (**A3:D6**).

Or:

Type **MINVERSE**. Press the Ctrl+Shift keys. With the mouse, highlight the [Σ] cell range. The range will appear in the formula box **Array1**.

Step 5. Move the cursor to **Array 2** and type the cell range of [Π], in our example: (**F3:F6**).

Or:

Move the cursor to **Array 2**. Press the Ctrl +Shift keys. With the mouse, highlight the [Π] cell range. The range will appear in the formula box **Array 2**.

Step 6. Press the Ctrl+Shift keys, click **OK,** and release the Ctrl+Shift keys.

The result for [*w*] will appear in the target cell array (**B11:B14**).

	Home	Insert	Page Layout	Formulas	Data	Review	View

J23 f_x | Function field

	A	B	C			F
1			$[\Sigma]$			Π
2						
3	0.06	0.063	0.023	0.033		0.054
4	0.063	0.09	0.043	0.04		0.072
5	0.023	0.043	0.035	0.02		0.038
6	0.033	0.04	0.02	0.028		0.037
7						
8						
9		$[w]$				
10						
11		0.296				
12		0.275				
13		0.375				
14	line 14	0.312				
15	$\sum$ =	1.258				
16	line 11					
17						

We now wish to normalize the $[w]$ vector of weights that we have obtained (so that they will add up to one) by dividing each asset weight by $\sum w_i = 1.258$.

Step 7. To get the sum of the assets weights in $[w]$, highlight cell **B15** and click the [**Σ Autosum**] button.[30]

Step 8. Highlight **D11:D14** target cells for the normalized weights vector $[w^{normal}]$.

Step 9. In the function field (as displayed in the figure above), type $f_x =$ (B11 : B14)/B15.

Press and hold the Ctrl+Shift keys.

Click on **Enter**. The normalized $[w^{normal}]$ will appear in the target field.

Release the Ctrl+Shift keys.

For control purposes only:

Step 10. Highlight cell **D15** and select the [**Σ Autosum**] button.

The result 1.00 should appear in the field and thus verify that the sum of the above cells is one; that is, we indeed got the normalized $[w^{normal}]$.

---

30. Click the **Home** tab. [Σ Autosum] is on the right-hand side of the menu tool bar.

	A	B	C	D	E	F
1			$[\Sigma]$			Π
2						
3	0.06	0.063	0.023	0.033		0.054
4	0.063	0.09	0.043	0.04		0.072
5	0.023	0.043	0.035	0.02		0.038
6	0.033	0.04	0.02	0.028		0.037
7						
8						
9		$[w]$		$[w^{normal}]$		
10						
11		0.296		0.24		
12		0.275		0.22		
13		0.375		0.30		
14	$line\ 14$	0.312		0.25		
15	$\sum$ =	1.258		1.00		
16	$line\ 11$					
17						

2. Calculate the expected premium and the standard deviation of portfolio P.

We may now add the column vector of normalized weights to our data.

Σ Variance-Covariance Matrix					$E(\pi_i)$	w_i^{normal}
Asset	I	II	III	IV		
I	0.06	0.063	0.023	0.033	0.054	0.24
II	0.063	0.09	0.043	0.04	0.072	0.22
III	0.023	0.043	0.035	0.02	0.038	0.30
IV	0.033	0.04	0.02	0.028	0.037	0.25

The portfolio's expected return premium, $E(R_p) = [w]^T \times [\Pi] = 0.049 = 4.9\%$, is calculated as follows:

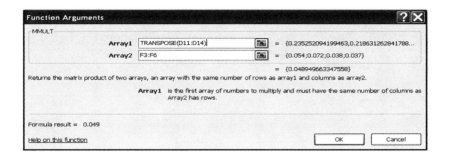

Highlight cell **B19**, click the **Insert Function** button f_x and choose the function **MMULT** (double click). In **Array 1**, type **TRANSPOSE (D11:D14)**, and in **Array 2**, type (**F3:F6**). Hold down the Ctrl+Shift keys and click **OK** to get the result.

	A	B	C	D	E	F
1			$[\Sigma]$				Π
2							
3	0.06	0.063	0.023	0.033		0.054
4	0.063	0.09	0.043	0.04		0.072
5	0.023	0.043	0.035	0.02		0.038
6	0.033	0.04	0.02	0.028		0.037
7						
8						
9			$[w]$		$[w^{normal}]$	
10						
11			0.296		0.24	
12			0.275		0.22	
13			0.375		0.30	
14	$\underset{Line\ 11}{\overset{Line\ 14}{\sum}}$ =		0.312		0.25	
15			1.258		1.00	
16						
17						
18						
19	$E(R_p) =$		0.049			
20						

We will calculate the variance $\sigma_p^2 = [w]^T \times [\Sigma] \times [w]$ in two steps:

Step 1. Calculate $[\Sigma] \times [w]$

Highlight the target range **F11:F14** for the result of $[\Sigma] \times [w]$.

	A	B	C	D	E	F
1			$[\Sigma]$			Π
2						
3	0.06	0.063	0.023	0.033		0.054
4	0.063	0.09	0.043	0.04		0.072
5	0.023	0.043	0.035	0.02		0.038
6	0.033	0.04	0.02	0.028		0.037
7						
8						
9			$[w]$	$[w^{normal}]$		$[\Sigma] \times [w]$
10						
11		0.296		0.24		0.04
12		0.275		0.22		0.06
13		0.375		0.30		0.03
14	line 14	0.312		0.25		0.03
15	$\sum$ =	1.258		1.00		
16	line 11					
17						
18						
19	$E(R_p) =$	0.049				
20						

(Cell reference F14, formula bar: `{=MMULT(A3:D6,D11:D14)}`)

Click the **Insert Function** button f_x and choose **MMULT**. Populate[31] **Array 1** with (**A3:D6**) and **Array 2** with (**D11:D14**). Hold down the Ctrl+Shift keys and click **OK** to get the result in the target range **F11:F14**.

Step 2. Calculate: $\sigma_p^2 = [w]^T \times \{[\Sigma] \times [w]\} = 0.39$

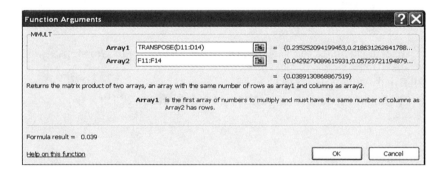

Function Arguments

MMULT

Array1 TRANSPOSE(D11:D14)   = {0.235252094199463,0.218631262841788...
Array2 F11:F14   = {0.0429279089615931;0.05723721194879...
                             = {0.0389130868867519}
Returns the matrix product of two arrays, an array with the same number of rows as array1 and columns as array2.

Array1 is the first array of numbers to multiply and must have the same number of columns as Array2 has rows.

Formula result =   0.039
Help on this function   OK   Cancel

31. Or hold down the Ctrl+Shift keys and highlight the [Σ] array range. The result will appear automatically in the **Array 1** field.

Highlight the target range **B21**.

Click the **Insert Function** button f_x and choose **MMULT**. Populate **Array 1** with **TRANSPOSE(D11:D14)**[32] and **Array 2** with **(D11:D14)**. Hold down the Ctrl+Shift keys and click **OK** to get the result in the target range **B21**.

	Home	Insert	Page Layout	Formulas	Data	Review	View	

	B21	▾	f_x	{=MMULT(TRANSPOSE(D11:D14),F11:F14)}			

	A	B	C	D	E	F
7						
8						
9		$[w]$		$[w^{normal}]$		$[\Sigma] \times [w]$
10						
11		0.296		0.24		0.04
12		0.275		0.22		0.06
13		0.375		0.30		0.03
14	line 14	0.312		0.25		0.03
15	$\sum$ =	1.258		1.00		
16	line 11					
17						
18						
19	$E(R_p) =$	0.049				
20						
21	$\sigma_p^2 =$	0.039	$\Rightarrow$ $\sigma =$	0.197		
22						

3. Calculate the normalized variance-covariance matrix $[\tau\Sigma]$

The normalized[33] variance-covariance matrix $[\tau\Sigma]$ will be extremely important and useful in the next chapter, when we present how to add our own expectations about future asset returns and variances.

We will multiply $[\Sigma]$ by an arbitrary constant τ and then repeat the same steps as in step 1 to get $[w^{normal}_{control}]$. Then we will change τ by trial and error until we obtain $[w^{normal}_{control}] = [w^{normal}]$, where $[w^{normal}]$ is the same value as received before, in the first part of the exercise. As you will see, this task can be achieved very quickly, in a few trial-and-error steps. (Solver may be handy here for those who master it.)

---

32. Or hold down the Ctrl+Shift keys and highlight the $[\Sigma]$array range. The result will appear automatically in the **Array 1** field.

33. Again, it is normalized in the sense that when we replace the original $[\Sigma]$ in our optimization process with the normalized variance-covariance matrix $[\tau\Sigma]$, we will automatically get $[w^{normal}]$.

	A	B	C	D	E	F	G	H	I	J	K	L	M
1		$[\Sigma]$				$[\Pi]$							
2													
3	0.06	0.063	0.023	0.033		0.054							
4	0.063	0.09	0.043	0.04		0.072							
5	0.023	0.043	0.035	0.02		0.038							
6	0.033	0.04	0.02	0.028		0.037							
7													
8													
9		$[w]$		$[w^{normal}]$		$[\Sigma]\times[w]$			$[\tau\Sigma]$				control
10													$[w^{normal}]$
11		0.296		0.24		0.043		0.076	0.079	0.029	0.042		
12		0.275		0.22		0.057		0.079	0.113	0.054	0.050		0.22
13		0.375		0.30		0.030		0.029	0.054	0.044	0.025		0.30
14		0.312		0.25		0.029		0.042	0.050	0.025	0.035		0.25
15	$\sum_{b w 11}^{bw14}$ =	1.258		$\sum_{bw11}^{bw14}$ =	1.00							$\sum_{bw11}^{bw14}$ =	1.00
16													
17													
18													
19	$E(R_p)$ =	0.049											
20													
21	σ_p^2 =	0.039	$\Rightarrow \sigma$ =	0.197									
22													
23	τ =	1.26											

Step 1. Put an initial value for τ (the value 1 is a good number to begin with) in cell **B23**.

Step 2. Select cell **H11**. In the function field, type[34] f_x =**A3*B23**. Copy cell **H11** (left click on the mouse), highlight the 4×4 cell area, that is, array (**H11:K14**), and right click on Paste.

Step 3. Create in array (**M11:M14**) the $[w^{normal}]^{control} = [\tau\Sigma]^{-1}[\Pi]$, following the same steps 1 to 10 as in the first part of the exercise for $[w^{normal}]$.

Step 4. Using your best estimate, change the content of cell **B23** a few times in a trial-and-error process until $[w^{normal}]^{control}$ in array (**M11:M14**) equals $[w^{normal}]$ in array (**D11:D14**). Watch $[\tau\Sigma]$ as it changes each step in your trial-and-error process.[35]

G. The Investment Opportunities Line

Finding the expected return[36] for portfolio P, R_p = 8.9% and its risk measure,[37] σ_p = 0.197, is not the end of the process. The investor must

---

34. The $ signs around B in **B23** mean the value content in cell B23 is fixed.

35. *Note:* it took me seven times (and less than one minute) changing B23 to reach the final result. There are ways to do the above process automatically in Excel.

36. Note that we have found the expected return premium, to which we have to add the risk-free return.

37. We may scale the risk measure as we wish: in decimal form, percentage, or even σ^2, as long as we are always consistent. It is only a question of scaling the x-axis.

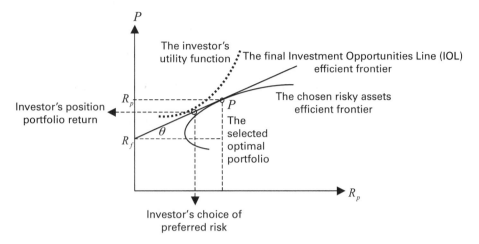

Figure 14.3
Establishing a Position between the Risk-Free Asset and the Risky Portfolio P

choose his preferred investment position between the risk-free asset (bonds) and the risky portfolio P, which was optimally constructed from the risky assets that were chosen, by calculating the vector $[w^{normal}]$ as their weights. Portfolio P was optimally constructed in the sense that the investment opportunities line (IOL) that the investor faces now ensures he may expect to get the maximum return R for any risk level he prefers to choose, where σ is his measure of risk.

The IOL equation is $R = 4 + 24.9 \times \sigma.$[38]

If, for example, the investor decided to invest in risky asset I alone, he could expect (according to the given data) a risk premium return of 5.4% (a total return of 9.4%) with a variance of 0.06, or a risk measure (standard deviation) of $\sigma = \sqrt{0.06} = 0.245$ (24.5%!). Keeping to the IOL, he could get, for the same risk (0.245), a risk premium return of 6.1% (a total return of 10.1%). The IOL will always be a better choice than investing in any other combination (weights) made from the four risky assets he selected initially.

The Excel efficient frontier optimizer template we constructed in the last section may be easily expanded for any number of risky assets. It may be combined with other worksheets on which the implied return vector of different assets and their variance-covariance matrix are

38. The slope of the line is $a = \dfrac{4.9}{0.197} = 24.9$.

calculated and the riskless rate (usually on one-year or less T-bills). We recommend starting with templates of ten risky assets or less, since the reader will find it difficult to find a large number of risky assets where the correlation between any two of them is small enough.

We might feed the final results automatically from one worksheet to another. Although building the templates is a somewhat tedious job, it need be done only once. We might import raw material from past history returns from a variety of online sources and change the content of our templates.[39]

These templates are a very powerful tool. Readers may play around with the different numbers—the implied expected return and the riskless return—replacing one asset with an alternative asset, and watch how their choices affect the final results on the spot. Readers may also learn much by playing around with the sensitivity of the model to changes in the expected return (and discover that it is quite sensitive). Understanding the sensitivity of expected return projections on the model may help readers better construct their own personal projections (views) about next period expected returns, and make them more sensible. We will elaborate on how to incorporate personal views into the model in the next chapter.

Chapter 14—Questions and Problems

Question 1

Re-do question 2 from chapter 12. Use this example to explain the problem of choosing risky assets for a practical investment portfolio with a limited number of highly correlated assets.

Question 2

Choose 10 risky assets, stocks, bonds, or ETFs, using the historical price of the last five years from the Internet.

Example—Yahoo Finance: http://finance.yahoo.com/q/hp?s=YHOO.

---

39. You can copy and save several copies of the templates for comparisons of different options.

Date	Open	High	Low	Close	Volume	Adj. Close
Apr. 8, 2011	17.08	17.11	16.77	16.77	13,114,200	16.77
Apr. 7, 2011	16.91	17.10	16.79	17.00	12,778,700	17.00
Apr. 6, 2011	17.17	17.20	16.94	17.05	13,298,700	17.05
Apr. 5, 2011	16.81	17.29	16.79	17.11	18,464,500	17.11
Apr. 4, 2011	16.90	17.05	16.81	16.87	9,560,800	16.87
Apr. 1, 2011	16.83	16.98	16.72	16.84	12,382,900	16.84
Mar. 31, 2011	16.71	16.88	16.65	16.68	15,131,500	16.68
Mar. 30, 2011	16.83	16.92	16.68	16.74	12,944,600	16.74
Mar. 29, 2011	16.60	16.78	16.53	16.75	10,037,900	16.75
Mar. 28, 2011	17.01	17.06	16.58	16.58	16,066,700	16.58
Mar. 25, 2011	16.94	17.05	16.70	16.96	21,047,200	16.96

Build an Excel file that, from the data for the past five years, calculates:

1. The monthly return on the 10 risky assets (translated to annual return).

2. The average riskless annual return, calculated monthly, on an additional one-year treasury bond of your choice.

3. The monthly return on the market portfolio derived from a representative index of your choice (e.g., S&P 500).

Question 3

Calculate β_i for the ten assets of your choice.

1. Calculate the implied expected return for the ten assets of your choice.

2. Calculate the variances for the ten assets of your choice.

3. Calculate the 50 covariances of each couple of the ten assets of your choice.

4. Calculate the 50 correlation coefficients for each of the couples.

Question 4

1. Build an MS Excel file "Mean-Variance"[40] optimization template for four risky assets, similar to the one presented in this chapter.

---

40. Efficient frontier method.

2. Expand and add three templates that can handle six, eight, and ten risky assets.

Question 5

Choose six assets that have the smallest correlation out of the ten risky assets of your choice. Feed the proper information into the optimization template for the six risky assets you have prepared.

1. Check how close the correlations to the recommended 0.2 figure are.

2. Find the structure of the optimal portfolio P, its expected risk premium, and its expected return.

3. Find the optimal portfolio P risk in terms of σ^2 and in terms of σ.

4. Explain the results briefly, as compared with holding each asset individually.

5. "Play around" with the assets' expected risk premiums, and watch the effect on the optimal portfolio structure. Report your experience briefly.

Question 6

1. Calculate the IOL. Choose your desired position. Explain your choice briefly using professional terms (even where you cannot quantify!).

2. Calculate τ and the normalized variance-covariance matrix. Explain.

Further Reading

Benninga, S. 2008. *Financial Modeling*. 3rd ed. Cambridge, MA: MIT Press.

Best, J. J., and R. R. Grauer. 1991. On the Sensitivity of Mean-Variance-Efficient Portfolios to Changes in Asset Means: Some Analytical and Computational Results. *Review of Financial Studies* 4: 315–342.

Bevan, A., and K. Winkelmann. 1998. *Using the Black-Litterman Global Asset Allocation Model: Three Years of Practical Experience*. New York: Goldman Sachs.

Black, F. 1990. Universal Hedging: Optimizing Currency Risk and Reward in International Equity Portfolios. *Financial Analysts Journal* (July/August).

Black, F., and R. Litterman. 1990. Asset Allocation: Combining Investor Views with Market Equilibrium. New York: Goldman Sachs Fixed Income Research.

Black, F., and R. Litterman. 1992. Global Portfolio Optimization. *Financial Analysts Journal*, 48: 28–43.

Blume, M. E. 1970. Portfolio Theory: A Step towards Its Practical Application. *Journal of Business* (April).

Blume, M. E., and R. Stambaugh. 1983. Biases in Computed Returns: An Application to the Size Effect. *Journal of Financial Economics* (November): 387–404.

Board, J. L. Q., and C. M. S. Sutcliffe. 1985. Optimal Portfolio Diversification and the Effects of Differing Intra Sample Measures of Return. *Journal of Business Finance and Accounting* (Winter).

Brealey, R. A., and S. D. Hodges. 1975. Playing with Portfolios. *Journal of Finance* (March).

Chan, L., J. Karceski, and J. Lakonishok. 1999. On Portfolio Estimation: Covariances and Choosing the Risk Model. *Review of Financial Studies*: 12.

Chen, S. N. 1987. Simple Optimal Asset Allocation under Uncertainty. *Journal of Portfolio Management* (Summer).

Chopra, V., and W. Ziemba. 1993. The Effect of Errors in Means, Variances, & Covariances on Optimal Portfolio Choice. *Journal of Portfolio Management*: 19.

Cooley, P. L., R. L. Roenfeldt, and N. K. Modan. 1977. Interdependence of Market Risk Measures. *Journal of Business* (June).

Disatnik, D. J., and S. Benninga. 2007. Shrinking the Covariance Matrix: Simpler Is Better. *Journal of Portfolio Management*: 33.

Elton, E. J., Gruber, M. J. and Padberg, M. W. 1978. Simple Criteria for Optimal Portfolio Selection: Tracing Out the Efficient Frontier. *Journal of Finance* (March).

Fama, E. F. 1968. Risk, Return and Equilibrium: Some Clarifying Comments. *Journal of Finance* (March): 29–40.

Fama, E. F. 1971. Risk, Return and Equilibrium. *Journal of Political Economy* (January/February): 30–55.

Fama, E. F., and J. D. MacBeth. 1973. Risk, Return and Equilibrium: Empirical Test. *Journal of Political Economy* (May/June): 607–636.

Friend, I., and M. Blume. 1970. Measurement of Portfolio Performance under Uncertainty. *American Economic Review* (September): 561–575.

Frost, P. A., and J. E. Savarino. 1986. Portfolio Size and Estimation Risk. *Journal of Portfolio Management* (Summer).

Green, R. C. 1986. Benchmark Portfolio Inefficiency and Deviations from the Security Market Line. *Journal of Finance* (June).

Green, R. C., and B. Hollifield. 1992. When Will Mean-Variance Efficient Portfolios Be Well Diversified? *Journal of Finance*: 47.

Gressis, N., G. C. Philippatos, and J. Hayya. 1976. Multiperiod Portfolio Analysis and the Inefficiency of the Market Portfolio. *Journal of Finance*.

Idzorek, T. M. 2002. A Step-by-Step Guide to the Black-Litterman Model. Zephyr, NV: Zephyr Associates.

Jacob, N. L. 1974. A Limited Diversification Portfolio Selection Model for the Small Investor. *Journal of Finance* (June).

Jobson, J., and B. Korkie. 1981. Putting Markowitz Theory to Work. *Journal of Portfolio Management*: 7.

Johnson, K. H., and R. C. Burgess. 1975. The Effects of Sample Sizes on the Accuracy of EV and SSD Efficiency Criteria. *Journal of Financial and Quantitative Analysis* (December).

Kandel, S., and R. F. Stambaugh. 1987. On Correlations and Inferences about Mean-Variance Efficiency. *Journal of Financial Economics* (March).

Kraus, A., and R. H. Litzenberger. 1975. Market Equilibrium in a Multiperiod State Preference Model with Logarithmic Utility. *Journal of Finance* (December).

Ledoit, O., and M. Wolf. 2003. Improved Estimation of the Covariance Matrix of Stock Returns with an Application to Portfolio Selection. *Journal of Empirical Finance*: 10.

Ledoit, O., and M. Wolf. 2004. Honey, I Shrunk the Sample Covariance Matrix. *Journal of Portfolio Management*: 31.

Lehmann, B. N. 1987. Orthogonal Frontiers and Alternative Mean-Variance Efficiency Tests. *Journal of Finance* (July).

Li, Y., and W. T. Ziemba. 1989. Characterizations of Optimal Portfolios by Univariate and Multivariate Risk Aversion. *Management Science*: 35.

Litterman, B., and Quantitative Resource Group (Goldman Sachs). 2003. *Modern Investment Management: An Equilibrium Approach*. New York: Wiley.

Lorie, J. H., P. Dodd, and M. H. Kimpton. 1985. *The Stock Market: Theories and Evidence*. 2nd ed. Homewood, IL: Richard D. Irwin.

Markowitz, H. M. 1990. Risk Adjustment. *Journal of Accounting Auditing and Finance* (Winter/Spring).

Merton, R. C. 1980. On Estimating the Expected Return on the Market: An Exploratory Investigation. *Journal of Financial Economics* (December): 323–361.

Roll, R. 1981. A Possible Explanation of the Small Firm Effect. *Journal of Finance* (September): 879–888.

Schwartz, R. A., and D. K. Whitcomb. 1977. The Time-Variance Relationship: Evidence on Autocorrelation in Common Stock Returns. *Journal of Finance* (March).

Statman, M. 1987. How Many Stocks Make a Diversified Portfolio? *Journal of Financial and Quantitative Analysis* (September).

15 Adding Subjective Views to Portfolio Allocation (the Black-Litterman Model)

A. Introduction

Many research papers have shown that statistically, it is impossible to beat the benchmark[1] of the implied equilibrium excess return vector $[\Pi]$ as the best estimator (predictor) of future returns. So, a logical, quantitative-oriented investor should at least start by considering allocating the assets in his portfolio (setting their weights w_i) according to the capital asset pricing model (CAPM) expected returns of the assets in an equilibrium market, using a mean-variance optimizer either in its matrix form, as introduced in chapter 14, or the Solver feature in MS Excel. Then, and only then, he might wish to add his personal opinions about future returns in the form of a basic views vector $[Q]$. In the last chapter, we found that the assets' weights w_i, derived using the efficient frontier technique, are very sensitive to small changes in the expected

---

1. But we also believe we are smarter and can beat the statistics.

returns premium vector [Π]. The newly derived weights w_i^* that are the result of such changes will often contradict straightforward intuition. Having worked so hard to convince the reader that the best estimator for [Π] derived from a historical data sample is the CAPM implied equilibrium returns, we now wish to modify our estimators for future returns by adding in subjective personal views.

In the last chapter we stated that we sought "neutral" estimators to forecast future returns, in the sense that they would offer us balanced results w_i when constructing our portfolio. Now, adding personal views, we should extend our definition and require that the revised estimator returns be highly correlated with the estimators at market equilibrium, thus leading us to a new (hopefully) balanced portfolio allocation, w_i^*. Once we incorporate this approach, then our basic views vector [Q] should be formulated *retrospectively*[2] and relative to the implied equilibrium excess return vector [Π].

Trying to find the best revised (new) retrospective joint estimator $E(R)$ for future returns, we may consider two distinct sources of information — the CAPM implied expected returns [Π] (based on the past data sample D) and the investor's opinion about future returns [Q]. Both sources of information for future returns are uncertain and therefore may at best be expressed as probability distributions. To incorporate our personal views using the Black-Litterman approach, we need to have all the involved parameters in their matrix form. That is why we insisted on presenting the mean-variance optimizer in its matrix form and did not simply let the black-box solution Solver so conveniently do the hard work for us.

The Black-Litterman model (1990) is a mathematical model that sets down a procedure combining both sources of information, using the Bayesian statistical approach to form a new joint estimator for the expected future returns $E(R)$ and its variance-covariance matrix $\left[\overline{\Sigma}\right]$ around the forecasted new mean. Remember that computing the variance $\left[\overline{\Sigma}\right]$ of the *retrospective* mean $E(R)$ around the forecasted new mean is not the same as computing a retrospective estimate of the variance $\left[\overline{\overline{\Sigma}}\right]$ from the assets' random returns $\left[\tilde{R}\right]$, which are easily calculated: $\left[\overline{\overline{\Sigma}}\right]=[\Sigma]+\left[\overline{\Sigma}\right]$.[3] Once we succeed in assessing the values of

---

2. The basic views vector [Q] is formulated retrospectively in the sense that the investor generates his personal view estimator [Q] only after knowing the values of the vector [Π].

3. I will elaborate on this point at the end of the chapter.

the new joint estimators $E(R)$ and $\overline{\overline{[\Sigma]}}$, we may find the new weights w_i^* for each asset in our revised portfolio, using the same efficient frontier optimizer template we set up in the previous chapter.

We may express the above approach by extending our notation:

$[\Pi]$ — Market-implied equilibrium risk premium estimator ($n \times 1$ column vector).

$P_r(\Pi)$ — The probability density function (PDF) of the equilibrium risk premium estimator (to prevail in the next time period = the future).

$[E(R)]$ — An investor's joint estimator for a future risk premium ($n \times 1$ column vector).

$P_r[E(R)]$ — The PDF of an investor's joint estimator for a future risk premium.

In basic statistics, we define *probability* as "a percentage of appearances in a large number of repeating trials." In the Bayesian statistical approach, we interpret probability as "a measure of a state of knowledge."[4] Whereas under the basic probability view, a hypothesis is typically rejected or not rejected without a probability being directly assigned to it, in a Bayesian approach, a probability is assigned to a hypothesis (subjective view). Thus, the Bayesian approach provides a standard set of procedures and formulas that suit the kind of calculations and procedures we need for formulating a model for our problem of how we should integrate our retrospective personal views.

The way the Bayesian approach measures a state of knowledge is by using Bayes' theorem for evaluating the probability that an event A will occur conditional on event B having occurred, and the converse probability of event B occurring conditional on event A having occurred. Denote $P_r(A)$ as the "prior" probability of event A, in the sense that it does not take into account any information about event B. $P_r(A \cap B)$ is the notation for the probability that both events A and B have occurred. $P_r(A|B)$ is the notation for the conditional probability of event A occuring if event B has occurred; i.e., if B yielded a specified value of $B = b$.

Bayes' theorem co-relates the conditional probabilities $P_r(A|B)$ with $P_r(B|A)$ and their prior probabilities $P_r(A)$ and $P_r(B)$ (figure 15.1):

---

4. Alternatively, in the Bayesian statistical approach probability may be defined as "a measure of rational personal belief."

Figure 15.1
The Overall Event A and Event B Space

$$P_r(A \mid B) = \frac{P_r(A \cap B)}{P_r(B)} \quad \Rightarrow \quad P_r(A \cap B) = P_r(A \mid B) \cdot P_r(B).$$

$$P_r(B \mid A) = \frac{P_r(A \cap B)}{P_r(A)} \quad \Rightarrow \quad P_r(A \cap B) = P_r(B \mid A) \cdot P_r(A).$$

Equating the right side of the above two formulas (since the left side is equal) results in the basic and important formula of Bayesian statistics:

$$P_r(A \mid B) \cdot P_r(B) = P_r(B \mid A) \cdot P_r(A),$$

or, as more commonly presented,

$$P_r(A \mid B) = \frac{P_r(B \mid A) \cdot P_r(A)}{P_r(B)}.$$

Defining the occurrence of event A as the probability of [Π] prevailing in the next time period (the future) and the occurrence of event B as the probability of [E(R)] prevailing in the next time period, we may expand the above notation of events A and B as:

$$P_r(E(R) \mid \Pi) \cdot P_r(\Pi) = P_r(\Pi \mid E(R)) \cdot P_r(E(R)).$$

$P_r(E(R) \mid \Pi)$ is the conditional PDF of [E(R)], the investor's joint estimator for a future risk premium given that the implied equilibrium risk premium estimator (which was derived from historical data) yielded a specific value [Π].

$P_r(\Pi)$ is the probability that under all the personal hypotheses about [E(R)] made by all the investors in the market, the implied equilibrium risk premium that will prevail in the next period will have the value [Π]. Thus, $P_r(\Pi)$ is a constant (between zero and one) that can be retrospectively incorporated into the integrating[5] constant of the probability distribution of $P_r(E(R) \mid \Pi)$.

---

5. In the final stage, the integrating constant C should be set so that $\int_{-\infty}^{\infty} C \cdot P_r(E(R) \mid \Pi) = 1.$

$P_r(\Pi|E(R))$ is the conditional PDF of the future returns to be the implied equilibrium risk premium [Π], based on the investor's view about future return [$E(R)$]. Since the different views in the market ultimately create the implied equilibrium risk premium, which vary [Σ], or, for our mean-variance optimizer purposes, the normalized [$\tau\Sigma$], around [Π], we may say that $[\Pi|E(R)] \sim N(E(R), \tau\Sigma)$.[6]

Our goal is to find the mean [$E(R)$] and variance-covariance $[\overline{\overline{\Sigma}}]$ estimators of the joint probability distribution $P_r(E(R)|\Pi)$ using the maximum likelihood method.

The likelihood function plays a key role in statistical inference. Whereas mathematical statistics allows us to predict unknown outcomes based on known parameters (of the PDF function), the likelihood function allows us to *estimate* the unknown parameters (of the PDF function) based on known outcomes (historical data). In principle, we choose an estimator that maximizes the likelihood function L on the estimated parameters vector θ, using a particular existing data sample, by setting the first derivative of L with respect to each θ_i[7] to equal zero, that is, $\dfrac{\partial L}{\partial \theta_i} = 0$. Often, deriving the maximum likelihood estimators is mathematically simplified by maximizing the log of the function, $\dfrac{\partial(\ln L)}{\partial \theta_i} = \dfrac{1}{L} \cdot \dfrac{\partial L}{\partial \theta_i} = 0$. The same estimator for θ will be obtained for any $L > 0$ by both methods.

As mentioned in chapter 14, the problem with the Black-Litterman model as presented in their publications is that they define only loosely the different mathematical parameters that play a role in their model and do not explore them on a practical level. This chapter seeks to provide readers with practical Excel tools that will allow them to implement the model. Therefore, we must patiently elaborate on each and every parameter, through the following steps.

We will first discuss how we generate (forecast) the personal view (i.e., opinion) vector [Q] assets' expected return values, both relative to [Π] and in absolute terms. Since [Q] is a random variable, we must also forecast its variance matrix, a task that is not simple. We will use a back-door

---

6. The expression $[E(\Pi)] = [E(R)]$ actually states the homogenous view of all investors in the CAPM-type world. Thus, we may assume that the probability density function of the estimator Π (based on historical data), subject to a particular investor's private view estimator $E(R)$, is also normally distributed, with a mean that reflects his personal views and with the same market-normalized variance $\Rightarrow [\Pi \mid E(R)] \sim N(E(R), \tau\Sigma)$, where N represents the normal distribution.

7. The parameters of θ in our case are either the mean vector [$E(R)$] or the variance-covariance matrix $[\overline{\overline{\Sigma}}]$.

technique and try to translate our confidence *level* in each of our personal views' (expected return values') forecast into a confidence *interval* for each forecasted value, which is mathematically comparable to the standard deviation from their mean. To be able to explain the translation procedure we will need to conduct a short review, discussing confidence in the quality of statistical estimators. Thereafter we will be able to define the variances for the forecasted values of our personal views.

Having the PDF parameter values (i.e., mean and variance parameters) for both $[\Pi]$ and $[Q]$, we can then use Bayesian statistics to derive the PDF parameters for the joint probability distribution, $[E(R)]$ and $[\Sigma]$. Next we will plug them into our mean-variance optimization Excel templates from chapter 14 to calculate the revised weights $[w^*]$ of our portfolio. Finally, we will discuss the resulting newly formed investment opportunities line.

B.   The Personal View Vector—Defining the Values of the Expected Returns

The model starts with a portfolio where asset allocation is executed using the implied equilibrium excess returns. Starting with the implied expected returns does not mean that we assume that the market is always in equilibrium. We do assume that returns tend not to move too far from their equilibrium state, and that when they do, the market will tend to push them back to equilibrium. Starting with the implied expected premiums of the assets makes formulating personal views easier. Rather than stating a view about the absolute return of each and every asset, investors may express an opinion about only some of the assets, and when they do, they give their opinion relative to the implied expected return. The returns of all other assets, those on which the investor does not have an opinion, will not be referenced in his views vector. As we noted in chapter 14, in the Black-Litterman model the investor is asked to specify not only a return expectation but also a degree of confidence in each of his views that differs from the equilibrium consensus. Stating the degree of confidence is a way to circumvent the need for forecasting the expected future standard deviation around the expectation, which is much less intuitive than forecasting future returns and is inversely related to the investor's confidence in the view. However, in their publications, Black and Litterman do not provide an intuitive way to quantify this relationship. It is up to the investor to compute the variance of his views

$[\Omega]$, one of the basic parameters in the Black-Litterman fundamental equations.

In this section we will first discuss the basic views vector $[Q]$'s expected return value properties and their interrelation as expressed by a vector (matrix) $[P]$. Since investors should prefer to express their personal views relative (and relatively close) to the market consensus $[\Pi]$, we will have to convert these relative views into a basic view vector $[Q]$ with absolute terms in order that $[Q]$ be compatible with $[\Pi]$ when we use both of them as sources of information.

We'll continue using the example for three assets from the previous chapter:

Variance-Covariance

Asset	I	II	III	Risk Premium
I	0.06	0.063	0.023	0.054
II	0.063	0.09	0.043	0.072
III	0.023	0.043	0.036	0.038

Let's proceed by processing the two most common basic types of views. At this stage we will ignore the investor's confidence level in each view, then afterward expand the model to include it:

A. In the next time period, asset I will have 0.5% more return than the market consensus (the implied equilibrium excess return). In our numerical example, where the market consensus is $\pi_1 = 5.4\%$, this means $[Q_1] = 5.9$.

B. In the next time period, asset II will outperform asset I by $x\%$. Although this basic view is expressed in absolute terms, and only indirectly relative to $[\Pi]$, that is, $[Q_2] = x\%$, it has a built-in problem as it concerns two assets at the same time.

To assess the result of this last view on our portfolio, we should compare the $x\%$ with the current market consensus (the mass of gravity) $[\Pi]$. The market consensus in our example is that asset II of the implied equilibrium excess return vector $[\Pi]$, with a return of 7.2%, outperforms asset I, with a return of 5.4%, by 1.8%.

So, if in our view $x\% = 1.5$, that is, $[Q_2] = 1.5$, it means that:

1. The expected return of asset I will increase by 0.3%, or

2. The expected return of asset II will decrease by 0.3%, or

3. The expected returns of asset I will increase and asset II will decrease, to a sum of –0.3% relative to the 1.8% market consensus.

As a result, we would expect that, in our revised portfolio, the weight of asset I should increase at the expense of asset II.

If $x\%$ in our view is such that $[Q_2] = 2.5$, it means that:

1. The expected return of asset II will increase by 0.7%, or

2. The expected return of asset I will decrease by 0.7%, or

3. Increase/decrease to a sum of 0.7% relative to the 1.8% market consensus.

As a result, we would expect that, in our revised portfolio, the weight of asset II should increase[8] at the expense of asset I.

We continue with another example combining the two basic views:

A. Asset II will outperform the market consensus by 0.5%.

B. Asset I will outperform asset II by 1.5%.

Thus, $[Q] = \begin{bmatrix} 5.9 \\ 1.5 \end{bmatrix}$.

Because of the type B view, the basic view vector $[Q]$ must be related to the revised estimator $[E(R)]$ through a transformation matrix $[P]$. Matrix $[P]$ relates each of the k basic views to one or more of the asset returns, or, in Black-Litterman terminology, must pose k linear constraints[9] on $[E(R)]$, as we will demonstrate shortly. Since $[E(R)]$ is a $1 \times n$ vector, $[P]$ should be a $k \times n$ matrix, where $[P] \times [E(R)] = [Q] + [\varepsilon]$. $[\varepsilon]$ is the uncertainty error term, related to the investor's confidence level in his personal view. $[\varepsilon]$ is also essentially the same idea that we stated earlier, that $[E(R)]$ may be at best represented as a probability distribution. To understand the role of $[P]$, let us first assume that the investor is 100% sure about his opinion. In this case there is no error, i.e., $[\varepsilon] = 0$ and $[P] \times [E(R)] = [Q]$. Afterward, we will modify it to include different confidence levels, and correspondingly, possible error terms $[\varepsilon]$.

8. In general, if the view is less (more) than the difference between the implied equilibrium returns, the weights of the underperforming (outperforming) asset should increase correspondingly.

9. The terminology of constraints comes from the optimization approach or process in the formal Black-Litterman model. We wish to minimize the variance of the difference between $[E(R)]$ and $[\Pi]$ for any given $[E(R)]$, subject to our views; that is,

$$\underset{[E(R)]}{Min}\left\{[E(R)-\Pi]\times[\tau\Sigma]^{-1}\times[E(R)-\Pi]^T\right\} \text{ s.t. } [P]\times[E(R)]=[Q].$$

This resembles the efficient frontier approach.

We will first introduce $[P]$ separately for each view and then jointly for all the views together.

The First Type of View (A)

Suppose we have only one view: "Asset I will outperform the market consensus by 0.5%"; that is, $[E(R)]$ will be related to the basic view vector $[Q_1] = [5.9]$ through a $1 \times n$ *row* transformation vector with 0's placed everywhere except where a view has been made on the asset, that is,

$$\begin{array}{ccc} Asset & I & II & III \end{array}$$
$$[P_1] = \begin{bmatrix} 1 & 0 & 0 \end{bmatrix}$$

$$[P_1] \times [E(R)] = [Q_1] \quad \Rightarrow \quad \begin{bmatrix} 1 & 0 & 0 \end{bmatrix} \times \begin{bmatrix} E(R_I) \\ E(R_{II}) \\ E(R_{III}) \end{bmatrix} = [5.9].$$

The Second Type of View (B)

Suppose we have only one view: "Asset II will outperform Asset I by 1.5%." $[E(R)]$ will be related to the basic view vector $[Q_2] = 1.5$ through a $1 \times n$ *row* transformation vector with 0's in every place except where a view has been made on the assets. Since this view can be written as $E(R_{II}) - E(R_I) = 1.5$, the corresponding row matrix will have the following form:

$$\begin{array}{ccc} Asset & I & II & III \end{array}$$
$$[P_2] = \begin{bmatrix} -1 & 1 & 0 \end{bmatrix}$$

$$[P_2] \times [E(R)] = [Q_2] \quad \Rightarrow \quad \begin{bmatrix} -1 & 1 & 0 \end{bmatrix} \times \begin{bmatrix} E(R_I) \\ E(R_{II}) \\ E(R_{III}) \end{bmatrix} = [1.5].$$

Combining the Two Views

We now wish to combine all the k *independent* views together. In our example of three assets $(n = 3)$ and two independent views $(k = 2)$, where $[P]$ is a $k \times n = 2 \times 3$ matrix, we may write:

$$[P] \times [E(R)] = [Q] \quad \Rightarrow \quad \begin{bmatrix} 1 & 0 & 0 \\ -1 & 1 & 0 \end{bmatrix} \times \begin{bmatrix} E(R_I) \\ E(R_{II}) \\ E(R_{III}) \end{bmatrix} = \begin{bmatrix} 5.9\% \\ 1.5\% \end{bmatrix}.$$

We could have elaborated more on the logic of how to build $[Q]$ or the transformation matrix $[P]$ for more complex basic views or considerations,[10] but since this book deals with fundamental models, we will conclude the discussion about $[Q]$ and $[P]$ here, and leave it for further study. I believe the reader now understands the role of $[Q]$, $[E(R)]$, and the transformation matrix $[P]$ that relates between them, in the Black-Litterman model. We can use them freely in further developing the model, assuming that finding the values for $[Q]$ and the transformation matrix $[P]$ are secondary and relatively easily solved problems.

Once we add personal views, we must also change (increase[11]) the corresponding variances of the future expected returns $[E(R)]$. Since it is most difficult to forecast variances, Black and Litterman suggested using the confidence level for each of the views.

We will now expand our example and add a confidence level to each of the views.

A. Asset II will outperform the consensus by 0.5%, at a 75% confidence level.

B. Asset I will outperform asset II by 1.5%, at a 40% confidence level.

When we were 100% sure of our view (and not 75% or 40%, as above), we could have solved the equation and found $[E(R)]$:

$$\begin{bmatrix} 1 & 0 & 0 \\ -1 & 1 & 0 \end{bmatrix} \times \begin{bmatrix} E(R_I) \\ E(R_{II}) \\ E(R_{III}) \end{bmatrix} = \begin{bmatrix} 5.9\% \\ 1.5\% \end{bmatrix}.$$

And, since $[E(R_{III})] = [\pi_{III}]$, as we had no view about asset III, then

$$\begin{bmatrix} E(R_I) \\ E(R_{II}) \\ E(R_{III}) \end{bmatrix} = \begin{bmatrix} 5.9\% \\ 7.4\% \\ 3.8\% \end{bmatrix}.$$

When we are 100% sure, we do not add any uncertainty with our views, and our revised estimator should have the same variance-covariance as those of the market consensus $[\Pi]$, that is, $[\tau\Sigma]$. Consequently, we may now use the efficient frontier optimizer we prepared in the previous chapter to solve for the new weight vector w_i^* (we leave it for the reader),

---

10. For example, we did not take into account the market capitalization (value) of each of the assets in our portfolio, and so treated a small firm (asset) the same way we treated a large firm (asset). This may be done through $[P]$.

11. Adding another random variable will always increase uncertainty, that is, the variance.

where in the new Excel sheet, $[E(R) \mid \Pi] \sim N[E(R), \tau\Sigma]$. That is, we should use the following tables:

Variance-Covariance [$\tau\Sigma$] New Premium Vector

Asset	I	II	III	
I	0.0690	0.0725	0.0265	0.059
II	0.0725	0.1035	0.0495	0.074
III	0.0265	0.0495	0.0414	0.038

We may now compare how w^* of the new Excel sheet replaces the weights w of the previous sheet:[12]

Asset	w		w^*
I	0.36		0.52
II	0.27	$\rightarrow$	0.10
II	0.37		0.38
Assets $\sum w_i$	1.00		1.00

I suggest readers play around with their personal views relative to Π, and watch how the portfolio becomes less and less balanced as we deviate from the equilibrium vector Π.

We are never 100% sure of our views!

Before we try to translate confidence levels into variances for our views, we will pause for a brief review of how mathematical statistics handles confidence levels and confidence intervals with respect to estimators' statistics derived from data samples, and how this can help us in transforming confidence levels into standard deviation (or variance).

C. Confidence in the Quality of Statistical Estimators

If we are willing to accept the assumption that the outcome of the future return R_i of each asset i are random variables that are the outcome from the same normal distribution with a known variance σ_i^2 but unknown[13] mean μ_i, then we may consider the past history data as random outcomes $R_i^1, R_i^2, ..., R_i^n$ from n independent experiments, where

12. Check: The weight of asset I increased at the expense of asset II, as we expected!
13. That is, μ is a constant of unknown value.

$E[R_i] \sim N(\mu_i, \sigma_i^2)$, or $\dfrac{(E[R_i] - \mu_i)}{\sigma_i} \sim N(0,1).^{14}$

Thus, we may use the standard normal distribution table to derive the probability that $\dfrac{(E[R_i] - \mu_i)}{\sigma_i}$ will be, for example, within the confidence interval $(-2, 2)$, which is derived from the table to be 0.95, that is, $P_r\left(-2 < \dfrac{(E[R_i] - \mu_i)}{\sigma_i} < 2\right) = 0.95$. This means we expect that 95% of future outcomes will be within this range.

The event $\left[-2 < \dfrac{(E[R_i] - \mu_i)}{\sigma_i} < 2\right]$, the event $[-2 \cdot \sigma_i < (E[R_i] - \mu_i) < 2 \cdot \sigma_i]$, and the event $[E[R_i] - 2\sigma_i < \mu_i < E[R_i] + 2\sigma]$ are identical.

Using $E[R_i]$ as an estimator[15] of μ_i for future projection means that, with a confidence level of 95%, we expect that the true mean return μ_i of the distribution, the value of which we do not know and try to assess based on the available historical data, will be within the interval $\pm 2\sigma_i$ away from our estimator $E[R_i]$, derived from the historical data (in our case, the implied return premium vector $[\Pi]$). About 68% of values drawn from a normal distribution are within one standard deviation σ away from the mean, about 95% of the values lie within two standard deviations, and about 99.7% are within three standard deviations. This fact is known as the *68–95–99.7 rule*, or the *empirical rule*, or the *3-sigma rule*. To be more precise, the area under the bell curves between $(\mu - n\sigma)$ and $(\mu + n\sigma)$ is given by $F(\mu + n\sigma) - F(\mu - n\sigma) = \Phi(n) - \Phi(-n) \equiv erf\left(\dfrac{n}{\sqrt{2}}\right)$:

n	$erf\left(\dfrac{n}{\sqrt{2}}\right)$	$(1 - P_r)$
1	0.68	0.32
2	0.95	0.05
3	0.99	0.00

14. Refer to a basic statistics book if you don't remember how to transform the left-hand equation into the right-hand equation. $N(0,1)$ is the standard normal distribution, for which there exists a distribution probability table.

15. $E[R_i] = \dfrac{\sum_{j=1}^{n} R_i^j}{n-1}$.

Or the mirror relation:

$erf\left(\dfrac{n}{\sqrt{2}}\right)$	n
0.66	1.00
0.80	1.28
0.90	1.64
0.95	1.96
0.997	3.00

When we wish to measure the quality of the estimators derived from sample data, we attach a probability that the statistics (the estimator) $E[R_i]$ will be close to the true parameter μ_i of the true probability distribution.

Proximity might be achieved when the variance σ^2 of $E[R_i]$ is as small as possible, because the variance of $E[R_i]$ is a measure of the concentration or intensity of the probability of the estimator $E[R_i]$ in the neighborhood of the point (center of gravity) μ_i. Since the confidence interval is given in relative units of σ, if we want to replace the confidence level with absolute terms of percentages of return, we may say that the confidence level is reciprocal to the confidence interval σ. The larger the interval σ, the lower our confidence level that $\mu_i = E[R_i]$, and vice versa. In Bayesian statistics, the inverse of the variance σ^2 is known as the *precision*.

The purpose of this review is to understand the basic logic behind the concept, and to acquire practical tools. Since the point should be clear by now, let us dispense with the mathematical formality and suggest two approximations to the problem of translating confidence levels to variances.

Suppose we know the total confidence interval range represented by the standard deviation ω_j that corresponds to $0 - 100\%$ of personal confidence level c_j in our view about the expected return of asset j; $j = 1$ ... k.

We want to "calibrate" ω_j to correspond to a certain personal confidence level c_j in our view about asset j (and not to the total range). Since the confidence level is reciprocal to the standard deviation, that is, the 100% confidence level corresponds to zero variance (standard deviation), we may apply a first-order approximation approach and multiply the "full-scale" ω_j by the $erf = (1 - c_j)$; thus, the standard deviation of our personal view j will be expressed as $\omega_j^{Personal} = (1 - c_j) \cdot \omega_j$.

We may also use the mirror functional relation and relate the total confidence interval range ω_j as (almost) equivalent to a 3σ range—the 95% confidence level is equivalent to $1.96/3 \approx 2/3$ of the range, the 90% confidence interval is equivalent to $1.96/3 \approx 0.55$ of the range, and so on—and apply some reciprocal mathematical relation on those last numbers to calculate the corresponding standard deviation and variance.

D. The Personal View Vector—Defining the Variances of the Expected Returns

Adding a personal view means introducing one more stochastic variable into the model, and thus by definition increasing the variance of the final result. Jay Walters in his 2008 revision of "The Black-Litterman Model: A Detailed Exploration" states, "Ω, the variance of the views is inversely related to the investor's confidence in the views, however the basic Black-Litterman model does not provide an intuitive way to quantify this relationship. It is up to the investor to compute the variance of the views" (p. 8). Walters presents few ways for translating confidence levels into variances. I will try to present an intuitive approach of my own.

Since uncertainty exists in our views, we present the uncertainty by a random, unknown, independent, normally distributed error term vector $[\varepsilon]$. The investor's basic views have the form $[Q] \pm [\varepsilon]$. In our example:

$$[Q] \pm [\varepsilon] = \begin{bmatrix} 0.059 \pm \varepsilon_1 \\ 0.015 \pm \varepsilon_2 \end{bmatrix}.$$

Since we have assumed that personal views are expressed around the "mass of gravity" $[\Pi]$, this means that the mean of the errors made by all the personal views expressed in the market must be zero.[16] Thus, the values of the error term vector $[\varepsilon]$ are normally distributed with a mean of zero and with the variance-covariance matrix $[\Omega]$, that is, $[\varepsilon] \sim N(0,\Omega)$. Since $[P] \times [E(R)] = [Q] + [\varepsilon]$, then $[P] \times [E(R)] \sim N(Q,\Omega)$.

$[\Omega]$ is a diagonal variance-covariance matrix with variances ω_j^2 on the diagonal, and 0's in all the off-diagonal positions. The off-diagonal elements of $[\Omega]$ are 0's because the model assumes that the views are independent of one another, that is, the covariances between the views are 0.

16. That is, by all investors.

$$[\Omega] = \begin{bmatrix} \omega_1^2 & 0 & \cdots & 0 \\ 0 & \omega_2^2 & \cdots & 0 \\ \vdots & \vdots & \cdots & \vdots \\ 0 & 0 & \cdots & \omega_k^2 \end{bmatrix} = \text{in our example} \begin{bmatrix} \omega_1^2 & 0 \\ 0 & \omega_2^2 \end{bmatrix}.$$

The standard deviation ω_j of the error terms ε_j represents the uncertainty about the jth view. The larger the standard deviation ω_j, the lower is our confidence about the jth view, and vice versa.

A 100% confidence level means $\varepsilon_j \overset{100\%}{=} 0$ and $\omega_j \overset{100\%}{=} 0$. The average of all the personal views $[E(R_i)]$ that exist in the market about the future return of asset i forms the market consensus π_i with normalized variances of $\tau\sigma_i^2$ (and covariances $\tau\sigma_{ij}$).[17] Thus, a 0% confidence level for a personal view about asset i means that the investor accepts the market consensus. Since the investor's view is a member of the same distribution of all the market personal views, $\omega_i \overset{0\%}{=} \sqrt{\tau}\sigma_i$ for his view, as well as for all other personal investor views that exist in the market. It is important to note that each asset in the portfolio has a different σ_i for the market consensus Π_i. This reflects the fact that all the investors in the market (together as a group) have a different confidence level about each of their mutual (consensus) estimators Π_i.

Since $[P] \times [E(R)] = [Q] + [\varepsilon]$, we should also apply the transformation matrix $[P]$ for the standard deviation ω. We should not calculate all the rows' $[P_i]$'s for all the views together in one step on our variance-covariance matrix $[\Omega]$, that is, $[P] \times [\tau\Sigma] \times [P]^T \neq \overset{0\%}{[\Omega]}$! As we have assumed that the views are independent, the off-diagonal ω_{ij} must equal zero. Using $[P] \times [\tau\Sigma] \times [P]^T = \overset{0\%}{[\Omega]}$ will result in having off-diagonal elements for $\overset{0\%}{[\Omega]}$ that are not zero; that is, $\omega_{ij} \neq 0$. Instead, we should apply each line of the transformation matrix $[P]$ separately to find the 0% confidence level $\overset{0\%}{[\Omega]}$:

$$\overset{0\%}{[\Omega]} = \begin{bmatrix} [P_1] \times [\tau\Sigma] \times [P_1]^T & 0 & \cdots & 0 \\ 0 & [P_2] \times [\tau\Sigma] \times [P_2]^T & \cdots & 0 \\ \vdots & \vdots & \cdots & \vdots \\ 0 & 0 & \cdots & [P_k] \times [\tau\Sigma] \times [P_k]^T \end{bmatrix}.$$

17. In the last chapter, we saw that $[\tau\Sigma]$ is normalized in the sense that it gives us the final solution directly for the weights vector $[w^{normal}]$ in the maximization process without the need to apply the constraint $\sum_1^n w_i = 1$.

In our three-asset portfolio example:[18]

$$[\Omega] = \begin{bmatrix} \overset{0\%}{\omega_1^2} & 0 \\ 0 & \overset{0\%}{\omega_2^2} \end{bmatrix} = \begin{bmatrix} 0.0762 & 0 \\ 0 & 0.0305 \end{bmatrix}.$$

We now know the total confidence interval (range) that corresponds to a 0–100% confidence level for any investor's jth view, $j = 1 \ldots k$.

	0%		100%
Confidence level for view Q_j	0%	–	100%
Confidence interval ω_j	$[P_j] \times \left[\sqrt{\tau}\sigma\right]$	–	0
Variance ω_j^2	$[P_j] \times [\tau\Sigma] \times [P_j]^T$	–	0

We may calibrate ω_j to correspond to our personal confidence level c_j in our view j. Since the confidence level is reciprocal to the standard deviation, we may apply a first-order approximation approach and multiply the full-scale $\overset{0\%}{\omega_j}$ by $(1 - c_j)$; that is, the standard deviation of our personal view j will be $\overset{Personal}{\omega_j} = (1 - c_j) \cdot \overset{0\%}{\omega_j}$. The reason we use $(1 - c_j)$ and not c_j is because of the inverse nature of the full confidence interval, which assigns the maximum $[P_j] \times \left[\sqrt{\tau}\sigma\right]$ to a 0% confidence level and zero to a 100% confidence level. Thus:

$$\overset{Personal}{[\Omega]} = \begin{bmatrix} (1 - c_1)^2 \cdot \overset{0\%}{\omega_1^2} & 0 \\ 0 & (1 - c_2)^2 \cdot \overset{0\%}{\omega_2^2} \end{bmatrix}.$$

$$\overset{Personal}{[\Omega]} = \begin{bmatrix} 0.25^2 \cdot 0.0762 & 0 \\ 0 & 0.6^2 \cdot 0.0305 \end{bmatrix} = \begin{bmatrix} 0.0048 & 0 \\ 0 & 0.011 \end{bmatrix}.$$

The above process is an approximation of the formation of $[\Omega]$. The exact calibration procedure should be done using the standard normal distribution table.[19] Other literature suggests calibrating τ with an arbitrary coefficient and thus scaling all the ω_j's with the same factor.

The above approximation procedure is simple and accurate enough[20] and takes into account, on the one hand, the investor's different confi-

---

18. In the final part of the chapter we will demonstrate the full calculation for a four-asset portfolio using Excel.

19. That is the formal part that we have skipped.

20. It is accurate enough, considering the nature and accuracy of personal level of confidence in general. In "A Step-by-Step Guide to the Black-Litterman Model," Tomas M.

dence levels for each view, and on the other, the market's relative confidence level about each of their mutual estimators π_i.[21]

To make the above presentation more intuitive, we may assume that, when forming view Q_j, the investor uses the average of some market analysts' opinions about future returns of Q_j and calculates his level of confidence in correlation with the average of those analysts' success in past projections. The investor might, of course, use other sources of information or other procedures (even intuition) to form his views.

The literature about personal views variance is fairly extensive. Some approaches do allow for covariances among the personal views. Since our goal is to understand the concept to an applicable degree, we will stop here and encourage curious readers to find their preferred approach from the vast literature.

E. Deriving $[E(R)]$ and $[\overline{\overline{\Sigma}}]$ of the Joint Probability Distribution

Let us summarize what we have achieved so far:

1. From a historical sample of market data D, we derived[22] the implied equilibrium excess return vector $[\Pi]$ and its variance-covariance matrix $[\Sigma]$ as the market consensus estimators for the next period returns.

2. The value of the utility function U depends on the choice of the asset weights $[w]$ when constructing our portfolio, given the above set of estimators $[\Pi]$ and $[\Sigma]$. We maximized our utility function with respect to the weights $[w]$ in order to get a minimum variance for any possible return. From this "efficient frontier," we obtained the normalized[23] optimal asset weights vector of our specific portfolio allocation: $[w^{normal}]$ = $[\tau\Sigma]^{-1}[\Pi]$, where τ is the normalization factor.

3. Then we presented our basic view vector $[Q]$ and the investor's best estimator for future excess return $[E(R)]$, which is based both

---

Idzorek (2002) suggests another calibration procedure, one that correlates the level of confidence with the magnitude of the deviation $\left[E(R_i)\right]^{100\%} - [\Pi_i]$ and the corresponding chance in the difference of weights. I suggest an *independent* projection of Q_j and an *independent* confidence level c_j.

21. Expressed by the different σ_j's of the different assets' returns.

22. In the previous chapter.

23. "Normalized" means $\sum_1^n w_i = 1$.

on the market consensus estimators $[\Pi]$ and $[\Sigma]$ and on the investor's views parameters $[Q]$ and $[\Omega]$. Next we defined a transformation matrix $[P]$ that translates $[E(R)]$ into terms of $[Q]$, that is, $[P] \times [E(R)]$ $= [Q] + [\varepsilon]$.

4. Each personal view Q_j has a personal confidence interval (standard deviation) $\omega_j^{Personal}$ that corresponds to an investor's personal level of confidence c_j about the investor's view Q_j. The confidence interval $\omega_j^{Personal}$ is the product of the market consensus confidence interval $[\omega_j^{0\%}] = [P_j] \times \left[\sqrt{\tau\sigma}\right]$ with the reciprocal of the personal confidence level, that is, with $(1 - c_j)$.

5. Thus, $\omega_j^{2\ Personal} = \left(1-c_j\right)^2 \cdot [P_j] \times [\tau\Sigma] \times [P_j]^T$. All the $\omega_j^{2\ Personal}$ of all the k views together form the diagonal elements of the personal views variance matrix $[\Omega]$.

Now that we have defined and demonstrated how to obtain all the variables we need for the Black-Litterman model, namely, $[\Pi]$, $[\tau\Sigma]$, $[Q]$, $[E(R)]$, $[P]$, and $[\Omega]$, we may address our goal to extract the new joint estimators for the future excess expected returns $[E(R)]$ and their variance-covariance matrix $[\overline{\Sigma}]$.

Both $[E(R)]$ and $[\overline{\Sigma}]$ of the future returns are parameters of the joint PDF and are based on both sources of information—the market consensus PDF—and our personal views PDF.

In the first section of the chapter we demonstrated that[24]

PDF of $P_r([E(R)]|[\Pi]) \sim$ PDF of $P_r([\Pi]|[E(R)]) \cdot P_r([E(R)])$.

We have also seen that $[P] \times [E(R)] \sim N(Q,\Omega)$. Since $[P]$ is ultimately a matrix of constants, which may also be reflected in the final retrospective integrating coefficient, we may replace the PDF of $P_r([E(R)])$ in the (right-hand side of the) above Bayesian formula with the PDF of $P_r([P] \times [E(R)])$.

Thus, we may write:

PDF of $P_r([E(R)]|[\Pi]) \sim$ PDF of $P_r([\Pi]|[E(R)]) \cdot P_r([P] \times [E(R)])$.

Both of the vectors' PDFs on the right-hand side, $P_r([\Pi] \mid [E(R)])$ and $P_r([P] \times [E(R)])$, have normal distributions. When we are talking about any single one of the returns' random variable r_i in the above vectors,

---

24. The $\sim$ sign means "proportional to."

it has a normal probability distribution, that is, the PDF of r_i is

$$f(r_i) = \frac{1}{\sigma_i \sqrt{2\pi}} \exp\left(-\frac{(r_i - \mu_i)^2}{2\sigma_i^2}\right).$$

To find an estimator $E(r_i)$ for the PDF's μ_i, we use the likelihood PDF $l(r_i)$, which is the product of the above density function that includes the past history values $r_{i,1}, r_{i,2}, r_{i,3} \ldots r_{i,n}$ of a g size sample:[25]

$$l(r_i) = f(r_{i,1}) \cdot f(r_{i,2}) \cdot f(r_{i,3}) \ldots f(r_{i,n}).$$

Since $l(r_i)$, is a product of exponential terms, it is easier to find the maximum of the log-likelihood function:

$$L(r_i) = Log(l(r_i)) = C \cdot \sum_{j=1}^{n} \left(-\frac{(r_{i,j} - \mu_i)^2}{2\sigma_i^2}\right).$$

Taking the first derivative of $L(r_i)$ with respect to μ_i and setting the derivative equal to zero, we get the well-known result $\mu_i = E(r_i) = \frac{1}{g}\sum_{j=1}^{g} r_{i,j}$. Similarly, we obtain the well-known form of the mean least square estimator for σ_i^2.

Note that in our equilibrium model, we used the implied return premium as our variable and sample data. Thus, $E(\pi_i) = \frac{1}{g}\sum_{j=1}^{g} \pi_{i,j}$.

$[R]$ is an $n \times 1$ vector of the future asset returns r_i, where each asset return r_i is normally distributed as above. As we already well know, our total portfolio variance is a result not only of each asset's return variances but also of the covariances among the $n \times n$ asset returns, that is, the variance-covariance matrix $[\Sigma]$. The PDF of the vector $[\tilde{R}] \sim N([E(R)]; [\Sigma])$ is written in linear algebra notation as

$$f([R]) = \frac{1}{(\sqrt{2\pi})^n \sqrt{\det[\Sigma]}} \cdot \exp\left\{-\frac{1}{2}\left([R - E(R)]^T \times [\overline{\overline{\Sigma}}] \times [R - E(R)]\right)\right\}.$$

Back to our Bayesian relation,

$$P_r([E(R)] \mid [\Pi]) \sim P_r([\Pi] \mid [E(R)]) \cdot P_r([P] \mid [E(R)]):$$

The PDF $P_r([\Pi] \mid [E(R)]) \sim N(E(R), \tau\Sigma)$, extracted from the data sample of size $n \times g$ vector of returns, will take the form

$$f(\Pi \mid E(R)) = \frac{g}{(\sqrt{2\pi})^n \sqrt{\det|\tau\Sigma|}} \exp\left\{-\frac{1}{2}\left([\Pi - E(R)]^T \times [\tau\Sigma]^{-1} \times [\Pi - E(R)]\right)\right\}.$$

---

25. Usually, we take the monthly returns over a five-year period; that is, $g = 60$.

For $[P] \mid [E(R)] \sim N(Q,\Omega)$, we may write:

$$f([P]\times[E(R)]) = \frac{h}{\left(\sqrt{2\pi}\right)^n \sqrt{\det|\Omega|}} \cdot$$

$$\exp\left\{-\frac{1}{2}\left(([P]\times[E(R)]-[Q])^T \times[\Omega]^{-1}\times([P]\times[E(R)]-[Q])\right)\right\}.$$

Writing the last equation above, we should ask ourselves what, in real-life terms, is the $k \times h$ sample size from which we can derive the parameters for this PDF of the personal views (where k is the number of views and h is the number of outcomes in the sample for that view). In 1992, Black and Litterman suggested two possible approaches:

1. Act as if we had a statistical summary from a data sample that is the result of the distribution of future returns. As we have previously suggested as an example, we may consider the views of h independent analysts regarding the future return of each of the k assets as the data sample of $k \times h$ size.

2. We will relate to the future returns probability distribution of the difference $[E(R)] - [\Pi]$ as if it were also normally distributed.

In both approaches, we need a measure of the investor's confidence in his views in order to be able to give a weight to the view. For the first approach, we may regard the relative size of the samples, that is, h/g, as a measure of the confidence level.[26] If we choose to accept the second approach, we may also adopt the approach we introduced before for the calibration of Ω through the investor's confidence level for each view.

We will apply the second approach since, as we will soon see, it is simpler (mathematically) to derive the desired final result. Moreover, we will obtain both estimators, the mean $[E(R)]$ and its variance-covariance $[\Sigma]$, in one step.

Summarizing once again, we have reached the following conclusions:

PDF of $P_r([E(R)] \mid [\Pi]) \sim$ PDF of $P_r([\Pi] \mid [E(R)]) \cdot P_r([P] \times [E(R)]$,

where

$$f(\Pi \mid E(R)) = \frac{g}{\left(\sqrt{2\pi}\right)^n \sqrt{\det|\tau\Sigma|}} \cdot$$

$$\exp\left\{-\frac{1}{2}\left([\Pi - E(R)]^T \times[\tau\Sigma]^{-1}\times[\Pi - E(R)]\right)\right\},$$

---

26. The measure h_i/g_i may be different for each view or asset.

$$f([P] \times [E(R)]) = \frac{h}{\left(\sqrt{2\pi}\right)^n \sqrt{\det|\Omega|}} \cdot$$

$$\exp\left\{-\frac{1}{2}\left(([P] \times [E(R)] - [Q])^T \times [\Omega]^{-1} \times ([P] \times [E(R)] - [Q])\right)\right\}.$$

Incorporating all the constants,[27] $P_r(\Pi)$, $\dfrac{g}{\left(\sqrt{2\pi}\right)^n \sqrt{\det|\tau\Sigma|}}$, and $\dfrac{h}{\left(\sqrt{2\pi}\right)^n \sqrt{\det|\Omega|}}$, into C_1, the retrospective integrating constant of the PDF $(\Pi \mid E(R))$, we may then say that the PDF of $P_r(E(R) \mid \Pi)$ is proportional to

$$\exp\left\langle\left[\left\{-\frac{1}{2}\left((\Pi - E(R))^T \times [\tau\Sigma]^{-1} \times (\Pi - E(R))\right)\right\}\right.\right.$$

$$\left.\left. + \left\{-\frac{1}{2}\left(([P] \times [E(R)] - Q)^T \times [\Omega]^{-1} \times ([P] \times [E(R)] - Q)\right)\right\}\right]\right\rangle.$$

We will spare the reader the tedious matrix algebra manipulation of the above[28] and will only give the final result for the PDF of $P_r(E(R) \mid [\Pi])$, which is:

$$P_r([E(R)] \mid [\Pi]) = C_2 \cdot$$

$$\exp\left\{-\frac{1}{2}\left(([A] \times [E(R)] - [B])^T \times [A]^{-1} \times ([A] \times [E(R)] - [B])\right)\right\}$$

Where $[A] = [\tau\Sigma]^{-1} + [P]^T \times [\Omega]^{-1} \times [P]$, and,
$$[B] = [\tau\Sigma]^{-1} \times [\Pi] + [P]^T \times [\Omega]^{-1} \times [Q]$$

C_2 is a constant (that includes C_1) that will be incorporated into the final integrating constant, to set $\displaystyle\int_{-\infty}^{+\infty} C_2 \cdot \exp\left\{-\frac{1}{2}\left(([A] \times [E(R)] - [B])^T \times [A]^{-1} \times ([A] \times [E(R)] - [B])\right)\right\} = 1$.

The above format for the PDF of $P_r(E(R) \mid \Pi)$ is also of a normal distribution.

Thus, we know that the maximum likelihood estimators should be

$$[E(R)] = [A]^{-1} \times [B] \text{ and } [\overline{\Sigma}] = [A]^{-1}.$$

---

27. Each of the following expressions is a different constant number.

28. For detailed mathematical manipulation, see George A. Christodoulakis (2002), "Bayesian Optimal Portfolio Selection: The Black-Litterman Approach," p. 8.

That is,

$$[E(R)] = \left([\tau\Sigma]^{-1} + [P]^{T} \times [\Omega]^{-1} \times [P]\right)^{-1} \times \left([\tau\Sigma]^{-1} \times [\Pi] + [P]^{T} \times [\Omega]^{-1} \times [Q]\right).$$
$$[\overline{\Sigma}] = [A]^{-1} = \left([\tau\Sigma]^{-1} + [P]^{T} \times [\Omega]^{-1} \times [P]\right)^{-1}.$$

We may give the above expressions intuitive interpretations:

$[\tau\Sigma]^{-1}$ is proportional to the confidence interval of the market consensus $[\Pi]$.

$[P]^{T} \times [\Omega]^{-1} \times [P]$ is proportional to the confidence interval of the personal view $[Q]$.

$[\tau\Sigma]^{-1} \times [P]^{T} \times [\Omega]^{-1} \times [P]$ is proportional to the confidence interval of the combined personal view $[E(R)]$.

$[\overline{\Sigma}]$, the retrospective variance of $[E(R)]$ around $[\Pi]$, is the inverse of the (retrospective) precision in evaluating $[E(R)]$. The retrospective precision of the $[E(R)]$ evaluator is thus the sum of the precision (square confidence interval) of $[\Pi]$ and the precision of $[Q]$.

The retrospective mean $[E(R)]$ is a weighted average between $[\Pi]$ and $[Q]$ where the above confidence intervals (the precisions) are used as the weights.

To acquire a more intuitive[29] feel for the $[E(R)]$ evaluator result, we may reformat it, the result, again, of tedious[30] matrix algebra manipulation, into

$$[E(R)] = [\Pi] + [\tau\Sigma] \times [P]^{T} \times \left([\Omega] + [P] \times [\tau\Sigma] \times [P]^{T}\right)^{-1} \times ([Q] - [P] \times [\Pi]).$$

We may check the above formula for two extreme cases:

1. For a 0% confidence level:

$$([Q] - [P] \times [\Pi]) = 0; \text{ thus, } [\overset{0\%}{E(R)}] = \Pi, \text{ as we have expected.}$$

2. For a 100% confidence level,[31] $[\Omega] = 0$.

Thus, $[\overset{100\%}{E(R)}] = \Pi + [\tau\Sigma] \times [P]^{T} \times \left([P] \times [\tau\Sigma] \times [P]^{T}\right)^{-1} \times ([Q] - [P] \times [\Pi]).$

---

29. If it is indeed possible to make these mathematical formulas intuitive.

30. For details of the mathematical manipulation, see Charlotta Mankert (2006), "The Black-Litterman Model: Mathematical and Behavioral Finance Approaches towards Its Use in Practice," pp. 40–41. Her paper also demonstrates the first approach proposed by Black and Litterman, namely, act as if we had a statistical summary from a sample data of future returns from which we derive $E(R)$.

31. Christodoulakis (2002, pp. 5–6) derives the same 100% confidence level result by $\underset{[E(R)]}{Min}\{[E(R) - \Pi] \times [\tau\Sigma]^{-1} \times [E(R) - \Pi]^{T}\}$ s.t. $[P] \times [E(R)] = [Q]$ using the conventional Lagrange multiplier method for constrained optimization.

To exercise the efficient frontier optimizer on $\left[\tilde{R}\right]$ we need $[E(R)]$ and the variance $\overline{\overline{[\Sigma]}}$ of the assets' random returns vector $\left[\tilde{R}\right]$. Computing the variance $\left[\overline{\Sigma}\right]$ of the mean $[E(R)]$ around $[\Pi]$ is not the same as computing the variance $\overline{\overline{[\Sigma]}}$ of the assets' random returns $\left[\tilde{R}\right]$ around $[E(R)]$. We introduced the error ε of $[Q]$ with a variance ω^2 around the market equilibrium $[\Pi]$ (with a mean of zero) $[\varepsilon] \sim N(0,\Omega)$. Since the error ε is independent of the variance $[\Sigma]$ of the returns $\left[\tilde{\Pi}\right]$, we can add the retrospective variance $\left[\overline{\Sigma}\right]$ of the retrospective mean $[E(R)]$ around $[\Pi]$ to the variance $[\Sigma]$ of the returns $\left[\tilde{\Pi}\right]$ and get the total variance $\overline{\overline{[\Sigma]}}$ of the assets' returns $\left[\tilde{R}\right]$, that is, $\overline{\overline{[\Sigma]}}=[\Sigma]+\left[\overline{\Sigma}\right]$.

Once we have succeeded in assessing the value of the new estimators $[E(R)]$ and $\overline{\overline{[\Sigma]}}$, we may now find the new weights w_i^* for each asset in our portfolio, using the same efficient frontier technique (template) that we formulated in the previous chapter.

All the above Black-Litterman model notations become clearer by way of a numerical example.

F. Adding Subjective Views Using Excel

Expanding the previous chapter's four-asset portfolio, and once again letting Excel do the hard work for us, we may find the new weights vector $\left[w^*\right]$ in two phases:

Stage 1. Calculate the new estimators for the joint distribution $[E(R)]$ and $\left[\overline{\overline{\Sigma}}\right]$.[32]

Stage 2. Use $[E(R)]$ and $\overline{\overline{[\Sigma]}}=[\Sigma]+\left[\overline{\Sigma}\right]$, and plug them into the efficient frontier optimizer template (from the previous chapter) to calculate the new weights vector $[w^{normal*}]$, as well as the $E^*(R_p)$, and σ_p^* of our newly allocated portfolio.

Continuing working on the four-asset Excel portfolio optimizer template from the previous chapter, we'll apply the two views we have used throughout this chapter:

---

32. In "The Intuition behind Black-Litterman Model Portfolios," Guanglian He and Robert Litterman (1999) adopt this convention of computing the variance of $\left[\tilde{R}\right]$. However, in "The Black-Litterman Model: A Detailed Exploration," Walters (2008) argues (p. 9) that the updated variance $\overline{\overline{[\Sigma]}}$ will be lower than either $[\Sigma]$ or $\left[\overline{\Sigma}\right]$ since the additional information should (intuitively) reduce the uncertainty of the model. I argue the opposite — see note 18. In any case, adding two "all positive value elements" matrixes will always result in larger value (diagonal) elements, that is, larger variances. The reader may check this point in the following Excel example.

1. Asset II will outperform the consensus by 0.5%, with a 75% confidence level.

2. Asset I will outperform asset II by 1.5%, with a 40% confidence level.

In the previous chapter, we detailed every step in building the Excel sheet. Now that the reader is familiar with Excel's array manipulation functions, our review can be more cursory, but still step by step. Once we have finished, the new part of the worksheet will look like the replica below. The replica is followed by an explanation of each part of the process in creating this worksheet.

At this stage, the reader is also advised to see the online Excel templates at http://finmodeling.com/en.

The spreadsheet replica contains the following labeled blocks:

$[P]$ (columns H–L, rows 18–22):

1	0	0	0
-1	1	0	0

$[\Sigma]$ (columns N–Q, rows 18–23):

0.076	0.079	0.029	0.042
0.079	0.113	0.054	0.050
0.029	0.054	0.044	0.025
0.042	0.050	0.025	0.035

$[\Sigma]^{-1}$ (columns S–W, rows 18–23):

83.491	-59.507	43.753	-44.643
-59.507	77.211	-55.423	-0.581
43.753	-55.423	78.126	-28.194
-44.643	-0.581	-28.194	101.927

$[P]^T$ (columns H–J, rows 26–31):

1	-1
0	1
0	0
0	0

$[P]^T \times [\Omega]^{-1} \times [P]$ (columns K–N, rows 26–31):

946.502	-734.862	0.000	0.000
-734.862	734.862	0.000	0.000
0.000	0.000	0.000	0.000
0.000	0.000	0.000	0.000

$[P]^T \times [\Omega]^{-1}$ (columns O–Q, rows 26–31):

211.640	-734.862
0	734.862
0.000	0.000
0.000	0.000

$k=$

$[\Sigma] \times [P_k]^T$ (columns S–T, rows 27–32):

	1	2
	0.076	0.004
	0.079	0.034
	0.029	0.025
	0.042	0.009

$(1 - c_j)^2$ (columns V–W, rows 31–33):

0.0625	0.0000
0.0000	0.3600

$[\Sigma]^{-1} \times \Pi$ (columns H, rows 34–39):

0.23
0.22
0.30
0.25

$[\Pi]$ (column J, rows 34–39):

0.054
0.072
0.038
0.037

$[Q]$ (column L, rows 34–39):

0.059
0.015

$[A] = [\tau\Sigma]^{-1} + [P]^T \times [\Omega]^{-1} \times [P]$ (columns N–Q, rows 35–39):

1029.993	-794.368	43.753	-44.643
-794.368	812.073	-55.423	-0.581
43.753	-55.423	78.126	-28.194
-44.643	-0.581	-28.194	101.927

$[P_k] \times [\tau\Sigma] \times [P_k]^T$ (columns S–T, rows 37–39):

0.076	0.000
0.000	0.004

$[\Omega]$ (columns V–W, rows 37–39):

0.0047	0.0000
0.0000	0.0014

$[B] = [\tau\Sigma]^{-1} \times [\Pi] + [P]^T \times [\Omega]^{-1} \times [Q]$

$[B(R)] = [A]^{-1} \times [B]$ (columns H, rows 43–47):

1.699
0.059
0.074
0.037
0.039

(column K, rows 43–47):

11.241
0.298
0.247

$[P]^T \times [\Omega]^{-1} \times [Q]$ (column M, rows 43–47):

1.46384
11.0229
0.00
0.00

$[\Sigma] = [A]^{-1} = ([\tau\Sigma]^{-1} + [P]^T \times [\Omega]^{-1} \times [P])^{-1}$ (columns N–Q, rows 43–47):

0.0044	0.0045	0.0015	0.0024
0.0045	0.0058	0.0026	0.0027
0.0015	0.0026	0.0156	0.0050
0.0024	0.0027	0.0050	0.0123

$[\Omega]^{-1}$ (columns V–W, rows 43–45):

211.640	0.000
0.000	734.862

Stage 1

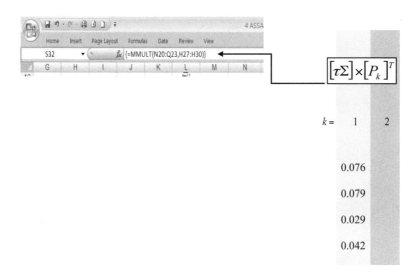

Step 1. For each P_k, separately (!) calculate $[\tau\Sigma] \times [P_k]^T$.

   Calculate for P_1, and fill in the left column.

   Repeat the same for P_2, and fill in the right column, $k = 2$.

Step 2. Calculate $[P_k] \times [\tau\Sigma] \times [P_k]^T$.

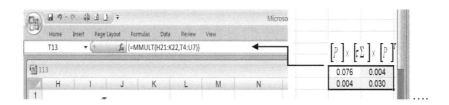

Step 3. Calculate $[\Omega]$ as demonstrated, and then calculate $[\Omega]^{-1}$, using **MIVERSE** (we skipped showing $[\Omega]^{-1}$).

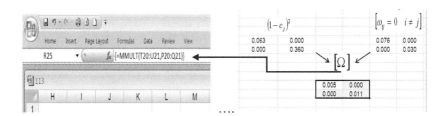

We are now ready to calculate $\left[\overline{\Sigma}\right] = [A]^{-1} = \left(\left[\tau\Sigma\right]^{-1} + [P]^{T} \times [\Omega]^{-1} \times [P]\right)^{-1}$ in a few steps, using the part of the worksheet displayed below:

	H	I	J	K	L	M	N	O	P	Q	R	S	T	U
17														
18		$[P]$					$[P]^{T}$		$(1-c_i)^2$				$[\omega_{ij}=0 \; i\neq j]$	
19														
20						1	-1		0.063	0.000			0.076	0.000
21	1	0	0	0		0	1		0.000	0.360			0.000	0.030
22	-1	1	0	0		0	0							
23						0	0				$[\Omega]$			
24														
25		$[P]^{T}\times[\Omega]^{-1}\times[P]$					$[\Omega]^{-1}\times[P]$				0.005	0.000		
26											0.000	0.011		
27														
28	303.119	-92.593	0.000	0.000		210.526	0.000	0.000	0.000					
29	-92.593	92.593	0.000	0.000		-92.593	92.593	0.000	0.000		$[\Omega]^{-1}$			
30	0.000	0.000	0.000	0.000										
31	0.000	0.000	0.000	0.000			$[\tau\Sigma]^{-1}$				210.526	0.000		
32											0.000	92.593		
33						83.491	-59.507	43.753	-44.643					
34						-59.507	77.211	-55.423	-0.581					
35						43.753	-55.423	78.126	-28.194					
36						-44.6426	-0.5807	-28.1943	101.9275					
37														
38					$A = [\tau\Sigma]^{-1} + [P]\times[\Omega]^{-1}\times[P]$					$\overline{\Sigma}=\left([\tau\Sigma]^{-1}+[P]^{T}\times[\Omega]^{-1}\times[P]\right)^{-1}$				
39														
40						386.610	-152.099	43.753	-44.643	0.004467975	0.004527036	0.001583	0.002421	
41						-152.099	169.803	-55.423	-0.581	0.004527036	0.012531624	0.007883	0.004235	
42						43.753	-55.423	78.126	-28.194	0.001582839	0.007882942	0.019743	0.006199	
43						-44.643	-0.581	-28.194	101.927	0.002420522	0.004234673	0.006199	0.01261	

Sheet1 / Sheet2 / Sheet3

Step 4. Calculate $([P]^{T} \times [\Omega]^{-1} \times [P])$ in two substeps (it can, however, be done in one step).

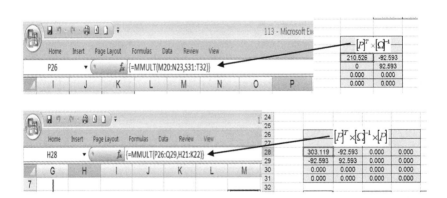

Step 5. Calculate $\left[\,\overline{\Sigma}\,\right] = [A]^{-1} = \left([\tau\Sigma]^{-1} + [P]\times[\Omega]^{-1}\times[P]\right)^{-1}$ in two substeps:

Calculate $[A] = [\tau\Sigma]^{-1} + [P] \times [\Omega]^{-1} \times [P]$:

Enter the **SUM** function into cell **N36 = SUM(T20,K28).**

To get the whole matrix array for $[A]$, copy **N36**, highlight array (**N36:Q39**), and paste:

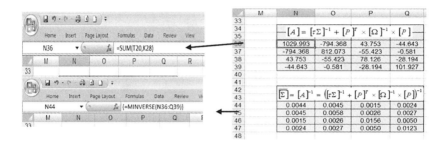

Step 6. Calculate $[B] = [\tau\Sigma]^{-1} \times [\Pi] + [P]^{T} \times [\Omega]^{-1} \times [Q])$ in three substeps:

First, calculate $[\tau\Sigma]^{-1} \times [\Pi]$:

Home	Insert	Page Layout	Formulas	Data	Review
	H35			f_x {=MMULT(T20:W23,J35:J38)}	
D	E	F	G	H	I
32					
33					
34				$[\tau\Sigma]^{-1} \times \Pi$	
35				0.23	
36				0.22	
37				0.30	
38				0.25	
39					

Since we have already calculated $([P]^{T} \times [\Omega]^{-1})$, we may now calculate $([P]^{T} \times [\Omega]^{-1}) \times [Q])$:

Home	Insert	Page Layout	Formulas	Data	Review	View
	L44			f_x {=MMULT(P29:Q32,L35:L36)}	
G	H	I	J	K	L	M
42					$[P]^{T} \times [\Omega]^{-1} \times [Q]$	
43					1.463845	
44					11.02293	
45					0.00	
46					0.00	
47						
48						

And finally, enter the **SUM(H35: L34)** function into cell **J43**. Copy **J43**, highlight array (**J43:J46**), and paste to attain the whole matrix array for [*B*]:

J43			f_x	=SUM(H35,L44)
G	H	I	J	K

39				
40			$[B] = [\mathcal{Z}]^{-1} \times [\Pi] + [P]^T \times [\Omega]^{-1} \times [\mathcal{Q}]$	
41				
42		$[E(R)] = [A]^{-1} \times [B]$		
43			1.699	
44	0.059		11.241	
45	0.074		0.298	
46	0.037		0.247	
47	0.039			

Step 7. Calculate $[E(R)] = [A]^{-1} \times [B]$.

H44				f_x	{=MMULT(N44:Q47,J43:J46)}	
D	E	F	G	H	I	

42					
43			$[E(R)] = [A]^{-1} \times [B]$	
44				0.059
45				0.074
46				0.037
47				0.039
48				

Step 8. Calculate $\overline{\overline{[\Sigma]}} = [\Sigma] + [\overline{\Sigma}]$.

Highlight cell **C44** and enter the **SUM** function **SUM(A3,N44)**.

Copy cell **C44**, highlight the cell array (**C44:F47**), and paste, to get the whole matrix array for $\overline{\overline{[\Sigma]}}$.

C44			f_x	=SUM(A3,N44)		
A	B	C	D	E	F	G

41						
42			$\overline{\overline{[\Sigma]}} = [\Sigma] + [\overline{\Sigma}]$			
43						
44			0.0644	0.0675	0.0245	0.0354
45			0.0675	0.0958	0.0456	0.0427
46			0.0245	0.0456	0.0506	0.0250
47			0.0354	0.0427	0.0250	0.0403
48						
49						

Stage 2

Now that we have $[E(R)]$ and $\overline{\overline{[\Sigma]}}$, we may use our efficient frontier optimizer template to calculate the new weights vector $[w^{normal*}]$, $E^*(R_p)$, and σ^*_p.

Open a new efficient frontier optimizer worksheet with $[E(R)]$ replacing $[\Pi]$ and $\overline{\overline{[\Sigma]}}$ replacing $[\Sigma]$. First copy your original optimizer and then replace $[\Pi]$ and $[\Sigma]$ with $[E(R)]$ and $\overline{\overline{[\Sigma]}}$ in a few substeps:

• On Worksheet 1 (from the previous chapter), highlight the whole area **A1:G22** of the efficient frontier optimizer and copy.

• Open a new Worksheet 2 (at the bottom of the screen), highlight **A1**, and paste, in order to get the new efficient frontier optimizer on Worksheet 2.

• To replace $[\Sigma]$ with $\overline{\overline{[\Sigma]}}$, highlight cell **A3** in Worksheet 2, choose the function **=VALUE**, then, on Worksheet1, highlight cell **C44** in order to transfer the new cell value of $\overline{\overline{[\Sigma]}}$ to **A3**. Copy cell **A3**, highlight the cell array (**A3:A6**), and paste — to replace the whole matrix array for $\overline{\overline{[\Sigma]}}$ into the optimizer on Worksheet 2.

• Replace $[\Pi]$ (on Worksheet 2) with $[E(R)]$ in the same manner as we replaced $[\Sigma]$ with $\overline{\overline{[\Sigma]}}$

We will automatically get the new weights vector $[w^{normal*}]$, $E^*(R_p)$, and σ^*_p in our new optimizer on Worksheet 2:

G.   Summary and Conclusions for the New Investment Opportunities Line

Once again, building the Excel templates is a tedious job! The good news is that, just as for the optimizer template of the previous chapter, we need only prepare them once. You can use the template for any future need; just plug in new personal views. Moreover, you can construct the template in such a way that only the relevant input data array and the relevant required results will be visible, while the irrelevant calculating parts remain hidden.[33]

The efficient frontier optimizer and the subjective views templates together are powerful instruments for playing around when constructing new portfolios, replacing and adding assets within the risky portfolio, or changing views.

Comparing the market consensus portfolio with the personal views portfolio from our example, we see the following:

	Consensus w^{normal}	Personal $w^{normal*}$
Asset 1	0.24	0.40
Asset 2	0.22	0.31
Asset 3	0.30	0.16
Asset 4	0.25	0.13
$E(R_P)$	8.9%	9.7%
σ_P	0.197	0.233
IOL slope	24.9	24.5

Although we have significantly increased the expected return of our portfolio (from 8.9% to 9.7%) by adding our personal expertise (views), we have also unintentionally increased the portfolio's expected variance σ_P from 0.197 to 0.233 (or increased σ_P^2 from 0.039 to 0.54). The final result is that the slope of the IOL has decreased from 24.9 to 24.5, which means that we get *less* risk premium for each unit of risk that we take.[34] This may suggest one reason why it is difficult to beat the benchmark (market consensus). It may also imply that we should not apply some of our views unless we have a considerable level of confidence in them, that is, usually in the range of over 70%.

---

33. On a different worksheet.
34. According to Sharpe's measure of portfolio management quality (see chapter 13).

Once again, since this is an introductory book concerned with fundamental models, we will stop at this stage and leave further discussion for more advanced curricula. We only wish to inspire readers to think about personal views concerning a change in the risk-free return, a change in investors' mutual risk aversion in a bullish or bearish future market (equivalent to a change in λ), etc.

The Black-Litterman model we presented in general, and the Excel templates we demonstrated in particular, provide us with powerful tools to understand the meaning and the consequences of applying personal views. The main conclusion is that we should always take into consideration that we are dealing with statistical models. Thus, we may (at best) project expected returns that have considerable variances. Whenever we wish to add personal views about future expected returns, we must find a built-in routine that will increase the expected variances. This is the only way we can judge whether it is worthwhile incorporating our personal views or whether it is better to use the consensus benchmark.

Further Reading

Christodoulakis, G. A. 2002. Bayesian Optimal Portfolio Selection: The Black-Litterman Approach. http://globalriskguard.com/resources/assetman/bayes_0008.pdf.

Frost, P. A., and J. E. Savarino. 1986. An Empirical Bayes Approach to Efficient Portfolio Selection. *Journal of Financial and Quantitative Analysis* 21.

He, G., and R. Litterman. 1999. The Intuition behind Black-Litterman Model Portfolios. *Investment Management Research*. New York: Goldman Sachs.

Idzorek, T. M. 2002. A Step-by-Step Guide to the Black-Litterman Model: Incorporating User-Specified Confidence Levels. Zephyr Cove, NV: Zephyr Associates.

Mankert, C. 2006. The Black-Litterman Model: Mathematical and Behavioral Finance Approaches towards Its Use in Practice. http://kth.diva-portal.org/smash/get/diva2:10311/FULLTEXT01.

Walters, J. 2008. The Black-Litterman Model: A Detailed Exploration. http://www.master272.com/finance/BL/JWalters_Black-Litterman.pdf.

16 Capital Structure—Maximizing Company Value

A. Capital Structure Effects on Corporate Value—Introduction
B. The Basic Assumptions and Model
C. Tax Shelter—Modigliani and Miller's First Proposition
D. Modigliani and Miller's First Proposition—Arbitrage

A. Capital Structure Effects on Corporate Value—Introduction

The equity required to set up or expand corporate operations can be raised through two financial instruments, shares (participation certificates) and bonds (debt certificates).[1] In the previous chapters we discussed share and bond valuation from the perspective of the individual investor. The next two chapters discuss the extent to which management (as agents on behalf of company owners[2]) can maximize share value by issuing shares and/or bonds. Maximizing share value will reduce the number of new shares issued when raising additional capital, thus minimizing the dilution of current shareholders' holdings. Maximizing bond value means minimizing the required risk premium (interest) payments on newly issued bonds, as the risk-free rate is defined exogenously, by the market.

---

1. Capital raised through bonds is denoted D (for "debt"), while capital raised through shares is denoted E (for "equity"). All other capital-raising financial instruments can be shown to be a linear combination of these two fundamental instruments.

2. Managers serve as agents for company shareholders. Just as shareholders seek to maximize the value of their shares, so too is this management's goal. For a discussion of agency problems and costs, see advanced curricula literature.

In the risk-return models discussed in the previous chapters, a share's value, and consequently that company's value,[3] is determined by investors according to their required return on the company's risky shares. According to these models, management should seek to maximize company value by expanding operations and financial results or by reducing the risk in the company's financial results, or both. Let's assume that the company's business is managed in the most effective way, that is, the best projects are chosen, and in the most efficient way, that is, at minimum expense, thereby maximizing its financial results (and the return on its shares).[4]

This chapter examines whether a particular capital structure (the ratio of bond-raised capital to share-raised capital)[5] can minimize risk on the company's shares, thus maximizing company value.

We'll use the debt-to-equity (D/E) capital structure ratio as the explanatory variable on the x-axis, while company value V (as a result of a specific capital structure) will be plotted on the y-axis (figure 16.1).

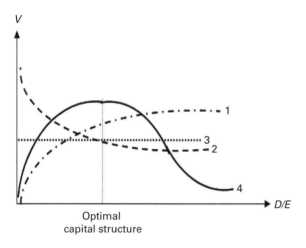

Figure 16.1
Prospective Functional Description(s) of a Firm's Value as a Function of Its Capital Structure

3. For a company financed by shares alone, company value = share price × number of shares. If the number of shares is fixed, then share value directly determines company value.
4. For a discussion of efficacy versus efficiency, see chapter 1.
5. Their ratio is denoted D/E.

We can expect one of the following scenarios:

1. Increasing function.
2. Decreasing function.
3. Constant function.
4. Increasing and then decreasing function.

Only the fourth type of function can explain a capital structure that maximizes company value. Strictly increasing or decreasing functions leads to a dichotomous solution,[6] while a constant function indicates that capital structure is irrelevant. We'll start off with basic assumptions and build a simple model, then ease some of these assumptions in order to develop a more complete and real-world-compliant model. Understanding the model's underlying assumptions and the arguments for and against these assumptions is no less important than understanding the model and its implications.

There are two fundamental approaches to the capital structure question, classic and modern.

The classic approach. The classic approach accords with the fourth type of functional correlation above, whereby a particular D/E ratio can be found that maximizes company value.

The modern approach. The modern approach, proposed by Modigliani and Miller, accords with the third type of functional correlation above, whereby capital structure is irrelevant to company value.

Consider a CEO at the beginning of a time period. Existing projects yield a known, constant, perpetual, and normally distributed revenue stream. This assumption includes a hidden assumption that an investment I is made at the beginning of each period that is equal to the last period's depreciation of the company's assets. Otherwise, after several periods, no capital assets would be left (machinery, structures, equipment) to provide the assumed perpetual revenue stream.

Now assume that this CEO wishes to expand operations and has a choice of new, investment-worthy projects. The company has profits, which it can distribute to its shareholders. Management can invest in new projects in several ways:

---

6. That is, capital is comprised only of shares or only of debt.

1. By not paying a dividend and using undistributed earnings to invest in new projects; or

2. By paying a dividend and raising new capital from external sources to invest in new projects.

This choice, known as a company's *dividend policy*, was actually discussed in chapter 4, even if it was not referred to by name.[7] In chapter 4 we saw how from an investor's standpoint, and subject to underlying assumptions, dividend payments have no effect on share price or company value. Indeed, dividends do not appear in the company valuation formula:

$$V_{(t)} = \frac{O_{(t+1)} - I_{(t+1)} + V_{(t+1)}}{1 + k_{(t+1)}}.$$

Therefore, we can assume that management may as well decide to distribute all earnings as dividends and raise new capital. The CEO now faces the question of how to raise this new capital in order to build a capital structure that maximizes company value:[8]

1. By issuing new bonds?

2. By issuing new shares?

3. A combination of both? In what ratio?

Remember that at some point in the past, existing projects were also new projects requiring investment. Therefore, past decisions to finance investments by new bonds or shares effectively determined the company's present capital structure.

B. The Basic Assumptions and Model

In chapter 4 we defined the term *operating income*, denoted O. This cash flow is comprised of revenues R, net of fixed costs (FC) and variable costs, which are always calculated as a constant percentage of revenue (VC). Thus, $O = R - FC - VC$.

Our first assumption is that revenues are distributed normally. The following example demonstrates that operating cash flows are also distributed normally.

7. In chapter 4, we discussed why dividend policies do not affect company or share valuation. Investors determine a company's value based on its net operating cash flow.

8. That is, issuing the minimum number of shares or bonds at the maximum price to raise the needed amount of money.

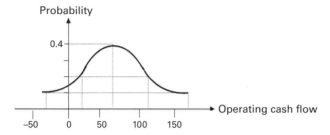

Figure 16.2
Operating Cash Flow—Normal Distribution

	Probability				
	0.1	**0.2**	**0.4**	**0.2**	**0.1**
Sales revenue	500	400	300	200	100
Fixed costs	80	80	80	80	80
Variable costs (50%)	250	200	150	100	50
Operating cash flow	170	120	70	20	(30)

As we are subtracting a constant (fixed costs) from a normally distributed value (revenues) and multiplying by another constant (variable costs), we are effectively performing a linear transformation of the probability distribution for revenues. This linear transformation of a normal distribution yields another normal distribution (figure 16.2).[9]

At this point, we must relax several assumptions to simulate more lifelike conditions, which include taxes. Initially, let's assume a world with only personal income tax (which may be different for wages than for capital gains) and corporate income tax. Income tax does not permit deduction of capital investments when an expense is incurred but rather recognizes *virtual* cash flow expenses over several years. These expenses are known as depreciation and are denoted by DP.

Now denote by T_C the corporate income tax rate. The fact that depreciation is recognized over several years means a reduction in a company's tax liability in those years. A company's payment to the income tax authority at the end of each period will equal

$$(O - DP) \cdot T_C = (R - FC - VC - DP) \cdot T_C.$$

---

9. Adding (or subtracting) a constant pushes the distribution curve to the right (or left), that is, it changes the mean value μ. Multiplying by a constant changes the units on the x-axis and thus the variance σ around the mean, but does not change the normal distribution's bell shape curve.

The fact that the payment made at the end of each period is reduced by $T_c \cdot DP$ (as compared to a scenario in which depreciation is not tax-deductible) means that although depreciation is a virtual expense, it (indirectly) increases a company's real post-tax net free cash flow. The model discussed in chapter 4 assumed a tax-free world, and so we defined the expression $O_i(t+1) - I_i(t+1)$ as company i's free cash flow.

In a world with taxes, we must take into account that investors consider a company's real free cash flow the one after income tax payments:[10]

$$O - (O - DP)\cdot T_C = (O - DP)\cdot(1 - T_C) + DP.$$

As explained above, to maintain a constant, perpetual revenue stream, in each period a company must invest an amount equal to the depreciation $(I = DP)$. Therefore, its net free cash flow (FCF)[11] is equal to

$$FCF = (O - DP)\cdot(1 - T_C) + DP - I = (O - DP)\cdot(1 - T_C).$$

C.   Tax Shelter—Modigliani and Miller's First Proposition

The interest a company pays to its bondholders is tax-deductible, while dividends to shareholders are not. Shareholders and bondholders are both corporate "capital holders." For the sake of simplicity, let's assume that one individual holds all the shares and bonds issued by a company. His only consideration is how to maximize his cash inflow from interest on the bonds written (issued) by the company and from the dividends paid on his holdings in the company's shares.

To this end, let's follow $1 generated by the company's operations when paid entirely as interest or as a dividend to the company's capital holder, after all tax payments have been made.

We denote the following

T_C—The corporate tax rate (in the following example,[12] 34%).

T_{PE}—The personal equity tax rate on capital gains (assume 25%).

T_P—The personal tax rate on other[13] income (assume 50%).

---

10. At that stage we assumed only the existence of corporate income tax. More generally, investors examine their net cash inflow after all applicable taxes, as discussed next.

11. Operating cash flow, O, should not be confused with net free cash flow, FCF.

12. The values in the following examples are realistic but vary among countries, and even between periods within the same country.

13. Wages, interest received on lending money (bondwriter), etc.

	Operating Cash Flow $1	
	Paid as Interest	**Paid as Dividend**
Corporate income tax	None	T_C
Earnings after corporate tax	$1	$1 - T_C$
Personal income tax (different rates for interest and for dividends)	T_P	$T_{PE}(1 - T_C)$
Net free cash inflow after all taxes	$1 - T_P$	$1 - T_C - T_{PE}(1 - T_C) = (1 - T_{PE})(1 - T_C)$

Government tax policy determines the similarity or difference of the final result offered on each track. Of course, if the T_{PE} on capital (dividends) is equal to the T_P on wages and interest gains (as is so often demanded by populists in the name of social equality), then the tax gap for each track would be greatest. Therefore, taxes on capital gains from shares are usually lower than the marginal personal tax rate on wages.

If we substitute numbers into the above example, then for every $1 of operating cash flow:

The left track yields a net cash flow of $1 - 0.5 = \$0.50$.

The right track yields a net cash flow of $(1 - 0.34) \times (1 - 0.25) = \$0.495$.

Therefore, the difference is negligible. The company's sole capital holder would be indifferent to its financing by share capital or by bonds. Either way, he alone endures the risk of owning that company.

To encourage capital investments, promote economic growth, or because of other constraints,[14] governments may grant the right track an advantage over the left one. In other words, government may provide incentives for share-based capital investments or bond-based capital investments (remember that governments are the largest issuers of bonds). Preference may also be given to a particular industry. Thus, for example, in many countries the tax rate for leasing apartments is lower than the tax rate on other capital investments, to encourage construction of residential apartments for rent. The government's considerations in determining the various tax rates are complex and sometimes contradictory. This matter is discussed in depth in the macroeconomic and taxation policy literature. Properly choosing the tax track through

---

14. Industry-specific constraints or populist political considerations.

which to finance company operations allows us to increase its free cash flow. The difference in the total amount paid to the tax authorities through the left track and the amount paid through the right track from each $1 of operating cash flow, presented in the last table, is referred to as a *tax shelter*.

To simplify their model, Modigliani and Miller assumed a world with only one kind of tax. The tax rate is equal to the difference between net cash flow on the left track and the right track for every $1 of operating cash flow. Modigliani and Miller referred to this tax difference as "corporate income tax."[15] Later, they examined the special case in which the corporate income tax is zero, that is, there is no material difference in free cash flows on the left track or the right track.

Let's demonstrate the tax shelter concept using the following example.

Two companies have completely identical operations. Both companies have a registered capital of $5,000, yielding a 20% return (operating cash flow). Company A finances its capital solely through shares, while company B issued $1,000 in bonds (to clarify the tax shelter concept, these bonds are also held by its shareholders) with an 8% interest rate, while the other $4,000 was raised as share capital. Assume that only corporate income tax applies, so that no personal taxes are charged on interest gains or dividends.

Parameter	Company A	Company B
Net operating cash flow (20%)	$1,000	$1,000
Interest paid to bondholders	$0	$80
Pretax earnings	$1,000	$920
Corporate income tax (34%)	$340	$312.8
Net cash flow to shareholders	$660	$607.2
Total net cash flow to capital holders[a]	$660	$687.2
Tax shelter[b]	$0	$27.2

a. Including interest earnings.
b. The difference between the left and right columns.

Company B capital holders, who financed part of the company's assets through bonds ("shareholders' loan"), recorded a greater profit (*FCF*)

15. This same term was used previously to refer to something else. Readers should take care not to confuse the two!

at the end of the period. They paid less income tax than company A owners. As mentioned, this difference constitutes a tax shelter. It is exactly equal to the tax savings afforded by the company recognizing the interest payment on the bonds as an expense: $80 \times 34\% = \$27.20$.

For historical reasons, the educational literature and even professional circles continued referring to the tax difference between the two tracks as constituting the "corporate income tax." In my experience, students tend to confuse it with the actual government-imposed corporate income tax. To avoid confusion, this book refers to the tax difference between the two tracks as a "segregating tax" (or sheltering tax), and denotes it with T_S.

We can calculate the T_S tax rate in the real world, which includes (for example) tax on ordinary income and on capital gains, using its definition as the percent difference between net cash flow on the left track and on the right track for every $1 in operating cash flow.

The difference in net cash flow between the left track and the right track is

$$\$(1-T_P)-(1-T_C)(1-T_{PE}).$$

On the left track, investors earn

$$\$(1-T_P).$$

The ratio (percent difference) of net cash flow on the left track[16] and the right track per $1 of operating cash flow is therefore

$$T_S = \frac{(1-T_P)-(1-T_C)(1-T_{PE})}{(1-T_P)} = \frac{(1-T_P)}{(1-T_P)} - \frac{(1-T_C)(1-T_{PE})}{(1-T_P)}$$
$$= 1 - \frac{(1-T_C)(1-T_{PE})}{(1-T_P)}.$$

Similarly, we can also calculate the segregating tax rate T_S for scenarios including a longer list of taxes, whether imposed on the right track or on the left one.

Modigliani and Miller's first proposition assumed zero bankruptcy cost.[17] Therefore, all companies issue two kinds of "participation certificates":

---

16. The lower tax bracket channel will always be used as the basis for calculation.

17. This assumption is not directly stated but is implied in Modigliani and Miller's development of their model.

- Risk-free bonds, and
- Shares whose risk is due to the distribution of company revenues.[18]

At first glance, this assumption seems far-fetched. The following example illustrates the criticism of this assumption and explains why it is usable nonetheless.

Success Inc. finances part of its assets through bonds, with an interest payment of 20. Its cash flow will be as follows:

	Probability				
	0.1	**0.2**	**0.4**	**0.2**	**0.1**
Operating cash flow	170	120	70	20	(30)
Bond interest payments	(20)	(20)	(20)	(20)	(20)
Post-interest cash flow	150	100	50	0	(50)

The post-interest cash flow is equal to shifting the probability distribution function axis to the right by 20, as compared to the zero-interest payment scenario (see figure 16.3).

The probability that the company will default on its interest payment (become insolvent) is calculated by the cumulative probability function $F(0) = \int_{-\infty}^{0} f(x)dx$ (the striped area in figure 16.3). The probability of a

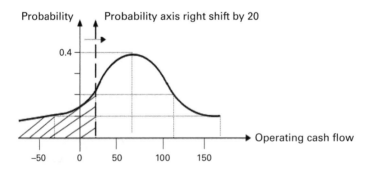

Figure 16.3
Post-Interest Operating Cash Flow—A Shifted Normal Distribution

18. And consequently, as discussed earlier, the net cash flow distribution is also normally distributed.

default is clearly not zero. The greater the interest rate, the more the *y*-axis moves to the right, and the greater the integral (signifying the probability of a default).

This argument, although both accurate and reasonable, assumes bondholders to be separate from shareholders. The problem can be temporarily[19] resolved by initially assuming that bonds and shares are both held by the same individuals. Therefore, the question facing a company's owners, who in any case bear all risk, is whether (for tax purposes) it is better to provide a company with its required capital by issuing additional shares or to register new money in the company's books as a shareholder loan.

As the owners are risking all the capital required to set up the company's operational assets, the question is reduced to the formal recognition of this capital as share or debt capital. In the above scenario, we can assume the debt to the owners to be risk-free, while all risk is borne by the shares.[20]

Modigliani and Miller's Model

Assume two companies with completely identical operations, in a world with a segregating tax of T_S.[21] The first company is leveraged[22] with debt and has a value of V^L, while the other unleveraged company, whose entire capital is financed by shares, has a value of V^U. Assuming both companies' net operating cash flows are perpetual and have a constant distribution, we can calculate the unleveraged company's value, V^U, by calculating its mean free cash flow, $F\tilde{C}F$. In other words, discounting a perpetual cash flow using a risk-adjusted discount factor:[23]

$$V^U = \frac{E(F\tilde{C}F)}{k} = \frac{E[(\tilde{O}-DP)\cdot(1-T_S)]}{k}.$$

The same operating cash flow $F\tilde{C}F$ is received by the leveraged company's shareholders. From this cash flow, the company must pay interest on the company's debt, $k_D \cdot D$. However, they also benefit from a

---

19. Later, we'll see that this assumption is not a prerequisite for the mathematical development of the model.

20. What would have been the case had the owners decided to finance the company entirely through shares?

21. As explained above, it is referred to by Modigliani and Miller as "corporate tax."

22. We will address the source of the term *leveraged* in the next chapter.

23. We can choose a risk-adjusted k factor as we wish, for example, β-adjusted, as per the market model.

tax shelter of $T_S \cdot k_D \cdot D$. As bondholders, they receive the interest payment $k_D \cdot D$.

The net cash flow to the company's capital holders is the sum of their cash flows as shareholders and as bondholders:

$$\underbrace{(\tilde{O}-DP)\cdot(1-T_S) - k_D\cdot D + T_S\cdot k_D\cdot D}_{\text{Dividend}} + \underbrace{k_D\cdot D}_{\text{Interest}}$$

$$= (\tilde{O}-DP)\cdot(1-T_S) + T_S\cdot k_D\cdot D$$

To calculate the company's value V^L, we must discount this perpetual cash flow. The first part of the above expression is random and has a constant distribution function. Therefore, to calculate its mean value, we must discount it using the risk-adjusted discount rate. The second part of the expression is constant and risk-free, and so can be discounted using the risk-free interest rate:

$$V^L = \frac{E[(\tilde{O}-DP)\cdot(1-T_S)]}{k} + \frac{T_S\cdot k_D\cdot D}{k_f}.$$

As we assumed that interest payments are made to bondholders at the risk-free interest rate (no default risk), so that $k_D = k_f$, we can rewrite the equation as[24]

$$V^L = \frac{E[(\tilde{O}-DP)\cdot(1-T_S)]}{k} + T_S\cdot D.$$

Comparing the expressions for the leveraged and unleveraged company values, we can correlate them as follows:

$$V^L = V^U + T_S\cdot D.$$

If the segregating tax T_S (which Modigliani and Miller refer to as "corporate tax" and notate as T_C) is zero, the leveraged and unleveraged company values are identical.

Therefore:
Capital structure does not affect company value, and their correlating function is a horizontal line.

---

24. If they are unequal, then $\dfrac{k_D\cdot D}{k_f}$ is the present value of future interest payments = the bonds' market value. Denoting by B the bonds' market value yields the expression $T_C\cdot B$. Note that this mathematical development does not require that $k_D = k_f$, and our initial assumption is not necessary.

Nonzero segregating taxes lead to dichotomous solutions, where higher D (debt) values increase (linearly) V^L. This additional value is due to the tax shelter on capital financed by debt. The greater the company's debt, the greater is its tax shelter, and consequently the greater is its value. Therefore, management should increase D as much as possible.

Conclusion

Modigliani and Miller's proposition makes perfect sense. If we examine a company's balance sheet, the left side details its productive assets and the right side details its liabilities, "certificates" issued by the company that indicate its contractual obligations to its shareholders or bondholders (who finance the purchase of productive assets).

A company's operating cash flow is derived from its asset operations, regardless of how these assets were financed.

In fact, Modigliani and Miller argue that, lacking a tax system giving preference to one kind of investor over the other, the tax rate and the net gain recorded by investors are identical on either track. In this case, a company's value is determined solely by the return on its assets, and its capital structure is irrelevant. If a difference exists between financing tracks that creates a tax shelter, a company's value is determined by the (post-tax) return on its assets plus the tax shelter value.

As demonstrated in the above numerical example, $T_S = 0$ is an approximately reasonable assumption that is observed in numerous markets. Moreover, in principle, a tax preference can exist not only on the debt interest track but also on the share-investment track (e.g., $T_{PE} = 0$). Any preference for one track over the other would lead investors to choose that track (i.e., 100% shares or 100% debt). A company's value is always determined by the post-tax return (cash flow) on its real assets plus any tax shelter value.

Finally, let's review the assumptions made in developing the model:

1. As we developed the model using $1 of operating cash flow, we made a hidden assumption that all companies are identical and differ only in size. Thus, a company with more assets will generate proportionately larger operating cash flows.

2. We may discard the assumption that bonds are issued at the risk-free interest rate. It was not required for formal development of the model since we have used k_D and not k_F until the very last stage. If the interest rates are not equal, $k_D \neq k_f$, company value will increase by $T_S \cdot B$, where B is the market value of a company's debt (as opposed to D, which is

the total face value of the bonds). Thus, this assumption does not change our conclusion and was made for convenience only.

3. Our hidden assumption that there is no (negative) premium on bankruptcy costs is the least reasonable of our assumptions. If such a premium were to exist and grow proportionately with debt, then a scenario is possible where an optimal capital structure does exist. For example, see question 6 at the end of this chapter.

D. Modigliani and Miller's First Proposition—Arbitrage

Modigliani and Miller's original article differs from our above discussion in its exceptional proof method. Their article is considered unique not only for its proposition (significant in itself) that $V^L = V^U + T_S \cdot D$ and that, when the segregating tax is zero, there is no difference in the value of leveraged and unleveraged companies, but also in their original method of proving their proposition. For the first time in the history of finance theory, a proposition (theory) was proved through arbitrage.

Hypothesis

In a perfect market at equilibrium (where no arbitrage is possible),

$$V^L = V^U + T_S \cdot D.$$

Proof

Position 1 Buy $x\%$ of the leveraged company's shares.[25] The cost of buying the shares from your own sources is $X \cdot E^L$.

Position 2 Borrow $X \cdot D(1 - T_S)$ dollars and buy $x\%$ of the unleveraged company's shares. The cost of buying the shares from your own sources is $X \cdot V^U - X \cdot D(1 - T_S)$.

With position 1, in each future period you can expect to receive a net cash flow from the company of $X \cdot (\tilde{O} - k_D \cdot D)(1 - T_S)$.

With position 2, in each future period you can expect to receive a net cash flow of $X \cdot (\tilde{O} - k_D \cdot D)$.

---

25. E = the market value of the company's shares, D = the market value of the company's debt, and V = the company's value ($V^L = E^L + D$ when leveraged, and $V^U = E^U$ when unleveraged).

However, you must also pay interest on your loan of $k_D \cdot X \cdot D(1 - T_S)$. Consequently, your total free cash flow in each period is

$$X \cdot (\tilde{O} - k_D \cdot D) - X \cdot k_D \cdot D(1 - T_S) = X(\tilde{O} - k_D \cdot D)(1 - T_S).$$

As your investment in position 1 yields the same net cash flow as an investment in position 2, their cost (the price paid for each investment position) must be identical, otherwise you could generate gains through arbitrage—short selling the "expensive" investment (position) and buying the "cheap" one (going long).

Therefore,

$$X \cdot E^L = X \cdot V^U - X \cdot D(1 - T_S).$$

$$E^L + D = V^U + T_S \cdot D,$$

since $E^L + D \equiv V^L$

$$\Rightarrow V^L = V^u + T_S \cdot D \qquad \text{QED}$$

The simplicity of the above proof clearly trumps any other rationalization. However, it is important to explain how our underlying concept that net cash flow is the only way of evaluating a financial asset also answers the question of capital structure. Although Modigliani and Miller used net cash flow in their article, their application of arbitrage arguments is so powerful a tool that it may distract readers from the underlying concept and the final conclusion, which was the goal of this chapter, and instead focus attention on the tool itself (arbitrage).

Chapter 16—Questions and Problems

Question 1

L Ltd. and U Ltd. are commercially identical companies with operating cash flows of $96 million each year into perpetuity. The companies operate in a tax-free market. The market value of L Ltd.'s debt is $275 million, with an 8% return. L Ltd. has 4.5 million shares with a market price of $100 per share. U Ltd. is debt-free and has 10 million shares with a market price of $80 per share. Assuming that the value of L Ltd.'s debt is at equilibrium:

a. In which of these shares should you invest? Explain.

b. If the risk-free rate is 6%, what can you say about L Ltd.'s debt?

Question 2

Music Inc. has one million shares priced at $10 each and yielding a return of 15%. Susan, the company's CFO, wants to buy 1% of the company, and has three options: to borrow 20%, 40%, or 60% of the amount required to buy these shares. The loan carries a 10% annual interest rate. Assume a tax-free market.

a. What is the annual return on investment on each financing track?

b. What is the return on equity for each financing track?

c. According to parts (a) and (b), what conclusion can Susan reach concerning the return on a leveraged company's share capital?

Question 3

Two identical companies operating in the meat industry and differing only in size have a free cash flow of $500,000 for company A and $1,500,000 for company B. Company A, which is financed only by shares, has a market value of $1,000,000.

What is the market value of company A's shares and company B's shares, if company B is financed by shares and bonds, and its bonds have a market value of $1,000,000 (assume that it is equal to the face value of the bonds)?

a. In a tax-free world.

b. If only a 40% income tax is applied.

Question 4

Under the Modigliani-Miller model, we assumed operating cash flows (O) to be constant.

Redevelop the model assuming operating cash flows grow at a constant rate g.

a. What is the value of an unleveraged company in a world with taxes?

b. What is the value of a leveraged company in a world with taxes?

c. What is the correlation between the value of leveraged and unleveraged companies?

d. Explain the reasoning behind your answer in part (c).

(*Hint*: The result stays the same, $V_L = V_U + T_S D$.)

Question 5

Two companies are traded on the capital market in Foolsland. The capital market is a perfect and tax-free market. The companies are identical in all respects except their financial structure:

Company A is unleveraged and trades at a market value of $10 million.

Company B has financial (risk-free) levering of $4 million and a market value of $8 million.

You are a wise traveler arriving in this land.

a. Through arbitrage, demonstrate how you can make money without investing a single penny of your own money.

b. Assuming a few more wise men came with you (let's say 100), what would happen? What is your conclusion?

(Assume that free cash flow from operations is distributed entirely as dividends.)

Question 6

In an economy that imposes an income tax on wages, a tax on capital gains, and a corporate income tax, experts studied the cucumber industry. They found that, contrary to Modigliani and Miller's assumptions, this industry does have bankruptcy costs, which increase as the value of a company's debt increases relative to its total market value.

These experts believe the mean bankruptcy cost to be $F = (a \cdot x^2 - b \cdot x) \cdot V^L$, where x is company's debt (bond) value as a percentage of its total value.

a. What is the optimal capital structure for companies in the cucumber industry? (Define a general expression.)

b. Assume $a = 4$, $b = 1.36$, the marginal income tax on wages and the tax on capital are identical and equal to 50%, and the corporate income tax is 36%. Calculate the optimal capital structure, that is, the percentage of capital financed by debt (and by shares) that maximizes the value of the firm.

c. What can you say about the cost-effectiveness of operating as a sole proprietor or as an LLC in a market where the tax on labor and the tax on capital gains are the same (in our case, 50%)?

d. How much will a company's value decrease if the market value of its bonds (debt) accounts for 50% of its total value, as compared to a company with an optimal capital structure?

Question 7

In Smartlandia, which historically had three taxes (personal, capital gains, and corporate income tax), the new finance minister has given in to the demands of the "riotous" sector and split the capital gains tax into two different taxes: a tax on capital gains from selling financial assets/shares (which will still be denoted T_{PE}), and a tax on dividends (denoted T_{Pd}). Assuming a perfect market:

a. Calculate the segregating tax rate T_S, assuming the minister's bill is approved by parliament.

b. How would the new law affect dividend distribution policies, assuming zero bankruptcy costs?

c. How would the new law affect dividend distribution policies, assuming there are bankruptcy costs (e.g., of the type described in the previous question)?

Question 8

Assume a Modigliani-Miller-compliant market where corporate income tax and personal income tax are identical and equal 50%, the capital gains tax equals 10%, and dividends are subject to 20% tax. If one company is financed partly by bonds with a $10 million market value and a second, identical company is financed entirely by shares, how much higher would the value of the first company be:

a. If they distribute 50% of their distributable operating profit as dividends.

b. If they enact an optimal dividend policy.

Further Reading

Aharony, J., and I. Swary. 1988. A Note on Corporate Bankruptcy and the Market Model Risk Measures. *Journal of Business Finance and Accounting* (Summer).

Altman, E. 1984. A Further Empirical Investigation of the Bankruptcy Cost Question. *Journal of Finance* (September): 1067–1089.

Ashton, R. K. 1986. Personal Leverage vs. Corporate Leverage: An Extension to the Debate. *Journal of Business, Finance and Accounting* (Winter).

Barges, A. 1963. *The Effect of Capital Structure on the Cost of Capital.* Englewood Cliffs, NJ: Prentice-Hall.

Baron, D. P. 1976. Default Risk and Optimal Capital Structure. *Journal of Finance* (December).

Becker, J. 1978. General Proof of Modigliani-Miller Propositions I and II Using Parameter-Preference Theory. *Journal of Financial and Quantitative Analysis* (March): 65–69.

Beranck, W. 1964. *The Effect of Leverage on the Market Value of Common Stock.* Madison, WI: Bureau of Business Research and Service.

Bhandari, L. C. 1988. Debt/Equity Ratio and Expected Common Stock Returns: Empirical Evidence. *Journal of Finance* (June).

Bierman, H., Jr., and R. West. 1966. The Acquisition of Common Stock by the Corporate Issuer. *Journal of Finance* (December): 687–696.

Boquist, J. A., and Moore, W. T. 1984. Inter-Industry Leverage Differences and the DeAngelo-Masulis Tax Shield Hypothesis. *Financial Management* (Spring).

Bowen, R. M., L. A. Daley, and C. Huber. 1982. Leverage Measures and Industrial Classification: Review and Additional Evidence. *Financial Management* (Winter).

Bradley, M., G. Jarrell, and E. H. Kim. 1984. On the Existence of an Optimal Capital Structure: Theory and Evidence. *Journal of Finance* (July): 857–878.

Brennan, M. J., and E. S. Schwartz. 1978. Corporate Income Taxes, Valuation, and the Problem of Optimal Capital Structure. *Journal of Business* (January): 103–114.

Castanias, R. 1983. Bankruptcy Risk and Optimal Capital Structure. *Journal of Finance* (December).

Chen, N. F., R. Roll, and S. Ross. 1986. Economic Forces and the Stock Market. *The Journal of Business* 59 (3): 383–403.

Cordes, J., and S. Shefrin. 1983. Estimating the Tax Advantage of Corporate Debt. *Journal of Finance* (March): 95–105.

DeAngelo, H., and R. W. Masulis. 1980. Leverage and Dividend Irrelevancy under Corporate and Personal Taxation. *Journal of Finance* (May).

DeAngelo, H., and R. W. Masulis. 1980. Optimal Capital Structure under Corporate and Personal Taxation. *Journal of Financial Economics* (March): 3–30.

Elton, E. J., and M. J. Gruber. 1968. The Effect of Share Repurchase on the Value of the Firm. *Journal of Finance* (March): 135–149.

Farrar, D., and L. Selwyn. 1967. Taxes, Corporate Financial Policy and Return to Investors. *National Tax Journal* (December): 444–454.

Fung, W. K. H., and M. F. Theobald. 1984. Dividends and Debt under Alternative Tax Systems. *Journal of Financial and Quantitative Analysis* (March).

Gordon, M. J. 1989. Corporate Finance under the MM Theorems. *Financial Management* (Summer).

Gorman, R., and E. Shields. 1986. Capital Structure, Corporate Taxes and the Clientele Effect. *Journal of Midwest Financial Association* 15.

Higgins, R. 1972. The Corporate Dividend-Saving Decision. *Journal of Financial and Quantitative Analysis* (March): 1527–1541.

Kalaba, R. E., T. C. Langetieg, N. Rasakhoo, and M. I. Weinstein. 1984. Estimation of Implicit Bankruptcy Costs. *Journal of Finance* (July).

Kane, A., A. Marcus, and R. McDonald. 1984. How Big Is the Tax Advantage to Debt? *Journal of Finance* (July): 841–853.

Kim, E. H., W. Lewellen, and J. McConnell. 1979. Financial Leverage Clienteles: Theory and Evidence. *Journal of Financial Economics* (March).

Kim, H. 1978. A Mean-Variance Theory of Optimal Capital Structure and Corporate Debt Capacity. *Journal of Finance* 33: 45–64.

Leland, H., and D. Pyle. 1977. Informational Asymmetrics, Financial Structure, and Financial Intermediation. *Journal of Finance* (May): 371–388.

Lev, B., and D. Pekelman. 1975. A Multiperiod Adjustment Model for the Firm's Capital Structure. *Journal of Finance* (March).

Marsh, P. 1982. The Choice between Equity and Debt: An Empirical Study. *Journal of Finance* (March).

Masulis, R. W. 1983. The Impact of Capital Structure Change on Firm Value: Some Estimates. *Journal of Finance* (March): 107–126.

Masulis, R. W., and B. Trueman. 1988. Corporate Investment and Dividend Decisions under Differential Personal Taxation. *Journal of Financial and Quantitative Analysis* 3 (4): 369–385.

Miller, M. H. 1977. Debt and Taxes. *Journal of Finance* (May): 261–275.

Miller, M. H., and F. Modigliani. 1961. Dividend Policy, Growth and the Valuation of Shares. *Journal of Business* (October): 411–433.

Miller, M. H., and F. Modigliani. 1966. Some Estimates of the Cost of Capital to the Electric Utility Industry 1954–57. *American Economic Review* (June): 333–348.

Miller, M. H., and M. Scholes. 1978. Dividends and Taxes. *Journal of Financial Economics* (December): 333–364.

Miller, M. H., and M. Scholes. 1982. Dividends and Taxes: Some Empirical Evidence. *Journal of Political Economy* 90 (6): 1118–1141.

Modigliani, F. 1982. Debt, Dividend Policy, Taxes, Inflation and Market Valuation. *Journal of Finance* (May).

Modigliani, F., and M. H. Miller. 1963. Corporate Income Taxes and the Cost of Capital: A Correction. *American Economic Review* (June): 433–443.

Morris, J. 1982. Taxes, Bankruptcy Costs and the Existence of an Optimal Capital Structure. *Journal of Financial Research* (December).

Robichek, A., and S. Myers. 1966. Problems in the Theory of Optimal Capital Structure. *Journal of Financial and Quantitative Analysis* (June): 1–35.

Schneller, M. 1980. Taxes and the Optimal Capital Structure of the Firm. *Journal of Finance* (March): 119–127.

Scott, J. 1981. The Probability of Bankruptcy: A Comparison of Empirical Predictions and Theoretical Models. *Journal of Banking and Finance* (September) 317–344.

Stiglitz, J. E. 1969. A Re-examination of the Modigliani-Miller Theorem. *American Economic Review* 59 (December): 784–793.

Stiglitz, J. E. 1974. On the Irrelevance of Corporate Financial Policy. *American Economic Review* (December): 851–866.

Talmor, E. 1984. The Determination of Corporate Optimal Capital Structure under Value Maximization and Informational Asymmetry. *Journal of Economics and Business* (February).

Titman, S., and R. Wessels. 1988. The Determinants of Capital Structure Choice. *Journal of Finance* (June).

Warner, J. 1977. Bankruptcy Costs: Some Evidence. *Journal of Finance* (May): 337–347.

17 The Cost of Corporate Capital

A.   Risk and Returns in Corporate Capital Structure

In the last chapter we discussed how, assuming a tax-free world (or, more generally, equal taxation under each financing track), Modigliani and Miller demonstrated that capital structure is irrelevant to a company's value. Their approach constituted a fundamental paradigm shift from the existing convention of classic financial theory. The disagreement between these two schools of thought reflects the practical aspects of choosing new projects. In the first part of this book, we discussed methods for ranking new projects. We discussed the internal rate of return (IRR), which led to the conclusion that a project is worthwhile if its IRR is higher than the cost of the capital required to finance that project. This leads us to ask, what capital cost should companies use to compare projects? Should they compare them to the cost of capital (interest) raised through bonds? The cost of capital required by the shareholders? The cost of capital in the last financing round (which depends on the ratio of bond to share-raised capital)? Or perhaps the average cost of capital?

The classic approach prior to Modigliani and Miller's proposition argued for an optimal capital structure. If such an optimal structure exists, then a "weighted average cost of capital" (WACC) can be defined thus:

$$WACC = \frac{D}{V} \cdot r_D + \frac{E}{V} \cdot r_E.$$

However, if Modigliani and Miller are right and capital structure is irrelevant, then the WACC under any given capital structure is constant. If that is the case, against which cost of capital should the company compare a potential project's IRR?

Going back to the previous chapter's example, we can immediately see that the greater the portion of a company's capital that is financed by bonds, the greater the risk incurred by that company's shareholders. If the company were to be financed solely by shares, the risk of a dividend not being distributed (i.e., if operating cash flow were less than zero) would be smaller than if the company were to be financed in part by bonds, and thus required to pay interest. The open (nonstriped) area below the curve in figure 17.1, denoting the free cash flow that can be distributed to shareholders, decreases as debt and interest payments grow. Bondholders' risk also increases along with debt (and, consequently, so does the interest paid on that debt). Only when the company's cash flow is greater than 20 will bondholders receive full payment. If the debt were to increase and push interest payments up to 30, for example, bondholders would receive full payment only when operating cash flows exceeded 30, which has a smaller cumulative probability, that is, a greater risk.

Shareholders' behavior is reasonable. Although the distributable net cash flow is smaller, it is distributed among fewer shareholders (as it is financed in part by debt). Returns per share increase along with risk. The following example illustrates this point for Success Inc.:

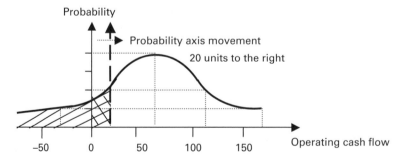

Figure 17.1
The Default Risk on Interest Payment from Operating Cash Flow

	Probability				
	0.1	**0.2**	**0.4**	**0.2**	**0.1**
Sales revenues	500	400	300	200	100
Fixed costs	80	80	80	80	80
Variable costs (50%)	250	200	150	100	50
Operating cash flows	170	120	70	20	(30)
Interest on bonds	(20)	(20)	(20)	(20)	(20)
Post-interest cash flow	150	100	50	0	(50)

Let's assume that an investment of $1,000 was required to set up Success Inc.'s operations. Furthermore, this investment was financed by issuing 1,000 shares of $1 par value each. The mean cash flow[1] is $70, that is, there is a mean return of 7% per share. Now let's assume that the shareholders decided to finance 50% of the investment ($500) through bonds offering a 4% return, for a total annual interest payment of $20. The mean cash flow goes down to $50, but as only $500 was raised through shares, this cash flow is distributed among only 500 shares. The mean return per share increases to 50/500 = 10%. Thus, although the shareholders incurred greater risk, their return per share also increased.

Bondholders are a bit harder to understand. Default risk, or the risk that a company will not be able to meet its interest payments in full, clearly grows as debt increases. Why should bondholders agree to lend $500, which obligates the company to pay $20 per period, at the same interest rate as a $250 loan with an interest payment of $10 per period? And, as bondholders should demand a higher interest rate as debt increases, this raises the question of what is the right rate.

As shareholder rate of return increases and new bondholders demand a higher interest rate, the WACC must increase the more a company is financed through debt. However, Modigliani and Miller's model from the previous chapter states that capital structure is irrelevant!

This apparent contradiction is resolved later in this chapter. However, readers can see why Modigliani and Miller's concept was so radically innovative and why it met such resistance among proponents of the classic approach.

Remember that Modigliani and Miller's first proposition dealt only with company value. The simple idea behind their argument begins and

1. Multiply each cash flow by its probability and sum up the multiples.

ends with operating cash flow. This cash flow is independent of the manner in which company operations are financed. It is generated strictly by a company's real operations.

Now let's examine the problem from an accounting perspective.

The company's balance sheet includes, on the left side, $1,000 in assets. These assets generate the cash flow going into the company's coffers. On the right side, the balance sheet presents the company's liabilities. If the company was financed only by shares, its entire operating cash flow would go to its shareholders. If the company was financed in equal parts by shares and bonds, its operating cash flow would be divided among its shareholders and bondholders. It would not be divided equally, as each group's risk is different. Bondholders would bear less risk, as they would have preference in receiving payment from the company—and they would receive a fixed $20 interest payment, regardless of the company's earnings. Shareholders would bear more risk, as they would receive only the remainder. Either way, the manner in which cash flows are distributed between shareholders and bondholders does not affect the cash flow generated by the company's operations.

Before answering the problem of the returns paid on shares and bonds and their effect on a company's WACC, there are a few more terms we must discuss, derived from the classic approach that preceded Modigliani and Miller's first formulation. Although these terms may increase readers' sympathy for proponents of classic financial theory, later on we will see how these contradictions were resolved in the article known as "Modigliani and Miller's Second Proposition".

B.   Corporate Business Risk—The Classic Approach

The question of which optimal capital structure (the debt/share capital ratio) can maximize share price while minimizing a company's weighted average cost of capital (WACC) was raised long before Modigliani and Miller became interested in the topic. We present this discussion for two reasons:

1. This approach, for the most part, does not contradict modern financial theory.

2. Businesses (and particularly accountants) still commonly use terminology derived from this classic approach, as it provides intuitive insight into a company's operational risk and capital structure.

Classic financial theorists approached this problem with the following definitions:

Commercial risk The percentage change in average net earnings[2] caused by a 1% change in average company revenues.

Operating leverage[3] The percentage change in average operating profits caused by a 1% change in average sales, resulting from the company's operating expense structure.[4]

We denote the following:

$EBIT$—Earnings before interest and tax; operating profit.[5]

S—Sales revenues.

Q—Quantity of units sold.

P—Price per unit.

VC—Variable cost per unit.

TVC—Total variable cost.[6]

FC—Fixed costs.

$$EBIT = S - TVC - FC = Q(P - VC) - FC.$$

A change in earnings can only be caused by a change in the quantity of units sold, as all other parameters are constant and given:

2. Before Modigliani and Miller, financial theory was concerned mainly with net earnings, not net cash flow.

3. The term "leverage" is derived from mechanics terminology.

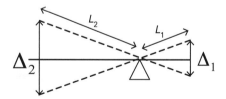

Small variations on one side, Δ_1, cause large variations on the other side, Δ_2. The ratio between these changes, $\dfrac{\Delta_2}{\Delta_1}$, is equal to the ratio $\dfrac{L_2}{L_1}$.

4. Denoted OL, for "operating leverage."

5. In modern financial theory, it is referred to as "operating cash flow." In principle, assuming that in each period an amount equal to the depreciation must be invested so that assets will continue generating profit into perpetuity, there is no difference between the two definitions.

6. $TVC = Q \cdot VC$.

$$\Delta EBIT = \Delta Q(P - VC)$$

$$OL = \frac{\dfrac{\Delta EBIT}{EBIT}}{\dfrac{\Delta Q}{Q}\bigg|=1\%} = \frac{Q(P-VC)}{Q(P-VC)-FC} = \frac{S-TVC}{S-TVC-FC}.$$

Following on our previous example, let's take the change in operating cash flow near Success Inc.'s average sales figure of $300. Let's assume that this average is due to the sale of 3,000 units at a unit price of $0.10 (ten cents), with variable costs (50% of sales) of $0.05 per unit. Fixed costs are $80.

Success Inc.'s operating leverage (OL) near its sales average is therefore

$$OL = \frac{300-150}{300-150-80} = 2.14.$$

Thus, every 1% change in the quantity of units sold would cause a 2.14% change in Success Inc.'s operating profit.

Let's assume another company, Status Corp., that is similar to Success Inc. but more conservative. This company decided to invest less in equipment and rely more on labor, with employees hired and dismissed according to demand. We can therefore assume that its fixed costs (due mainly to depreciation) are lower, say $50. However, as production is more labor-intensive, its variable costs are 0.7 cents per unit (its selling price does not change and is determined by the market).

Status Corp.'s operating leverage is therefore

$$OL = \frac{300-180}{300-180-50} = 1.71.$$

Thus, every 1% change in the quantity of units sold (around the average sales figure) would cause only a 1.71% change in its operating profit.

If sales volumes change, we could (at least theoretically) immediately decrease variable costs proportionately. The greater the weight of a company's fixed costs, the greater the percentage change in operating profit caused by a 1% change in sales, and consequently the greater the operational risk.

The smaller a company's operating leverage, the smaller is its risk.

The above example was crafted so that both companies have the same mean earnings of $70 at their average sales volume ($300). The companies differ in their deviation from this average. Above the average, Success Inc.'s earnings would be greater than Status Corp.'s, but below the average its earnings would be lower than Status Corp.'s (do the calculations and see for yourself).

Market fluctuations (economic expansion and depression cycles), although affecting both companies' sales the same way, would have a smaller impact on Status Corp.'s operating profit than on Success Inc.'s operating profit. The intuitive connection between operating leverage and risk is also reflected in the modern mean-variance model or market model by σ or β.

Let's define *balance point* as the sales volume at which operating profit is zero:

$$PQ - VQ - F = 0.$$

Figure 17.2 demonstrates that the smaller a company's fixed costs, the further away its sales average will be from the balance point, and thus

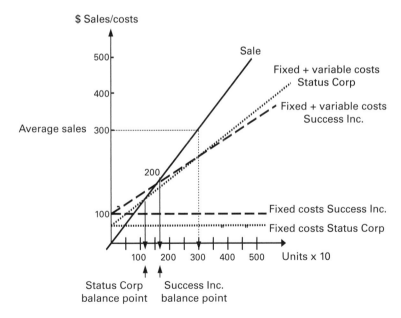

Figure 17.2
Operating Profit Balance Point

the smaller will be both the probability of loss and the operating risk (and vice versa for higher fixed costs).

Let's define:

Financial leverage (denoted FL)—The percentage change in earnings per share caused by a 1% change in operating profit, owing to the company's capital structure.

A company's capital structure affects the changes in earnings per share caused by changes in operating profit. Shareholders receive the leftover earnings after deducting interest payments (a fixed cost) from operating profit. The greater the part paid as interest on debt, the greater is the percentage change in earnings per share caused by a 1% change in operating profit. The higher the interest rate on debt, the greater is the "financing risk" borne by shareholders (in addition to operating risk).

Net earnings per share—Earnings after interest and taxes, divided by the number of shares.

Denote EPS as earnings per share, I as the total interest[7] paid on bonds, and T as the company's tax rate:

$$EPS = (EBIT - I)(1 - T) / N.$$

The change in earnings per share can only be caused by a change in operating profit and a change in the total interest payment:[8]

$$\Delta EPS = (\Delta EBIT - \Delta I)(1 - T) / N = \Delta EBIT \cdot (1 - T) / N.$$

$$FL = \frac{\dfrac{\Delta EPS}{EPS}}{\dfrac{\Delta EBIT}{EBIT}\Big|= 1\%} = \frac{EBIT}{EBIT - I}$$

$$= \frac{Q(P - VC) - F}{Q(P - VC) - F - I} = \frac{S - TVC - F}{S - TVC - F - I}.$$

The greater the financial leverage $\dfrac{D}{D+E}$, that is, the greater the interest I paid on a company's debt, the greater that company's risk as expressed in its financial leverage, FL.[9] Market fluctuations will affect operating

---

7. Note that in this chapter, I denotes interest (whereas in other chapters I refers to investment).

8. We assume debt to be constant, and so there is no change in the total interest payment: $\Delta I = 0$.

9. Interest I appears as a negative factor in the denominator.

profit, and the greater the financial leverage, the more operating profit fluctuations will affect net earnings per share. Here too we can see the intuitive connection between financial leverage and risk, as measured in σ or β in modern financial theory.

Readers should note that according to classic financial theory too, tax does not affect risk, as the tax rate does not appear in the financial leverage formula.

Let's go back to Success Inc., which is financed only by shares, so that interest $I = 0$ and $FL = 1$. In other words, every 1% change in operating profit will cause a 1% change in earnings per share. This makes sense, as operating profits are distributed entirely as dividends.

Status Corp., which is financed in equal parts by shares and by bonds, pays \$20 in interest. Around the \$300 sales average, where $EBIT = \$70$, its financial leverage is

$$FL = \frac{EBIT}{EBIT - I} = \frac{70}{70 - 20} = 1.4.$$

In other words, every 1% change in operating profit will cause a 1.4% change in net earnings per share. Note that even though Status Corp. took a more conservative risk than Success Inc. in determining its operating expense structure, its capital structure is more risky.

Total leverage (TL)—The percentage change in earnings per share caused by a 1% change in sales, owing both to a company's expense structure and to its capital structure.

Total leverage = operating leverage × financial leverage, as they have a serial effect on earnings per share (following a 1% change in sales). Operating leverage affects gross profit and financial leverage affects net earnings. Therefore,

$$TL = OL \times FL = \frac{S - TVC}{S - TVC - FC - I}.$$

Note that the total leverage equation has both fixed costs FC and fixed interest I as negative numbers in the denominator. The greater these costs, the smaller the denominator and the greater the total leverage!

Conclusion: The greater a company's fixed operating costs and the greater its fixed financing costs (interest), the greater its total leverage. Therefore, small fluctuations in sales will lead to greater changes in earnings per share.

We can calculate the total leverage near the average sales figure:

For Success Inc., $TL = 2.14 \times 1.0 = 2.14\%$.

For Status Corp, $TL = 1.71 \times 1.4 = 2.39\%$.

Thus, every 1% change in sales will cause a 2.14% change in earnings per share in Success Inc. and a 2.39% change in earnings per share in Status Corp. Ultimately, Status Corp.'s earnings have a greater fluctuation.

Let's summarize the difference between the classic approach and the modern approach according to Modigliani and Miller.

In the classic approach, a company's risk is determined on two levels:

1. Risk related to uncertainty in operating profits (operating cash flow, according to Modigliani and Miller) as a result of a company's operating expense structure, that is, the ratio of fixed to total costs (or fixed to variable costs).

2. Risk related to uncertainty in net earnings per share as a result of a company's capital structure, that is, the ratio of debt to total capital, which determines the ratio of the fixed interest payments to bondholders to the variable dividend payments to shareholders.

As a company's risk is determined by both factors combined, company value should likewise be determined by both factors.

Under Modigliani and Miller's first proposition, both a company's risk and its value are determined solely by the first factor, that is, by net operating cash flow.

We also saw how the return on the debt component and the return on the share component both increase as the D/E ratio increases. At first glance, it seems that the classical theorists are correct, and the WACC should also increase. This seems to contradict Modigliani and Miller's proposition discussed in the previous chapter, that company value is constant. In the following section we discuss Modigliani and Miller's second proposition, which offers a solution to this problem by relating it to the price of the company's capital sources.

C. The Cost of a Company's Capital Sources — Modigliani and Miller's Second Proposition

Let's compare the balance sheet for a company financed entirely by shares with that of a company financed in equal parts by shares and by bonds.

Denote A as assets, E as equity (shares), and D as debt-raised capital (bonds).

Balance Sheet

Financing Method	Liabilities	Assets
100% shares	$E = \$1{,}000$	$A = \$1{,}000$
Total	$1,000	$1,000
50:50 Shares-debt	$E = \$500$ $D = \$500$	$A = \$1{,}000$
Total	$E + D = \$1{,}000$	$1,000
In General	$E + D$ = A	

In the example presented in the previous section, the mean cash flow was $70, that is, a mean return on the $1,000 of assets of $r_A = 7\%$. If the company was 100% financed by shares, this would also be the return r_E per share, received by shareholders: $r_A = r_E = 7\%$.

When the company is financed by both bonds and shares, its total operating cash flow of $r_A \times A$ is utilized for interest payments $I = r_D \times D$, with the remainder being distributed as dividends of $r_E \times E$. Thus:

$$r_A \cdot A = r_D \cdot D + r_E \cdot E$$

$$\Rightarrow r_A = \frac{D}{A} \cdot r_D + \frac{E}{A} \cdot r_E = \frac{D}{D+E} \cdot r_D + \frac{E}{D+E} \cdot r_E = WACC.$$

Before we discuss Modigliani and Miller's second proposition, I would like to remind readers of the linearity of the returns and of the risk measure β, as discussed in chapter 7. When an investor holds several assets, each of which has different risk and different cash flows, the mean return and risk on the total portfolio cash flow are

$$\overline{R} = \sum w_i \overline{R}_i.$$

$$\beta = \sum w_i \beta_i.$$

This equivalency actually works both ways. For example, if we build one asset out of several assets and compare the total returns and risk on that asset's cash flow with those of its component assets, or if we split a combined cash flow into several sub-flows (which add up to the original cash flow), the above equations, correlating the return and risk on the composite asset with the returns and risks on its constituent assets, remain valid.

This equivalency is known as the law of cash flow value preservation.

We can now describe the mathematical ties between the different values as presented in Modigliani and Miller's second proposition:

$$r_A = \frac{D}{D+E} \cdot r_D + \frac{E}{D+E} \cdot r_E.$$

As the cash flow generated by the assets is divided into two cash flows, one going to shareholders and the other to bondholders, and as the total cash flow's risk is equal to the weighted sum of the risks on the constituent cash flows, then

$$\beta_A = \frac{D}{D+E} \cdot \beta_D + \frac{E}{D+E} \cdot \beta_E.$$

We can now factor out shareholder returns and risk, and bondholder return and risk,[10] as a function of D/E:

$$r_E = r_A + \frac{D}{E}(r_A - r_D)$$

$$\beta_E = \beta_A + \frac{D}{E}(\beta_A - \beta_D)$$

and graphically as shown in figure 17.3.

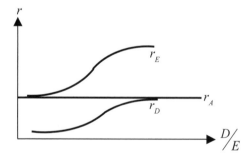

Figure 17.3
The Return on Assets, Equity, and Debt

10. As r_D is also a function of D/E, then r_E is correlated with D/E, both directly and indirectly, through r_D.

Note that, according to Modigliani and Miller, r_A is constant. According to figure 17.3, this seems unlikely, but if we remember that when calculating WACC, the return on debt and the return on shares is multiplied by their relative weights, $\dfrac{D}{D+E} \cdot r_D$ and $\dfrac{E}{D+E} \cdot r_E$, respectively — this is indeed possible.

This argument can be verified through the two end-case scenarios:

• With capital financed only by shares, and
• When capital is financed (almost) entirely by debt

If $D = 0$, the multiple $\dfrac{D}{D+E} \cdot r_D$ is zero and the return on the shares equals the return on the assets.

If $E \approx 0$,[11] the multiple $\dfrac{E}{D+E} \cdot r_E$ is zero and the return on the bonds equals the return on the assets.

As the functions for the return r_A (or r_E and r_D) and for the risk measure β_A (or β_E and β_D) (from the previous page) are similar, the result is graphically identical, and so there is no need to draw it again.

If $D = 0$, the multiple $\dfrac{D}{D+E} \cdot \beta_D$ is zero and the risk on the shares equals the risk on the asset's returns.

If $E \approx 0$, the multiple $\dfrac{E}{D+E} \cdot \beta_E$ is zero and the risk on the bonds equals the risk on the assets. As bondholders assume the role of shareholders, and incur all the company's risk, they can also be expected to demand all the return generated by its assets, as demonstrated in figure 17.3.

The statement, in Modigliani and Miller's first proposition, that in a tax-free world a company's value remains constant, is verbally equivalent to the statement that its WACC is independent of its capital structure.

The statement, in Modigliani and Miller's second proposition, in a tax-free world can be phrased as follows: In a perfect market, the mean return on shares will increase as debt increases according to the D/E ratio. The values for E and D are determined by the market price of the company's shares and bonds,[12] respectively. The rate at which returns increase is determined by the margin $(r_A - r_D)$, which decreases as debt increases, and the return demanded by bondholders nears the return on the company's assets.

---

11. E (equity) can be very small compared to D (debt), but never zero (except in cases of bankruptcy, when bondholders become owners of the company).

12. Remember that *interest* on the bonds is constant, while *return* on the bonds varies according to their market price. The market-determined cost of debt equals the bond price times the number of bonds issued.

Let's move on to a world with taxes. For simplicity's sake, let's keep the assumption that debt is risk-free (even though we've shown that this assumption is not necessary for developing the model and all we need to do is substitute D, the face value, with B, the market value).

In chapter 14, we discussed post-tax net cash flow $FCF = (O - DP) \cdot (1 - T_S)$, which in unleveraged companies is distributed only among shareholders. FCF was used to calculate the value of unleveraged companies, which is also the value of all shares on the market, by discounting an infinite series:

$$E^U = V^U = \frac{E(\tilde{FCF})}{r_E} = \frac{E[(\tilde{O} - DP) \cdot (1 - T_S)]}{r_E}.$$

From this last equation we can derive the return required by shareholders, which is also the return on assets:

$$r_A = r_E = \frac{E[(\tilde{O} - DP) \cdot (1 - T_S)]}{V^U}.$$

Similarly, shareholders in leveraged companies will receive the remaining cash flow after payment of interest to bondholders. By discounting an infinite series, this amount equals:

$$r_E = \frac{[E(\tilde{O} - DP) - r_D \cdot D](1 - T_S)]}{E^L}.$$

We also know that $V^L = V^u + T_S \cdot D$, from which we can conclude that

$$V^U = V^L - T_S \cdot D = E^L + D - T_S \cdot D = E^L + D(1 - T_S).$$

Substituting the second and fourth equations into the third equation yields

$$r_E = r_A + (r_A - r_D)(1 - T_S)\frac{D}{E}.$$

Similar to our calculation for a tax-free world, in a world with taxes, the return on assets A is $WACC = r_A \cdot (1 - T_S)$. Assets are financed by both bonds and shares. As the interest payment is tax-deductible and the company has a tax shelter of $T_S \cdot r_D \cdot D$, its net cash flow (post-tax) from its assets equals $WACC \cdot A + T_S \cdot r_D \cdot D$, and is used both to pay interest $I = r_D \cdot D$, with the remainder distributed as dividends of $r_E \cdot E$. Therefore, $WACC \cdot A + T_S \cdot r_D \cdot D = r_D \cdot D + r_E \cdot E$:

$$WACC = \frac{D}{E + D} \cdot r_D(1 - T_S) + \frac{E}{E + D} \cdot r_E.$$

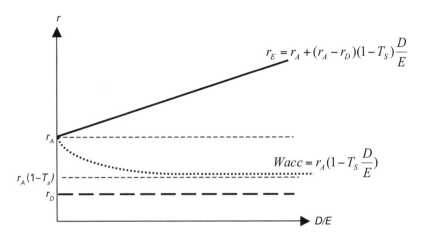

Figure 17.4
The Return on Assets, Equity, and Debt in a World with Tax

Note that *WACC* is the weighted average of the net costs[13] of a company's capital sources.

Substituting our equation for r_E from the previous page into the last equation and rearranging the equation yields $WACC = r_A(1 - T_S \dfrac{D}{E + D})$.

Again, remember that all the above returns are *net after taxes*: in other words, return r_E, as calculated by a company's shareholders (according to the net dividend inflow), and the net post-tax return on assets r_A.

D. Corporate Business Risk—Classic versus Modern Financial Theory

Under the classic approach, commercial risk is comprised of two components:

1. Risk from operating leverage, and
2. Risk from financial leverage.

Let's analyze the connection between operating leverage and risk measure β.

As discussed earlier, operating cash flow is generated by a company's assets. Therefore, we can write:

13. The net cost of debt for the company is only $r_D (1 - T_S)$ because of the tax shelter.

$PV(\text{Asset}) = PV(\text{Cash Flow}) = PV(\text{Sales}) - PV(\text{Variable Cost})$
$- PV(\text{Fixed Cost})$.

Switching sides and using the abbreviated notation for the various values, the equation can be rewritten as

$PV(S) = PV(A) + PV(VC) + PV(FC)$.

Since β is a linear measure, then the sales revenues β is actually the weighted average of each of the above components:

$$\beta_S = \beta_A \frac{PV(A)}{PV(S)} + \beta_{VC} \frac{PV(VC)}{PV(S)} + \beta_{FC} \frac{PV(FC)}{PV(S)}.$$

β_{FC} for fixed costs is zero as their correlation with the market is zero.

β_S for sales revenues and β_{VC} for variable costs are equal, as variable costs are calculated as a fixed percentage of sales (multiplying by a constant), and so are perfectly correlated.

Substituting into the above equation and factoring out the asset β on the left side of the equation yields

$$\beta_A = \beta_S \frac{PV(S) - PV(VC)}{PV(A)} = \beta_S (1 + \frac{PV(FC)}{PV(A)}).$$

In other words, the assets' risk is equal to the risk from sales multiplied by the operating lever.[14] If fixed costs are zero, then the operating lever is 1 and the β values will be identical.

The connection between the financial lever and risk measure β was discussed in the previous chapter:

$$\beta_A = \beta_D \frac{D}{D+E} + \beta_E \frac{E}{D+E}.$$

We also developed the expression for share-related risk as a function of the financial leverage from this last equation:

$$\beta_E = \beta_A + \frac{D}{E}(\beta_A - \beta_D)$$

If we want to further examine the connection between the total leverage and the share risk measure β_E, we can substitute β_A, calculated as a

14. We can define operating leverage as $1 + \dfrac{PV(FC)}{PV(A)}$.

function of the operating leverage, into this last equation. However, we will not perform this calculation here as it provides no significant insight whatsoever, other than a simple mathematical exercise.

Modigliani and Miller's theory of corporate WACC led to a fierce debate with proponents of classic financial theory. We will present this debate in terms drawn from modern financial theory, and afterward examine its practical significance.

Over the years, most arguments in this debate were resolved through reasoning and empirical study. Here we will discuss only the reasons for the difference between the two approaches, generally referred to as "actual market efficiency." Readers are reminded of our discussion of perfect markets and efficient markets in chapter 4, where we provided a general definition of market efficiency as the extent to which the real market approximates perfect market conditions.

One of the most problematic assumptions in the models discussed so far is information symmetry, that is, the extent to which all information is available to all market participants in form, time, and content. Chapter 4 provided a brief discussion of studies by Nobel laureates on asymmetric information and presented the used-car market as an example. Now let's discuss how asymmetric information was used to support the proponents of classic financial theory.[15]

The first explanation presented by classical theorists is that markets are not perfect and information is asymmetric. Management knows better than investors the risks inherent in expected cash flows from assets. At lower risk levels, investors will underestimate the risk and so will demand a lower return than they should (according to Modigliani and Miller's graph). On the other hand, at higher risk levels, as investors are aware of the information asymmetry, they will demand a higher return than predicted by Modigliani and Miller, in order to safeguard against surprises arising out of lack of perfect knowledge. At low risk levels, bondholders will demand the risk-free interest rate. As the debt ratio increases, bondholders will be "late" in updating their required return and will continue to demand the risk-free rate. After a certain D/E ratio, the return required on bonds will be updated at a faster rate than predicted by Modigliani and Miller until it coincides with Modigliani and

15. Historically, the debate between the two schools of thought did not use the same terminology as we are using here, which is mainly derived from modern financial theory. However, if the debate is considered from our present perspective and translated into modern terminology currently in use, it can be presented as in this book.

Miller's graph and even exceeds it owing to information asymmetry as explained above.

In this case, the WACC will indeed reach a minimum and then increase, and so company value (and share value) will have a maximum value at that point.

A second explanation put forward by classical theorists is that because the market is inefficient, it includes expenses that do not exist in a perfect market. These include bankruptcy costs, agency costs,[16] floatation costs, and so on. Let's explain this point by focusing on one type of cost, bankruptcy costs.

As debt increases, along with interest payments, the risk that bondholders will not receive full payment also increases.[17] If a company becomes insolvent, its bondholders will wish to file for bankruptcy. In extreme scenarios, in which a company's entire capital is financed by bonds, bondholders should clearly receive the entire return generated by that company's assets, in the same way that shareholders would have received that return had the company been financed only through shares. However, when a company enters bankruptcy proceedings,[18] the process whereby ownership of the company is transferred from its shareholders to its bondholders takes place in court.

This process involves significant expenses, such as receiver fees, attorney fees, and auditor fees, and can also include a reduction in productivity owing to layoffs, diminished employee morale, and the like. Bondholders must account for the mean value (probability times cost) of these expenses as a company's debt increases, and subtract them from the value of a company that may unintentionally come under their ownership.

According to Modigliani and Miller, if a tax shelter exists, companies should increase their debt as much as possible so as to maximize the added value (generated by the tax shelter) over unleveraged companies.

Graphically speaking, the cost of capital goes down while company value goes up the more we increase the D/E ratio because of tax shelter

---

16. Agency costs have been mentioned in previous chapters and are mainly due to the fact that companies are not managed by their shareholders but by professional managers. In principle, managers, as shareholder agents, should maximize the shareholders' utility function by maximizing share price. However, as managers also have personal utility functions that they seek to maximize, a gap is created, which is reflected in share prices. This gap is known as "agency cost."

17. Operating cash flow does cover interest payments.

18. Which would happen well before all of a company's capital was financed by bonds.

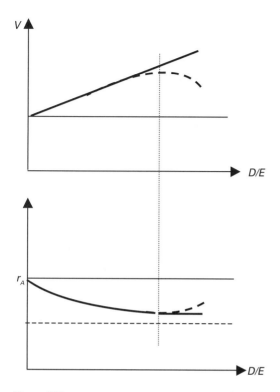

Figure 17.5
Firm Value and Return on Assets in a "Real" World with Tax Shelter and Bankruptcy Cost

effects (see figure 17.5). Classic financial theory argues that at a certain point, the mean bankruptcy cost becomes significant, and it will continue to increase with debt. A minimum/maximum value will be obtained when it equals the added value generated by the tax shelter.

Having understood the disagreement, we are still left with the question of who is right. We can answer this question theoretically or through empirical observation.

1. Theoretical solution

The argument between Modigliani and Miller and classic financial theory can be summarized as revolving around actual market efficiency. We will not go into this matter in depth, but suffice it to say that it is a conflict between Modigliani and Miller's normative model of how one should act assuming an efficient and near-perfect market and the classic descriptive model, which presents an imperfect market. Some theorists go so far as to say that market efficiency should be defined as the degree to which the market complies with Modigliani and Miller's propositions. Thus, it is no longer a disagreement but merely a question of definitions.

The Modigliani-Miller model can be relaxed on a number of assumptions. Current research in this field aims to develop a mathematical model for optimal capital structure that takes into account additional parameters. For the time being, the debate rages on.

2. Empirical studies

From previous chapters, we know that empirical studies are no simple task. Assume, for example, that we want to study capital-raising rounds, such as those that changed a company's capital structure, and calculate the WACC before and after these rounds. The problem is that issues are accompanied by company prospectuses, which specify how proceeds are to be used. Only a small number of capital-raising rounds are aimed at changing capital structure. The goal is usually to finance a new project, and a change in capital structure is the result of the financing method. It is possible that the change in a company's cost of capital after an issue (of shares or bonds) was not caused by a change in its capital structure but by investors' expectations concerning the risks and rewards offered by the new project and their impact on the company's financial results. One possible solution to this problem is to perform a cross-sectional study of companies with similar risk profiles. For example, utility companies are characterized by a capital structure relying heavily on debt. This is also clear considering that their financial results are usually rather stable and predictable.[19] On the other hand, service-oriented companies usually have a capital structure with a small debt component, and their financial results are usually relatively volatile. Studies employing this approach, that is, studies of a particular industry with a similar risk profile, were limited in the variability of examined capital structures. The matter can be approached from numerous other directions as well,[20] with each approach offering its own advantages and disadvantages.

Unfortunately, studies of corporate capital structure do not lead to clear-cut conclusions. Modigliani and Miller themselves published several empirical studies whose findings indicate that capital costs are flat or

19. Utility consumption is characterized by relatively inelastic demand. Financial results vary mainly as a result of government intervention in determining prices.

20. For example, by checking the return on different-risk bonds, rated by credit rating agencies such as Moody's.

linearly decreasing. Other works have presented findings supporting a conclusion that an optimal capital structure can be found.

If we were to assume that Modigliani and Miller's approach is correct, we should have been able to find corporate capital structures spanning the entire range of 0–100% (or at least most of that range). The fact that no companies can be found whose debt exceeds a certain percentage of their capital indicates that the above classic reservations (and others that we did not discuss) are well-founded. As mentioned, current research is seeking a more complete model that might explain the existence of an optimal capital structure.

E. The Cost of Capital—Capital Budgeting under Uncertainty

In the first part of the book, when discussing effective project selection, we accounted only for the time value of capital and ignored the effects of risk. The fact that a project's return exceeds the WACC according to its IRR does not guarantee that the project will be chosen. It is possible for a project's risk to increase along with its returns, so that when we discount the cash flow generated by that project using a risk-adjusted rate, its net present value (NPV) will turn out not to be attractive at all, or even negative. This is another good reason to prefer NPV to IRR in project selection. In this section we discuss how adding risk considerations affects investment project ranking and selection.

In principle, we may look at companies as a collection of projects. Every production line or every product can be considered a project "title." Therefore, much as an investor's portfolio contains different types of securities, companies hold a "project portfolio," as follows:

$$PV(\text{Firm}) = PV(\text{Project A}) + PV(\text{Project B}) + PV(\text{Project C}) + \dots.$$

The first question is: Should each project be discounted using the same discount rate?

To better understand this question, let's consider the following three projects, A, B, and C, in which a company can invest:

A = a building that the company is constructing for its offices.

B = another project within the company's line of business.

C = a project in a new segment that the company wishes to enter.

Each project has a materially different cash flow. An office building that would replace the company's current rent payments can be attributed a future cash flow that is equal to these current payments. This cash flow is relatively constant and has a low correlation with general market performance, and so has a low risk level. A project in the company's line of business can be expected to have a similar risk profile to the company itself, while a project in a new segment can be expected to carry a different risk.

Conclusion: The true cost of capital for discounting each project depends on the project itself, and not on the company's cost of capital. The discount rate for each project will therefore be calculated using the risk-adjusted rate with a CAPM-based risk measure:

$$k_{Project} = r_f + \beta_{Project} (r_m - r_f).$$

As a company's total operating cash flow is the sum of the cash flows from each separate project, the company's risk measure β_A derives from the weighted sum of all project β's:[21]

$$PV(\text{Firm}) = PV(\text{Project A}) + PV(\text{Project B}) + PV(\text{Project C}) +\dots .$$

$$\beta_{Firm} = \beta_A = \beta_{Proj.A} \frac{PV_{Proj.A}}{PV_{Firm}} + \beta_{Proj.B} \frac{PV_{Proj.B}}{PV_{Firm}} + \beta_{Proj.C} \frac{PV_{Proj.C}}{PV_{Firm}} + \dots$$

It is now clear how each project's risk should be characterized. We must calculate β for its expected cash flow. Although not simple, this calculation is doable. For example, if considering a new project in the meat industry, we can calculate the β for companies operating in this industry and use it to calculate the new project's discount rate. Or we could calculate the historically required rate of return in this industry (which is already risk-adjusted). The new project's expected cash flow can then be discounted using this new risk-adjusted discount rate. Such a calculation is not always so direct or simple, but there are various ways of circumventing obstacles and deriving the β or the risk-adjusted return for the project. When considering projects within a company's line of business, it is quite common to discount the project using the company's WACC or the industry average cost of capital.

Using the market model's β measure as a project risk measure seems counterintuitive: if we use the risk-adjusted discount rate determined by the market (i.e., on the market line), then the project's price I_0 is also determined by the market and, by definition, equals the cash flow discounted using that same risk-adjusted discount rate, $\sum \frac{C_i}{(1+k)^i} = I_0$.

---

21. We saw the law of value preservation in action when splitting/consolidating cash flows: if $\bar{R} = w_i \bar{R}_i$, then $\beta = \Sigma w_i \beta_i$.

In this case, NPV will by definition be zero: $NPV = \sum \dfrac{C_i}{(1+k)^i} - I_0 = 0.$
How can a company invest in a project if the model it uses by definition yields a net present value of zero?

The answer is simple. Remember that the model is a market equilibrium model, while the market is not always at equilibrium. As discussed earlier, in practice, shares may not be located on the market line, and the same holds true for projects. Management's job is to identify and seize such opportunities. An example of such a situation might be a temporary market shortage due to natural disasters such as an earthquake in Asia, which destroyed a large FAB[22] facility that manufactured computer components. The excess demand doubled component prices.[23] Other manufacturers, which could quickly increase their production capacity, enjoyed a significant NPV on their investment.

It is also possible for a company to benefit from competitive advantages. For example, in Israel, Wissotsky, which produces and markets tea, entered the coffee market that historically was dominated by Elite (more than 85% market share). The project could have yielded a positive NPV for Wissotsky, as it already had the relevant equipment, warehouses, and marketing chain at its disposal.[24] In this case, the positive NPV derived mainly from fixed costs.[25] Wissotsky could utilize part of its fixed assets, and its market penetration costs were also lower as it was already marketing its tea products. Therefore, its operating leverage was smaller than is common in the coffee industry, which also reduced its operating risk.

We also saw how when we use the market model to define a project's risk measure, we can use NPV to rank and choose investments. However, using this model raises a new problem: if management chooses projects that maximize NPV, this does not guarantee that these projects will carry the same risk as the company. Management can choose to invest in an office building, thereby reducing the company's average overall risk, or expand into a new and riskier segment, thereby increasing average

22. FABs are facilities equipped with clean rooms where electronics components are fabricated. The setup costs for such facilities amount to billions of dollars. As a result, only a very small number of manufacturers supply the entire global market. For example, Intel and AMD manufacture processors for virtually all computer manufacturers in the world.

23. This is a true historical example!

24. Wissotsky quickly obtained a 20% market share.

25. This is an example of synergistic operations—coffee was synergistic to Wissotsky's manufacturing and marketing operations.

overall risk. Moreover, management acts as agents on behalf of share-holders. Obviously, different shareholders have different utility functions according to their individual risk aversion. How can management choose projects, when no one project mix could ever satisfy all shareholders' risk preferences?

Here we can employ Fisher's separation theorem.[26] Although it can be presented mathematically, because it is simple to understand we will present it only in words.

Fisher's separation theorem requires a perfect market. The only assumption required is that the interest rate for borrowing and that for lending be identical. In this case, management must take on all projects with an NPV greater than zero. It makes no difference to shareholders if, by doing so, management increases a company's risk. This is due to the fact that all investors can obtain the risk level that maximizes their individual utility functions by building a portfolio that includes a risk-free asset and shares in the company, and compensate for any increase or decrease in risk on the company's shares by changing the ratio of their holdings in the risk-free asset and the company's shares.

Fischer's separation theorem also means there is no connection between problems facing a company's CFO when investing in new projects and financing problems when raising new capital for the company. Management should maximize company value generated by the net cash flow of the chosen projects. Note that this refers to maximizing company value, not maximizing cash flow. Cash flows are discounted using a risk-adjusted discount rate. It is possible for one cash flow to be greater, but because it carries greater risk, it would then yield less value to the company after discounting. After maximizing company value on the operational level, investors can choose their holdings and investments according to their personal preferences.

As mentioned earlier, the first step in assessing a project is calculating its net future cash flow. In the previous chapter we learned that

$$EBIT = S - VC - FC = Q(P - VC) - FC,$$

where

- Q denotes the quantity of units sold;
- P denotes the price per unit;

---

26. Irving Fisher (1867–1947) was one of the greatest American neoclassical economists, though his later work on debt deflation is often regarded as belonging instead to the post-Keynesian school. Fisher produced various investment-related inventions.

- *VC* is the variable cost per unit; and
- *FC* denotes fixed costs.

As we are dealing with forward-looking assessments, we must account for errors in each of the predicted values. Thus, if in the previous chapter we only defined the percentage change in operating profit[27] caused by a 1% change in sales, in *sensitivity testing* we must also examine the following:

- The percentage change in operating profit caused by a 1% change in *price per unit*.
- The percentage change in operating profit caused by a 1% change in *fixed costs*.
- The percentage change in operating profit caused by a 1% change in *variable costs*.

Remember that the three values italicized are best-judgment predictions. For example, fixed costs are estimated according to equipment quotations received from various suppliers. It is possible that, on acquisition, competition among bidding suppliers will cause equipment prices to be lower. Conversely, it may be necessary to buy additional equipment or make other investments that the company did not anticipate.

A product's selling price and variable costs are likewise subject to change.

The change in operating profit can be calculated around any given point. In the previous chapter, we demonstrated the change in operating cash flow around Success Inc.'s average sales value of $300. For that same point, we can also calculate the effect of a 1% change in the other parameters. Another important point to consider is the equilibrium point. It indicates where we start earning a profit or, from a more pessimistic perspective, where we start losing.

The above approach is known as the scenario method. In this method, we change all the parameters and check the results in at least three scenarios:

1. The average (or mean) scenario—the calculation point according to our best estimate for all the above values.

27. As discussed in the previous chapter, under certain assumptions, the definition for operating profit is equivalent to the definition for net operating cash flow.

2. The best-case scenario—the most optimistic forecast, that is, maximum expected quantity and price and minimum expected fixed and variable costs.

3. The worst-case scenario—the most pessimistic forecast, that is, minimum expected quantity and price and maximum expected fixed and variable costs.

The scenario method allows us to calculate the range of possible outcomes for a project. As discussed earlier, the mean alone is not a sufficient measure, and variance is an important factor to consider. The scenario method supersedes the variance[28] measure and serves the same purpose. We can also change our estimates for a project's β and see how these changes affect the NPV.

Summary: All the methods above seek to aid investors in making informed choices when assessing investment projects. Although a formal project-ranking model was presented in this chapter, remember that all values used in that model are based on judgment and are subject to error. Therefore, some form of sensitivity testing is required before making an educated selection of projects.

Chapter 17—Questions and Problems

Question 1

Recruitment Corp. finances 40% of its capital through consol bonds with a 6% interest, traded at 80% of their face value. The market return on the company's shares is 15% and their β risk measure is 1.5. Assume that only a 34% corporate income tax applies, the return on the market portfolio is 11.7%, and both shares and bonds are traded at equilibrium.

a. Should the company invest in a project within its normal area of business, whose IRR before taxes is 18.2%?

b. What is the risk measure β of the bonds when calculating WACC? What does this example teach you about the assumptions in Modigliani and Miller's model?

c. How sensitive are the company's financial results to market changes?

d. The company is considering construction of a headquarters building instead of signing a 20-year, fixed-rate lease. The company's comptroller

28. Similar to the confidence interval in statistics.

calculated annual rental costs to be 7% of the cost of the new building. Annual maintenance costs for the building (incurred by the owner) are 2% of its value. Should the company invest in the building's construction?

Question 2

Ultra More Ltd. operates in a market where the risk-free rate is 4%, the return on the market portfolio is 12%, and only a corporate income tax is applied, at 25%.

Twenty percent of the company's capital is financed by debt (risk-free), and its shares have a β risk factor of 1.75. The company is considering a project in its line of business (same risk profile) offering a 14.5% post-tax return. The company can finance the project by raising new capital, comprised 40% of risk-free debt.

a. Calculate the cost-effectiveness of investing in this project considering the structure of its financing capital.

b. Should the company invest in the project if the new capital has the same structure as the company's existing capital?

c. In light of your answers to parts (a) and (b) above, is your calculation in part (a) correct for all capital amounts required for the project? Should the project be implemented according to part (a) or part (b)?

Question 3

Rapid Growth Inc.'s shares are traded with an 18% return. Management has determined that the company's optimal capital structure consists of 25% debt, which, at that D/E ratio, can be raised at a cost of 8%. Corporate income tax is 40%. Management is considering a project, within the company's line of business, that requires new capital and an investment of $1.2 million, and is expected to yield operating profits of $300,000 a year for many years to come (assume perpetuity), provided that $50,000 is invested each year to renew equipment.

a. The company's CFO examined the project and used the operating rate of return required on the market for similar projects. What is his recommendation? Calculate and explain.

b. The company's COO examined the project and used the company's weighted average cost of capital. What is his recommendation? Calculate and explain.

c. What is the difference between their calculations, and what causes this difference? Calculate and explain.

d. Who is right? Explain.

Question 4

Company U has one million shares with a market value of $6.60 per share and current operating income of $1 million. Company L has an identical operational structure but its capital structure includes debt, whose market value is 30% of the company's market value and bears 5% interest. Corporate income tax is 36%. What is the market rate of return for Company L's shareholders?

Question 5

John and Jack, who both study fundamental financial theory, are arguing how an increase in the corporate income tax would affect the value of leveraged companies and their share price according to Modigliani and Miller. John says that the tax shelter would increase, and so both values would increase, while Jack holds that distributable cash flows would decrease, and therefore both values would decrease, too. Who is right?

Further Reading

Ang, J. S., and W. G. Lewellen. 1982. Risk Adjustment in Capital Investment Project Evaluations. *Financial Management* 11 (2): 5–14.

Arditti, F. D., and H. Levy. 1977. The Weighted Average Cost of Capital as a Cutoff Rate: A Critical Analysis of the Classical Textbook Weighted Average. *Financial Management* (Autumn).

Baumol, W. S., and R. E. Quandt. 1965. Investment and Discount Rates under Capital Rationing. *Economic Journal* (June): 317–329.

Ben-Horim, M. 1979. Comment on the Weighted Average Cost of Capital as a Cutoff Rate. *Financial Management* (Summer).

Benzion, U., and J. Yagil. 1987. On the Discounting Formula for a Stream of Independent Risky Cashflow. *Engineering Economist* (Summer).

Beranek, W. 1977. The WACC Criterion and Shareholder Wealth Maximization. *Journal of Financial and Quantitative Analysis* (March): 17–32.

Bernhard, R. H. 1969. Mathematical Programming Models for Capital Budgeting: A Survey, Generalization and Critique. *Journal of Financial and Quantitative Analysis* (June): 111–158.

Bierman, H., Jr., and S. Smidt. 1975. *The Capital Budgeting Decision.* 4th ed. New York: Macmillan.

Bogue, M. C., and R. R. Roll. 1974. Capital Budgeting of Risky Projects with "Imperfect" Markets for Physical Capital. *Journal of Finance* (May): 601–613.

Booth, L. 1982. Correct Procedures for the Evaluation of Risky Cash Outflows. *Journal of Financial and Quantitative Analysis* (June): 287–300.

Brigham, E. F., and T. C. Tapley. 1985. Financial Leverage and the Use of the Net Present Value Investment Criterion: A Reexamination. *Financial Management* (Summer).

Butler, J. S., and B. Schachter. 1989. The Investment Decision: Estimation Risk and Risk Adjusted Discount Rates. *Financial Management* 18 (Winter): 13–22.

Casey, C. J., and N. J. Bartezak. 1984. Cashflow: It's Not the Bottom Line. *Harvard Business Review* (July/August).

Celec, S., and R. Pettway. 1979. Some Observations on Risk-Adjusted Discount Rates: A Comment. *Journal of Finance* (September): 1061–1063.

Chambers, D. R., R. S. Harris, and J. J. Pringle. 1982. Treatment of Financing Mix in Analyzing Investment Opportunities. *Financial Management* (Summer).

Constantinides, G. 1978. Market Risk Adjustment in Project Valuation. *Journal of Finance* (May): 603–616.

Durand, D. 1981. Comprehensiveness in Capital Budgeting. *Financial Management* 10 (5): 7–13.

Durand, D. 1989. Afterthoughts on a Controversy with MM, Plus New Thoughts on Growth and the Cost of Capital. *Financial Management* (Summer).

Fama, E. 1974. The Empirical Relationships between the Dividend and Investment Decisions of Firms. *American Economic Review* 64 (3), 304–318.

Fama, E. F. 1977. Risk-Adjusted Discount Rates and Capital Budgeting under Uncertainty. *Journal of Financial Economics* (August): 3–24.

Gahlon, J. M., and J. A. Gentry. 1982. On the Relationship between Systematic Risk and the Degrees of Operating and Financial Leverage. *Financial Management* (Summer).

Gehr, A. K., Jr. 1981. Risk-Adjusted Capital Budgeting Using Arbitrage. *Financial Management* 10 (5): 14–19.

Gitman, L. J. 1977. Capturing Risk Exposure in the Evaluation of Capital Budgeting Projects. *Engineering Economist* (Summer).

Gitman, L. J., and V. A. Mercurio. 1982. Cost of Capital Techniques used by Major U.S. Firms: Survey and Analysis of Fortune's 1000. *Financial Management* (Winter).

Hamada, R. S. 1969. The Effect of the Firm's Capital Structure on the Systematic Risk of Common Stocks. *Journal of Finance* (May): 435–452.

Hoskins, C. G. 1978. Capital Budgeting Decision Rules for Risky Projects Derived from a Capital Market Model Based on Semivariance. *Engineering Economist* (Summer).

Klammer, T. P., and M. C. Walker. 1984. The Continuing Increase in the Use of Sophisticated Capital Budgeting Technique. *California Management Review* (Fall).

Lewellen, W. 1977. Some Observations on Risk-Adjusted Discount Rates. *Journal of Finance* (September): 1331–1337.

Lintner, J. 1965. The Valuation of Risky Assets and the Selection of Risky Investments in Stock Portfolios and Capital Budgets. *Review of Economics and Statistics* (February): 13–37.

Lorie, J. H., and L. J. Savage. 1955. Three Problems in Capital Rationing. *Journal of Business* (October): 229–239.

Mandelker, G. N., and S. G. Rhee. 1984. The Impact of the Degrees of Operating and Financial Leverage on Systematic Risk of Common Stocks. *Journal of Financial and Quantitative Analysis* (March).

McConnell, J., and C. Muscarella. 1985. Corporate Capital Expenditure Decisions and the Market Value of the Firm. *Journal of Financial Economics* (September): 399–422.

Modigliani, F., and M. H. Miller. 1958. The Cost of Capital, Corporation Finance, and the Theory of Investment. *American Economic Review* 47 (June): 261–297.

Myers, S. C. 1968. Procedures for Capital Budgeting under Uncertainty. *Industrial Management Review* (Spring): 1–20.

Myers, S. C. 1984. The Capital Structure Puzzle. *Journal of Finance* (July): 575–592.

Myers, S. C., and S. M. Turnbull. 1977. Capital Budgeting and the Capital Asset Pricing Model: Good News and Bad News. *Journal of Finance* (May): 321–332.

Osteryoung, J. S. 1973. A Survey into the Goals Used by Fortune 500 Companies in Capital Budgeting Decisions. *Akron Business and Economic Review* (Fall).

Perrakis, S. 1979. Capital Budgeting and Timing Uncertainty within the Capital Asset Pricing Model. *Financial Management* (Autumn).

Robichek, A., and J. C. Van Horne. 1967. Abandonment Value and Capital Budgeting. *Journal of Finance* (December): 577–590.

Ross, M. 1986. Capital Budgeting Practices of Twelve Large Manufacturers. *Financial Management* (Winter).

Ross, S. A. 1979. A Simple Approach to the Valuation of Risky Streams. *Journal of Business* (July): 254–286.

Rubinstein, M. E. 1973. A Mean-Variance Synthesis of Corporate Financial Theory. *Journal of Finance* 28 (March): 167–182.

Sick, G. A. 1986. Certainty Equivalent Approach to Capital Budgeting. *Financial Management* (Winter).

Stiglitz, J. E. 1972. Some Aspects of the Pure Theory of Corporate Finance: Bankruptcies and Take-Overs. *Bell Journal of Economics* 3 (2): 458–482.

Williams, J. 1987 Prerequisites, Risk and Capital Structure. *Journal of Finance* (March).

18 Risk Trading

A. Pure Risk Trading—Future Contracts

B. The Consumption-Based Capital Asset Pricing Model

C. Hedging Interest and Currency Risk

D. Hedging Equity Holding Risk

A. Pure Risk Trading—Future Contracts

In the first part of this book, we discussed how trading in the "time value of financial assets" enhances utility for all market participants. When a financial asset (bonds) has a market where participants ultimately trade the timing of actual consumption, individuals do not have to consume their entire income when it is generated and can postpone or advance consumption according to their utility functions. Bond-type financial assets (and a market where such assets are traded) are used to smooth consumption over time. Advancing (postponing) consumption requires paying (receiving) a risk-free fee (interest) of r_f per time unit (year).

In the second part of the book we discussed risk, and demonstrated how a fee is required on the inherent risk of holding a financial asset, in terms of a premium required in excess of the risk-free interest rate. In the single-period capital asset pricing model (CAPM), investors maximize their mean utility in a world that defines financial assets according to only two parameters, the asset's mean return and β, the asset's covariation with the market portfolio. The return required on a risky asset is comprised of the price required for postponing (advancing consumption) by one time period, denoted r_f (the pure interest rate for trading in time), plus a premium of $\beta(r_m - r_f)$ required for incurring a risk of β, according to the equation:

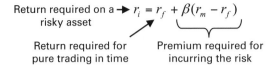

Return required on a → $r_i = r_f + \beta(r_m - r_f)$
risky asset

Return required for   Premium required for
pure trading in time   incurring the risk

In practice, a specific market exists for trading in time value—the bond market.[1] Would the existence of a market for trading in "risk value" also increase participants' utility?

To answer this question, let's return to our fundamental definition of interest as the cost of money.

In chapter 2, we defined the goal of individual investors as seeking to maximize their wealth, with the aim of meeting a more basic need—maximizing utility from consumption. Utility is maximized by smoothing consumption over time, owing to the mismatch between an individual's income (output) at each point in his life and his actual consumption over time. Later we developed models to convert actual consumption (e.g., of wheat) to a cash equivalent, required to buy the same amount of consumption C (of wheat). Our basic assumption was that individuals always prefer present consumption to future consumption. For individuals to forgo a certain amount of present consumption, they will demand a larger amount of future consumption (money). We defined "interest" as this required extra consumption, in monetary terms. Our initial, basic model was a two-period model, present and future. This model was easily expanded into a multiperiod model or a continuous model.

Having since discussed Sharpe and Treynor's capital asset pricing model, defining the β risk measure correlated to the market overall performance and the premium required for incurring that risk, $\beta(r_m - r_f)$, let's reexamine individuals' goals and revisit our definition of interest. If we view the CAPM as a model for smoothing consumption over time, financial assets are then used owing to discrepancies between the time of generating the personal income (output) and its actual consumption time, compensated by R_f, and arbitrary overall economy output irregularities in bad periods of time and good periods, compensated by $\beta(r_m - r_f)$.

Accordingly, individuals will buy financial assets during good periods and sell them in difficult ones. This statement requires proof, and such

1. Such a market for trading in time value exists, at least theoretically. In practice, it is not perfect, that is, it is not completely risk-free. However, we can define the real interest rate on short-term U.S. Treasury bonds as practically risk-free.

proof for a consumption-based capital asset pricing model (CCAPM) was put forth in Robert Lucas's 1978 article "Asset Prices in an Exchange Economy," discussed in depth in the next section.

We can thus expand our definition of interest rate:

Interest rate k The additional consumption (money) required:

1. To postpone consumption from the present to the future; and

2. As a premium for reducing the dependency of consumption on future output (economic conditions).

Until Lucas presented the CCAPM model, financial theorists relied on a classic normative economics-based model. This model explained the need to trade in pure risk (using wheat as an example), and can be summarized through the following example.

Two tribes are identical in size, in consumption habits, and in their wheat-farming members' utility functions. The tribes live on opposite sides of the same mountain. In each period, it rains on only one side of the mountain. The chance of rain falling on a particular side in each period is 50%.

Let's assume that wheat can be stored, but half the wheat spoils in each storage period. Let's further assume that the harvest is four times the amount sown when it rains and zero when it does not rain.

A normal consumption unit is defined as the quantity consumed by each tribe member (multiplied by the number of members). For the sake of simplicity, let's also assume that all tribe members have an identical consumption-utility function, which is a classic function with decreasing marginal utility, as detailed in figure 18.1.

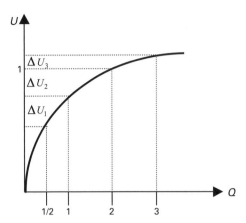

Figure 18.1
Classical (Marginal Decreasing) Utility from Consumption

In time $t = 0$, each tribe has six units of wheat. What would be the optimal consumption, sowing, and storage strategy for a tribe seeking maximum consumption at minimum effort?

One option is for the tribe to consume one unit, sow one unit, and store four units. As we do not know whether or not it will rain in the next period, it is possible that no harvest will be available.

Therefore, if it rains, the tribe will have four units from the harvest plus two units from storage (after half the amount spoils), and the cycle can repeat.

If it does not rain, the tribe will have two units left from storage and can consume one and sow the other.

However, what would happen if one side of the mountain remained dry for two consecutive periods? What would that tribe eat and sow in the third period? As there is an independent 50% chance for rain in each period, then the chance for two consecutive dry periods is $1/2 \times 1/2$, or a relatively large chance of 25%. The tribe would need to consume less and store and sow more!

However, we do not really need all six units given to us at $t = 0$—four units will suffice! The tribes can reach the following agreement: each time it rains on one side of the mountain, that tribe will provide the other tribe with two units, one for consumption and one for sowing. As statistically it rains 50% of the time on each side, then over time, the number of units given by each tribe to the other will be equal. In each period, one tribe will have a harvest of four units, which can be used as follows: two for consumption (one for each tribe) and two for sowing (one for each tribe), without storage/spoilage and without risk for the future.

The above solution is an example of trading in pure risk. The contract proposed for the two tribes is known as a *future contract*. The above proposal clearly increases the mean utility (maximizes consumption and minimizes labor) for both tribes over time and demonstrates how pure risk trading can increase utility for all market participants.

The risk trading in the above wheat-based model is not strictly theoretical and has many real-world economic applications. Consider two companies, one located in the United States and the other in Europe, each of which separately wins a contract in the other's country to supply their product (which does not have to be identical); that is, the American company wins a contract in Europe, and vice versa. The contracts are worth one million dollars or euros, respectively. For the sake of simplicity, let's further assume that when the contracts are won, one dollar equals one euro. Both companies need to manufacture the goods and supply them within three months. Payment is made against delivery of the goods. Vast numbers of such transactions occur every day on the international markets, for different amounts but under identical conditions.

To secure their respective contracts, as in any real-world competitive market, both companies reduced their profit to a minimum, leaving no room for unforeseen surprises. They now face a serious problem: their expenses are incurred in advance in their local currency,[2] while payment is made in the other country's currency at the end of the period. At the end of the period, each company must convert its payment to its local currency, so that it can repay the loan it received from a local bank in order to manufacture the order.[3] However, neither company knows the future currency exchange rate at the time of payment. The rate can go up or down. For each of these companies' shareholders, the marginal increase in utility[4] from an improved exchange rate is smaller than the marginal decrease in utility from an inferior exchange rate (diminishing marginal utility). In other words, the mean utility from both possible scenarios is lower than the utility from the certainty equivalent of receiving one million in local currency.

As in the wheat-based model, the solution is for each company to sign a future contract with the other: if the exchange rate changes, the company that benefits from such change will compensate the other for the difference. Thus, in every case, each company will receive exactly one

2. They must pay for raw materials and wages in their local currency.

3. Their calculations included interest on the loan and exchange fees.

4. As usual, we assume shareholders (investors) to be risk averse (their utility function is similar to that in the wheat-based model).

million in local currency. This demonstrates how risk trading increases utility for both companies. All that is left now is to find a floor for such trading (e.g., banks), so that both companies on either side of the ocean can trade their risk. Note that in this example, trading in time, as reflected in the interest rate on the loan taken by each company from its local bank to finance its respective project, is completely separate from the companies' future contract, which they use to cancel out the future risk posed by currency rate fluctuations. Currency risk trading systems are designed to serve as a floor where standard units of currency can be sold for exchange, for a specified time (e.g., a three-month contract for one thousand units of currency). Supply and demand, as well as currency rate expectations for the end of the period, determine the price of these contracts. Contract costs and bank commissions can be factored in beforehand when pricing the product so as to avoid any possible surprises.

Future exchange rates in exports are only one of many examples of risk trading. In many fields, including financial asset (shares) trading, risk trading is worthwhile. Because the market for trading in time allows better management of consumption timing, the risk trading market allows better management of risk, with each individual (or company, in the above case) undertaking risk according to its own utility function.

As demonstrated, a future contract is a contractual obligation between two parties according to which one party sells and the other buys a real or financial asset at a given future time and at a specified price, to be paid upon delivery.[5] In the above example, the American company commits to selling to the European company (and the latter commits to buying) one million euros in exchange for one million dollars.[6] This is an example of a financial contract. However, similar contracts can be made for commodities. For future contracts to be traded in predefined units and specified dates, commodities must be homogenous. Thus, for example, future contracts are traded for various types of commodities: oil, wheat, soy, and even pork. Through these transactions, traders can mitigate the risk of future price fluctuations. The farmers growing the wheat know that they will receive a fixed price and can plan their expenses accordingly. Bakers know they can buy the wheat or flour at a specified price and supply the goods to which they have committed at a given price.

---

5. The fact that the payment is made against delivery effectively neutralizes the time cost of money.

6. The contract can also be written the other way around, with the European company selling one million dollars for one million euros.

Thus, the farmers reduce the risk on their revenues, and the bakers reduce the risk on their expenses. Even more "everyday" transactions, such as buying a car to be delivered in two months' time at a predetermined price, are actually future contracts. The contractual right to receive a car at a predetermined date and price can be sold to a third party.

When a future contract is made between two parties, the contract itself becomes a financial asset that can be traded. The party actually holding the contract on its exercise date is entitled to exercise the contract at the specified conditions.[7] The contracted product's price, however, is not fixed or certain over time. Consider a contract for supplying a specified quantity and type of oil in six months at a predetermined price: if oil prices go up, everyone would want to buy the contract offering oil at a discounted price, and the contract will have a value and price of its own. The future contract, which has no value or price when drafted (excluding brokerage fees), becomes an asset that may have value over time and that carries only risk. At any given time the "commodity" (real or financial) stated in the contract has a *spot price*. The future contract's market price will be linked both to the commodity's spot price at a given point in time and the expectations of all market players concerning the commodity's future price at the contract's exercise date.

We will now discuss a number of financial instruments (and principles for determining their price) designed for risk trading. These instruments are conceptually equivalent to another financial instrument we discussed—bonds that are used to trade in time. Later, these tools will allow us to mitigate and hedge[8] risks related to interest rates, currency rates, and share price fluctuations over time. An in-depth discussion of models for future contracts on commodities exceeds the scope of this book, and appears in advanced course curricula.

Before discussing models for hedging financial instruments, let's discuss Lucas's modern financial model, the CCAPM.[9] This model relates the risk on a given quantity of future output to the required extra future consumption, according to our new definition of interest as the cost of money.

---

7. It makes no difference if the right is to receive a car against a payment specified in that contract or a tanker full of oil of a specified type and at a specified price (per ton). Remember that bonds are also contracts between two parties, but once signed (issued) they become a financial asset that is marketable to third parties.

8. "Hedging" here means limiting to a predefined range.

9. There are different ways of presenting this concept. This is one of the simpler ways in terms of mathematical complexity.

B. The Consumption-Based Capital Asset Pricing Model

The model presented in chapter 2 for defining interest as the cost of money, according to which individuals seek to maximize their combined utility from present and future consumption, can now be expanded to a random market. The mean (average) utility from "future[10] consumption" is translated to "present value" using the discount rate $\kappa = \dfrac{1}{1+r}$, which matches our new definition of interest:

$Max\{U(c_0) + \kappa \cdot E[U(c_1)]\}$.

In chapter 2, individuals could only lend or borrow money. Now, individuals can invest part of their available income at the start of the period, e_0,[11] not only by borrowing or lending at the risk-free rate but also by buying or selling n participation certificates (shares) in a productive asset whose price and end-of-period dividends are uncertain. In contrast to our model from chapter 2, the end-of-period return, e_1, is uncertain (figure 18.2).[12]

The price of each participation unit at time zero is p_0, and each participation unit distributes a dividend of d_1 at the end of the period. The joint dividend payments equal the return e_1 (independent of an individual's start-of-period investment) that individuals have at their disposal at the end of the period. Individuals must choose the number of participation certificates n they want to buy to maximize their mean consumption utility across both periods.

$\underset{n}{Max}\{U(c_0) + \kappa \cdot E[U(c_1)]\}$,

where $\begin{array}{l} c_0 = e_0 - n \cdot p_0 \\ c_1 = e_1 + n \cdot (p_1 + d_1) \end{array}$.

Thus, $\underset{n}{Max}\{U(e_0 - n \cdot p_0) + \kappa \cdot E[U(e_1 + n \cdot (p_1 + d_1))]\}$.

To find the number of participation units that maximizes utility, let's find the first derivative by n and equate to zero:

---

10. At $t = 0$, there is no uncertainty, and therefore $U(c_0) = E[U(c_0)]$.

11. Since I am using E as the "expected" (mean) operator, in this chapter I will use e as the "earnings" symbol, and to maintain uniformity, I will use lowercase for all the rest of the symbols.

12. The model discussed in chapter 2 uses the notation E_0. To avoid confusion with the mean operator E we will use the lowercase e_0.

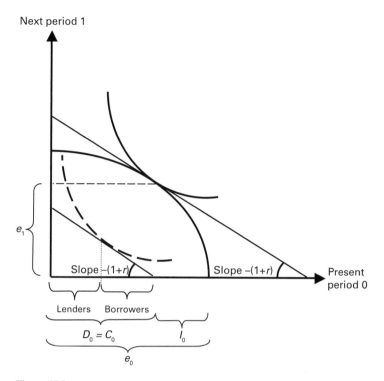

Next period 1

e_1

Slope $-(1+r)$ Slope $-(1+r)$ Present
period 0

Lenders   Borrowers

$D_0 = C_0$ I_0

e_0

Figure 18.2
Investment Production and Consumption over Two Periods

$$[U'(c_0)] \cdot (-p_0) + \kappa \cdot E\{[U'(c_1)] \cdot (p_1 + d_1)\} = 0.$$

$$p_0 = \frac{\kappa \cdot E\{[U'(c_1)] \cdot (p_1 + d_1)\}}{U'(c_0)} = \kappa \cdot E\left\{\left[\frac{U'(c_1)}{U'(c_0)}\right] \cdot (p_1 + d_1)\right\}.$$

$$1 = \kappa \cdot E\left\{\frac{U'(c_1)}{U'(c_0)} \cdot \left(\frac{p_1 + d_1}{p_0}\right)\right\}.$$

Define $m_{0,1}$ as the ratio of the marginal utility from consumption at the end of the period to that at the start of the period: $m_{0,1} = \dfrac{U'(c_1)}{U'(c_0)}$.

We recall that by definition, the r_j return on participation certificates is given by

$$1 + r_j = \frac{p_1 + d_1}{p_0}.$$

Both $m_{0,1}$ and r_j are random variables whose values are known only at the end of a period. Substituting them into the last equation gives us[13]

$$1 = \kappa \cdot E\{m_{0,1} \cdot (1 + r_j)\} = \kappa \cdot \{E[m_{0,1}] \cdot E[1 + r_j] + \text{Cov}[m_{0,1}; (1 + r_j)]\}.$$

$$\frac{1}{\kappa \cdot E[m_{0,1}]} = E[1 + r_j] + \frac{\text{Cov}[m_{0,1}; (1 + r_j)]}{E[m_{0,1}]}.$$

This last equation is true for all r_j, and thus also for r_f = risk-free asset. However, as the r_f return is certain, then

$$\text{Cov}[m_{0,1}; (1 + r_f)] = 0 \text{ and } E[1 + r_f] = 1 + r_f.$$

Therefore, $1 + r_f = \dfrac{1}{\kappa \cdot E[m_{0,1}]}$.

Substituting this last equation into the previous equation yields

$$1 + r_f = E[1 + r_j] + \frac{\text{Cov}[m_{0,1}; (1 + r_j)]}{E[m_{0,1}]}.$$

$$E[r_j] - r_f = -\frac{1}{E[m_{0,1}]} \cdot \text{Cov}[m_{0,1}; (1 + r_j)].$$

Insert the definition $m_{0,1} = \dfrac{U'(c_1)}{U'(c_0)}$ back into this last equation, and remember that $U'(c_0)$ is certain and so can be factored out of the statistical operators (mean and covariance) as a constant:

$$E[r_j] - r_f = -\frac{1}{E[U'(c_0)]} \cdot \text{Cov}[U'(c_1); (1 + r_j)].$$

The literal interpretation of this last equation leads us to conclude that the risk premium[14] $E[r_j] - r_f$ on a risky asset j is inversely (negatively) correlated with the covariance (correlation) between r_j, the risky asset's return, and $U'(c_1)$, an individual's marginal consumption utility: $\text{Cov}[U'(c_1); (1 + r_j)]$.

This conclusion accords with our new definition of interest, where financial assets are used not only to over time as a result of a (temporal)

---

13. Reminder: for any two random variables x and y, $E[x \cdot y] = E(x) \cdot E(y) + \text{Cov}(x,y)$.

14. The risk premium here refers to the mean return, exceeding the risk-free interest rate.

discrepancy between output consumption timing but also to smooth consumption between bad time periods, when return e_1 is low, and better time periods. The last equation indicates that individuals will indeed buy financial assets in good times and sell them in more difficult times.

Financial assets with a high inverse correlation to general economic conditions (output) will have a low risk premium, and vice versa: assets with a high positive correlation to general economic conditions (output) are less useful during difficult times and so will demand a higher risk premium.

Caution: Although Sharpe and Treynor's CAPM and Lucas's CCAPM lead to the same conclusions regarding the nature of the return premium required for risk, they are fundamentally different models. Their basic definition of risk-free interest and the variable correlated with the return on the risky asset r_j are totally different (in CAPM, correlation is measured with the market portfolio, while CCAPM measures correlation with marginal consumption utility) and should not be confused. Accordingly, the numbers obtained for those parameters (risk-free interest rate and correlation coefficient) by empirical tests are completely different.

C. Hedging Interest and Currency Risk

One of a CFO's most important responsibilities is risk management. It is inconceivable for a business not to be insured against burglary, fire, employee injury, liability toward customers because of faulty products, and so on. Companies pay premiums on all such insurance policies. These premiums are worthwhile because if no such insurance is in place, a liability event could put the company's very existence at risk. All the above examples (involving interest and currency fluctuations) can also be considered from a similar perspective. Companies pay the bank a fee for buying a financial asset, which is intended to limit risk in case of market fluctuations, and such fees should be seen as insurance premiums. A currency collapse may cause companies to go bankrupt no less than uninsured fire damage may.

The guiding principle in risk management is known as hedging risk.[15] Insuring against risks that a company might incur without going bankrupt is not worthwhile. The mean damage value[16] is always smaller than the

---

15. "Hedging" here means limiting to a known range, or fencing in.

16. Mean damage value is figured as the probability of an insurance event multiplied by the cost of damages.

insurance premium, as insurance companies must also add their administrative overhead and profit on top of this value. Companies should "self-insure" against these risks up to the point where they threaten stability, and make sure to cover all risks beyond this point.

CFOs hedge against the following risks:

1. Changes in cash inflows (not caused by actual changes in sales, but rather by currency exchange rate fluctuations).

2. Changes in cash outflows (mainly due to changes in raw material prices).

3. Changes in the value of financial assets held by the company (surplus cash investments).[17]

4. Changes in the value of the company's outstanding liabilities.

Earlier in this chapter we discussed how companies can protect themselves against changes in raw material prices (buying on the futures market) and against currency fluctuations. In all the above examples, the risk management strategy was based on linking liabilities with revenue. For example, if we receive an order at a fixed local price, we want all the expenses used in calculating that price to remain constant and be linked to the same base.

It is emphasized that all the instruments discussed above are not intended to "go against the market" in the long term. They are designed as short-term hedges for a company's existing operational commitments. Market fluctuations that can be predicted and acted against do not fall under this category, and so do not require hedging; for example, a change in product prices due to a change in raw materials for future sales for which no binding contract has yet been signed.

Let's go back to the previous example of the two companies that secured contracts in each other's native country. We said that each company takes a loan from its local bank. Let's assume that delivery is in nine months' time. However, each company will start processing the order only six months from now (until then they are working on meeting previous orders). Thus, they must take out a three-month loan, but only six months from now. When calculating costs, each company's CFO used present interest rates and must now find a way to hedge against changes in financing costs caused by changes in the market interest rate. The practical solution is to buy a three-month loan contract from the bank, to be exercised only six months from now.

---

17. Private investors may also want to hedge their financial asset holdings' risks.

Such contracts are known as *forward contracts*.[18] Banks, which lend and borrow money extensively and for different periods and interest rates, cover themselves against risks transferred to them by companies, as detailed below.

Let's assume that we need to borrow $100 for one year, but we do not need the loan until one year from now. We sign a forward contract with the bank for $100 to be given in one year's time, for a period of one year, at a predetermined interest rate of 14.04%.

How did the bank calculate the required interest rate? To avoid exposure to interest rate fluctuations, the bank conducts the following borrowing/lending transactions at the current interest rates (R_{Spot}) on the market (interest and principal paid at the end of the period) against our forward contract.[19]

Let's assume that the term structure of interest rates on signing the contract is 10% for one-year loans and 12% (annually) for two-year loans. The bank borrows $90.91 for two years at 12% interest and lends (to a third party) $90.91 for one year at 10% interest.

Thus, on signing the contract, the bank did not record any change in its cash flow (both loaned and borrowed $90.91).

In one year, the bank will receive payment of $100 on its one-year loan plus interest, and will give you this $100 as agreed. At the end of the first year, again the bank did not record any change in its cash flows.

In two years' time, you will pay back your (one-year) loan plus interest, for a total amount of $114.04. The bank will also need to pay back its (two-year) loan plus interest, for a total amount of $114.04.

After two years, again the bank did not record any change in its cash flows.

The bank's cash flow will be as follows:

	Year		
	0	1	2
Give one-year loan	−$90.91	+$100.00	$0
Take two-year loan	+$90.91	$0	−$114.04
Resulting cash flow for bank	$0	+$100.00	−$114.04
Forward contract loan	$0	−$100.00	+$114.04
Net cash flow for bank	$0	$0	$0

18. The contract's method is based on fixing an interest rate. If at the end of the period actual interest payments are higher, the bank pays the company the difference. If actual interest payments are lower, the company pays the bank the difference.

19. Assuming no fees apply.

A mirror image of this scenario can be created by swapping borrowing and lending transactions.

Thus, the bank calculated its required interest rate for the forward contract as follows:

$$R_{Forward} = \frac{(1 + R_{2Years,Spot})^2}{(1 + R_{1Year,Spot})} - 1.$$

$$R_{Forward} = \frac{(1.12)^2}{(1.1)} - 1 = 0.1404 \Rightarrow 14.04\%.$$

Remember that this interest is *certain* and immune to any market interest rate changes. The bank derives its profit only from a fee charged on the contract, without taking any position on the risky interest rates.

In a similar fashion, the companies could also buy a forward currency contract from their respective banks, instead of signing a future contract between them, without either bank incurring any currency-related risk.

Let's assume that the company wants to fix the dollar to euro exchange rate one year from now. The present exchange rate is 1:1. The American company wants to exchange (buy) dollars for 100 euros[20] one year from now. The bank is willing to commit to a predetermined exchange rate of 1:1.0192 euro to the dollar. Let's see how the bank calculated this rate.

To hedge currency risks, the bank takes/gives loans according to the currency-specific spot interest rates on signing the contract (R_{Spot})[21] (interest and principal paid at the end of the period) and covers itself against any risk that might be transferred from the company to the bank as follows.

Let's assume that the annual interest rate on signing the contract is 6% for dollars and 4% for euros. The bank borrows €96.15 for one year at 4% interest, exchanges the euros for dollars at the present rate of 1:1 ($96.15), and lends them out for one year at 6% (principal and interest are paid at the end of the period).

Thus, on signing the contract, no change is recorded in the bank's cash flow (both borrowed and loaned out: $96.15 = €96.15).

In one year's time, the euro loan must be repaid (principal plus interest) for 96.15 × 1.04 = €100. The bank receives €100 from the American company according to their forward contract, and uses the money to

20. The example originally involved €1 million.
21. Assuming no fees apply.

repay its loan. On its dollar loan, the bank receives $96.15 \times 1.06 = \$101.92$, and gives them to the company at the forward exchange rate of 1:1.0192 euros to the dollar.

The above example illustrates how future exchange rates are determined according to present currency-specific interest rates:

$$X_{ChangeRate,Future} = X_{ChangeRate,Spot} \times \frac{1 + R_{\$,Spot}}{1 + R_{\text{€},Spot}}.$$

$$X_{ChangeRate,Future} = \frac{1}{1} \times \frac{1.06}{1.04} = 1.0192 \quad \$: \text{€}.$$

The future exchange rate *must* be as calculated above, to prevent arbitrage!

When the bank offers a forward contract on an interest rate or an exchange rate, its cash flow at any given moment is zero, and so its risk is also zero.[22] The bank makes a profit not by taking a risky position but by charging transaction fees. Of course, theoretically the company could make the same transactions itself, but the bank has an advantage as it extends and receives credit during the normal course of its operations. It is less expensive for the company to pay the bank a known fee for its brokerage services than to try to build a "do-it-yourself" contract.

Above, we discussed how companies can hedge interest and currency risks at a given time in the future through forward contracts. Companies' operations usually consist of a series of inflows and outflows over several points in time in the future (and not only at one point in time). Companies wishing to hedge this chain of risks contact their banks and sign *swap contracts* converting the series of uncertain future liabilities into a series of fixed and predetermined amounts. The bank, which incurs these companies' risk, covers itself through a series of future contracts or forward contracts, as detailed above.

Swap contracts hedge (cancel) exposure to interest rate risk, currency risk, or any mixture of the two. Swap contracts are conceptually identical to our above discussion. Effectively, it's just a name for a contract that transfers the headache of handling a series of uncertain future events from companies to banks in exchange for a fee.

---

22. In practice, banks may not be able to balance the process perfectly, and are then left with a residual gain/loss position. The central bank dictates rules for reporting and managing these residual risks. In extreme cases, the central bank is forced to intervene.

D. Hedging Equity Holding Risk

From the above list of activities requiring risk management, we have yet
to discuss changes in the value of financial assets held by a company.
Companies invest their surplus cash (earmarked for future investment
in commercial opportunities) in financial assets, bonds,[23] and shares
traded on the market.

During the 2000–2002 capital market crisis, many shares[24] shed as
much as 90% of their peak value in 2000. The overall NASDAQ index
of technology company shares fell by 65%. The S&P 500 (an index comprised of the 500 largest companies in the United States) fell by more
than 35%. Similar or greater drops were even more prevalent during the
2008 crisis.

Future contracts can be drafted as an option (not an obligation) for
party A to conduct the transaction, while party B commits to the transaction (if party A wishes to exercise its option). Such contracts are referred
to as options and warrants.[25] For a quick definition, an option is a contract
granting its holder a right[26] to buy from or sell to a third party a specified
asset (either real or financial) at a specified price, quantity, and future time.

In the above example, each company could have written an option
offering to sell one million units of the other party's currency in exchange
for one million units of its local currency, and then traded these contracts.
In other words, each party would submit its contract to the other party
in exchange for that company's contract.[27] Of course, at the exercise date
(after three months), only one company would exercise its contract.[28]
Contrary to common belief, options are not speculative instruments.
Quite the opposite: they are designed to mitigate risk, thereby increasing
utility. When options are traded on the free market, they can be bought
by those seeking to reduce their risk exposure (e.g., the baker wishing to
secure the price of wheat to be supplied in a few months' time). However,

23. Hedging against interest risk was discussed in the previous section.
24. It happened in the United States and across most of the world markets.
25. Using the term "option" or "warrant" does not change the nature of the contract.
26. But not an obligation.
27. Each contract effectively constitutes a financial asset. If rate-change expectations are
symmetrical and homogenous, the prices on the contracts will be identical, and the companies could swap contracts, or sell and buy them at the same price.
28. The contract would be exercised only by the company that was adversely affected by
the rate change. The other party should not exercise its option as it can obtain better terms
on the spot market. Essentially, one million dollars and one million euros will change hands,
exactly as if a regular future contract were signed instead of two option contracts.

they can also be bought by speculators who expect the price of wheat to go up so that they may profit from selling the contract prior to its exercise date.

Options can be written for a broad range of financial and physical assets, and they then become marketable financial assets in their own right, just like future contracts. Shares are one type of asset for which options can be written.

Generally, options fall into two categories:

1. Option holders are granted the right to buy from the option issuer a specified quantity of shares at a specified price and date. These are known as *call options.*

2. Option holders are granted the right to sell to the option issuer a specified quantity of shares at a specified price and date. These are known as *put options.*

Options fill a great many different needs. Below is one example of a company's[29] need to grant an option.

A high-risk company is looking to raise debt. In order to reduce the interest rate on its bonds, for every $1,000 par value bonds it offers an option[30] to buy 10 shares in the company at a specified exercise price,[31] five years from now. The assumption is that in five years' time, the share price will exceed the exercise price,[32] and bondholders can exercise their option and buy the shares at the predetermined price, thus making a profit on the difference.

The question is, what should the value of this option be at any given moment prior to the exercise date? The option's price will be equal to at least the expected profit from exercising the option immediately, which is its naive approach value. This value reflects the difference between the share's market price and the option's exercise price/value.

We'll first discuss which parameters should influence the value/price of a call option.

Assume that when a call option was written on a share, its spot price was $S = \$20$. The option is granted for one year from its issue, at a strike

---

29. Options can be granted by either a company or third parties. For example, parties may wish to hedge shareholding risk (as demonstrated below).

30. Such an option is referred to as a warrant. Companies can also issue convertible bonds, bonds that can be converted into shares at a specified ratio at a specified date.

31. For example, $100, whereas the share price was $60 when the bond was issued.

32. In professional terms, such scenarios, in which the share price exceeds the option's exercise price, are referred to as "in the money options."

price[33] of X = \$30. Denote the gain from immediately exercising the option as W (assuming that it can be exercised at any given moment), that is, its naive value, and denote by V the value/price at which the option is traded on the market.

As holders of call options profit only when the share price is higher than the strike price, so long as the share price is lower than the strike price, the options' market price will be close to zero. It will not equal zero because as long as there is a chance that the share price will exceed the strike price during the option period,[34] there is some probability of earning a profit, and so the price will be equal to the mean value of that profit. This last observation leads us to conclude that even if the option is an "American option," that is, exercisable at any given moment, it should only be exercised at the end of the period, as though it were a "European option."[35] Therefore, both options must be priced the same.

Figure 18.3 plots the price V on a call option, as a function of share price S.

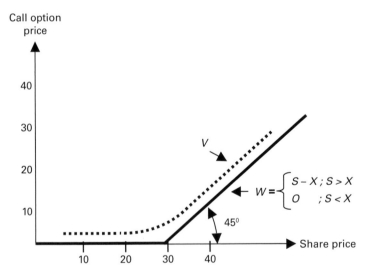

Figure 18.3
Call Option Naive (W) and Real (V) Price

33. X is referred to as either the strike price or the exercise price.

34. This is true even if the option is in the money; that is, the share price exceeds the exercise price.

35. An "American option" is exercisable at any given moment, while a "European option" may only be exercised at the end of the period.

The graph for an identical put option would look like figure 18.4.[36]

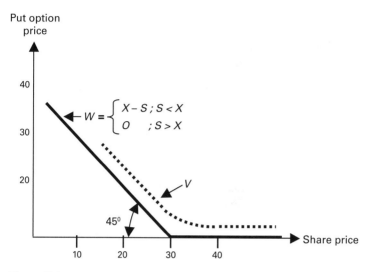

Figure 18.4
Put Option Naive (*W*) and Real (*V*) Price

V, the value of a call option (dotted line in figures 18.3 and 18.4), must be a function of share price *S*, the strike price *X*, the time remaining until the option expiration *T*, the risk-free interest rate r_f, and the variance of the share's return σ^2, as detailed below.

The connection between the first three parameters (T, S, X) and the option value *V* is quite intuitive:

1. The smaller the difference between the exercise price and the share price[37] $(X - S)$, the greater the option price *V*, so that as the share price *S* goes up, or the exercise price *X* goes down, the option value *V* goes up.

2. The longer the exercise time *T*, the greater the option value *V*, as the chance for the share price *S* to exceed the exercise price *X* increases with a longer exercise time T.[38]

36. The graph depicted is not accurate! It will be amended in the following chapter. This description is only intended to provide an understanding of the principle involved!

37. $(S - X)$ is greater.

38. In principle, if the exercise time is infinite, then the option is an American option, that is, it can be exercised at any moment, and will never be exercised (why is that?), and its price will be equal to the share price (explain!).

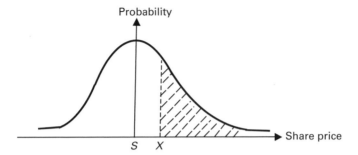

Figure 18.5
The Cumulative Probability of a Share's Price Exceeding X Next Period

The effect on the option's price V caused by the risk-free interest rate r_f and the σ^2 variance on the share's return is less intuitive:

3. When we hold a share directly, part of its required return is due to the "time value," that is, the risk-free interest rate, of the capital "locked" by our holding the share.[39] The share price constitutes interest on the capital that is "saved" while holding the option, as opposed to holding the share directly. Therefore, the higher the risk-free interest rate, the greater the advantage offered by holding an option rather than a share. The higher the risk-free rate r_f, the greater the option's value V.

4. The greater the share's return variance σ^2, the greater the variance of that share's price. The cumulative probability that the share price will exceed the strike price X (the option will be in the money) is the area marked by dashes in figure 18.5.

When, at a given moment, we have two shares with the same price S, both of which have an option with an identical exercise price X and exercise time T, then the share with the greater variance will have a thicker tail, and thus the cumulative probability of that share's price exceeding the exercise price will be greater. The difference between the cumulative probabilities for the two shares' options being in the money is the area marked by dashed lines in figure 18.6.

Conclusion: The value of call options increases along with all the parameters listed above, except for its exercise value.[40]

---

39. The money invested in buying the share could otherwise have carried interest (bond).

40. The first derivative of the option value for each variable is positive, excluding the strike price X, for which the first derivative of the option price is negative.

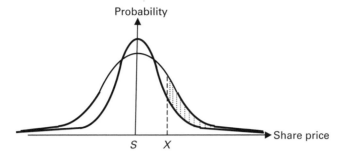

Figure 18.6
The Probability of a Share's Price Exceeding X Is Larger for a Share with a Greater Price Variance (a Thicker Tail)

Before discussing a number of positions[41] designed to hedge share-holding risks through options, we'll introduce another important financial instrument, the short sale.[42]

Short selling is the selling of a financial asset (e.g., shares) that one does not own. Such sales are conducted as follows: we "borrow" the share for a specified period, promising to return it at the end of the period.[43] We sell this borrowed share and buy it back at the end of the period to return the "loan." Obviously, if the share's price goes down during this time, we earn a profit on our position. In principle, the result of a short sale is the mirror image of going long on a share (figure 18.7).

In principle, we can short sell any financial asset: shares, call options, put options, and even bonds. The position's value will always be a mirror image of the original asset (mirrored on the x-axis).

An option's income structure makes it an effective tool in hedging various risks, when held together with the underlying financial asset.[44] Below we discuss two strategies for hedging an investment in shares, using options.

The most basic scenario that we would like to hedge is a drop in share price exceeding a given percentage. One of the ways to do this is to issue an automatic sell order. For example, if we bought a share at $100 and we wish to limit our possible loss to 20%, we can issue an automatic sell

---

41. Position—the possible results from holding (a combination of) financial assets.

42. Not all financial markets permit this kind of financial asset. It was unofficially presented in chapter 12, question 4, and expanded in chapter 14 (see note 6).

43. Of course, this requires collateral (as in any loan), and a fee is charged in addition to interest.

44. The underlying asset is the asset on which an option was written.

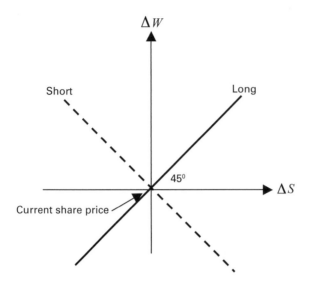

Figure 18.7
A Short Sale Is the Mirror Image of Going Long on a Share

order to be executed the instant the share price hits $80.[45] Alternatively, we can buy an $80 put option. That way, the minute the share price drops below $80 we can exercise this option. Figure 18.8 plots the profit inflow from a position consisting of a share (long) and a put option.

As illustrated in figure 18.8, a position consisting of a share plus a put option, called a *protective put strategy*, creates a bottom hedge that limits losses to 20%.[46]

Let's assume that we expect major volatility in the share price in the coming period (e.g., owing to changes in the company's management). However, we don't know whether these changes will cause the share price to go up or down. We can therefore implement a *straddle strategy*, which allows us to earn a profit regardless of whether the share goes up or down by buying a call option with an exercise price exceeding the share price and a put option with an exercise price below the share price.[47] This strategy is demonstrated in figure 18.9.

---

45. For automatic sell orders, it is possible that no buyers will be available at the specified price, and so the sale will actually take place at a price lower than $80.

46. The protection is time-limited to the expiration date, after which a new option should be bought. Option costs (insurance fee) should be added to the maximum potential loss.

47. When both options have the same exercise price, the position has a V shape.

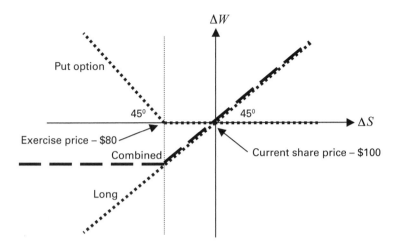

Figure 18.8
A Bottom Hedge Protective Put Strategy

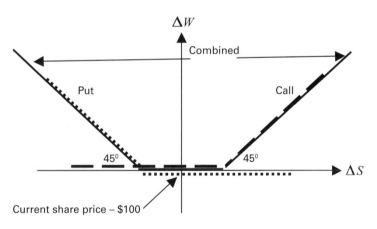

Figure 18.9
A Straddle Strategy

We will exercise our put option once the share price goes down, and if it goes up, we will exercise our call option.

This strategy is expected to incur a loss if the share price does not change. In this case, our loss will be reflected in the purchasing price of the two options—our "insurance fee."

These are only a few of the many possibilities offered by options for hedging share-holding risk. Readers are referred to the extensive literature on option strategies for more information.

The only unanswered question now is how a traded option's price should behave over time, from the moment it is issued and until it expires. This point is discussed in the following chapter.

Chapter 18—Questions and Problems

Question 1

A company has an order backlog for several years. Cost calculations for the third year's orders were based on a forward loan contract secured from the company's bank. The contractual interest rate on the local currency is derived from the returns in a market where zero-coupon government bonds are traded as follows:

Years to maturity	1	2	3	4	5
Return	10%	13%	15%	16%	16.5%

a. What is the interest rate reflected in the company's calculations for orders placed in the third year?

b. Demonstrate how the bank can offer this rate without incurring any interest rate risk.

Question 2

All orders placed with the company in question 1 during the third year are denominated in dollars and paid at the end of the year. As virtually all of the company's expenses are in its local currency, the ruby, costs for the third year's orders were calculated based on a forward dollar-to-ruby exchange contract secured from the company's bank.

The exchange rate on signing the contract is four rubies to the dollar.

The U.S. interest rate curve derived from the return in a market where zero-coupon U.S. government bonds are traded is as follows:

Years to maturity	1	2	3	4	5
Return:	6%	8%	9%	9.5%	9.75%

a. What is the exchange rate reflected in the company's calculations for its third-year orders?

b. Demonstrate how the bank can offer this exchange rate without incurring any currency risk.

Question 3

A foreign real estate company that issued CPI-linked bonds carrying 4% interest in its local market bought an income-generating property in the United States yielding an 8% annual return. The company's bonds are repaid over a 10-year period in annual payments of both principal and interest. The company wishes to reduce its exposure to both its local CPI and to currency exchange rate fluctuations. Therefore, the company contacts its bank and asks to buy a swap contract. Demonstrate how the bank will determine the CPI/currency rates without incurring any risk (demonstrate using standard contracts of one million currency units/ year).

Question 4

In this chapter, we discussed option-based buy/sell strategies for hedging underlying assets with uncertain, and therefore risky, future cash flows. These are known as hedging strategies.

A naked strategy is a speculative investment strategy that includes investing in only one option.

a. When should you buy a naked call option?

b. What is the cost and what is the profit of this strategy, and what are the limits of its profits and losses?

c. What is its equilibrium point?

d. How does the option's value behave over time?

Question 5

A *combined strategy* is a speculative investment strategy comprised of investment in more than one option. After explaining your market expectations for the near future to your investment consultant, the latter (who is familiar with your risk preferences) suggests that you buy a one-month put option on the market index at an exercise price of $X = 330$, at a premium of 800, and sell (issue) a put option at an exercise price of $Y = 300$, at a premium of 400 ($X > Y!$). The options multiplier is 100.

a. What is the cost of this strategy?

b. Plot the strategy's profit and loss behavior ΔW (including strategy cost) as a function of the market index (in the range 280–340 points, with 10-point intervals).

c. What is the strategy's equilibrium point?

d. Plot your expected change in wealth ΔW as a function of the base index S (the naive value).

e. What were your market expectations on which your investment consultant based his recommendation?

f. Could you obtain the same profit/loss through a different strategy?

g. Add the market value V of your strategy to your graph from part (d), and its behavior over time.

Question 6

One month after question 5, having presented your updated market expectations to your investment consultant, the latter suggests you buy a one-month C(310) option on the market index at a premium of 800, and buy a one-month P(310) option at a premium of 400. The options multiplier is 100.

a. What is the cost of this strategy?

b. Plot the strategy's profit and loss ΔW (including strategy cost) as a function of the market index (in the range 280–340, with 10-point intervals).

c. What is the strategy's equilibrium point?

d. Plot your expected change in wealth ΔW as a function of the base index S (the naive value). Add the market value V and its behavior over time.

e. What were your updated market expectations on which your investment consultant based his recommendations?

f. Could you obtain the same profit/loss through a different strategy?

Question 7

Your friend Tony had completely different expectations concerning the market's behavior, and so his investment consultant suggested he buy and sell one-month options as follows:

Sell C(310) = 800 and buy C(330) = 600.

Sell P(300) = 500 and buy (P280) = 300.

The options multiplier is 100.

a. What is the cost/reward for this strategy?

b. Plot the strategy's profit and loss ΔW (including strategy cost) as a function of the market index (in the range 270–340, with 10-point intervals).

c. What is the strategy's equilibrium point?

d. Plot the expected change in Tony's wealth ΔW as a function of the base index S (the naive value), and plot the market value V on the same graph.

e. How does the market value V behave over time?

f. What were the expectations on which Tony's investment consultant based his recommendation?

g. What can you say about Tony's risk preference?

h. Could Tony have obtained the same profit/loss through another strategy?

Question 8

Two markets offer options on two different underlying assets (multiplier of 10).

1. P(310) = 80, P(300) = 190.
2. C(330) = 80, C(310) = 100, C(300) =150, C(290) = 180.

Demonstrate (explain) how you can create arbitrage in each of these markets.

Question 9

A market has the following options: C(310) = 1,000, C(300) = 1,500. You are offered an option yielding the index rate above 300 (multiplier of

100), up to a maximum of 1,500, at a price of 40. Should you buy the option?

Question 10

Assume that two European options, one put and one call, are offered on a share S. The exercise price equals the share price, that is, $S = X$, and both options have the same exercise date.

The call option's market price is higher than the put option's price (as discussed in the following chapter).

a. Using a graph, demonstrate how a portfolio comprised of the share and the put option on that share and the sale (issue) of a call option has the same value (possible cash flow) as a bond.

b. If the company also issued a bond (zero default risk), what can you say about its value? Explain.

Further Reading

Anderson, R., and J. Danthine. 1983. The Time Pattern of Hedging and the Volatility of Futures Prices. *Review of Economic Studies* 50 (April): 249–266.

Bodie, Z., and V. Rozansky. 1980. Risk and Return in Commodities Futures. *Financial Analysts Journal* 36 (3): 27–31, 33–39.

Breeden, D. T. 1970. An Intertemporal Asset Pricing Model with Stochastic Consumption and Investment Opportunities. *Journal of Financial Economics* (September): 265–296.

Breeden, D. T. 1980. Consumption Risks in Futures Markets. *Journal of Financial Economics* (May): 503–520.

Carlton, D. 1984. Futures Markets: Their Purpose, Their History, Their Growth, Their Successes and Failures. *Journal of Futures Markets* (Fall): 237–271.

Cornell, B., and M. Reinganum. 1981. Forward and Futures Prices: Evidence from the Foreign Exchange Markets. *Journal of Finance* (December): 1035–1045.

Cox, J. C., J. E. Ingersoll, and S. A. Ross. 1981. The Relation between Forward Prices and Futures Prices. *Journal of Financial Economics* (December): 321–346.

Fama, E. F. 1970. Multiperiod Consumption-Investment Decisions. *American Economic Review* (March): 163–174.

Fama, E. F. 1972. Perfect Competition and Optimal Production Decisions under Uncertainty. *Bell Journal of Economics* 3 (2): 509–530.

French, K. 1986. Detecting Spot Price Forecasts in Futures Prices. *Journal of Business* (April): 539–554.

Hansen, L. P., and R. J. Hodrick. 1980. Forward Exchange Rates as Optimal Predictors of Future Spot Rates: An Econometric Analysis. *Journal of Political Economy* (October): 829–853.

Hazuka, T. 1984. Consumption Betas and Backwardation in Commodity Markets. *Journal of Finance* (July): 647–655.

Jagannathan, R. 1985. An Investigation of Commodity Futures Prices Using the Consumption-Based Intertemporal Capital Asset Pricing Model. *Journal of Finance* (March): 175–191.

Lucas, R., Jr. 1978. Asset Prices in an Exchange Economy. *Econometrica* 46 (6): 1429–1445.

Modest, D., and M. Sundaresan. 1983. The Relationship between Spot and Futures Prices in Stock Index Futures Markets: Some Preliminary Evidence. *Journal of Futures Markets* (Spring): 15–41.

Mueller, P. A. 1981. Covered Options: An Alternative Investment Strategy. *Financial Management* (Autumn).

Paddock, J., D. Siegel, and J. Smith. 1988. Option Valuation of Claims and Physical Assets: The Case of Offshore Petroleum Leases. *Quarterly Journal of Economics* 103 (3): 479–508.

19 Option Pricing

A. Statistical Tools

In 1973, Black and Scholes were the first to develop and present a mathematical model for pricing call options. Theirs was a continuous model, in which time and share prices at any given moment were continuous and share prices were normally distributed. However, advanced mathematical tools were needed to develop the model, and their approach did not allow much room for intuition in understanding the final result/ formula. Several years later, Cox, Ross, and Rubinstein (1979) developed a model with discrete time periods and share prices, where prices at the end of each period had a binomial distribution. This model can be expanded to account for continuous time and share prices (the Black-Scholes model) by decreasing the time intervals to zero ($\Delta t \rightarrow 0$), thus increasing the number of "gambles" on the share price binomial distribution to infinity ($n \rightarrow \infty$). This model leads to the same result as presented by Black and Scholes, but the process is easier to understand and the intermediate and final results are easier to interpret.

As mentioned, the Cox-Ross-Rubinstein (CRR) model is binomial, and therefore requires that we review a number of basic concepts in statistics and binomial distribution:

Permutations

Definition: The number of different ways of ordering n different objects.

Example: The number of different ways of ordering the letters a, b, and c is six: abc, acb, bac, bca, cab, and cba. With n objects, the first can be placed in any of n places, the second in any of the $n - 1$ remaining places, the third in any of the $n - 2$ remaining places, and so on.

Thus, the number of ways of ordering n different objects is given by $n \cdot (n - 1) \cdot (n - 2)... \cdot 3 \cdot 2 \cdot 1 \equiv n!.$[1]

Combinations

Definition: The number of groups of m elements that can be selected out of n different objects.

Example: Find the number of three-element groups that can be selected out of five elements, a, b, c, d, and e.

The first can be chosen out of five options, the second out of the four remaining options, and the third out of the three remaining options, so that the number of possibilities will be $5 \cdot 4 \cdot 3 = 60$.

However, as the order of the elements (the number of permutations) within the group is irrelevant, we must divide by the number of permutations for three elements, which according to our above example is $3! = 6$. Thus, the final result is $\dfrac{5 \cdot 4 \cdot 3}{3!} = \dfrac{60}{6} = 10.$

Generally, when required to select a group of m elements out of n different elements:

$$\frac{n \cdot (n-1) \cdot ... \cdot (n-m+1)}{m!} = \frac{n!}{(n-m)!m!} \equiv \binom{n}{m} ; 0 \le m \le n.$$

Here, $\binom{n}{m}$ is the notation indicating the number of m-sized groups that can be selected out of n different elements.

Bernoulli Distribution[2]

Definition: A gamble with two possible results: u = up, with probability P, or d = down, with probability $(1 - p)$.

For example, a coin toss where heads = u, and tails = d.

---

1. The symbol $\equiv$ means equal by definition. By definition, $0! = 1$.
2. Named after the Swiss mathematician James Bernoulli.

The probability distribution function for a Bernoulli distribution is therefore

$$P(u) = p$$
$$P(d) = (1-p) \; ; \; 0 < p < 1.$$

Binomial Distribution

Definition: The probability of obtaining an "up" result m times out of n independent gambles, each of which has a Bernoulli distribution function.

The probability of obtaining an "up" result m times (and therefore a "down" result $n - m$ times) is $p^m \cdot (1-p)^{(n-m)}$.

The number of possibilities of obtaining "up" m times is $\binom{n}{m}$.

The probability distribution function for a binomial distribution[3] is therefore

$$B(m|n,p) = \binom{n}{m} \cdot p^m \cdot (1-p)^{(n-m)}$$

$$= \frac{n!}{(n-m)!m!} \cdot p^m \cdot (1-p)^{(n-m)}; \; m = 0, 1, \dots n.$$

$$E(m) = n \cdot p.$$

$$\sigma(m) = n \cdot p \cdot (1-p).$$

The cumulative probability distribution ($m \leq k$) of a binomial distribution, that is, the probability of obtaining an "up" result once, and up to k times, out of n attempts is given by

$$B(m \leq k) = \sum_{m=0}^{k} \frac{n!}{(n-m)!m!} \cdot p^m \cdot (1-p)^{(n-m)}; \; k = 0, 1, \dots, n.$$

Further, the probability of $m \geq k$,[4] or the probability of obtaining an "up" result k or more (up to n) times out of n attempts, is given by

$$B(m \geq k) = \sum_{m=k}^{n} \frac{n!}{(n-m)!m!} \cdot p^m \cdot (1-p)^{(n-m)}.$$

---

3. $B(m|n,p)$: The probability of obtaining m "up" results out of n gambles, each with a probability p. The graph of a binomial distribution function is similar to the normal distribution's bell curve, but instead of a continuous line the graph is comprised of discrete columns.

4. The cumulative probability that $m \geq k$ is the complementary cumulative probability $B(m \geq k) = 1 - B(m \leq k)$.

B. Call Option Pricing

The Black-Scholes model for a call option price formula, at $t = 0$ from which T is defined, is

$$C_0 = S \cdot N(d_1) - X \cdot e^{-r_f \cdot T} \cdot N(d_2),$$

where $N(*)$ is the value obtained from a normal distribution table[5] and

$$d_1 = \frac{\ln(S/X) + r_f \cdot T}{\sigma\sqrt{T}} + \frac{1}{2}\sigma\sqrt{T};$$

$$d_2 = \frac{\ln(S/X) + r_f \cdot T}{\sigma\sqrt{T}} - \frac{1}{2}\sigma\sqrt{T} = d_1 - \sigma\sqrt{T}.$$

The underlying concept in Black and Scholes's work, which is also applied in the CRR binomial model, is that a risk-free (i.e., with a certain result) portfolio can be built by going long on a share and going short on a corresponding number of call options on that same share (as will be demonstrated below). Thus, such a portfolio must have a risk-free return of r_f to avoid arbitrage between this portfolio and the risk-free interest rate (asset) prevailing in the market.

As usual, let's first review the model's underlying assumptions.[6]

1. There is a perfect market,[7] where short selling is possible.

2. There is continuous (uninterrupted) trading.

3. The price of financial assets over time is continuous and smooth (there are no price jumps).

4. Companies do not pay dividends during the option period.

5. The statistical distribution of asset prices is constant over time.

6. The risk-free rate is constant over time.

Following Cox, Ross, and Rubinstein, let's begin with a simple single-period model. We will then move to a two-period model, which can then

---

5. Because of the symmetry around the origin, normal distribution function tables are given for the range $0 \to \infty$, and not for $-\infty \to \infty$. Therefore, we must add 0.5, the cumulative probability for the range $-\infty \to 0$, to our result from the table.

6. These assumptions are aimed at simplifying the model and our discussion and apply to a continuous model. Later, we will relax restrictions 2–6 so as to allow, for example, a finite number of jumps in a financial asset's price; the payment of known, predetermined dividends, and so forth.

7. See the perfect market assumptions.

be generalized as an *n*-period model. Finally, we will increase *n* to infinity ($n\rightarrow\infty$) so as to compare this model with Black and Scholes's continuous model.

Denote	**Example**
S—The share price (binomial distribution)	$S = \$10$
X—The option's exercise price	$X = \$11$
r_f—The continuous risk-free interest rate	$r_f = 10\%$
u—The share price upward multiplier ($u > 1 + r_f$)	$u = 1.2$
d—The share price downward multiplier ($d < 1$)	$d = 0.7$
C_0—The option's price (value) at the start of the period	

Single-Period Model

If the share goes up, its price will be $u \cdot S = 1.2 \cdot 10 = \$12$.

If the share goes down, its price will be $d \cdot S = 0.7 \cdot 20 = \$7$.

An investor who buys the option at the start of the period at a price C_0 will see an end-of-period cash flow (profit) according to the following.

If the share goes up: The investor will exercise the option for an expected payoff C_u of $C_u = u \cdot S - X = 12 - 11 = \$1$.

If the share goes down: The investor will not exercise the option, and the expected payoff C_d will be $C_d = d \cdot S - X < 0 \Rightarrow 0$.

As said earlier, the basis for the Black-Scholes model was to build a portfolio comprised of a share and *w* call options to be sold on that share. The value (cash flow) of this portfolio at the end of the first period will therefore be as follows.[8]

If the share goes up: $u \cdot S - w \cdot C_u$.

If the share goes down: $d \cdot S - w \cdot C_d$.

To build a risk-free portfolio, we must hold or sell *w* options so that the payoff under both up and down scenarios will be identical:

$$u \cdot S - w \cdot C_u = d \cdot S - w \cdot C_d$$

$$\Rightarrow w = \frac{S \cdot (u-d)}{C_u - C_d} = \frac{10(1.2-0.7)}{1-0} = 5.$$

Therefore, for every share held, the risk-free portfolio will include five options.[9] Let's calculate the portfolio's payoff for our above example:

8. The option buyer's gain is the option writer's (seller's) loss on his portfolio, and will therefore be entered as a negative number.

9. We need to assume a short sale as we are selling a quantity *w* of options, which is larger than the number of shares held.

If the share goes up: $u \cdot S - w \cdot C_u = 10 \cdot 1.2 - 5 \cdot 1 = \$7.$
If the share goes down: $d \cdot S - w \cdot C_d = 10 \cdot 0.7 - 5 \cdot 0 = \$7.$

Indeed, this is a risk-free portfolio, as it yields an identical (certain) payoff of \$7 for both up and down scenarios!

As the portfolio at $t = 0$ (comprised of the share price minus w times the price of the option sold) is risk-free, its price, multiplied by the risk-free interest rate $(1 + r_f)$, must be equal to its end-of-period value: $(1 + r_f)(S - w \cdot C_0) = u \cdot S - w \cdot C_u.$

Therefore, $C_0 = \dfrac{S[(1+r_f) - u] + w \cdot C_u}{w \cdot (1 + r_f)}.$

Substituting $w = \dfrac{S \cdot (u - d)}{C_u - C_d},$

we get $C_0 = \dfrac{C_u \left(\dfrac{(1+r_f) - d}{u - d} \right) + C_d \left(\dfrac{u - (1+r_f)}{u - d} \right)}{1 + r_f}.$

Define q as the "hedging probability":[10]

$q = \dfrac{(1+r_f) - d}{u - d} = \dfrac{(1+0.1) - 0.7}{1.2 - 0.7} = 0.8;$

$1 - q = \dfrac{u - (1+r_f)}{u - d} = \dfrac{1.2 - (1+0.1)}{1.2 - 0.7} = 0.2.$

We can then define the option price in a single-period model as

$$\boxed{C_0 = \dfrac{q \cdot C_u + (1-q)C_d}{1 + r_f}.}$$

Let's calculate the specific option price in our example:

$C_0 = \dfrac{q \cdot C_u + (1-q)C_d}{1 + r_f} = \dfrac{0.8 \cdot 1 + 0.2 \cdot 0}{1 + 0.1} = \$0.73.$

Indeed, a portfolio consisting of one share and five options meets the risk-free portfolio requirement:

---

10. The idea of defining the coefficients that multiply C_u and C_d in the developed equation as "probability" is due to the fact that their sum always equals 1, and so the expression matches a Bernoulli distribution. The fact that their sum is 1 does not represent probability in the classic sense of the word, that is, the chance of a certain event occurring, but is rather only a mathematical definition derived from the fact that it meets the mathematical requirement for "probability."

$$(1+r_f)(S-w\cdot C_0) \qquad = \qquad u\cdot S - w\cdot C_u$$

$$\downarrow \qquad\qquad\qquad\qquad \downarrow$$

$$(1+0.1)(10-5\cdot 0.73) = 1.1\cdot 6.35 = \$7 \qquad = \qquad 10\cdot 1.2 - 5\cdot 31 = \$7$$

Note that hedging probability q is completely unrelated to investors' subjective probability p that the share price will go up. It is related only to the share's up and down multipliers[11] and the risk-free interest rate.

Two-Period Model

For two consecutive increases, the share price will be

$u\cdot u\cdot S = 1.2\cdot 1.2\cdot 10 = \$14.40.$

For two consecutive decreases, the share price will be

$d\cdot d\cdot S = 0.7\cdot 0.7\cdot 10 = \$4.90.$

For an increase followed by a decrease (or vice versa),[12] the share price will be

$u\cdot d\cdot S = 1.2\cdot 0.7\cdot 10 = \$8.40.$

An investor buying the option at the start of the second period (end of the first), after the share price went up in the first period, will buy it at a price C_u. At the end of the second period, that investor's payoff would be the following:

• If the share price went up,[13] the investor would exercise the option for an expected payoff C_{uu} of $C_{uu} = u \cdot u \cdot S - X = 14.4 - 11 = \$3.10$.

• If the share price went down, the investor would not exercise the option, for an expected payoff C_{ud} of $C_{ud} = u \cdot d \cdot S - X < 0 \Rightarrow 0$.

We can now apply the single-period model initially to the first period, and again, separately, to the second period: $C_u = \dfrac{q\cdot C_{uu} + (1-q)C_{ud}}{1+r_f}$.

Likewise, an investor who buys the option at the start of the second period (end of the first), after the share price went down in the first

---

11. For example, derived from a historical average or future expectations. Note that the $u - d$ has a similar connotation as σ.

12. Note that we have only one result for *uu* or *dd*, but two possible scenarios with identical results for *ud* or *du*.

13. In the second period.

period, would buy it at a price of C_d. At the end of the second period, that investor's payoff C_{dd} (two decreases) and C_{du} (decrease and increase) would be $C_d = \dfrac{q \cdot C_{du} + (1-q)C_{dd}}{1+r_f}$.

Now let's apply the single-period model to the first period $C_0 = \dfrac{q \cdot C_u + (1-q)C_d}{1+r_f}$, and then apply our results for C_u and C_d so as to obtain a two-period pricing model:

$$C_0 = \frac{q^2 \cdot C_{uu} + 2 \cdot q \cdot (1-q) \cdot C_{du} + (1-q)^2 C_{dd}}{\left(1+r_f\right)^2}.$$

This process can easily be transformed into a computer algorithm yielding a numerical solution. However, we wish to develop Black and Scholes's equation, and will therefore seek a general model for n periods.

n-Period Model

For an investor holding an option (bought at a price of C_0), the probability of the share price going up m out of n times (periods) with a binomial distribution and a probability q is

$$B(m|n,q) = \frac{n!}{(n-m)!m!} \cdot q^m \cdot (1-q)^{(n-m)},$$

where q is the hedging probability for investors holding a risk-free portfolio.

After going up m times (thus going down $n - m$ times), the share price is $u^m \cdot d^{n-m} \cdot S$.

Option holders will exercise their options only when $u^m \cdot d^{n-m} \cdot S > X$.

For this to happen, the share price must go up some minimum number k of the times!

The mean payoff in these cases will be the product of:

• the probability of the share price going up exactly m times:

$$\frac{n!}{(n-m)!m!} \cdot q^m \cdot (1-q)^{(n-m)},$$

• and the return from each such event:

$$u^m \cdot d^{n-m} \cdot S - X.$$

Summing up all these events for which $m \geq k$:[14]

$$\sum_{m=k}^{n} \frac{n!}{(n-m)!m!} \cdot q^m \cdot (1-q)^{(n-m)} \left(u^m \cdot d^{n-m} \cdot S - X \right).$$

As the mean payoff is paid after n periods, it must be discounted[15] to the time of buying the option, in order to calculate its price:

$$C_0 = \frac{\displaystyle\sum_{m=k}^{n} \frac{n!}{(n-m)!m!} \cdot q^m \cdot (1-q)^{(n-m)} \left(u^m \cdot d^{n-m} \cdot S - X \right)}{(1+r_f)^n}.$$

The option's price in the multiperiod model is therefore

$$\boxed{\begin{aligned} C_0 &= \frac{S}{(1+r_f)^n} \cdot \sum_{m=k}^{n} \frac{n!}{(n-m)!m!} \cdot q^{.m} \, (1-q)^{n-m} \cdot u^m \cdot d^{n-m} \\ &+ \frac{X}{(1+r_f)^n} \cdot \sum_{m=k}^{n} \frac{n!}{(n-m)!m!} \cdot q^m \cdot (1-q)^{n-m} \end{aligned}}$$

Let's try to understand the meaning of this last equation. $\sum_{m=k}^{n} \frac{n!}{(n-m)!m!} \cdot q^m \cdot (1-q)^{n-m}$ is the *complementary* cumulative distribution function, that is, the probability of the option being in the money, and therefore being exercised.

$\sum_{m=k}^{n} \frac{n!}{(n-m)!m!} \cdot q^m (1-q)^{n-m} \times u^m \cdot d^{n-m}$ is therefore the weighted average of the share price multiplier only for cases in which the option is in the money.

When multiplied by $\frac{S}{(1+r_f)^n}$, the expression yields the mean (average) share price after n periods, discounted to the start of the period.

The first expression, $\frac{S}{(1+r_f)^n} \cdot \sum_{m=k}^{n} \frac{n!}{(n-m)!m!} \cdot q^m (1-q)^{n-m} \cdot u^m d^{n-m}$, is the mean (average) share price (after n periods) for those cases in which the option is in the money, discounted to the start of the period.

The expression $\frac{X}{(1+r_f)^n}$ is the exercise value, discounted to the start of the period.

---

14. For all other cases, the return is 0.

15. It is discounted using the risk-free interest rate, as in these cases the exercise price is lower than the share price, and so holders of the option will certainly exercise it.

The second expression, $\dfrac{X}{(1+r_f)^n}\cdot\sum_{m=k}^{n}\dfrac{n!}{(n-m)!m!}\cdot q^m\cdot(1-q)^{n-m}$, is the mean payment when exercising the option (after n periods) for those times when the option is in the money, discounted to the start of the period.

The option's price (at the start of the first period) C_0 is the difference between the mean share price and the mean payment when exercising the option (after n periods), both discounted to the start of the first period, and obviously only in those cases in which the option is in the money.[16]

Comparing the CRR Model with the Black-Scholes Model

The final result of Black-Scholes continuous model is as follows:

$$C_0 = S\cdot N(d_1) - X\cdot e^{-r_f\cdot T}\cdot N(d_2),$$

where

$$d_1 = \frac{\ln(S/X)+r_f T}{\sigma\sqrt{T}} + \frac{1}{2}\sigma\sqrt{T} \;\; ; \; d_2 = d_1 - \sigma\sqrt{T},$$

and $N(d)$ is taken from the standard normal distribution table.

To convert the CRR binomial option pricing model into the Black-Scholes continuous model, we must first define a standard time unit, for our purposes a year, and divide it into n events (periods), as in the binomial model. As $n\to\infty$, the binomial scenario becomes a continuous scenario.

In order not to limit our option expiration period by choosing a year as our standard time unit, we can delineate T as the number of standard units for the option's lifetime; for example, $T = 1.5$ for an 18-month option and $T = 0.25$ for a 91-day option.

Accordingly, all values in the resulting equations must conform to our choice of one year as the standard unit. Thus, r_{fc} is the *continuous* risk-free interest rate derived from the *annual*[17] risk-free rate r_f (this calculation was demonstrated[18] in chapter 3): $1+r_{fc} = e^{r_f}$.

16. Here we take into account that when an option is not in the money, its value is zero.

17. When the term structure of interest rates is not a straight line, we must reflect the annual interest rate in the interest paid on risk-free bonds traded for a similar period as the option, and only then convert it to a continuous rate. In principle, option prices are not particularly sensitive to interest rate changes, and small changes can be disregarded.

18. Where we had marked R_{ef} as the continuous interest rate.

The standard deviation calculation must also be annualized. As there are 253 trading days[19] in one year, $\sigma_{Year}^2 = 253 \cdot \sigma_{Day}^2$.

Now let's compare the equation derived by Black and Scholes with that developed by Cox, Ross, and Rubinstein for the binomial options pricing scenario.

We begin with the CRR equation:

$$C_0 = \frac{S}{(1+r_f)^n} \cdot \sum_{m=k}^{n} \frac{n!}{(n-m)!m!} \cdot q^m (1-q)^{n-m} \cdot u^m d^{n-m}$$

$$+ \frac{X}{(1+r_f)^n} \cdot \sum_{m=k}^{n} \frac{n!}{(n-m)!m!} \cdot q^m \cdot (1-q)^{n-m}.$$

We will define a new and "nameless"[20] probability g, where

$$g = \frac{u}{(1+r_f)} \cdot q \text{ and } 1-g = \frac{d}{(1+r_f)} \cdot (1-q).$$

Here, too, the definition of g as a probability is strictly derived from its mathematical properties, that is, $\frac{u}{(1+r_f)} \cdot q + \frac{d}{(1+r_f)} \cdot (1-q) = 1.$[21]

The first expression in the binomial equation for n periods in the CRR model can be rearranged as

$$\frac{S}{(1+r_f)^n} \cdot \sum_{m=k}^{n} \frac{n!}{(n-m)!m!} \cdot q^m (1-q)^{n-m} \cdot u^m \cdot d^{n-m}$$

$$= S \cdot \sum_{m=k}^{n} \frac{n!}{(n-m)!m!} \cdot \frac{u^m}{(1+r_f)^m} \cdot q^m \cdot \frac{d^{n-m}}{(1+r_f)^{n-m}} \cdot (1-q)^{n-m}$$

$$= S \cdot \sum_{m=k}^{n} \frac{n!}{(n-m)!m!} \cdot \left[\frac{u}{(1+r_f)} \cdot q\right]^m \cdot \left[\frac{d}{(1+r_f)} (1-q)\right]^{n-m}$$

$$= S \cdot \sum_{m=k}^{n} \frac{n!}{(n-m)!m!} \cdot g^m \cdot (1-g)^{n-m} = S \cdot B(m > k \mid n, g).$$

Substituting both q, the hedging probability, and g, our new probability,[22] into the CRR equation yields the following:

---

19. There are 253 independent events, each and all having the same distribution.

20. We did not give a name to this probability since its only use is to compare the Black-Scholes model with the CRR model, and it has no further practical application.

21. See for yourself: substitute q and (1 − q) as defined above.

22. Note that we are using the first term of the mathematical expression in g and the second term in q. These are purely mathematical exercises that only serve to allow us to compare the two models/expressions.

$$C_0 = \frac{S}{(1+r_f)^n} \cdot \sum_{m=k}^{n} \frac{n!}{(n-m)!m!} \cdot q^m (1-q)^{n-m} \cdot u^m d^{n-m}$$

$$+ \frac{X}{(1+r_f)^n} \cdot \sum_{m=k}^{n} \frac{n!}{(n-m)!m!} \cdot q^m \cdot (1-q)^{n-m}$$

$$= S \cdot \sum_{m=k}^{n} \frac{n!}{(n-m)!m!} \cdot g^m \cdot (1-g)^{n-m}$$

$$+ \frac{X}{(1+r_f)^n} \cdot \sum_{m=k}^{n} \frac{n!}{(n-m)!m!} \cdot q^m \cdot (1-q)^{n-m}$$

$$= S \cdot B(m > k \mid n, g) + \frac{X}{(1+r_f)^n} \cdot B(m > k \mid n, q).$$

In their work, Cox, Ross, and Rubinstein demonstrated that when $n \to \infty$, then

$$\frac{1}{(1+r_f)^n} = e^{-r_f \cdot T}$$

$$B(m > k \mid n, g) \quad \to \quad N(d_1),$$
$$B(m > k \mid n, q) \quad \to \quad N(d_2),$$

where

$$d_1 = \frac{\ln(S/X) + r_f T}{\sigma\sqrt{T}} + \frac{1}{2}\sigma\sqrt{T} \; ; \; d_2 = d_1 - \sigma\sqrt{T}.$$

Thus, we can rewrite the "continuous" binomial scenario in the CRR model as in the Black-Scholes model:

$$C_0 = S \cdot N(d_1) - X \cdot e^{-r_f \cdot T} \cdot N(d_2).$$

As mentioned previously, when Black and Scholes presented their work, it was difficult to interpret their mathematical expressions. Their work, however, can now be interpreted through the CRR model.

The first expression, $S \cdot N(d_1)$, is the mean (average) end-of-period share price only when the option is in the money, discounted to its start of period T value.

The second expression, $X \cdot e^{-r_f \cdot T} \cdot N(d_2)$, is the mean payment for exercising the option in those instances in which the option is in the money, discounted to its start of period T value.

C_0, the option price (in start-of-period T terms), is the difference between the mean share price and the mean payment for exercising the option after T periods, discounted to the start of period T, only when the option is in the money.[23]

In this way, we can also interpret $N(d_1)$ and $N(d_2)$:

$N(d_1)$ is the discounted average share price multiplier, for those occasions when the option is in the money.[24]

$N(d_2)$ is the cumulative probability that the option will be in the money and will therefore be exercised.[25]

Let's demonstrate this model through the following example.

You hold 50,000 shares in Meatball Inc., with a present share price of $S = \$2.60$. You wish to hedge against share price fluctuations in the next three months by issuing options. At your request, your investment consultant checked and found that the annualized continuous interest r_f (for the next three months) is 3%. The average daily change, σ_{Day}, in the share's price over the last year was 4.53% (a standard year has 253 trading days).

First we must translate the daily standard deviation σ_{Day} into annualized terms: $\sigma = \sigma_{Year} = 4.53 \times \sqrt{253} = 72\%$.

We will calculate the option's price[26] using three separate tables in MS Excel (each colored a different shade) for periods of $T = 0.2, 0.25,$ and 0.3, that is, the next 2.4, 3.0, and 3.6 months, respectively, and for changes in share price of 30%, 40%, and 50%, that is, $X/S = 1.3, 1.4,$ and $1.5,$ respectively:

---

23. Here we take into account that when an option is not in the money, its value is zero.

24. Similar to the expression $\dfrac{1}{(1+r_f)^n} \cdot \sum_{m=k}^{n} \dfrac{n!}{(n-m)!m!} \cdot q^m (1-q)^{n-m} \cdot u^m d^{n-m}$, the weighted average share multiplier, for those occasions when the option is in the money, discounted to the start of the period.

25. Similar to the expression $\sum_{m=k}^{n} \dfrac{n!}{(n-m)!m!} \cdot q^m \cdot (1-q)^{n-m}$, which is the complementary cumulative distribution function, that is, the probability that the option will be in the money and thus exercised.

26. According to the equation

$$C_0 = S \cdot N(d_1) - X \cdot e^{-r_f T} \cdot N(d_2)$$
$$d_1 = \frac{\ln(S/X) + r_f T}{\sigma\sqrt{T}} + \frac{1}{2}\sigma\sqrt{T} \quad ; \quad d_2 = d_1 - \sigma\sqrt{T}.$$

	T(Year) = 0.2			T(Year) = 0.25			T(Year) = 0.3		
	T(Month) = 2.4			T(Month) = 3			T(Month) = 3.6		
X/S	1.3	1.4	1.5	1.3	1.4	1.5	1.3	1.4	1.5
X^{27}	3.38	3.64	3.9	3.38	3.6	3.9	3.38	3.64	3.9
d_1	−0.635	−0.865	−1.08	−0.528	−0.703	−0.925	−0.445	−0.633	−0.808
d_2	−0.957	−1.187	−1.402	−0.888	−1.063	−1.285	−0.84	−1.028	−1.203
$N(d1)^{28}$	0.263	0.193	0.14	0.299	0.241	0.177	0.328	0.263	0.21
$N(d2)$	0.169	0.118	0.081	0.187	0.144	0.099	0.201	0.152	0.115
Pr/Op	0.1143	0.0776	0.0523	0.1485	0.1125	0.0767	0.1812	0.136	0.1018

The table indicates that as T increases, the option price goes up, and as X (or X/S) increases, the option price goes down, as expected.

Having calculated the option's prices under various different scenarios, the question is, what level of hedging do we apply to the portfolio? We saw that holding w options would result in a perfect, risk-free portfolio, but what is this w?

The option price in the multiperiod model is

$$C_o = \frac{S}{(1+r_f)^n} \cdot \sum_{m=k}^{n} \frac{n!}{(n-m)!m!} \cdot q^m \cdot (1-q)^{n-m} \cdot u^m \cdot d^{n-m}$$
$$+ \frac{X}{(1+r_f)^n} \cdot \sum_{m=k}^{n} \frac{n!}{(n-m)!m!} \cdot q^m \cdot (1-q)^{n-m}.$$

The change in option value ΔC caused by the change in share price ΔS alone is

$$\frac{\Delta C}{\Delta S} = \frac{1}{(1+r_f)^n} \cdot \sum_{m=k}^{n} \frac{n!}{(n-m)!m!} \cdot q^m (1-q)^{n-m} \cdot u^m d^{n-m} = Q.$$

If we want to hedge the portfolio so as to eliminate risk, then a portfolio comprised of Q_s shares requires Q_c options, and the portfolio's value would be $Q_s \cdot S - Q_c \cdot C$.

We know that, when moving from a period division of $n - 1$ periods to n periods, and when $n \to \infty$ (periods get progressively shorter), changes in such a portfolio's value should be negligible.[29]

27. This row is calculated from line X/S above, given that $S = 2.6$.

28. In Excel, the **NORMDSIT(Z)** function returns the standard cumulative distribution function for z.

29. Remember that this is for a fixed period T, which is simply divided into a larger number of Bernoulli trials.

$$Q_s \cdot \frac{\Delta S}{\Delta n} - Q_c \cdot \frac{\Delta C}{\Delta n} = 0$$

$$\Rightarrow \frac{\Delta S}{\Delta C} = \frac{1}{Q_c / Q_s} = Q \; ; \; \Rightarrow \frac{Q_c}{Q_s} = \frac{1}{Q}.$$

In a risk-free portfolio, each share ($Q_s = 1$) requires that we hold $w = Q_c$ options. Therefore, $w = \frac{1}{Q}$.

The expression denoted before by Q is the same one denoted by $N(d_1)$ in our comparison of the CRR binomial model with the Black-Scholes continuous model. Therefore, in the Black-Scholes continuous model,

$$w = \frac{1}{N(d_1)}.$$

If instead of w options we hold only one option for every share in the portfolio, then we have perfectly hedged (eliminated risk) only $1/w$ of the portfolio.

Therefore, $N(d_1)$ is also a measure of the "hedging ratio"—the percentage of a portfolio that is perfectly hedged (risk-free) by holding one option for every share in the portfolio.

Summary

In their article, Cox, Ross, and Rubinstein also demonstrated the connection between the parameters used in their binomial model and Black and Scholes's continuous model, that is,

$$u = e^{\sigma\sqrt{n/m}} \; ; \; d = e^{-\sigma\sqrt{n/m}}.$$

Knowing these parameters allows us to use an automated numerical model as demonstrated earlier.[30] Employing such a model (algorithm) on a small number of periods (e.g., $n = 20$) yields results that are very close to those derived from the continuous model. The CRR model seems redundant and too complex for practical applications compared with the Black-Scholes model. However, later in this chapter we'll see that the binomial model does have practical applications, in cases where the Black-Scholes model cannot be used directly owing to various constraints.

---

30. See the end of the two-period model.

C. Put Option Pricing

Put option prices can be determined using the straddle strategy for hedging against share-related risk, as discussed in chapter 18.[31] We'll examine a position that includes, in addition to a share, a call option and a put option on that share, with identical exercise prices X and expiration terms T. Both options are European options, which can only be exercised at the end of the period. Stoll (1969) demonstrated that in this case, we can determine a put option's price by knowing the call option's price, calculated as per the previous section. The connection between the two options' price is known as put-call parity.

The expected future results from such a position that includes one share, priced S_0, one call option, priced C_0, and one put option on that share (with identical X and T values), priced P_0,[32] can be classified into two scenarios:

1. The future share price is higher than the option's exercise price, $S \geq X$.
2. The future share price is lower than the option's exercise price, $S < X$.

The following table summarizes possible future results:

	$S \geq X$	$S < X$
Share value	S	S
Call option value	$-(S - X)$	0
Put option value	0	$(X - S)$
Total portfolio value	X	X

The final result, which is identical for all future scenarios, indicates that we are in fact holding a risk-free portfolio. The portfolio's end-of-period return must therefore match the risk-free interest rate for each period, to prevent arbitrage:

$$S_0 + P_0 - C_0 = \frac{X}{1 + r_f} .$$

Therefore, we can derive a put option's price from the put-call parity:[33]

$$P_0 = C_0 - \frac{S_0(1 + r_f) - X}{1 + r_f} .$$

---

31. A straddle strategy entails holding a call option and a put option with the same exercise price.

32. The period does not necessarily have to be one year.

33. Price S_0 is given, and price C_0 is given by the market or can be calculated.

Substituting the above for continuous conditions:

$$P_0 = C_0 - S_0 + X \cdot e^{-r_f \cdot T}.$$

The graphical description of call and put options presented in the previous chapter included the note, "The graph depicted is not accurate! It will be amended in the following chapter. This description is only intended to provide an understanding of the principle involved!"

We can now understand the amendment required for the graph, using a straddle strategy expecting a given moment t, when the exercise price (for both options) will be equal to the share's spot price $S = X$ ($30 in the example from chapter 16).

According to the table above, the naive value W for the two options will be zero. The value V at moment t results from the fact that the mean value derived from possible future changes in the share's price (after this specific point in time), for both call and put options, is greater than zero. Although both options have an identical exercise price X and expiration time T, according to the equation $C_0 = P_0 + \dfrac{r_f \cdot S_0}{1 + r_f}$, the call option's market price[34] C_t must also be greater than P_t, the put option's price at time t.[35]

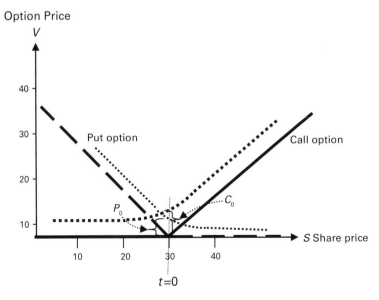

Figure 19.1
A Call Option Price C_t Is Always Greater Than the Same Put Option Price P_t

---

34. We are referring to market prices in absolute values! Remember that we are selling the call option and buying the put option.

35. Any given moment may be the "start" of a future period.

In contrast to European options, American options can be exercised at any time throughout their term. Pricing these options requires us to return to the CRR model, but this time for put options. Our previous example is no longer usable, as American put options cannot be issued at an exercise price that is higher than the share's spot price on issue, otherwise everyone would want to buy the option and exercise it immediately (arbitrage).

Therefore, we'll use the same scenario and method as in our call option pricing example but change the option's exercise price to $X = \$10$.

Single-Period Model for American Put Options

Denote   **Example**

S—The share price (binomial distribution) $S = \$10$
X—The option exercise price $X = \$10$
r_f—The risk-free rate $r_f = 10\%$
u—The share price multiplier when going up ($u > 1 + r_f$) $u = 1.2$
d—The share price multiplier when going down ($d < 1$) $d = 0.7$
P_0—The option price (value) at the start of the period

If the share price goes up, its expected value will be $u \cdot S = 1.2 \cdot 10 = \$12$.
If the share price goes down, its expected value will be $d \cdot S = 0.7 \cdot 20 = \$7$.

An investor who buys the option at the start of the period at a price of P_0 will record an end-of-period payoff (profit) calculated as follows.

If the share goes up: The investor will not exercise the option, and his expected payoff P_u will be: $P_u = X - u \cdot S < 0 \Rightarrow 0$.

If the share goes down: The investor will exercise the option, and his expected payoff P_d will be $P_d = X - d \cdot S = 10 - 7 = \$3$.

To build a risk-free portfolio, we must hold[36] a number of options, w, so as to record an identical payoff, whether the share goes up or down:

$$u \cdot S + w \cdot P_u = d \cdot S + w \cdot P_d$$
$$\Rightarrow w = \frac{S \cdot (u - d)}{P_d - P_u} = \frac{10(1.2 - 0.7)}{3 - 0} = 1.67.$$

This risk-free portfolio will therefore include 1.67 put options on each share.

---

36. As opposed to the call option pricing model, where we bought shares and sold call options, yielding a portfolio exercise value of $u \cdot S - w \cdot C$, in the put option pricing model, we buy both the share and the option, for an exercise value of $u \cdot S + w \cdot P$.

Let's calculate and check the portfolio payoff for our current example:
If the share goes up: $u \cdot S + w \cdot P_u = 10 \cdot 1.2 + 0 = \$12$.
If the share goes down: $d \cdot S + w \cdot P_d = 10 \cdot 0.7 + 1.67 \cdot 3 = \$12$.

The portfolio is risk-free as it yields an identical (certain) result of \$12 for both up and down scenarios! Since the portfolio is risk-free, its price (comprised of the share price plus w times the price of the options purchased), multiplied by the risk-free interest rate $(1 + r_f)$, must be equal to the portfolio's end-of-period value:

$$(1+r_f)(S+w \cdot P_o) = u \cdot S + w \cdot P_u$$

$$P_o = \frac{S[u-(1+r_f)] + w \cdot P_u}{w \cdot (1+r_f)}.$$

Substitute $w = \dfrac{S \cdot (u-d)}{P_d - P_u}$,

so that $P_o = \dfrac{P_u\left(\dfrac{(1+r_f)-d}{u-d}\right) + P_d\left(\dfrac{u-(1+r_f)}{u-d}\right)}{1+r_f}.$

The hedging probability q is[37]

$$q = \frac{(1+r_f)-d}{u-d} = \frac{(1+0.1)-0.7}{1.2-0.7} = 0.8;$$

$$1-q = \frac{u-(1+r_f)}{u-d} = \frac{1.2-(1+0.1)}{1.2-0.7} = 0.2.$$

The option price in a single-period model can be written as

$$P_o = \frac{q \cdot P_u + (1-q) \cdot P_d}{1+r_f}.$$

Calculating the specific option price in our example:

$$P_o = \frac{q \cdot P_u + (1-q) \cdot P_d}{1+r_f} = \frac{0.8 \cdot 0 + 0.2 \cdot 3}{1+0.1} = 0.545.$$

Two-Period Model for American Put Options

If the share goes up for two consecutive periods, its expected price is

---

37. This definition is identical to that for the call option hedging probability.

$u \cdot u \cdot S = 1.2 \cdot 1.2 \cdot 10 = \$14.40.$

If the share goes down for two consecutive periods, its expected price is

$d \cdot d \cdot S = 0.7 \cdot 0.7 \cdot 10 = \$4.90.$

If the share goes up and then down (or vice versa),[38] its expected price is

$u \cdot d \cdot S = 1.2 \cdot 0.7 \cdot 10 = \$8.40.$

An investor who buys the option at the start of the second period (end of the first), after the share went up in the first period, will buy the option at a price of P_u, and will record the following payoff at the end of the second period.

If it goes up,[39] the investor will not exercise the option, for an expected P_{uu} of

$P_{uu} = X - u \cdot u \cdot S = 10 - 14.4 < 0 \Rightarrow 0.$

If it goes down, the investor will exercise the option, for an expected P_{ud} payoff of

$P_{ud} = X - u \cdot d \cdot S = 10 - 8.4 = \$1.60.$

We can apply the single-period model employed for the first period, for the second period (only):

$$P_u = \frac{q \cdot P_{uu} + (1-q) \cdot P_{ud}}{1+r_f} = \frac{0.8 \cdot 0 + 0.2 \cdot 2.8}{1.1} = \$0.51.$$

Likewise, an investor who buys the option at the start of the second period (end of the first), after it went down in the first period, will buy the option at a price of P_d, and will record the following payoff:

Two consecutive decreases: $P_{dd} = X - d \cdot d \cdot S = 10 - 3.6 = \$6.40.$

A decrease followed by an increase:[40] $P_{du} = \$1.60.$

Therefore: $P_d = \dfrac{q \cdot P_{du} + (1-q) \cdot P_{dd}}{1+r_f} = \dfrac{0.8 \cdot 2.8 + 0.2 \cdot 5.1}{1.1} = \$2.96.$

---

38. Note that here too, we have only one result for *uu* or *dd* but two identical results for either *ud* or *du* scenarios.

39. In the second period.

40. $P_{ud} = P_{du}.$

It seems that, here too, the above process can easily be translated into an automated algorithm providing a specific numerical solution, as for call options. However, this is not the case.

In the two-period model, if the share price went down in the first period and we exercise the option at the end of the first period (start of the second), our expected payoff will be $X - d \cdot S = 10 - 7 = \$3.00$.

Whereas, if we continue to hold the option for the second period, its price at the start of the second period will be $P_d = \$2.96$.

Clearly,[41] it would be better to exercise the option at the end of the first period and not hold it for a second period (or exercise it and sell for $3 and buy a new one for $2.96).

This does not prevent us from deriving an automated algorithm from the above process. However, we will need to examine our results at each stage and exercise the option if it is not worthwhile holding it for an additional period.

The above leads us to three conclusions:

1. An investor holding an American put option may exercise it during its lifetime.[42]

2. An American put option's price will always be higher than a European put option's price issued under the same terms.

3. It is not possible to develop a general formula for pricing American options, only an algorithm providing a specific numerical solution.

D. Additional Applications of the Option's Model—Bonds

What sense could issuing options on bonds have, when in chapter 16 we saw how interest rate risks can be hedged without options? Our principal approach to determining option values/prices—that is, to building a risk-free portfolio[43]—is also applicable to a broad range of other problems that seem completely unrelated to options but nevertheless share the same principal approach. For example, some variable rate mortgages specify a maximum interest rate.[44] In this case, it is possible to use a

---

41. One can think of an example where the difference between the two possibilities is greater and more convincing. However, even this result is sufficient to reach the correct principal conclusion.

42. As we saw, an investor holding an American call option would have an incentive to hold it until expiration.

43. Whose return must be equal to the risk-free interest rate to prevent arbitrage.

44. The borrower will not be charged an interest rate exceeding that specified in the contract, even if the market interest rate exceeds this rate.

variation of the binomial option pricing model to calculate the bank's
required premium (above the risk-free rate), given the maximum interest
rate specified for the loan.[45] We used the option pricing model on bonds
to demonstrate that the basic approach is identical, even though at first
glance the expected payoff seems quite different:

1. While share prices diverge over time, bond prices converge toward a
bond's face value at maturity.

2. When interest rates increase, a bond's value decreases, and vice versa:
when rates decrease, a bond's value increases.

3. Most bonds pay coupons every period (as opposed to shares, where
we required zero dividend payments).

4. At the end of the final period n (at maturity), there is only one possible result (face value plus coupon). Since this result is certain, the call
option's value at the start of the last period (which is also the end of the
previous period) must be zero. Therefore, an option's lifetime must be at
least one period shorter than the underlying bond's lifetime.

To avoid repetition, we'll discuss only how the binomial model (which
has already been presented twice before) can be used to build an automated model. We'll use the same numbers from our previous examples
(although we will not calculate in full).

Denote	**Example**

r_f—The risk-free interest rate (binomial distribution) — $r_f = 10\%$

p—The probability that r_f will go up — $p = 0.5$

u—The interest rate's upward multiplier — $u = 1.2$

d—The interest rate's downward multiplier — $d = 0.7$

R—The periodic coupon payment

B_n—The (expected) bond price at the end of period n

$$B_n = \frac{p \cdot B_{n+1}^u + (1-p) \cdot B_{n+1}^d + R}{(1+r_f)}$$

C_n—The value of a call option written on that bond, at the
end of period n

C_n^u—The value of a call option at the end of period n after
the bond's value went up in period n

C_n^d—The value of a call option at the end of period n after
the bond's value went down in period n

---

45. The cash flow will be identical to that of an ordinary mortgage loan plus issuing a call
option with an exercise price as per the maximum interest rate.

Again, we'll build a risk-free portfolio by issuing[46] w call options on each bond in our portfolio, so as to obtain an identical payoff in any given scenario:

$$B_n^d + R - w \cdot C_n^d = B_n^u + R - w \cdot C_n^u$$

$$\Rightarrow w = \frac{B_n^d - B_n^u}{C_n^d - C_n^u}.$$

As the result is certain, the expected payoff at the end of the period is discounted, using the risk-free rate, and is equal to the portfolio's start-of-period value:

$$B_n + R - w \cdot C_n = \frac{B_{n+1}^d + R - w \cdot C_{n+1}^d}{1 + r_{f,n}}.$$

Substitute the above w value (adjusted for period $n + 1$):

$$C_n = \frac{\left[B_{n+1}^d + R - \left(1 + r_{f,n}\right) \cdot B_n\right] \cdot C_{n+1}^u - \left[B_{n+1}^u + R - \left(1 + r_{f,n}\right) \cdot B_n\right] \cdot C_{n+1}^d}{\left(B_{n+1}^d - B_{n+1}^u\right) \cdot \left(1 + r_{f,n}\right)}.$$

Again, we can obviously build a recursive computer algorithm for the above process, to calculate a numerical solution. This algorithm starts from an option's expiration date (remember, one period before the bond's maturity) and works backward until it calculates the loan value at the grant date, C_0.

Many attempts have been made, and many more will be made, to apply the principle behind the option-pricing model to other fields. The option pricing model is the only model so far that relates "the cost of risk" to "time" (expiration). The mean-variance model and CAPM do not account for time.

This section seeks to spark the reader's imagination about the possibilities offered by the principle and applications of building a risk-free portfolio in arbitrage-free markets, on which the option pricing model is based, as a basis for a variety of other uses.

E. Structured Product Pricing

New financial instruments are currently being introduced in the capital markets under the generic term "structured products." These securities

---

46. The payoff will be negative.

are actually bonds issued by existing financial institutions that guarantee a much higher rate of return than the market average. This excess return is contingent on (limited to) minor events with rare probability.[47]

This section serves two purposes:

1. To explain the risks involved in these products (which are often wrongly marketed as "risk-free"); and

2. To demonstrate how such instruments can be priced as a combination of the fundamental pricing models discussed so far.

We will explain this topic through the following examples.

Commerzbank, a large, reputable German bank,[48] offered 15-year bonds at a contingent interest rate of 7.5% (three times the risk-free market rate at that time!), paid quarterly pro rata according to the number of days in the quarter in which the USD LIBOR rate was below 7% (otherwise, no interest was paid). The issuer was also granted an early repayment option at the end of each quarter.

This instrument belongs to a family of structured products known as "range notes." In other words, their return depends on the underlying asset[49] (in our case, the USD LIBOR) staying in a given range (in our case, 0–7%). The financial instrument is clearly not risk-free, and we can use the models at our disposal to price the interest premium required in addition to the (risk-free, for our purposes) USD LIBOR rate.

First, the instrument is subject to the "regular" bond-related risks discussed in the first part of this book. These include a default premium, as the product was issued by a commercial bank and not the U.S. government. As discussed in chapter 5, we can calculate the default premium by comparison with other instruments on the market, such as the default premium charged for regular 15-year bonds issued by the same (or similar) bank.

Second, we can use the option models to calculate the premium required as a result of a maximum interest rate condition, as demonstrated in the previous section. Note that in this case, the instrument would not pay the maximum interest rate but 0%!

Third, we can calculate the liquidity premium, which will be the weighted average of the probability that the interest rate on the underly-

---

47. In principle, this is legitimate.
48. With an A credit rating.
49. The underlying asset is actually a 15-year risk-free bond.

ing asset will exceed 7%, which means, highly unmarketable, that is, a liquidity premium required on a virtually zero-liquidity bond, with a "regular" liquidity premium.[50]

After calculating all the above, we can also calculate and add the price of the early repayment option granted the issuer, measured as a required return premium.

We started by saying that the instrument in the above example was marketed as an alternative to a risk-free bond,[51] and demonstrated this claim to be false. Investors' losses would include both losses through lower returns and possible losses on invested capital. In addition to the risk of the issuer's default within the next 15 years[52] and the risk of inability to cash the bond during those 15 years (even if it was certain to be repaid at the end of the period),[53] there was always the risk that, during the 15 years, the market interest rate could have exceeded 7%, at which time the bond would have yielded a 0% return (as per its terms). We've already discussed how to calculate the capital loss on a bond when the bond interest coupon is lower than the market interest rate.

Below is another example of a structured bond, with a share as an underlying asset.

A well-established financial-sector company[54] issued one-year bonds with a contingent return of 17%. The underlying asset was SanDisk shares,[55] traded at $47.20 at the bond's issue date. The condition: if, during the bond's lifetime, the share price dropped below $28.30 (–40%), investors would receive only part of their initial investment, prorated to the share price at that time and its price at the bond's issue date.

This was effectively a "reverse convertible"[56] bond—its return was limited to 17%, while its loss was equal to that on the share.[57]

---

50. These instruments' marketability is several orders of magnitude smaller than that of U.S. government bonds.

51. This is how it is usually promoted by people charged with marketing and distributing it on the capital market.

52. This is a very long time, and even a reliable A-rated company may experience difficulties.

53. And the need to lower its sale price significantly so that people will still want to buy it.

54. As the company has an AA rating, the chance of a default in the next year is small and negligible.

55. SanDisk is a market leader in the development and manufacture of flash memory modules for electronic appliances.

56. Ordinary convertible bonds have a "minimum" return, and potential earnings are unlimited if the share price exceeds the conversion price.

57. In case of losses of more than 40%.

A statistical examination of the share's historical data indicates that the share had a 5% probability of shedding more than 40% of its value in one year. The historical data can be used to numerically calculate the probability distribution for a price drop of more than 40%. However, as the calculation is based on sample data, it would be more accurate to use the tail of a standard normal distribution, based on the fact that 95% of the events (returns) are higher than a negative return of –40%.

Another option for calculating the price for the above bond is to build a portfolio that yields a similar return, using option pricing methods: Let's assume that we hold such a bond, and buy w put options on SanDisk[58] for each bond, so that the portfolio yields the same return as a risk-free bond (the other side of the equation). We can perform the calculation based on the price of put options traded on the market (if there are no –40% options, we can use the closest options available), or calculate specifically, as demonstrated in the previous sections. Either way, such a calculation exceeds the scope of this book. Therefore, we have only demonstrated the approach underlying the solution, without going into full details.

Finally, there are three things to remember when discussing risk trading:

1. In principle, risk trading is designed to reduce risk. Issuing entities should not incur risk (which is not always the case in practice) but should only serve as intermediaries, earning brokerage fees! The German bank in the above example was (apparently) seeking to cover itself against a risky position created during the ordinary course of business. The financial institution in the second example was seeking to hedge a risk incurred in the course of business, and cover itself against any decrease of more than 40% in SanDisk's share price, incurred through put options (apparently) issued[59] at a customer's request (for which he paid the option price plus profit).

2. Hedge funds usually hold financial assets based on strategies similar to those discussed above. Apparently, as the chance of a negative scenario is very small, it would be easy to build a diversified portfolio yielding a high return. However, if some of these assets are highly correlated with a particular (rare) market event, it is possible for a large number of

---

58. Buying/holding these bonds is equivalent to issuing (selling) put options.

59. If prices drop, bondholders will bear the results, and if not, the bank will have to pay them the return on the bonds. Note that the bank can invest the proceeds from the bonds in standard bonds, thereby reducing the cost of returns payments to bondholders.

the assets to collapse at the same time, if and when such an event occurs. Such a scenario led to the collapse of hedge funds managed (or consulted) by leading capital market experts. Remember, even if statistically the odds of a particular event are extremely low, if that event does occur, the catastrophic consequences would account for 100% of the affected parties' results.

3. There is no free lunch! The fact that it is difficult to calculate the risk and premium required on a structured product does not mean that its higher return does not come with risk. On the contrary: as uncertainty increases owing to the lack of accurate calculations, a greater premium is required. In any case, structured securities portfolio management is best left to the experts (who are themselves not invulnerable). The risk in these portfolios is significant, and investors should account for that fact in their utility functions.

F. An Empirical Review

The Black-Scholes model was first presented in 1973, and the first empirical studies of that model were performed by Black and Scholes themselves. Since then many studies have been carried out, using a variety of different methods. It is noted that the Black-Scholes model provides a calculation formula that is particularly astonishing in what it *does not* include:

1. It is not dependent on the expected return on the underlying asset but only on its variance. In the binomial model, it is not dependent on the probability of an increase/decrease in the underlying asset's price but only on the price multiplier (conceptually equivalent to variance).

2. It is not dependent on an individual's utility function.

The reason for this surprising result is that the model is based on building a perfectly hedged portfolio—a portfolio comprised of two assets where by definition the price of one asset is determined by the price of the other (the underlying asset). Once these two assets can be combined to build a portfolio that yields an identical result in any scenario, its price must be equal to the price of a risk-free bond portfolio, to avoid arbitrage. Conceptually, such a portfolio indeed does not depend on the behavior of the underlying asset's price (which mathematically and functionally defines the other asset's price) or on an individual's utility function.

CAPM defines a risk-free asset as one whose correlation with the market portfolio must be zero. In other words, when tested empirically, a perfectly hedged portfolio's β should not be significantly different (statistically speaking) from zero. Most empirical studies actually were based on the concept of building a perfectly hedged portfolio, where the connection between the two portfolio assets (the underlying asset and the option) is based on Black and Scholes's formula.

Before conducting empirical studies, it is necessary to discuss possible reasons for findings not coinciding with the model, so as to try and neutralize these factors. These possible reasons (besides the possibility that the model is simply wrong) can be classified into two main categories:

1. The first is general. The market is not perfect. We know ahead of time that the market is not perfect and includes (among other things) taxes and transaction costs. If results do not support our model, we need to adjust for transaction costs. This adjustment is relatively simple, and only if our results still do not support the model will we check the basis for our assumption that taxes are uniform for all types of securities and that they do not affect net payoff.[60]

2. The parameters we use in calculating the Black-Scholes formula might not be accurate enough. In chapter 18 we discussed five parameters affecting an option's value: the continuous price of the underlying share, the continuous variance of the share price, the exercise price, the time remaining until the option expires, and the continuous risk-free interest rate. Only one parameter, the continuous variance of the share price, is not directly given but must be calculated. This raises two problems (actually, the same problem from different angles): Should we use the historical variance known on buying the option at t_0 (ex-ante), that is, known variance; or should we account for the actual variance recorded during the option's lifetime and measured at the end of the period T (ex-post), so that an investor who bought the option should have predicted it when buying the option (i.e., predicted variance)? Because the predicted variance differs from the known variance, in calculating a portfolio's average return (through statistical analysis of historical data), should we account for variance changes during the option's lifetime and correct the w ratio (between the number of shares and the number of options in the portfolio) dynamically so that the portfolio remains perfectly hedged con-

---

60. As in our discussion of corporate capital structure.

tinuously? Or should we maintain a constant ratio, calculated when buying the option at time t_0?

As discussed previously, most studies have examined whether the β of a perfectly hedged portfolio, constructed according to the Black-Scholes formula, is significantly different from zero. Furthermore, studies have examined whether such a portfolio can be arbitraged against a risk-free portfolio traded on the market, when the options in the portfolio were bought at a time when their market price was lower than calculated using the Black-Scholes formula and sold when their share price was higher than calculated using the formula.

The conclusions were as follows:

1. The perfectly hedged portfolio's β is not significantly different (statistically) from zero. This result was also observed when w was chosen at t_0 and remained constant throughout the option's lifetime.

2. Using predicted variance yields better results than using known variance. In other words, in determining an option's price, people take into consideration more than the variance of the underlying share's price at that point in time.

3. Excessive returns can be obtained through arbitrage, as described above. However, as they are less than 1%, transaction costs do not allow their translation into real profit.

4. Option prices calculated by the Black-Scholes model are on average lower than option prices on the market when they are in the money and higher, on average, when they are out of the money.

5. The difference between the calculated price and the actual market price, as detailed in section 4 above, increases as the time to expiration decreases.

Conclusion: The assumption that the market does not allow arbitrage[61] was found to be empirically true. This assumption is absolutely paramount as a principal concept.

No definitive answer was found to the question of whether the difference between the calculated price and the actual market price, as detailed in item 4 above, is the result of faulty statistical analysis or of the need for a more finely tuned model. When no suitable assets (options) are available on the market that can be used to directly obtain price data,

61. In practical economic forms.

the model provides a reasonable price estimate for practical purposes of the option's value (not necessarily its market price).

Chapter 19 — Questions and Problems

Question 1

Assume a binomial model for two periods. A share's price at time zero is $100, and can increase or decrease by 20% each period. The risk-free interest rate is 1% per period.

a. Calculate the price of a European call option and a European put option with an exercise price of $110.

b. Repeat part (a) for an exercise price of $90.

Question 2

A share is traded at $7. Using historical data regarding the relative daily change in the share's price[62] in the past six months, you calculated a daily standard deviation of 0.0445. The (annual) risk-free interest rate is 6%. According to the Black-Scholes formula, what is the calculated value of a six-month European call option with an exercise price of $10?

Question 3

A share is traded at $10. You calculated the annual standard deviation of the continuous relative change in the share's price as 0.5. The risk-free interest rate is 6%. Using the Black-Scholes formula, what is the calculated value of a six-month European put option with an exercise price of $10?

Question 4

We demonstrated that $C_0 = f\{(S - X), T, r_f, \sigma\}$. Define an option price's sensitivity to parameter changes as follows:

Delta Δ   The change in an option's price caused by a (small) change in the share price: $\Delta = \dfrac{\partial C}{\partial S} = N(d_1)$.

---

62. "Relative change in share price" and "return" are two names for the same expression, $\dfrac{P_{t+1} - P_t}{P_t}$.

More interesting is to calculate the percentage change in an option's price caused by a 1% change in share price: $\dfrac{\frac{\partial C}{C}}{\frac{\partial S}{S}} = \dfrac{\partial C}{\partial S} \cdot \dfrac{S}{C} = N(d_1) \cdot \dfrac{S}{C}$.

Theta θ The change in an option's price caused by a (small) change in its expiration time:[63] $\theta = \dfrac{\partial C}{\partial T}$.

Rho ρ The change in a share's price caused by a (small) change in the risk-free interest rate: $\rho = \dfrac{\partial C}{\partial r_f}$.

Vega v The change in an option's price caused by a (small) change in the standard deviation: $v = \dfrac{\partial C}{\partial \sigma}$.

Except for Δ, which has a simple mathematical expression, the best way to calculate the change in an option's price is using MS Excel, reducing the option period by one day ($T \approx -0.003$), or increasing/decreasing the risk-free rate by 1%, or increasing/decreasing the return's standard deviation by 1%.[64]

a. Calculate an option price's sensitivity to its various parameters using the data from question 2.

b. How should the parameters affect an option's price when it is deep in the money/deep outside the money and as its expiration period gets shorter?

Question 5

This question is designed to demonstrate the practical application of option-based hedging:

a. What is the principle underlying the call option pricing model?

b. Using the data from question 2, how many options should an investor hold in a portfolio, including the underlying share, to construct a risk-free portfolio?

---

63. The expiration period grows shorter with every passing day.

64. A 1% increase in the risk-free interest rate is considered very large under ordinary market conditions, while an increase in the annual standard deviation of the relative share price is not considered particularly large. Indicative values are $r_f = 5\%$; $\sigma = 50\%$; that is, σ is one order of magnitude greater than r_f.

c. Using the data from question 1, how many options should an investor hold at the start of the first period in order to build a risk-free portfolio for the end of the first period? How many options should an investor hold at the start of the second period in order to build a risk-free portfolio for the end of the second period? Demonstrate that the portfolio is indeed risk-free at each stage.

d. What can you conclude about option-based hedging according to the Black-Scholes formula in part (a) above?

Question 6

The option pricing model has many uses. This question demonstrates its application in calculating the market value of a company's debt capital.

Assume that a company has risky zero-coupon[65] bonds with a market value B (the debt's face value is D), which are guaranteed by the company's assets. The debt (including interest payments) is paid at the end of period T, and so bankruptcy claims can be made only at the end of the period. As discussed in chapter 14, if the market value of the company's shares is S, then the company's market value is $V = S + B$.

In question 10 of chapter 18, we demonstrated that buying a share S (or for our present purposes, any risky asset) and a put option on that share (or that risky asset), and selling a call option on that share (or risky asset), where both options have the same exercise time T and where the exercise price is equal to the share price $S = X$, we will obtain the same result as holding a risk-free zero-coupon bond D where $S + P - C = D$.

Using the end-of-period payment schedule for shareholders and bondholders, and for scenarios where asset values at the end of the period are either higher or lower than the debt $V \leq D; V > D$, demonstrate that the following:

a. A leveraged company's shares can be considered an option on that company's value (Black and Scholes 1973). In other words, the share price S is actually a call option on the company's assets V left over at the end of the period (after payment of the company's debt).

b. Using part (a) above and the equation $S + P - C = D$, demonstrate that the risky debt's value B is equivalent to the risk-free debt's value D plus the sale of a put option on the company's assets.

---

65. This is not a common type of bond, but it is interesting as a theoretical discussion demonstrating possible applications of the option pricing model.

Question 7

Use your conclusions from the previous question. The market value of a utilities company is $3 billion, and their continuous annual standard deviation is 40%.[66] The company financed its assets through a zero-coupon bond with a face value of $2 billion, with interest and principle to be repaid in nine years. Assume that the company does not distribute dividends.[67] The risk-free interest rate is 4%.

a. Calculate the value of the company's shares as a call option on its assets.

b. What is the market value of the company's debt?

c. How would the company's share value and debt value change if the risk-free rate increased to 6%? Explain the significance of your results.

Question 8

a. Calculate the prices of three-month Call(1800) and Put(1800) options on an 1800-point Dow Index if the risk-free interest rate is 8% and the annual standard deviation is 70%.

b. In New York, the Dow closed at 1800 points. The following day in Tokyo (well before the start of trading in the United States), options were traded, as follows—Call(1800) = $254, and Put(1800) = $238. What is the rate of increase/decrease that the Tokyo market expects for the Dow Index on the following day of trading in New York? What happened to the gap between these two options as compared with part (a)?

c. The Chicago Board Options Exchange Volatility Index (CBOE VIX)[68] reflects market expectations concerning short-term volatility (next 60 days). Originally, the index was measured by the average standard deviation of in-the-money put and call option pairs on the S&P 500 index, from the present month, as compared to pairs from next month. Later, the VIX was changed to include a wider range of exercise prices X and

---

66. This is equivalent to saying that the continuous annualized standard deviation of the r_A return on the company's assets is 40%.

67. As mentioned earlier, the model can be modified for call options so as to allow for dividend payments. Utilities companies usually distribute a fixed dividend.

68. The CBOE Volatility Index was developed in 1993 and measures expectations for σ volatility (as opposed to measured historical volatility). Its lowest level, 9.48, was recorded in December 1994. Its average value between 1990 and 2008 was around 19 points, and peaked at 89.53 points during the credit crunch in late October 2008. The VIX index itself is used as an underlying asset for both put and call options.

not only options which are in the money. Explain the logic behind the CBOE VIX, based on the previous sections in this question.

Question 9

a. In developing the pricing model for American put options, we concluded that an American option's price must always be higher than that of a European option. Explain why.

b. A company is about to issue new one-year options. Currently, an older series of one-year options is traded on the market. In pricing these options, should the company use the historical variance or the expected variance according to the previous option series currently on the market? Explain.

c. In chapter 18, we demonstrated how risk trading (e.g., currencies) is a win-win situation that inherently increases the utility of both parties to a transaction. Explain how, in capital market risk trading, option writers and option buyers are in a win-win situation even though one party's loss is the other's gain (in both cases we are ignoring speculator trading).

Question 10

We demonstrated how American options can be priced using a multiperiod model. We also demonstrated that scenarios are possible in which the expected payoff from exercising an option at the end of a certain period will be higher than the option's calculated price for the start of the next period (according to the expected results for this next period), and so the option should be exercised.

a. Find the minimum share price for which it is clearly worthwhile to exercise the option for the continuous case as well.

b. Use your conclusions from the above to explain (in addition to the mathematical explanation provided in this chapter) why put option prices should be lower than those of call options with the same parameters (i.e., even when the chances for an increase or decrease are identical).

Further Reading

Ball, C. A., and W. N. Torous. 1984. The Maximum Likelihood Estimation of Security Price Volatility: Theory, Evidence and Application to Option Pricing. *Journal of Business* (January).

Benninga, S., R. Steinmetz, and J. Stroughair. 1993. Implementing Numerical Option Pricing Models. *Mathematica Journal* 3.

Black, F., and M. Scholes. 1973. The Pricing of Options and Corporate Liabilities. *Journal of Political Economy* (May/June): 637–654.

Blomeyer, E. C., and H. Johnson. 1988. An Empirical Examination of the Pricing of American Put Options. *Journal of Financial and Quantitative Analysis* (March).

Boyle, P., and A. L. Anathanarayanan. 1977. The Impact of Variance Estimation in Option Valuation Models. *Journal of Financial Economics* (December).

Brenner, M., G. Courtadon, and M. Subrahmanyam. 1985. Options on the Spot and Options on Futures. *Journal of Finance* (December): 1303–1317.

Brenner, M., and D. Galai. 1984. On Measuring the Risk of Common Stocks Implied by Options Prices: A Note. *Journal of Financial and Quantitative Analysis* (December).

Capozza, D., and B. Cornell. 1979. Treasury Bill Pricing in the Spot and Futures Markets. *Review of Economics and Statistics* (November): 513–520.

Chang, J. S. K., and L. Shanker. 1987. Option Pricing and the Arbitrage Pricing Theory. *Journal of Financial Research* (Spring).

Courtadon, G. 1982. The Pricing of Options on Default-Free Bonds. *Journal of Financial and Quantitative Analysis* (March).

Cox, J. C., and S. A. Ross. 1976. The Valuation of Options for Alternative Stochastic Processes. *Journal of Financial Economics* 3:145–166.

Cox J. C., S. A. Ross, and M. Rubinstein. 1979. Option Pricing: A Simplified Approach. *Journal of Financial Economics* 7: 229-263.

Cox, J. C., and M. Rubinstein. 1985. *Options Markets*. Englewood Cliffs, NJ: Prentice-Hall.

Evnine, J., and A. Rudd. 1985. Index Options: The Early Evidence. *Journal of Finance* (July).

Fischer, S. 1978. Call Option Pricing When the Exercise Price Is Uncertain, and the Valuation of Index Bonds. *Journal of Finance* (March).

Galai, D., and R. W. Masulis. 1976. The Option Pricing Model and the Risk Factor of Stock. *Journal of Financial Economics* (March): 53–82.

Geske, R. 1977. The Valuation of Corporate Liabilities as Compound Options. *Journal of Financial and Quantitative Analysis* 12: 541–552.

Geske, R., and H. E. Johnson. 1984. The American Put Option Valued Analytically. *Journal of Finance* (December).

Geske, R., and R. Roll. 1984. On Valuing American Call Options with the Black-Scholes European Formula. *Journal of Finance* (June).

Grinblatt, M., and H. Johnson 1988. A Put Option Paradox. *Journal of Financial and Quantitative Analysis* (March).

Latane, H. A., and R. J. Rendleman, Jr. 1976. Standard Deviations of Stock Price Ratios Implied on Option Prices. *Journal of Finance* (May).

MacBeth, J. D., and L. J. Melville. 1980. Tests of the Black-Scholes and Cox Call Options Valuation Models. *Journal of Finance* (May).

Martin, D. W., and D. W. French. 1987. The Characteristics of Interest Rates and Stock Variances Implied in Option Prices. *Journal of Economics and Business* (August).

McDonald, R., and D. Siegel. 1984. Option Pricing When the Underlying Asset Earns a Below Equilibrium Rate of Return: A Note. *Journal of Finance* (March).

Merton, R. C. 1973. Theory of Rational Option Pricing. *Bell Journal of Economics and Management Science* 4: 141–183.

O'Brien, T. 1988. Portfolio Insurance Mechanics. *Journal of Portfolio Management* (Spring).

Omberg, E. 1987. A Note on the Convergence of Binomial-Pricing and Compound-Option Models. *Journal of Finance*: 42.

Paskov, S. H. 1997. New Methodologies for Valuing Derivatives. In *Dempster Mathematics of Derivative Securities*, eds. S. Pliska and M. Dempster, 545–582. Cambridge, UK: Isaac Newton Institute and Cambridge University Press.

Perrakis, S., and P. Ryan. 1984. Option Pricing Bounds in Discrete Time. *Journal of Finance* (June).

Pye, G. 1966. The Value of a Call Option on a Bond. *Journal of Political Economy* (April): 200–205.

Rendleman, R. J., Jr., and R. W. McNally. 1987. Assessing the Costs of Portfolio Insurance. *Financial Analysts Journal* (May/June).

Rubinstein, M. 1984. A Simple Formula for the Expected Rate of Return of an Option over a Finite Holding Period. *Journal of Finance* (December).

Schmalensee, R., and R. R. Trippi. 1978. Common Stock Volatility Expectations Implied by Option Premia. *Journal of Finance* (March).

Stapelton, R. C., and M. G. Strahmanyan. 1984. The Valuation of Options When Asset Returns Are Generated by a Binomial Process. *Journal of Finance* (December).

20 Summary, Insights, and Further Study

A. Summary
B. Insights
C. Further Study

A. Summary

A financial asset is a piece of paper granting its holder contractual ownership rights over a future cash flow C_t, which may consist of interest, dividends, or the sale of the asset itself. The last case requires the buyer and the seller to assess the asset's present value at the time of sale. The basic financial asset valuation model is founded on discounting the future cash flow using a discount rate k, the cost of capital, which is defined as the present value of $1 expected to be received at a given future time (day, month, year). The cost of capital is determined by the duration until payment is received $\equiv$ the time value, and the probability of receiving the payment, also called the risk value (premium).

In this book, we have discussed fundamental concepts and models for valuing bonds, shares, and their derivative financial assets. The aphorism that for every complex problem there is a solution that is simple, clear, and wrong serves as a fitting conclusion to this book. The paradigm of using a mathematical model to try to correlate real-world measurements with mathematical formulas so as to reach conclusions about expected future results (even if these are not intuitive) relates better to physics research, where phenomena have a small number of measured parameters. Not all physics models are as deterministic as those of classical mechanics. Some models apply statistical tools based on the law of large numbers to the measured data, and make excellent predictions. In physical phenomena, where each of a large number of subelements (molecules, electrons, etc.) participates *absolutely randomly* in the process, their *joint behaviors still have a systematic outcome*. The modern financial models discussed in this book try to replicate this concept in the field of economics.

The assumption that the unpredictable and therefore random individual behaviors of a large number of capital market participants together form a strict system with defined rules that can be used to predict process outcomes has proved to be only partially true.

This way of thinking flourished during the final decade of the twentieth century. Mathematicians and physicists were recruited by leading financial entities to develop mathematical models, which were then applied using supercomputers. The weaknesses of this approach became evident toward the end of the first decade of the twenty-first century, with the onset of the largest financial crisis since the Great Depression. In the real world, where the capital market operates, the number of measurable parameters is staggering. We can only search for approximate, adequate solutions, with what is "adequate" being determined by our own preferences. The models presented in this book assume uncertainty in the short term, which is characterized by narrow-variance fluctuations around a steady state, but do not account for chaotic movements. Economists refer to these chaotic phenomena as "business cycles" or "bubbles"; they occur when the steady state around which the market fluctuates is slowly shifted owing to normal (Gaussian) statistical behavior or non-normal (or perhaps normal?) human behavior to the point that the entire system becomes unstable. The system is brought back to the normal steady state chaotically, in a way that is not reflected in the models discussed in this book. It should be remembered that even in nonchaotic conditions, we are still applying statistical models. As discussed in the first chapter of this book, understanding the advantages and disadvantages of probabilistic models is paramount to properly using financial models. Even if the probability of losing 90% or more of our investment is only a thousandth of a thousandth of a percent, it is still present, and if the event does occur, it will account for 100% of the future result!

However, this book seeks to provide means for conceptualizing financial ideas and to present fundamental models in finance theory in a holistic manner. As an introductory-level book, it does not presume to provide an exhaustive discussion but only to present the relevant topics at their basic level. Later in this chapter we review the rationale common to all the various models presented in this book and discuss the important insights gained and the problems left unsolved. We endorse practical ways to apply the models, being attentive not only to their benefits but also to their limitations, all so as to transform the theories discussed in this book into practical, usable tools.

B. Insights

1. Net Present Value

The basic definition on which all the other models are based is the discount rate k, which we termed the cost of capital. In the first part of this book we discussed the effect of time on the cost of capital as congruent with the time value of money, while the second part of the book discussed the effect of risk on the cost of capital as congruent with the risk value (premium). In such a model, the present value (PV) of a financial asset that is expected to yield a future net cash flow[1] C_t can be calculated using the equation

$$PV = \sum_{t=1}^{n} \frac{C_t}{(1+k)^t}.$$

The net present value (NPV) for investors is the difference between the market price P that must be paid for a financial asset and its calculated PV: $NPV = P - PV$.

When we finance a business under our direct, private, and exclusive ownership, then clearly we must discount the net cash flow generated by that business when calculating its value. Once a business is incorporated, financed, and owned indirectly through shares and bonds, then (as demonstrated by Modigliani and Miller) the manner of incorporation does not affect the way in which owners calculate the business's acquisition or sale value. Owners look neither at dividends, which are determined arbitrarily by the board of directors, nor at earnings, which are determined by accounting principles and tax laws (and which are identical to gains calculated using the dividend model). Instead, when valuing a company, owners examine its net cash flow, exactly as though it were under their individual, exclusive ownership. The company's value is distributed among its debtholders and shareholders according to its capital structure and the risk incurred by each capital holder.

---

1. "Net cash flow" refers to the actual inflows to the financial asset owner.

At first glance, the use of the market model's β risk measure in calculating NPV seems self-contradictory. We use a risk-adjusted discount rate determined by the market (i.e., located on the market line), and the asset price P is also determined by the market. The asset price P is by definition equal to the cash flow discounted using the risk-adjusted discount rate, and so NPV will by definition be zero. However, we must remember that the model is an equilibrium model. Not every asset in the market is in equilibrium at all times, and, as demonstrated earlier, shares may not be located on the market line. Projects also may not be located on the market line, and thus both investors in stocks and managers seeking projects for investment are required to identify and seize these opportunities.

2. Risk Measures

When a future cash flow is uncertain, we can no longer refer to anticipated returns but only to expected (mean) returns. Two financial assets with an identical mean return are still differentiated by their individual risk levels. The definition of risk is not only a question of measurement methodology but also and mainly a matter of determining a standard "risk unit" or "risk norm."

For example, when measuring distance, the standard length is derived from a stick kept in a museum in France under controlled climatic conditions and defined as one meter. The length of this stick is the standard—the basic measurement unit—and all other distances are measured as multiples (or fractions) of its length.

The mean-variance model defines risk as the magnitude of variation of the returns around their average value, that is, their standard deviation σ. The capital asset pricing model (CAPM) defines risk as the magnitude of the relative covariation of the asset's return with the general market return, that is, the regression coefficient β, where the general capital market variance σ_m^2 serves as the standard.

In both these risk-defining models, the mean-variance model and the market model, it is not worthwhile holding a single financial asset. Holding an asset along with other assets in a portfolio, however, reduces part of its specific variance risk. For an efficient portfolio, that is, a portfolio in which all the participating assets' specific variances cancel out, and only then, the two models converge and measure exactly the same risk for that portfolio or asset: $\sigma_p = \beta_p \cdot \sigma_m.$[2]

2. In this case, the difference in risk measurement units is similar to the difference between inches and centimeters.

Our goal was to develop a simple model where the cost of capital k equals the time value of money (R_f) plus the risk value (premium) of money. In both models, we accomplished this goal for efficient portfolios located on the securities market line.

In the mean-variance model, a portfolio's return accords with

$$k_i = R_f + \frac{\sigma_i}{\sigma_m}(R_m - R_f),$$

while in the market model, a portfolio's return accords with

$$k_i = R_f + \frac{\sigma_{im}}{\sigma_m^2}(R_m - R_f) = R_f + \beta_i(R_m - R_f).$$

The general market variance σ_m is the standard risk unit ($\beta = 1 \Rightarrow \sigma_i = \sigma_m$). Under the market model, the risk of all financial assets on the market is measured as a multiple (or fraction) of the market variance, which is then identical to that obtained under the mean-variance model. With a perfectly efficient portfolio, both models yield the same result, and using β is more convenient as it is a linear measure.[3] However, it should be kept in mind that in contrast to the meter stick in Paris, which has a constant length, market variance is not constant and varies over time. Accordingly, at equilibrium, all models provide "relative prices" to the prevailing market variance at a specific point in time.

In practice, most investors do not hold perfectly efficient portfolios—their portfolios are not a linear combination of the market portfolio and a risk-free portfolio but comprise a limited number of financial assets. Therefore, the market model ceases to apply. Investors can still use the mean-variance model's efficient frontier and try to construct a portfolio that minimizes variance for any possible required return. To optimize portfolios using the efficient frontier method, investors should use the mean inferred return premium, derived from the market model at equilibrium. This is based on the assumption that when asset prices (returns) in the market are not at equilibrium, they do not deviate significantly from their equilibrium levels, and when they do deviate significantly, market forces tend to push them back toward equilibrium. The Black-Litterman model provides us with both a theory and tools (easily implemented using MS Excel functions) for managing such real-world portfolios, even when we wish to deviate from those parameters of

---

3. The σ variance measurement is nonlinear. See the discussion in the "Law of Cash Flow Value Conservation" section in this chapter.

inferred return premium and use "better" parameters that account as well for an investor's subjective views.

3. The Law of Cash Flow Value Conservation

The relative convenience of modern financial models arises from the linear nature of both returns and the risk measure β on future cash flows. When dealing with several assets, each of which has a separate cash flow with discrete mean return and risk values, then, when all such assets are held together, the mean return and risk of their joint cash flow[4] conform to the following linear equations:

$$\overline{R} = \sum w_i \overline{R}_i.$$
$$\beta = \sum w_i \beta_i.$$

These equations are two-directional: whether we build one asset out of several constituent assets and examine the return and risk of the overall cash flow or separate an asset's overall cash flow into several constituent cash flows, the above linear equations correlating the risk and return of the overall asset with its constituent parts remain valid.

This property, as expressed in the above set of linear equations, is referred to as the law of cash flow value conservation.

4. Perfect Market and Efficient Market

The capital market's function is to allow individuals and companies to trade in both the timing and risk of consumption, both of which are traded through cash equivalents. Buyers and sellers benefit from the existence of a market for consumption timing and risk in general, and from the existence of an efficient market in particular. A capital market's efficiency is measured relative to that of a perfect market, where the following conditions or assumptions obtain:

1. There are no transaction costs (no brokerage fees), no taxes, and no administrative restrictions.

2. Market participants may buy any quantity whatsoever (even fractional quantities).

---

4. If we view a portfolio as a black box whose contents are unknown, we see that it has a cash flow with returns and a risk measure $(\overline{R}; \beta)$.

3. The capital market, like the commodities market, is competitive.

4. Perfect, free information is immediately available to all market participants.

5. All market participants make rational decisions seeking to maximize their mean utility from wealth (consumption).

When comparing a market's efficiency against the first two requirements, we are actually checking the efficiency of its operational aspects. Obviously, the market is not operationally perfect, and the question revolves around the measure of its efficiency, or, in other words, the extent to which its inefficiency distorts resource allocation. When discussing the optimal capital structure model, we relaxed the assumption concerning taxes (see next section), although "distribution cost" and "agency cost" are also clearly liable to distort such optimal allocation. A market's efficiency is expressed in reduced costs; real-world markets are currently experiencing a trend in this direction, for example, through online securities trading.

Requirements 3 and 4 define conditions for perfect resource allocation (in an operationally perfect market, as per requirements 1 and 2). In practice, information is not perfect, and neither is it free. As an example of imperfect information we discussed the famous Enron scandal, which implicated Arthur Anderson LLP.[5] Anderson, one of the largest accounting firms in the world, was expected to serve as a watchdog for adequate and reliable disclosure. The assumption that information is free is clearly unrealistic. This is evidenced by the thousands of well-paid analysts whose salaries are paid for by investors.

Information quality can and should be improved through legislation. For example, President George W. Bush issued a directive requiring executives to sign their company's financial statements, subjecting them to personal liability. Information pricing also has its own set of problems. As in every industry, if prices are above normal, more and more people will enter the market until profits are more normal. Adding to the equation the existence of arbitrage traders, we can assume that the market tends toward equilibrium. Comprehensive models that would describe how equilibrium is broken and how market bubbles form have yet to be formulated.[6]

5. Arthur Anderson LLP was actually implicated in a number of scandals, the most famous of which was the Enron case.
6. There is no shortage of partial concepts and models, however.

5. Optimal Capital Structure and the Cost of Capital Sources

The operating cash flow generated by a company's real assets is independent of whether the purchase of these assets was financed through bonds or through shares. A company's value is determined only by the present value of the cash flows generated by these assets.[7] As a company's value V should be equal to the value of its shares E plus the value of its debt D, $V = E + D$, the present value of a company's cash flow determines the market value of its shares and debt. A company's value will be highest in a tax-free world, where all cash flows generated by real assets are pocketed by a company's capital holders (investors who financed the purchase of these assets). If a tax applies, part of the company's cash flow is assigned to the tax authorities. The leftover, the net cash flow, is then distributed to the company's capital holders. The difference between a company's value in a tax-free world and its value in a world with taxes is exactly the present value of the cash flow transferred to the tax authorities.

Modigliani and Miller argued that in a world with taxes where no segregating tax is applied (i.e., the tax rate is identical regardless of the financing method, bonds or shares), the net return to capital holders is independent of the financing method chosen for acquiring the income-generating assets. Therefore, a company's value is determined strictly by the return on its real assets (net of taxes calculated as a fixed percentage), and a company's capital structure is irrelevant: $V^L = V^u$.

When taxation segregates the various investment tracks and creates a "tax shelter," in other words, reduced tax payments under a particular method, a company's value V^L is determined by the value of the cash flow generated by its real assets after payment of the maximum tax track V^u, plus the tax shelter's value as reflected in the tax rate difference T_S between the maximum taxation track and the preferred tax track.[8]

In other words, $V^L = V^u + T_S \cdot D$.

As noted earlier, the return and risk on the assets, r_A and β_A, respectively, are independent of the financing structure, and it is this return on the assets that supplies the cash flow used to pay capital holders and tax authorities alike. Therefore, the law of cash flow value conservation can be used to analyze the value (price) of cash flows paid to

7. In other words, a company's value is unrelated to the profit margin or to the dividend percent distributed by management.

8. In our example, the tax difference T_S promotes (direct) bond-based financing.

shareholders and bondholders. In fact, returns and risk are divided between both financing sources, with increased returns on shares (or bonds) accompanied by a corresponding increase in risk, according to the market equilibrium trade-off between risk and return (the market line).

We discussed how, in a tax-free world, the returns and risk for shareholders are given by

$$r_E = r_A + \frac{D}{E}(r_A - r_D),$$

$$\beta_E = \beta_A + \frac{D}{E}(\beta_A - \beta_D).$$

In a world with taxes, the return to capital holders (shares plus bonds), that is, the weighted average cost of capital, is no longer the return on the assets, as part of these returns are diverted to the tax authorities and only the rest is paid to capital holders: $WACC = r_A(1 - T)$.

When a segregating tax of T_S persists, the above weighted average cost of capital depends on the tax shelter created by a company's capital structure:

$$WACC = \frac{D}{E+D} \cdot r_D(1-T_S) + \frac{E}{E+D} \cdot r_E = r_A\left(1 - T_S \frac{D}{E+D}\right).$$

$WACC$ is the net weighted average cost of all capital sources. The net cost of the debt capital to the company is only $r_D(1 - T_S)$ because of the tax shelter. The return recorded by the shareholders in a world with tax will therefore be

$$r_E = r_A + (r_A - r_D)(1-T_S)\frac{D}{E}.$$

6. Capital Budgeting under Uncertainty

The cost of capital used to discount a project depends on the project itself, and not on the price of the capital raised to finance that project. The discount rate for each project is its risk-adjusted discount rate: $k_{Project} = r_f + \beta_{Project}(r_m - r_f)$. In other words, the discount rate depends on $\beta_{Project}$, the correlation of the project's cash flow with the market portfolio's performance. A company's overall operating cash flow is actually the sum of all its individual projects' cash flows. Therefore, a company's value in a tax-free world is the sum of the present value of all its projects. Thus,

β_{Assets}, the risk of that company's overall cash flow, is determined by the weighted sum of all the projects' betas:[9]

$$PV(\text{Firm}) = PV(\text{Project A}) + PV(\text{Project B}) + PV(\text{Project C}) +$$

$$\beta_{Firm} = \beta_{Assets} = \beta_{Proj.A} \frac{PV_{Proj.A}}{PV_{Firm}} + \beta_{Proj.B} \frac{PV_{Proj.B}}{PV_{Firm}} + \beta_{Proj.C} \frac{PV_{Proj.C}}{PV_{Firm}} + \dots .$$

In a world with taxes, we must use the operating cash flows generated by a company's projects, post-tax.

Calculating the return and the β risk measure of a project's expected cash flow is no easy task, but it is possible. For example, if we intend to invest in a new project in the meat industry, we can directly find the historical return required in this industry (which is already risk-adjusted) and use it to discount the project's expected net cash flow.[10] Things are not always so simple, but there are various ways of overcoming the different obstacles and estimating the risk-adjusted return for a given project.

The value added to the company from a new project results from the following:

1. The net present value of the project, discounted using a project-specific risk-adjusted discount rate.

2. The additional tax shelter resulting from the structure of the additional capital raised by the company to finance the project.

If, when discounting a project, we use the company's net weighted average cost of all capital sources (for a project within its line of business) instead of the project-specific cost of capital, the result would reflect the value added by both components together (i.e., tax shelter). Note that in this case we may obtain a positive NPV increment, even if the project itself has a negative net present value, because of the value of the tax shelter generated by that project.[11]

Management examines projects based on maximum NPV, but this does not guarantee that such projects will have the same risk level as the company. According to Fisher's separation theorem, if in selecting new investments management changes the company's overall risk, each inves-

9. According to the law of cash flow value preservation.

10. We must adjust the historical equation so as to account for tax rates across different periods, as necessary.

11. Of course, this scenario is of less merit than the alternative option of raising capital (with the same structure) and depositing it in a bank deposit earning an interest of R_f!

tor holding shares in that company can compensate for such increased or decreased risk and obtain the risk level that maximizes his or her individual portfolio's utility function. Investors do this by changing the ratio between their risk-free holdings and their holdings in the company's shares. Different shareholders have different utility functions, derived from their different risk-aversion profiles. Fisher's separation theorem allows us to separate the discussion of the problems facing capital market investors from the problems managers face, both when investing in real projects and in determining the mix of a company's financing sources on the capital market. This separation is not contradictory but rather leads to a common solution through capital market efficiency.

7. Future Contracts — Risk Trading and Hedging

Risk trading allows the transfer and sharing of risk, thereby increasing utility for both individuals and the market at large. As trading in time allows consumption to be smoothed over time, trading in risk allows consumption to be smoothed between periods when output is randomly lower and periods when output is randomly higher. In contrast to common belief, risk trading is not intended for speculators but for businesses that, in the ordinary course of their operation, expose themselves to risks they would like to mitigate. A sharp change (drop) in currency rates may cause a company that is not "insured" against currency fluctuations to go bankrupt, just as uninsured fire damage might. Following the same logic, where companies are willing to pay an insurance premium to protect against a specific event (fire, burglary, etc.), they are also willing to pay their bank an insurance (brokerage) fee against catastrophic financial events. The guiding principle in corporate risk management strategy is associating future liabilities to future revenue on the same basis (interest, currency, etc.) so as to hedge (limit) risk. In this book, we discussed a number of financial instruments for trading in risk and several hedging strategies employed by companies and capital market investors to hedge the risk arising from:

1. Changes in the value of a company's financial assets and liabilities (e.g., interest rate changes).

To avoid possible changes in financing costs caused by changes in the market interest rate, companies can contact their banks and "buy" a loan for a predetermined period (e.g., one year), which will come into effect in the future (e.g., the loan will be granted in one year's time). The interest is fixed, and therefore certain and immune to market interest rate fluctuations in the coming year.

$$R_{Forward} = \frac{(1+R_{2Years,Spot})^2}{(1+R_{1Year,Spot})} - 1.$$

2. Changes in cash flows not caused by changes in sales (e.g., changes in revenues caused by currency rate fluctuations).

Companies can buy contracts (issued in standardized amounts) that fix the future exchange rate between two currencies. These future rates are determined according to the currency-specific spot interest rates for the required future period: $X_{ChangeRate,Future} = X_{ChangeRate,Spot} \times \frac{1+R_{\$,Spot}}{1+R_{€,Spot}}$.

In principle, a bank that offers a forward contract on an interest or exchange rate records zero cash flow at any given point in time and so does not incur any risk through the transaction. Banks profit not from assuming a risky position but from fees they charge on "pairing" complementary contracts.

3. Changes in cash outflows (e.g., raw material prices).

Risk management is achieved by trading future contracts on commodities. Contracts are standardized, issued for homogenous products, in predefined quantities, and with specified delivery times.

4. Changes in capital market investments (shares and bonds).

The value of shares and bonds in a company's or an individual's portfolio may fluctuate drastically. Investors can buy future contracts to buy or sell shares or bonds at a predetermined price. These contracts are known as options and allow investors to hedge against losses.

There are two types of options:

1. The option holder has the right to buy from the issuer a predetermined number of shares, at a specified price X, at a specified future date[12] T. These are known as *call options*.

12. The right to buy can be exercised contractually *at* a specified date or *until* a specified date. Options exercisable only at a specified future date are known as European options. Options exercisable at any moment until a specified future date are known as American options.

2. The option holder has the right to sell to the issuer a predetermined number of shares, at a specified price X, at a specified future date T. These are known as *put options.*

By holding a combination of shares and options, investors can hedge (limit) their expected return range.

8. Option Pricing

Four parameters affect the expected mean profit (=price C_0) on call options:

1. The lower an option's exercise price X relative to the share price S, the higher is that option's value.

2. The longer an option's exercise or expiration period T, the higher is its value.

3. The higher the cost of the risk-free interest rate r_f, the higher is an option's value.

4. The higher the σ^2 variance of an underlying share's returns, the higher is the corresponding option's price.

Thus, $C_0 = f(S,X,T,r_f,\sigma^2)$.

Investors holding a call option will profit only when the underlying share's price is higher than the exercise price. So long as the share price is below the exercise price, the option's market price C_0 will be almost zero. It will not be zero as long as there is a chance that the share's price will exceed the exercise price during the option period, and so the option has a mean profit value. Since an option's market price will always equal the mean profit value, and there is always a chance that the share's price will go up, it is worth while holding the option until its expiration date T.

The equation for calculating a call option's value was developed by Black and Scholes in 1973: $C_0 = S \cdot N(d_1) - X \cdot e^{-rf \cdot T} \cdot N(d_2)$.

S and X are the share price and the exercise price, respectively, and r_f is the risk-free interest rate for period T, derived from the annual continuous risk-free rate r_{fc}:

$1 + r_{fc} = e^{rf}$.

$N(*)$ is the value derived from the normal distribution table, where d_1 and d_2 are

$$d_1 = \frac{\ln(S/X)+r_f \cdot T}{\sigma\sqrt{T}} + \frac{1}{2}\sigma\sqrt{T} ; d_2 = d_1 - \sigma\sqrt{T} = \frac{\ln(S/X)+r_f \cdot T}{\sigma\sqrt{T}} - \frac{1}{2}\sigma\sqrt{T}$$

$N(d_1)$ is the average of the share price multiplier,[13] discounted to the start of the period, for those times when the option is in the money.

$S \cdot N(d_1)$ is the mean (average) share price, for those times when the option is in the money, discounted to the start of the period.

$N(d_2)$ is the cumulative probability that the option will be in the money, and will therefore be exercised.

$X \cdot e^{-rf \cdot T} \cdot N(d_2)$ is the mean payment for exercising the option, discounted to the start of the period, for those times when the option is in the money.

C_0 is the option price in start-of-period terms, which is the difference between the share's mean market price and the mean payment for exercising the option at time T, both discounted to the start of the period, and only for those times when the option is in the money.[14]

To price a European put option, which can only be exercised at the end of the period, we used a position where an underlying share is held in conjunction with a corresponding call option and put option, both of which have the same exercise price X and expiration date T. Stoll (1969) demonstrated that through this position, known as "put-call parity," investors can find out the price of a put option by knowing the call option price, which is determined as detailed above. Therefore,

$$P_0 = C_0 - S_0 + X \cdot e^{-(1+r_{fc} \cdot T)}.$$

Investors holding an American put option can exercise it at any point during its lifetime. Therefore, no definite formula can be derived for pricing American put options, only an automated numerical solution. Thus, an American put option's price will always be higher than a European put option issued under the same terms.

C. Further Study

1. Single-Period Model or Multiperiod Model?

The discount rate k was defined mathematically based on a single-period CAPM. In other words, the model assumes that at the start of a period,

---

13. The share price multiplier is the factor by which the share's price will increase.
14. When an option is not in the money, its value is zero.

investors have expectations about end-of-period results. The NPV model, on the other hand, discounts cash flows across several time periods. How can we calculate a risk-adjusted discount rate for different periods when even r_f changes from period to period?[15] Why shouldn't investor expectations, like other parameters, also change between periods?

As this is the case, we must expand the model, combining the NPV model with the single-period CAPM model into a multiperiod model. This is possible, but it was not covered in this book, which is dedicated to fundamental models. Technically, the model is expanded using the "certainty equivalent" discussed in the utility function chapter, as applied on CAPM. The problem is not only technical but, first and foremost, requires a reevaluation of our assumptions for the multiperiod model. The conclusions derived from the multiperiod model are not materially different from those derived from the single-period model, and in any case, this topic is best left to advanced curricula.

2. Dynamic Portfolio Management

In this book, we have mostly discussed equilibrium models. Only the Black-Litterman model assumed nonequilibrium conditions. When using CAPM methodology, we effectively assume that a company holds an efficient project portfolio, like an investor holding an efficient asset portfolio. Only through this assumption can we assume that random (nonsystematic) changes in project cash flows cancel each other out. Moreover, we assume that the projects' cash flows are related to general economic conditions, and yet there are numerous companies whose β has a miniscule R^2 coefficient of determination.[16] This indicates that general economic conditions do not play a decisive role in determining these companies' performance. The use of multiple-parameter models, as discussed in this book, does not materially improve this correlation, owing to problems in defining these explanatory parameters. The methods discussed in this book, although logical and understandable, do not provide an absolute, final, and practical solution but set forth conceptual and mathematical methods. These reservations notwithstanding, and in the absence of a better alternative, the methods discussed in this book are statistically better than coin-toss decision making.

---

15. The term structure of interest rates.

16. The R^2 parameter correlation coefficient under CCAPM is much better than that for parameters under CAPM.

Companies should invest in projects with a positive NPV. We discussed the economic cost (the return) required from a project under CAPM, which by definition does not allow for positive NPV. We also discussed how nonequilibrium conditions can be exploited to invest in such projects. How, then, do some companies manage to record economic gains, while others do not? Why do some companies decide to invest in a particular project, while others reject the very same investment? Is it the result only of inefficiency or bad management, or maybe there are additional factors at play? And if the positive NPV is indeed attributable to lack of equilibrium, how long will it take a competitive market to return such an investment to equilibrium? In light of all the above, is there even any point in calculating NPV?

This point also came up in our discussion of financial asset investment management. We saw how skillful management is perceived as the ability of financial asset managers to predict market behavior and leverage their expertise to generate profit by buying and selling securities. Numerous studies conducted around the world have found that there is no point in looking for underpriced shares and buying and selling them accordingly (as opposed to project selection, where that is exactly what we proposed). Such a search is extremely costly and not worthwhile. Expert management essentially consists of predicting market behavior (or that of a particular industry, such as real estate, transportation, or communications), identifying imminent market behavior, and changing a portfolio's structure and β accordingly. Unmanaged portfolios will have the same β in both a bull market and a bear market. Well-managed portfolios will decrease their β when the market is expected to go down and increase their β when the market is about to go up. We discussed how portfolio manager performance can be evaluated based on this dynamic principle, but we did not discuss models for changing β *prospectively* (as opposed to performance assessment, which is retrospective).

Modern finance theory must concede that it does not offer theoretical models for predicting market increases or decreases.[17] Our models are therefore relativistic models for general market performance and do not model absolute performance. There is still a great deal of art in predicting market behavior and choosing investments, activities based more on experience than on scientific calculations.

---

17. Pure (theoryless) statistical models, which use "leading parameters" to predict market behavior, are limited in their practical prediction ability.

3. Inefficient Market

In 2001 the Nobel Prize Committee broke with tradition and awarded the Nobel Prize in Economics to three individuals, Michael Spence from Stanford, George Akerlof from Berkeley, and Joseph Stiglitz from Columbia University, for their separate work on asymmetric information. Their studies demonstrated that capital markets are not perfect in their information distribution and that people do not always make rational decisions. Therefore, markets do not always match supply and demand perfectly, and may distort financial asset prices. Let's assume that a company's management has better information than investors concerning the value of a certain financial asset, and investors know this to be the case. Under these conditions, competent financial asset managers would not want to sell or issue new share capital.

We recall that in the last 20 years of the twentieth century, the world of finance was dominated by conservative policies, and governments and central banks always went "by the book"—that is, they followed the World Bank's recommendations. In fact, the Keynesian model that most readers are familiar with predicts that certain conditions may cause a drop in investments, leading to an economic slowdown and unemployment. It is possible that the capital market has an inherent trait of under-investment or overinvestment, as demonstrated only too well by the price bubble bursts of the late twentieth century and early twenty-first century. Such price bubbles also characterized earlier economic crises.

All modern finance theories are based on the assumption of a perfect or efficient market, and also assume that individuals seek to maximize their wealth utility function (make rational decisions). We know these assumptions to be false, but such arguments against modern finance theory bring us back to the discussion presented in chapter 1 of what constitutes a good model. Currently, no other comprehensive and measurable theory based on another set of assumptions is available. However, we must take care not to become entrenched in our perceptions that having found a torch, we are sure to find the treasure. It is quite possible that in the future, new models will be developed, based on another set of assumptions, that will make our present theories a special case of a broader theory (see, e.g., attempts by physicists to find one unified theory that will explain both Einstein's relativity theory and quantum theory[18]).

18. Currently, each theory is based on a separate and different set of assumptions.

4. The Dispute Concerning Dividends and Capital Structure

The Modigliani-Miller models, which argue that dividend payments and capital structure are irrelevant, are extremely seductive in their straightforward logic. Moreover, they can possibly be defined as normative models, describing how rational managers *should* behave, even if actual behavior is different. Real-world observations do not necessarily support the theory, and I am not referring to empirical studies, which are objectively an extremely difficult undertaking and their results are subject to pointed criticism. I refer to the many executives whom I believe to be seasoned, experienced professionals who disagree with M&M's models for a variety of different reasons. Do these executives take other factors into account, such as the value of their options (until exercised)?[19] Or is it a market imbalance that undermines efficiency?

The very fact that leading executives behave differently than predicted must lead us to consider that these issues have yet to be fully explored. The gap between expectation and reality indicates that we must review and fine-tune our assumptions, or reform the capital market so as to better approximate Modigliani and Miller's normative model. Such regulatory actions, implemented in the past and present (e.g., the recognition of options as a corporate expense, or directives such as the one issued by President Bush requiring executives to personally sign their company's financial statements), are steps in this direction.

Further Reading

Bodie, Z., A. Kane, and A. J. Marcus. 2004. *Investments*. 6th ed. New York: McGraw-Hill/Irwin.

Brealey, R. A., S. C. Myers, and F. Allen. 2005. *Principles of Corporate Finance*. 8th ed. New York: McGraw-Hill.

Copeland, T. E., and F. J. Weston. 1988. *Financial Theory and Corporate Policy*. 3rd ed. Reading, MA: Addison-Wesley.

Elton, E. J., M. J. Gruber, S. J. Brown, and W. N. Goetzmann. 2004. *Modern Portfolio Theory and Investment Analysis*. 6th ed. New York: Wiley.

Fama, E. F. 1976. *Foundations of Finance*. New York: Basic Books.

Fama, E. F., and M. H. Miller. 1971. *The Theory of Finance*. New York: McGraw-Hill.

19. Preliminary work carried out after the bankruptcies (including the bankruptcies of corporate giants) that followed the bubble burst of the late 2000s found that many executives sold their shares and pocketed hundreds of millions of dollars shortly before their company's value collapsed almost to zero.

Hsia, C. C. 1981. Coherence of the Modern Theories of Finance. *Financial Review* 16 (Winter): 27–42.

Haley, C. W., and L. D. Schall. 1973. *The Theory of Financial Decisions*. New York: McGraw-Hill.

Levy, H., and M. Sarnat. 1984. *Portfolio and Investment Selection*. Englewood Cliffs, NJ: Prentice-Hall.

Markowitz, H. M. 2006. Samuelson and Investment for the Long Run. In *Samuelsonian Economics and the Twenty-First Century*, eds. M. Szenberg, L. Ramrattan, and A. A. Gottesman, 252–261. Oxford, UK: Oxford University Press.

Petty, W. J., and O. D. Bowlin. 1976. The Financial Manager and Quantitative Decision Models. *Financial Management* 5 (4): 32–41.

Index